The Literacy Dictionary

The Vocabulary of Reading and Writing

Theodore L. Harris

Richard E. Hodges

Editors

Frank Greene, Senior Associate Editor

Dianne Monson, Associate Editor

International Reading Association
800 Barksdale Road, PO Box 8139
Newark, Delaware 19714-8139, USA

Director of Publications   Joan M. Irwin
Assistant Director of Publications   Wendy Lapham Russ
Associate Editor.   Christian A. Kempers
Assistant Editor   Janet Parrack
Production Department Manager   Iona Sauscermen
Graphic Designer   Boni Nash
Design Consultant   Larry Husfelt
Desktop Publishing Supervisor   Wendy Mazur
Desktop Publishing   Anette Schütz-Ruff
                          Cheryl Strum
Production Services Editor   David Roberts

Photo Credits   Michael Siluk, pp. 1, 25, 169, 177, 199; CLEO Freelance Photo, pp. 17, 67, 103, 125, 131, 147, 161, 201, 251, 277; Mary Loewenstein Anderson, pp. 53, 269; Robert Finken, pp. 81, 265; Top Shots, p. 93; Laima Druskis Photography, p. 111; Skjold Photographs, pp. 127, 225; Little Bighorn Photos, p. 287

Library of Congress Cataloging in Publication Data
   The literacy dictionary: The vocabulary of reading and writing/Theodore L. Harris, Richard E. Hodges, editors.
      p.   cm.
   Includes bibliographical references.
   1. Reading—Dictionaries.   2. English language—Composition and exercises—Study and teaching—dictionaries.   3. Literacy—Dictionaries.   4. Language arts—Dictionaries.   5. English language—Dictionaries.   6. Reading teachers—Handbooks, manuals, etc.   7. English teachers—Handbooks, manuals, etc.   I. Harris, Theodore Lester.   II. Hodges, Richard E. III. International Reading Association.
LB1049.98.L58   1995   95-20233
372.4'03—dc20   CIP
ISBN 0-87207-138-3 (pbk.)

Second Printing, February 2005

Dedication

Ted Harris, my friend and colleague, died February 14, 1995, the day that the final revised manuscript for this dictionary was completed and ready for editorial production. After two and a half years of work, I am tempted to say that Ted, at age 85, saw this event as his "last hurrah." But that is not an appropriate metaphor. For Ted's mind was keen and active, and he was ready to move on to reading books and materials other than a dictionary manuscript and enjoying other well-deserved activities; but his body let go.

Ted had a long-standing interest in lexicography. In his early years, he worked as an editor on the Thorndike–Barnhart dictionaries. He brought to this field the broad interests and knowledge that lexicography requires from his years at the University of Chicago where he earned PhB (1931), A.M. (1938), and PhD (1941) degrees. Ted had studied with William S. Gray and other "giants" of the reading field during the Chicago era in his fields of specialization, developmental and remedial reading and psychology of learning.

Ted served his chosen profession in many ways. In addition to writing scholarly and professional publications, he was a well-regarded teacher, advisor, and mentor to numberless students at the University of Wisconsin (1946–1967), Washington State University (1967–1968), and the University of Puget Sound (1969–1974). He was President of the International Reading Association (1971–1972). He was elected to the Reading Hall of Fame (1977) for his scholarly and service contributions to the reading field. And, he coedited two dictionaries—*A Dictionary of Reading and Related Terms* (1981) and this volume.

Whatever endeavors Ted undertook in his professional life he undertook with commitment, vigor, and rigor. He held high standards for himself and for the persons and organizations with whom he worked. Ted had the personal qualities necessary for dictionary making: he was efficient, industrious, tough-minded, and he loved language—especially literary language.

The *Oxford English Dictionary* lists a term, first documented in 1856 but now rarely used—**orismology**—meaning the study or practice of defining technical terms. I have added this term to *The Literacy Dictionary* and devised a corresponding term, **orismologist**, in honor of Ted. He would have enjoyed this addition; for he truly regarded himself as an orismologist in the field of literacy. This dictionary is both a testimony of and, now, a tribute to his contributions to the field to which he dedicated his talents and energy for over half a century.

Richard E. Hodges

Contents

Editorial Advisory Board

Invited Essay Authors

Censorship	M. Jerry Weiss	Jersey City State College, Jersey City, New Jersey
Dyslexia	Doris Johnson	Northwestern University, Evanston, Illinois
Emergent Literacy	William H. Teale	University of Illinois at Chicago, Illinois
Evaluation in Education	Robert C. Calfee	Stanford University, Stanford, California
Functional Literacy	John Ryan	United Nations Educational, Scientific, and Cultural Organization, Paris
Genre	Richard Beach	University of Minnesota, Minneapolis, Minnesota
Grammar and Grammatical	Joseph M. Williams	University of Chicago, Chicago, Illinois
Literacy	Richard L. Venezky	University of Delaware, Newark, Delaware
Literary Criticism	Francis L. Cousens	University of Puget Sound, Tacoma, Washington
Phonemic Awareness	Joanna Williams	Teachers College, Columbia University, New York, New York
Readability	George R. Klare	Ohio University, Athens, Ohio
Reader Response	Sam Leaton Sebesta	University of Washington, Seattle, Washington
Problems in Translation	Takahiko Sakamoto	University of Tsukuba, Tokyo
Whole Language	Dorothy Strickland	Rutgers University, New Brunswick, New Jersey

Lexicographic Consultants

Sol Steinmetz and Leonore Crary Hauck, Random House Dictionaries, New York, New York; Richard L. Venezky, University of Delaware, Newark, Delaware

International Literacy Consultants

Vincent Greaney, The World Bank, Washington, DC; Mogens Jansen, The Danish Institute for Educational Research, Copenhagen; John Ryan, United Nations Educational, Scientific, and Cultural Organization, Paris; Takahiko Sakamoto, University of Tsukuba, Tokyo; Renate Valtin, Humboldt–University of Berlin; Ralph C. Staiger, Emeritus, International Reading Association and University of Delaware, Newark, Delaware

Introduction

The primary purpose of *The Literacy Dictionary* is to provide a resource to help educational practitioners, researchers, and other interested persons in the national and international community to understand terms used in contemporary and historical writings about literacy. We define literacy as competence in reading and writing, with full recognition that such competence ordinarily rests upon an extensive experience base in the use of spoken language. Within this context, we seek to provide authenticated definitions of the technical terminology of the nature, study, and practice of literacy. Although popular conceptions of literacy often include arithmetic competence, or numeracy, the focus of this dictionary is on language rather than numerical literacy.

The Need for a Dictionary of Literacy

Extensive changes in educational theory and practice since the publication of *A Dictionary of Reading and Related Terms* in 1981 call for a new kind of dictionary. Among these changes are deeper understandings of the social nature of language development and of the constructive nature of learning, the development of holistic views of curriculum and instruction, and more comprehensive, innovative ways of assessing learning. As a result of theoretical and practical advances, a reconceptualized dictionary that views the theory and practice of reading and writing development in relation to the broader concept of literacy appears warranted at this time.

Conceptualization of *The Literacy Dictionary*

The figure on the next page shows graphically the conceptualization of the nature and scope of this dictionary in relation to the core concept of literacy. The vertical dimension of the chart represents the primary focus of the dictionary on curricular, instructional, and linguistic domains in literacy education, to which the majority of dictionary entries are related. The horizontal dimension represents the foundational and technical domains that are involved in studies of literacy to which a substantial number of new entries have been added from the current literature on literacy. The scope of this chart suggests that literacy is not a singular conception but one that is both multidimensional and multidisciplinary.

The specific categories within the domains represented in this dictionary are indicated in the table on page xi. The greatest increase in dictionary terminology since 1981 is in the fields of literacy, language, sociology, and supporting technology. New fields not present in the 1981 dictionary that contribute additional terminology are those of writing, literacy criticism, student assessment, print and graphic design, and semiotics. The elimination of many terms considered nonfunctional in relation to literacy led to a slight decline in the number of psychological terms and to a reduction of more than 50 percent of the terms in physiology, a field that is now the province of specialists in learning disability. The names of persons and of reading tests, other than certain clinical instruments, have also been excluded as main entries, although many such references remain within definitions and notes where appropriate.

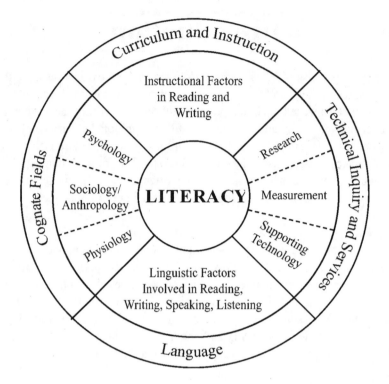

The Selection of Terms and Definitions

Two factors strongly influenced the selection of terms for inclusion in this dictionary: the audience for whom the dictionary is intended and the criteria for entry selections and their definitions.

The Audience. *The Literacy Dictionary* is directed toward a more sharply defined professional audience than was the case in the 1981 dictionary. Namely, the dictionary should serve persons who are involved in the study or teaching of literacy, such as those engaged in graduate study, research, college teaching, or advanced independent inquiry. The greater specificity of audience has led to the deletion of many general, nontechnical terms and definitions contained in the 1981 dictionary and the addition of other terms that have a direct functional relation to literacy.

Criteria for Entry Selection. The development of specific criteria for the inclusion of entries to meet the needs of a professional audience has permitted a more judicious selection of technical terms. Three criteria were used to judge the suitability of each term in relation to the concept of literacy and its study:

1. Is the term relevant?
2. Is the term specific and technical rather than general and nontechnical?
3. Does the term have well-established or expected longevity in the literacy literature?

Categories Involved in the Study of Literacy

The Field of Literacy

General literacy	Adult literacy	Emergent literacy
Politics of literacy		

Curriculum and Instruction

Reading	*Common*	*Writing*
Word identification	Instructional status	Orthography
Comprehension	Instructional levels:	Print/graphic design
Children's literature	Elementary	Writing processes
Literary analysis	High school	
Literary criticism	College	
Young adult literature	Curriculum theory &	
	instructional practice	
	Interests & preferences	
	Readability	
	Word knowledge	
	Historically significant terms	

Cognate Fields

Psychology	*Sociology/Anthropology*	*Physiology*
Learning	Sociology	Learning disability
Development	Cultural anthropology	Neurology
Cognition	Readership	Speech & hearing
Perception	Content analysis	Vision
Clinical psychology	Linguistic diversity	Atypical learners
Remedial & corrective		
reading		
Research models		

Language: Reading, Writing, Speaking, Listening

General linguistics	Psycholinguistics	Semantics
Grammar	Sociolinguistics	Semiotics

Technical Inquiry and Services

Research	*Measurement*	*Supporting Technology*
General research methods	Tests & measurement	Instructional materials &
	Statistics	technology
	Educational evaluation	Library science
	Student assessment	

When we considered the complex nature of the concept of literacy, its study, and its teaching, the application of these general criteria proved far from easy. Relevance, for example, often proved to be a matter of considered judgment. Similarly, the more general, familiar terminology of curriculum and instruction, of language, and of literature caused many problems of choice. In such cases, core terms were considered essential in spite of their general nature.

Criteria for Definitions. Five criteria were used for judging the adequacy of entry definitions:

1. Is the definition understandable?
2. Is the definition adequate in scope?
3. Is the definition free from wordiness?
4. Is the definition precise and authentic?
5. Is the definition relevant as demonstrated by verbal or graphic example?

The Dictionary as a Reference Tool

We have designed *The Literacy Dictionary* to be a reference tool of literacy terms beyond the scope of its 1981 predecessor by introducing or extending several innovative features that expand the function of standard dictionaries. These features include the Wordex, clusters of related terms and concepts, collective terms, notes, illustrative contexts, editorial essays, and invited essays.

The Wordex. The Wordex, beginning on page 291, is an index to more than 650 important terms that are not main entries but are included within definitions of main entries to which they are closely related. The intent of the Wordex is to provide users of *The Literacy Dictionary* with a ready reference with which to access terms that are not main entries but occur in meaningful context within main entry definitions. Types of words listed in the Wordex include (1) alternative terms, as *deep meaning* for *deep structure*; (2) subentry terms, as *acrolect* in *creole*; (3) synonyms, as *superordinate* for *hypernym*; (4) antonyms, as *living language* versus *dead language*; and (5) alternative spellings of main entries, as *aphaerisis* versus *apherisis*. The Wordex has been designed for easy use. If a word is not found as a main entry, one looks for that word in the Wordex and, if included in the dictionary, the main entry term(s) in which it is included is provided.

Clusters of Related Terms and Concepts. Throughout the dictionary will be found boxed groups, or clusters, of terms and concepts closely associated with selected main entries. The boxes graphically display these items for easy identification and quick reference and are intended to provide the user with collections of conceptually related terms found in *The Literacy Dictionary*. The four types of boxes are described on the next page.

Types of *Correlation*
biserial correlation
intercorrelation
multiple correlation
partial correlation
point-biserial correlation
product-moment correlation
rank-order correlation
tetrachloric correlation

---

*Terms are all defined in this dictionary.

1. Related main entry terms that share the more general factor under which they are grouped. For example, the box on the left accompanies the general main entry *correlation* and lists the types of correlation that are defined in main entries in the dictionary.

2. Subsets of undefined terms associated with a main entry for which illustrative examples are provided. For example, accompanying the general grammatical term *aspect* will be found the box of types of aspect used in English verb formation, as shown here.

Types of *Aspect*
Perfect
past perfect (also pluperfect):
   Joan *had read* the book.
present perfect: Joan *has read* the book.
future perfect: Joan *will have read* the book.

Progressive
past progressive: Joan *was reading* the book
present progressive: Joan *is reading* the book.
future progressive: Joan *will be reading* the book.

Main Subcategories of *Government/Binding Theory*

• *Binding theory* describes the referential relationships among noun phrases in a sentence.

• *Bounding theory* describes the rules that restrict the movement of sentence constituents.

• *Case theory* describes the assignment of cases, or functions, to noun phrases in a sentence.

• *Theta theory* assigns semantic roles to elements of a sentence.

• *X-bar theory* describes phrase structures.

3. Subsets of terms associated with a main entry that are briefly defined within the box rather than as main entries. For example, this box shown collects and briefly defines main subcategories of *government/binding theory*.

4. Brief, illuminative extensions of selected main entry definitions, such as examples and comparisons, that broaden the meaning or meanings of a term, as the boxes that accompany the entries *reading-writing relationships* and *reading*, respectively.

Collective Terms. Collective terms are categories of subordinate, complementary terms that are defined within a main entry in order to highlight their meaning relationships. For example, within the main entry *text processing* the theoretical perspectives of *top-down processing*, *bottom-up processing*, and *interactive processing* are defined in order to point out their similarities and differences. Collective terms are referenced in the Wordex.

Notes. Frequent use is made of notes incorporated within main entries. These notes serve to clarify and extend the meaning of the term with which they are associated.

Illustrative Contexts. Many illustrative phrases and sentences are used in definitions of main entries to clarify the meanings of definitions and to indicate typical usage.

Editorial Essays. We have prepared brief introductory essays to selected terms. These essays are designed to provide a more encyclopedic commentary of crucial literacy terms. Examples of introductory essays will be found in the main entries for *critical literacy*, *meaning*, *reading*, and *word*.

Invited Essays. *The Literacy Dictionary* also contains 14 invited essays written by noted scholars (see page vii) who offer their personal views on topics of particular relevance to the field of literacy. These contributions are an especially noteworthy feature of the dictionary, and we are indebted to these colleagues for their contributions on the topics of censorship, dyslexia, emergent literacy, evaluation in education, functional literacy, genre, grammar and grammatical, literacy, literary criticism, phonemic awareness, readability, reader response, problems in translation, and whole language.

International Aspects of *The Literacy Dictionary*

In preparing this dictionary, we have been aware that a work of this scope sponsored by the International Reading Association ought to reflect and be responsive to the international community. Wherever practicable, illustrative examples and names from different nationalities have been used in definitions; and authors and scholars worldwide have been cited where appropriate.

We have also been aware that, for those with a good command of English, carefully constructed, comprehensible definitions are the most obvious solution to a shared understanding of terms. For others, however, the solution is neither obvious nor easy. For example, the matching of word meaning equivalents in several languages, as was attempted in the 1981 dictionary, does not serve the needs of its users, in large part because word meanings are both linguistically and culturally influenced.

To address this problem, an invited group of International Literacy Consultants, chaired by Ralph Staiger, suggested that international scholars be queried (1) to determine which English literacy terms needed clarification and which might then be translated in the UNESCO official languages and (2) to identify literacy terms in other languages that have meanings unique to a given language that might then be included in *The Literacy Dictionary* to broaden international understandings of literacy terms for both English and non-English users. Accordingly, a questionnaire was prepared and sent to 53 active members of the International Reading Association in 43 countries. The results were valuable, but limited, showing that literacy concepts vary greatly among different cultures and languages. Further, difficulties in communication involving translations were revealed in the questionnaire returns, an issue that the eminent Japanese scholar, Takahiko Sakamoto, addresses in his essay on problems in translation in this dictionary.

The questionnaire returns revealed that it was not possible in this edition to identify a sufficient number of terms that would justify translation into the UNESCO official languages. However, we have included information from the questionnaires and the names of those volunteering the information in notes to main entry terms wherever appropriate. In all, IRA members in 14 countries provided valuable information about the use and translation of technical terms in several languages. The dictionary is a richer one for the contributions of our international colleagues. Suggestions that will enlarge the international scope of the next edition will be welcomed and should be directed to the Dictionary Revision Project, in care of International Reading Association.

Guide to the Dictionary

Entries. Main entry headings are in boldface. Undefined subentry headings in boldface are typically added at the end of the entry.

Variant Spellings. As a general rule, spellings found in the Random House dictionaries are followed, except when other specialized sources indicate otherwise. British spellings, such as *centre* and *programme*, are limited to main entries and subentries.

Pronunciation. Pronunciations for main entries have been discontinued in this edition of the dictionary. However, pronunciations and sound symbols continue to appear in main entry contexts as needed as examples to clarify speech and writing terminology.

Parts of Speech. The part(s) of speech for each main entry and subentry heading of single words and hyphenated two-word compounds are given immediately before each definition or subentry, as noun (*n.*), verb (*v.*), adjective (*adj.*), and adverb (*adv.*).

Definition Order. In entries with multiple definitions, the most common or most pertinent meaning with respect to literacy is usually given first. In some instances, a generic or historical meaning is given first to clarify following definitions.

Idioms and Defined SubEntries. Such entries are in boldface and are given definitions.

Special Type Signals. Italicized type is used to indicate citations, illustrative phrases and sentences, non-English word entries, and occasionally to emphasize a point, as in a note. Italicized type is also used in definitions to refer to a letter or letter cluster as *a* in hat, or *oa* in boat. (By contrast, the sound represented by such a letter or letters is indicated by virgules, as /a/ in *hat*, or /ō/ in *boat*.)

Cross References. Cross references are indicated by either the words See or See also. In addition to the standard symbols of synonym (*Syn.*) and antonym (*Ant.*), this dictionary also uses *Cp.* (compare) when such references serve to clarify, contrast, or extend the meaning of the particular terms.

Restrictions. A minimal number of restrictions are used in this dictionary, chiefly *cap.* (capitalized), informal, *Brit.* (British), archaic, *pl.* (plural), and *sing.* (singular).

Acknowledgments

International Reading Association. As with the 1981 edition, *The Literacy Dictionary* is the result of the involvement of many persons during a three-year period whose contributions deserve special recognition. We are especially grateful to the International Reading Association—its Board of Directors, Executive Director, Director of Publications and her staff, and international membership—for continued support for a publication of this nature.

Editorial Advisory Board. We feel privileged as well as thankful to have gained the expertise of the stellar members of the Editorial Advisory Board. The contributions of this board have been indispensable in the construction of this dictionary, ranging from initial entry selection and definition to critical editorial comments on terms and definitions that were submitted to them for review. With the range of fields and topics that *The Literacy Dictionary* encompasses, it is only through the collective expertise shared by scholars in these areas that a work of this nature is made possible. We are grateful to them for the time and effort taken from their already busy professional pursuits and given to this undertaking.

Lexicographic Consultants. Special thanks go to these consultants for their contributions. For lexicographic assistance, we acknowledge Sol Steinmetz, Editor in Chief, and Leonore Crary Hauck, Managing Editor (retired), Random House Dictionaries. We are appreciative of the assistance that Richard Venezky has provided in overseeing the general field of literacy terms and in offering technical assistance on a number of lexicographic problems that we raised.

International Cooperation. As mentioned earlier, many persons active in the international literacy scene participated directly or indirectly in the preparation of this dictionary. The work of the International Literacy Consultants was especially helpful in exploring the parameters of international cooperation within the two-year time span allotted to this project. We are grateful for the tireless efforts of its chair, Ralph Staiger, in soliciting the advice and counsel of literacy leaders worldwide by telephone, mail, e-mail, and personal contact. The consultants are Vincent Greaney, Mogens Jansen, John Ryan, Takahiko Sakamoto, and Renate Valtin.

While all cannot be acknowledged, special thanks are due to the IRA members in 14 countries who provided valuable information about the use and translation of technical terms in 12 languages other than English. We wish to acknowledge the contributions of Alfred Asiamah, Ghana; Adelina Arellano-Osuna, Venezuela; Anna Adamic-Jászó, Hungary; Man Boonprasent, Thailand; Judit Kádár-Fülop, Hungary; Peter Gavora, Slovakia; Hideo Kiyokawa, Japan; Jutta Kleedorfer, Austria; Anna Maulina, Latvia; Safia Oswan, Malaysia; Ng Seok Moi, Brunei; Antra Purina, Latvia; Vytautas Rimsa, Lithuania; Katri Sarmavvori, Finland; Tuanchi Tan-ngarmtrong, Thailand; Rosa Marie Torres, Ecuador and UNICEF; and Rosmarie Tschirky, Switzerland.

University of Puget Sound. The University of Puget Sound and several members of its faculty and staff deserve special thanks. Carol Merz, Dean of the School of Education, graciously provided ample office space for the editors and their assistants. Constructive assistance was provided on entry selection and on problem entries by John English, Professor of Education; John Woodward, Associate Professor of Education; Michel Rocchi, Professor of Foreign Languages and Literature; and Francis Cousens, Professor of English. We wish also to thank the staff of the Center for Writing and Learning for their help concerning literacy issues at the college level; namely, Julie Neff-Lippman (Director), Sharon Kennedy, Sharlyn Russell, Ivey West, and Barbara Price.

Volunteer Help from the Field. Thanks go to Monica Dashen, graduate assistant to Joanna Williams in the area of cognition, and to Filiz Edizer, graduate assistant to Johanna DeStefano in the area of sociolinguistics, for their contributions in preparing terms. Thanks also go to J. David Grisham, a consultant to Herbert Simons in the area of vision, and to Denise Kelly-Ballweber, Audiologist. We wish to thank Robert Barker of Tacoma, Washington, editor of *The Social Work Dictionary*, for his expertise (and occasional hand holding) in matters pertaining to dictionary construction.

Project Implementation. The work of the editors and associate editors was greatly enhanced by the active participation of the IRA Director of Publications, Joan Irwin, in the planning and implementation of *The Literacy Dictionary*, especially in emphasizing a need for a professional, technical dictionary of literacy. Her associates, Anne Fullerton and Christian Kempers, and others of her staff provided efficient production management of the project.

During the dictionary preparation, the IRA Publications Division conducted a field review of provisional dictionary entries in early 1994. A questionnaire was sent to more than 400 persons in the IRA community. Responses from more than 37 percent of this group were helpful in identifying approximately 100 additional terms for consideration by the editors as well as reaffirming the general representativeness, currency, and usefulness of the proposed set of dictionary entries. We wish to express our gratitude for these contributions to the IRA colleagues listed on pages xviii–xix.

Unlike the 1981 dictionary, *The Literacy Dictionary* manuscript was produced by computer. The chief architect of this computer operation was Frank Greene, Senior Associate Editor, whose expertise in designing the computer program needed for composing a dictionary has our deep respect and admiration. We are indebted to Frank for his enormous expenditure of time and effort in this and many other aspects of the building of the new dictionary.

We are also indebted to Vicki Moll, our Assistant Editor and Office Manager. Equipped with a great degree of computer proficiency, she also brought intelligence, good humor, and patience to a complex editorial process. Vicki made many suggestions for the improvement of the manuscript while carefully monitoring the countless additions, deletions, and corrections made by the editors. We wish also to thank her predecessor, Grace Mashie, who in the initial phase of the project helped us organize the office and get started on the preliminary stages of dictionary construction.

Finally, we express a deep personal thanks to our compatriots in this project, Senior Associate Editor Frank Greene and Associate Editor Dianne Monson, and to Sam Weintraub and Johanna DeStefano who, for quite understandable reasons, found it impossible to continue in their roles as Associate Editors due to demanding commitments at their respective universities. In the same spirit as in the 1981 dictionary, we want to say this: In a project that required much sharing of responsibility, tough intellectual decisions, and hours of concentrated effort, the group worked together with good humor and sound judgment. Each participant brought different but complementary kinds of expertise and experience to the task. It has been a personal and professional privilege to work with such a fine group on this truly cooperative project.

Theodore L. Harris
Richard E. Hodges
Editors

Tacoma, Washington, 1995

Word List Reviewers

The editors and publisher wish to thank the following individuals who participated in a review of the dictionary's word list while it was being developed.

Donna Alvermann, National Reading Research Center, University of Georgia; Carolyn Andrews-Beck, Miami University; Betty Conway Archambeault, Baylor University; Eunice N. Askov, Pennsylvania State University; Betsy Baker, Missouri State Council of IRA; Jo Ann F. Bass, University of Mississippi; Maria Ruth Pardo Belgrano, Argentina Reading Association; Allen Berger, Miami University; Janet Ramage Binkley, Retired, International Reading Association; Morton Botel, University of Pennsylvania; Susan Burks Brennan, Cedar Hill School; Carol Brown, Oregon Reading Association; Janet Busboom, Mercer University; Trevor Cairney, Australian Reading Association; Ruth M. Caswell, Texas Woman's University; Arnold B. Cheyney, Emeritus, University of Miami; Tanna Clark, Arkansas State Reading Council; Desmond C. Clarke, International Development in the Caribbean Committee of IRA; Mabel Condemarín, Chile Ministry of Education; Maggie Corboy, University of South Carolina–Aiken; Bernice E. Cullinan, New York University; Nancy A. Custer, Natrona County School District #1; Delva Daines, Brigham Young University; Dale D. Downs, Eastern Illinois University; Mary Anne Doyle, University of Connecticut; John Elkins, University of Queensland; Warwick B. Elley, University of Canterbury; Joan Elliott, Indiana University of Pennsylvania; Nancy Farnan, San Diego State University; Ruth D. Farrar, Bridgewater State College; Gay Fawcett, Summit County Board of Education; Karen M. Feathers, Wayne State University; Joan C. Fingon, Vermont Council on Reading; Peter Fisher, National–Louis University; Ros Fisher, University of Plymouth; Rona F. Flippo, Fitchburg State College; James Flood, San Diego State University; Nora Forester, Archdiocese of San Antonio, Diocese of Victoria; Nancy V. Fox, University of Colorado at Denver; Marcie Frevert, Emmetsburg Community Schools; Victor Froese, University of British Columbia; Regina Leite Garcia, Fluminese Federal University; John George, University of Missouri–Kansas City; Cindy Gillespie, Ball State University; Susan Mandel Glazer, Rider University; Francisco Gomes de Matos, Federal University of Pernambuco; Alvin Granowsky, World Book Educational Products; M. Jean Greenlaw, University of North Texas; Margaret M. Griffin, Texas Woman's University; Priscilla L. Griffith, University of South Florida; Thomas G. Gunning, Southern Connecticut State University; Barbara Guzzetti, Arizona State University; Bill Hammond, Georgia Department of Education; Margaret Pope Hartley, The Psychological Corporation; Kay I. Hays, International Reading Association; Judith Hendershot, Field Local Schools; Alastair Hendry, United Kingdom Reading Association; Margaret Henrichs, Westminster College; Arlene Hett, College of Great Falls; Barbara L. Hiles, Missouri State Council of IRA; Jim Hoffman, University of Texas at Austin; Torleiv Høien, Stavanger College of Education; Jack Humphrey, University of Evansville; Judith W. Irwin, University of Connecticut; Peg Isakson, Colorado Council of IRA; Amy Jahner, North Dakota Reading Association; Dale D. Johnson, University of Northern Iowa; Robert A. Kaiser, Memphis State University; Wendy C. Kasten, University of South Florida at Sarasota; Francis E. Kazemek, St. Cloud State University; Marilyn Keerak, Saskatchewan Reading Council; Sharon B. Kletzien, West Chester University; Darlene

Kramer, Wisconsin State Reading Association; Diane Lapp, San Diego State University; Libby Limbrick, New Zealand Reading Association; Wayne M. Linek, East Texas State University; James M. Macon, California Reading Association; Dolores B. Malcolm, St. Louis Public Schools; Leona Manke, Albertson College of Idaho; Miriam Marecek, Boston University; Lydia Marlow, Missouri State Council of IRA; Leslie McClain-Ruelle, University of Wisconsin–Stevens Point; Michael C. McKenna, Georgia Southern University; Donna Mealey, Louisiana State University; Jane Medwell, College of St. Mark and St. John; Barbara Moore, University of the South Pacific; Lori Morgan, Orange Unified School District; Lesley Mandel Morrow, Rutgers University; Olga Nelson, Eastern Michigan University; Heide Niemann, German Association for Reading and Writing; Dale E. Norton, College of the Sequoias; Rafael Olivares, Queens College, City University of New York; Lloyd O. Ollila, University of Victoria; James R. Olson, Georgia State University; Mary Olson, University of North Carolina–Greensboro; Nancy D. Padak, Kent State University; P. David Pearson, University of Illinois at Urbana–Champaign; Roberta G. Pearson, Guilford County Schools; Ulla-Britt Persson, Swedish Council of IRA; Margaret Yatsevitch Phinney, University of Minnesota; John C. Pitman, New Jersey Department of Education; Kathy Ransom, consultant; Peggy E. Ransom, Ball State University; Timothy Rasinski, Kent State University; Colleen Rickert, Aurora Public Schools; Frances Harlene Robbins, Colorado Council of IRA; Betty D. Roe, Tennessee Technological University; Doris Roettger, Heartland Area Education Agency; Marie C. Roos, Jackson State University; Tonja L. Root, Valdosta State University; Kathy Roskos, John Carroll University; Elaine J. Ruggieri, West Warwick Schools; Terry Salinger, International Reading Association; Barbara R. Schirmer, Lewis & Clark College; Mary Dunn Siedow, The Literacy Center; Mary Jett Simpson, University of Wisconsin–Milwaukee; Yvonne Siu-Runyan, University of Northern Colorado; Kathy G. Short, University of Arizona; Judith Pollard Slaughter, McGill University; Jane Barber Smith, New York State Reading Association; Karen Smith, National Council of Teachers of English; Linda Snyder, Franklin College; Maha Sripathy, Singapore Society for Reading and Literacy; Norman A. Stahl, Northern Illinois University; Ralph C. Staiger, Emeritus, International Reading Association and University of Delaware; Jacquelyn W. Stephens, Reading and Speech Institute of Savannah; Joan C. Stevenson, The R.L. Bryan Co.; Betty Stewart, Manitoba Reading Association; Rosemarie Stocky, Liberty Middle School; Barbara D. Stoodt, University of North Carolina–Greensboro; Shauna Tateoka, Mastery Learning Special Interest Group of IRA; Denny Taylor, University of Arizona; Dana G. Thames, University of Southern Mississippi; Richard A. Thompson, University of Central Florida; Robert Tierney, Ohio State University; Richard T. Vacca, Kent State University; Karen Van Eaton, Teaching as a Researching Profession Special Interest Group of IRA; Sylvia Vardell, University of Texas at Arlington; MaryEllen Vogt, California State University, Long Beach; Barbara Walker, Eastern Montana College; Kate Tyler Wall, International Reading Association; Lillian Ward, Tennessee Reading Association; M. Jerry Weiss, Jersey City State College; Sharon Wentzell, Canadian Special Interest Group on Literacy of IRA; Sandra J. White, Ontario Reading Association; Karen D. Wood, University of North Carolina–Greensboro; Carol Zacharias, Manitoba Reading Association

ABC book **1.** See **alphabet book**. **2.** a book used in the British Isles from at least the 15th century for combined reading and religious instruction, originally including the alphabet, syllabarium, Pater Noster, Hail Mary, and creed. Also ABC; ABC-book; **abcee-book**; **absey-book**; **battledore**. See also **abecedarium**; **hornbook**.

ABCS *n.* **1.** the letters of the English alphabet. **2.** the rudiments of a school subject, especially of reading, writing, and spelling. Also ABC's.

abduction *n.* **1.** in semiotics, the process by which new hypotheses or conclusions are reached through intuition or a cognitive leap. *Cp.* **induction** (def. 2). **2.** the result of such a process; a hypothesis or conclusion. *Cp.* **deduction** (defs. 3, 4). *v.* **abduce**.

abecedarian **1.** *n.* one who is learning the fundamentals of anything. **2.** *adj.* alphabetic. **3.** *n.* (17th to 19th century) a beginning reader. **4.** *n.* (17th to 19th century) one who teaches beginning reading.

abecedarium *n.* a type of book used from about the 9th to the 18th century for combined reading and religious instruction, containing the alphabet, columns of syllables, creeds, and prayers. Also **abecedary**. See also ABC **book** (def. 2); **hornbook**; **spelling book** (def. 2).

ability-achievement discrepancy the difference between an individual's expected or potential level of performance and the actual level of performance, often used in operational definitions of reading and learning disability.

ability grouping the placement of students according to similar levels of intelligence or achievement in some skill or subject, either within or among classes or schools; tracking; homogeneous grouping. See also **streaming**. *Cp.* **heterogeneous grouping**.

ablaut *n.* a systematic alternation of vowels in roots of words that affects grammar and meaning, as in *sing, sang, sung*; gradation.

absolute *n.* a sentence part that is unconnected or awkwardly connected to the rest of the sentence, as *However* in *However, she was pleased to see him.*

abstract noun a word describing a quality, state, action, or other intangible, as *joy, idea, movement*. Also **value word**. *Cp.* **concrete noun**.

abstract reasoning the use of higher mental processes to identify and manipulate qualities and make generalizations based on these qualities, as in advanced literacy and comprehension tasks. Also **abstract thinking**. *Cp.* **concrete reasoning**.

academic ability an estimate of an individual's actual or potential power to perform well in school tasks. Also **academic aptitude**; **scholastic ability**; **scholastic aptitude**.

academic literacy book learning. See also **literacy**. *Cp.* **workplace literacy**.

accent **1.** *n.* in speaking, prominence or emphasis given to a word or syllable through one or more of these factors: loudness, change of pitch, and longer duration. **2.** *n.* orthographic marks used in text to show the nature and placement of spoken accent, as: **a.** a symbol (') placed above a vowel grapheme or adjacent to a syllable to indicate either primary or a secondary stress. See also **primary accent** (def. 2); **secondary accent** (def. 2). **b.** a symbol placed above a vowel grapheme to indicate that the vowel quality is not identical with that of the nonaccented vowel, as French *élève*. See also **acute accent**; **circumflex**; **grave accent**. **c.** a symbol placed above or below Hebrew consonants to indicate vowel quality or tone. **d.** in the metrical analysis of verse, a symbol that indicates if a syllable is strongly stressed (–) or weakly stressed (˘), as *How do I love thee?* See also **diacritic mark**; **prosodic sign**; **stress** (def. 2). **3.** *v.* to utter or mark with accent; accentuate. **4.** *n.* a manner of speech, especially pronunciation, particular to an individual, region, or social group, as *a foreign accent*, *a Southern accent*. *Cp.* **dialect**. **5.** *n.* the manner in which anything is said, particularly to emphasize emotions; tone of voice. See also **prosody** (def. 1). **6.** *n.* rhythm or meter of verse in poetry forming more or less regular intervals or beats. *v.* **accentuate**. *adj.* **accentual**.

accidence *n.* in traditional grammar, the study and system of inflection as a grammatical device. *Cp.* **inflectional morphology**.

accommodation *n.* **1.** the changes persons make in their speech to approximate the speech of those with whom they are talking, as adults who use simple syntax and vocabulary when talking with young children. See also **linguistic convergence**. **2.** in Piagetian theory, cognitive activity that involves the modification of mental structures; adapting one's way of thinking to fit the world. **3.** the changes made by an organism to fit a situation. **4.** the normal focusing adjustments of the eye, especially of the crystalline lens, for clear vision. *v.* **accommodate**. *adj.* **accommodative**.

accommodative convergence a reflexive change in the convergence of the eyes that accompanies changes in normal focusing adjustments, as the turning in of the eyes when focusing on near-point targets.

accountability *n.* the idea that schools or teachers are responsible for educational outcomes and should be evaluated, traditionally through examination of students' test scores.

accusative case in traditional grammar, the case of the direct object of a transitive verb or preposition, as *ball* and *him* in *I hit the ball toward him*. *Note*: In English, the object of a verb generally follows the verb, as *Mary likes books*, with pronouns changing case from the nominative to the accusative, as *Mary likes her*.

achievement test a test of knowledge of or proficiency in something learned or taught; especially, a test of the effects of specific instruction or training. *Cp.* **aptitude test**.

acoustic phonetics the study of the physical structure of speech sounds, as vibration, resonance, intensity, etc. *Cp.* **articulatory phonetics**; **auditory phonetics**; **phonetics**.

acoustics *n.* **1.** (*with pl. v.*) the characteristics of a room that affect sound loudness and distortion. **2.** (*with sing. v.*) the study of sound; specifically, the transmission, reception, and modification of sound waves. See also **acoustic phonetics**.

acquisition *n.* **1.** the gaining of a skill, as in learning handwriting. **2.** in some theories of language development, the innate process by which children learn a first language. **3.** in learning, an increase in response strength following reward. *v.* **acquire**.

acronym *n.* a word formed from the initial letters of words in a phrase, as UNESCO from *United Nations Educational, Scientific, and Cultural Organization*.

acrophonic principle in the development of writing systems toward an alphabetic script, the use of the name of a symbol for its initial sound only, as a picture of a butterfly used to represent the letter *b*. *Note*: The acrophonic principle introduces phonetic representation into a writing system, as in ancient Egyptian.

across the curriculum the theory and practice of extending key functional areas of one discipline or subject into other curricular areas, as *reading across the curriculum, mathematics across the curriculum, literature across the curriculum. Note*: The current trend to holistic curricula is a reaction to a long-standing practice of treating functional areas as isolated entities. It is not, however, a new concept in reading instruction. In the 1930s, several basal series experimented with it, while in the 1940s and 1950s *Every teacher is a teacher of reading* was a popular slogan, although one that was not always translated into effective practice.

acrostic *n.* a kind of puzzle sometimes used as a teaching tool in vocabulary development in which lines of verse or prose are arranged so that words, phrases, or sentences are formed when certain letters from each line are used in a certain sequence.

action research research, usually informal, designed for direct application to behavior or to a situation, as research by teachers in their classrooms. *Cp*. **applied research**; **basic research**.

active reading constructing meaning from text by transforming and integrating textual information into existing networks of knowledge and experience.

activity curriculum a curricular approach in which students' active investigations of problems of genuine interest to them take precedence over the study of prescribed subject areas. See also **child centered**; **curriculum**. *Cp*. **subject centered**.

actual development level an estimate of mental ability based on performance; "the level of a child's mental functions that has been established as a result of certain already completed developmental cycles" (Vygotsky, 1978). *Note*: Vygotsky commented that a test of mental age reveals what a child can actually do but not what a child can potentially do. See also

performance (def. 5); **zone of proximal development**. *Cp*. **potential developmental level**.

acuity *n.* **1.** clarity or keenness of reception of sensory stimuli. **2.** the extent to which the senses can detect the duration, intensity, position, and other properties of a target stimulus or array. *Note*: Special types of acuity, as *auditory acuity*, are given under the describing term.

acute accent an orthographic symbol (´) placed directly above a vowel grapheme to indicate that the vowel is rising in pitch (Greek), closed or tense (French), or stressed (Spanish). *Note*: In English, when written words borrowed from other languages contain this accent mark, it is generally retained in writing in order to preserve pronunciation, as *café*. See also **accent** (def. 2); **diacritic mark**.

adaptation *n.* **1.** the rewriting or alteration of an original work. **2.** change or adjustment to meet environmental demands. *Note*: In biological adaptation, changes in structure enable an organism to survive. In social adaptation, behavioral changes permit personal-social adjustment within a culture. **3.** the regulation by the pupil of the amount of light entering the eye. *v.* **adapt**. *adj*. **adaptive**.

adjacency pair two related utterances in a conversation between two speakers, the second always being a response to the first, as *"You forgot your homework." "No, I didn't." Note*: Forms of adjacency pairs include complaint-denial (as above), greeting-greeting, question-answer, and invitation-acceptance (or rejection). Analysis of adjacency pairs is a tool in the broader study of the social nature of communication. See also **ethnography of communication**.

adjective *n.* a word or word group that modifies or provides qualities or attributes to a noun, as *good* in *a good book* or *very interesting* in *a very interesting story*. *Cp*. **adverb**. *adj*. **adjectival**.

adjustment inventory a series of self-report items used to gauge emotional reactions.

adnominal *n.* a word or phrase that contributes to the meaning of a noun to which it is related, as *stormy* in *stormy weather* or *on the shelf* in *that book on the shelf.*

adult basic education (ABE) a comprehensive term applied to "the education of adults in the areas of primary knowledge such as literacy and numeracy, of social and life skills, and of understanding of community life necessary to responsible participation in society" (UNESCO, 1978).

adult literacy a level of literacy that enables a person in or about to enter the workforce to function effectively both as an individual and as a member of society; functional adult literacy. *Note*: "The issue that the term 'adult' raises derives from the need to include social relevancy in the definition of literacy" (Venezky et al., 1990). Numerous agencies exist for the study of adult literacy and the dissemination of information about adult literacy resources. See also **functional literacy**; **literacy**.

Adult Performance Level (APL) **Study** a comprehensive national survey in the United States of adult coping skills, including reading, writing, computation, problem solving, and interpersonal skills (Northcutt, 1975).

advance organizer an instructional tool in which brief written text is presented prior to other text for the purpose of enhancing the comprehension of that text. *Note*: The advance organizer may be constructed simply to suggest connections between the presumed background knowledge of the reader and the new material, or it may intentionally restate the new material at higher levels of abstraction, generalizability, and inclusiveness, as in Ausubel's original (1960) concept of the term.

adventure story a narrative that features the unknown, uncharted, or unexpected, with elements of danger, excitement, and risk.

adverb *n.* a word that modifies or specifies the mode of action of a verb (as *steadily* in *run steadily*), an adjective (as *very* in *a very beautiful dress*), or an adverb (as *rather* in *go rather quickly*). *Cp.* **adjective**. *adj.* **adverbial**.

aesthetic reading in transactional theory, a type of reading in which attention is focused on "what is being lived through, the idea and feelings being evoked during the transaction" (Rosenblatt, 1978). *Cp.* **efferent reading**.

affective domain the psychological field of emotional activity. *Cp.* **cognitive domain**; **psychomotor domain**.

affective fallacy in literary criticism, the error of judging a literary work primarily by its emotional appeal. *Cp.* **intentional fallacy**; **pathetic fallacy**.

affix *n.* a bound (nonword) morpheme that changes the meaning or function of a root or stem to which it is attached, as the prefix *ad-* and the suffix *-ing* in *adjoining*. See also **derivational affix**; **inflectional suffix**; **prefix**; **suffix**.

affixing language a language that primarily uses affixes to express grammatical relationship, as Latin or Greek.

affricate a speech sound that starts as a stop but ends as a fricative, as the /ch/ in *watch*. Also **affricative**.

age equivalent a type of derived score based on the age in the test standardization population at which the average person earns a given score. *Note*: The International Reading Association (1981) has issued a formal statement deploring the use of comparisons based on age-equivalent scores in education. See also **grade equivalent** *Note*: **age norm**.

age norm   **1.** normal or average performance for a given chronological age. **2.** *pl.*, the distribution of scores on a test by chronological age.

agent   *n.*   **1.** the person or thing doing, or responsible for the doing of, an action expressed by a verb. **2.** the part of a clause, usually a noun or noun phrase, that specifies who is responsible for an action; agentive. **3.** a person who acts on another's behalf.

agentive case   in case grammar, the noun or noun phrase that initiates the action of a verb, as *Charles Fillmore* in *Charles Fillmore developed case grammar.*

agglutination   *n.*   a type of word formation characterized by easily distinguishable morphemes that undergo little change when combined, as the English *un-natur-al-ist-ic-al-ly.* *Note*: Languages in which agglutination is predominant are called *agglutinative languages*, as Japanese, Turkish, and Swahili. *Cp.* **analytic language**.

agnosia   *n.*   the whole or partial loss of the ability to recognize sensory information when sensory acuity is intact. *Note*: Agnosia refers to higher order cognitive loss. Blind persons, for example, are not said to have a visual agnosia. *Cp.* **aphasia**.

agrammatism   *n.*   a form of aphasia in which the use of words is grammatically distorted or incorrect.

agraphia   *n.*   the loss of the ability to produce handwriting because of neurological factors, as those related to visual-spatial-motor integration.

agreement   *n.*   the grammatical correspondence of syntactically related words; concord; as

the noun plural ending *-s* and the plural verb *are* in *The trees are in bloom.*

alexia   *n.*   **1.** an aphasic condition marked by virtually complete inability to read, in which reasonable vision, intelligence, and language functions other than reading remain intact. **2.** the loss, usually from central nervous system dysfunction, of reading ability. See also **agnosia**; **aphasia**; **dyslexia**; **word blindness**.

aliteracy   *n.*   lack of the reading habit in capable readers. *n., adj.* **aliterate**.

allegory   *n.*   a metaphorical narrative in prose or verse in which the characters and often parts of the narrative usually represent moral and spiritual values, as in John Bunyan's *Pilgrim's Progress. Cp.* **fable** (def. 1); **parable**. *adj.* **allegorical**.

alliteration   *n.*   the repetition of the initial sounds in neighboring words or stressed syllables, as "The fair breeze blew, the white foam flew / The furrow followed free" (Samuel Taylor Coleridge, "The Rime of the Ancient Mariner"). *v.* **alliterate**. *adj.* **alliterative**.

allograph   *n.*   **1.** one of the variant shapes of a grapheme, as *B, b. Cp.* **graph** (defs. 1, 2); **grapheme**. **2.** a piece of writing, especially a signature, made by someone for another person. *adj.* **allographic**.

allomorph   *n.*   an alternate form of a morpheme, as the plural in English represented by *s* in *books* and *es* in *classes*. See also **morph**. *Cp.* **variant**.

allophone   *n.*   **1.** any of a class of speech sounds that constitute a phoneme, as the *p* sounds in *pot, spot,* and *top,* which are allophones of the phoneme /p/. *Cp.* **variant**. **2.** in Quebec, anyone whose mother tongue is neither French nor English.

alphabet *n.* **1.** the complete set of letters or other graphic symbols representing speech sounds used in writing a language or in phonetic transcription. **2.** a writing system in which graphic symbols represent speech sounds. **3.** the sequential arrangement of the letters used to write a given language. See also **letter** (def. 1); **orthography**; **script** (def. 1); **writing system** (def. 1). *n.* **alphabetization**. *v.* **alphabetize**. *adj.* **alphabetic**; **alphabetical**.

alphabet book a book for helping young children develop the concept and sequence of the alphabet by pairing given letters with pictures of objects that begin with the sounds they represent. Also ABC **book**. *Cp.* **counting book**.

alphabetic principle the assumption underlying alphabetic writing systems that each speech sound or phoneme of a language should have its own distinctive graphic representation. See also **alphabetic writing**; **one-to-one correspondence** (def. 2).

alphabetic writing a writing system in which one or several letters represent one speech sound or phoneme but not a syllable, morpheme, or word. See also **alphabetic principle**; **writing system**. *Cp.* **ideography**; **logography**; **logosyllabic writing**; **pictography**; **syllabary** (defs. 1, 3).

alphabet method **1.** a method of teaching reading and spelling in nearly universal use from ancient times until the early part of the 19th century in Europe and the 1870s in the United States. *Note*: In this method, students first identified letters by their names, then they spelled out syllables (see **syllabarium**) and then words containing from one to eight syllables (see **cumulative spelling**) before reading short sentences and finally stories. When students met an unfamiliar word, they spelled it out in order to decode it. See also **synthetic method**. *Cp.* **word method**. **2.** the technique of naming the letters of a word in sequence and then pronouncing the word for the learner. Also ABC **method**.

alphabet verse **1.** a short poem constructed around words that illustrate the letters of the alphabet. **2.** a religious or moral verse, usually in couplets, designed to teach the alphabet, as "In Adam's Fall, / We sinned all. / Thy Life to mend, / This *B*ook attend" (from *The New England Primer*).

alphanumeric *adj.* referring to sets of characters containing both letters and numbers, and often additional special characters. Also **alphameric**.

alpha risk in statistics, the possibility of rejecting as false or unacceptable something that is true or acceptable; the chance of making a Type I error. *Note*: If, for example, it is important that no one who might pass a course be rejected from that course, the alpha risk will be made small by using a loose acceptance level. *Cp.* **beta risk**.

alternate form any of two or more forms of a test or test series that are similar in content, item difficulty, and test results; equivalent form; parallel form.

alternate-form reliability the consistency of scores obtained by a group when reexamined with a different set of comparable items. *Note*: The correlation between the scores obtained on the two forms represents one type of reliability coefficient of the test.

alternation *n.* systematic linguistic variations: **a.** in related derived forms, as the present tense *think* with the past tense *thought*. **b.** in distinctive speech sounds, as the /k/ and /s/ sounds represented by the second *c* in *critic* vs. *criticize*. *v.* **alternate**.

alternative assessment the use of means of assessment other than standardized tests to achieve "direct, 'authentic' assessment of student performance on important learning tasks" (Warther et al., 1993). See also **authentic assessment**.

alternative discourse writing that uses unconventional patterns of rhetoric, as in James Joyce's *Ulysses*. *Note*: Alternative discourse is seen by some as a means of helping writers express their personal voice.

alveolar **1.** *n.* a consonant speech sound made when the tongue and the alveolar ridge stop or constrict the air flow, as /t/, /s/. **2.** *adj.* having to do with such a sound.

alveolar ridge the ridge of the upper and lower jaw that is covered by the gums and contains the tooth sockets.

amalgamation theory a theory of word recognition in reading in which experienced readers who are knowledgeable of grapheme-phoneme correspondences integrate in memory the spelling units of specific words with their phoneme equivalents without a need to first phonologically recode these words. "Seeing the spelling activates connections that lead directly to the pronunciation of that word in memory, where the meaning is found" (Ehri, 1994).

amblyopia *n.* reduced visual acuity, not correctable by refractive lenses and not due to injury or defects in the structure of the eye; dimness of sight. See also **visual suppression**. *n.* **amblyope**. *adj.* **amblyopic**.

American Sign Language (ASL) a communication system of coded hand movements used among and with the deaf to express meaning that would otherwise be expressed by speech. See also **sign language**.

ametropia *n.* a refractive condition in the eye that causes an unclear image because light rays

do not focus exactly on the retina, as in farsightedness, nearsightedness, and astigmatism. See also **refraction** (def. 1). *adj.* **ametropic**.

anagram *n.* **1.** a word or phrase whose letters form other words or phrases when rearranged, as the words *notes*, *tones*, and *onset* created from *stone*. **2.** a rearrangement of the letters in a word or phrase that results in a different word or phrase. **3.** a game sometimes used in vocabulary or spelling instruction in which letters of words or phrases are transposed to form new words. *Note*: In some versions, only selected letters of a word are rearranged to form other words, as *red*, *ear*, *dear*, and *err* from *reader*. See also **palindrome**. *v.* **anagrammatize**.

analogy *n.* **1.** a partial similarity, as *the computer is like the brain*. **2.** a general comparability or likeness, as *Your analogy of verbs as operators is useful*. **3.** *pl.*, a vocabulary development game designed to elicit associations between a concept and students' background knowledge. **4.** in reasoning, the inference that if things are similar in known ways, they are probably similar in other ways. **5.** in linguistics, a change of irregular grammatical forms to conform to regular patterns, as a young child's use of *mans* for *men* or *goed* for *gone*.

analysis *n., pl.* **-ses** **1.** the process or result of identifying the parts of a whole and their relationships to one another. *Ant.* **synthesis**. **2.** the use of this process as a method of study, as *word analysis*. **3.** See **statistical analysis**. **4.** psychoanalysis. *v.* **analyze**. *adj.* **analytic; analytical**.

analysis-by-synthesis a theory of speech perception that proposes that listeners have an internal language mechanism that selects acoustic features from incoming speech and tries to synthesize a replication of them.

analysis of covariance (ANCOVA) a form of analysis of variance for partialing out the effect of correlated variables so that dependent variables can be considered one at a time, a procedure that may be used, for example, to equate experimental groups by adjusting posttest scores for initial group differences. See also **analysis of variance**.

Types of *Analysis**

Measurement and statistics
analysis by synthesis
analysis of covariance (ANCOVA)
analysis of variance (ANOVA)
bivariate analysis
factor analysis
item analysis
multiple-regression analysis
multivariate analysis
path analysis
pattern analysis
regression analysis
sequential analysis
trend analysis

Language related
cluster analysis
content analysis
contextual analysis
conversational analysis
critical analysis
discourse analysis
feature analysis
linguistic analysis
literary analysis
perceptual analysis
phonemic analysis
phonetic analysis
phonic analysis
propaganda analysis
semantic feature analysis
structural analysis
task analysis
text (structure) analysis
word analysis

*Terms are all defined in this dictionary.

---

analysis of variance (ANOVA) a statistical procedure for testing the significance of the difference between the means of two or more groups. See also **analysis of covariance**.

analytic language a language in which syntactic features are expressed primarily by words and their order rather than by affixes, as Vietnamese; isolating language. *Cp.* **agglutination**; **synthetic language**.

analytic method a way of teaching beginning reading that starts with whole units of language and later breaks these down into their parts, as sentences into words or words into sounds; global method; look-and-say method. See also **word method**. *Cp.* **synthetic method**.

analytic phonics a whole-to-part approach to word study in which the student is first taught a number of sight words and then relevant phonic generalizations, which are subsequently applied to other words; deductive phonics. See also **whole-word phonics**. *Cp.* **synthetic phonics**.

analytic scoring in writing, the assignment of scores to different aspects of a writing sample to identify its specific strengths and weaknesses in areas such as ideas, style, grammar, organization, spelling, etc. *Cp.* **holistic scoring**.

Anansi tale a series of folktales of African origin that flourish in Jamaica describing the adventures of Anansi, a spider and trickster; often used to promote multicultural awareness. *Note*: "These tales have a rhythm and cadence found in no other stories in the world. They ring of the oral tradition and are frequently written in the storyteller's voice" (Huck et al., 1993).

anaphora *n.* **1.** the use of a word, usually a pronoun, as a substitute for a preceding word or group of words; backward reference; as *it* in *Her name is Marie, but I didn't know it*. See also **ref-**

erence (def. 5). *Cp.* **cataphora**; **endophora**; **exophora**. **2.** a literary device of repeating initial sounds or words or phrases to achieve a certain effect. Also **anaphor**. *adj.* **anaphoral**.

anastrophe *n.* the deliberate inversion of the usual order of the parts of a sentence for literary effect. See also **inversion**.

anecdotal record a description of behavior; a reporting of observed behavioral incidents.

angular gyrus a small area of the cerebral hemisphere involved with the comprehension of oral and written language. *Note*: Lesions in this area may lead to some forms of receptive aphasia and to poor spelling performance and decoding in reading.

animate noun a subclass of nouns referring to living things. *Cp.* **inanimate noun**.

anisometropia *n.* a differing refractive condition in the two eyes; differential ametropia. *Note*: Anisometropia, one of the major causes of amblyopia, may refer to different degrees of the same refractive condition or to different types of conditions, as one farsighted eye and one nearsighted eye.

anomia *n.* aphasia that involves the loss of ability to recall words, as the names of objects, persons, activities, etc.

antagonist *n.* a character that opposes the hero(-ine); villain. *Cp.* **protagonist**.

antecedent *n.* a word, phrase, or clause to which a following pronoun refers, as *Iris* is the antecedent of *she* in *Iris tried, but she couldn't find the book*. *Cp.* **anaphora** (def. 1).

anthropomorphism *n.* the attribution of human characteristics to animals, plants, or objects, as to the wolf in *Little Red Riding Hood*. *adj.* **anthropomorphic**.

antonym *n.* a word opposite in meaning to another word. *Cp.* **synonym** (def. 1). *adj.* **antonymous**.

aphasia *n.* any receptive or expressive disorder in language use caused by disease of or injury to the brain, often following a major stroke or head injury. *Note*: Alexia, dyslexia, and other symbolic processing disorders are considered aphasic language disorders. *Cp.* **agnosia**. *adj.* **aphasic**.

Types of *Aphasia**
expressive aphasia
receptive aphasia
semantic aphasia

---

*Terms are all defined in this dictionary.

---

apherisis *n.* the loss or deletion of an initial sound of a word, as the once pronounced /k/ in *knife*. Also **aphaerisis**. *Cp.* **aphesis**; **apocope**; **syncope**.

aphesis *n.* in historical linguistics, the loss of an unstressed vowel at the beginning of a word, sometimes leading to the creation of a new word, as *cute* from *acute*. *Cp.* **apherisis**; **apocope**; **syncope**. *adj.* **aphetic**.

aphonia *n.* loss of voice, usually completely. *Cp.* **dysphonia**.

apocope *n.* the loss of one or more sounds or letters at the end of a word, as the once pronounced "silent e" in *name*. *Cp.* **apherisis**; **aphesis**; **syncope**.

appellation *n.* **1.** a proper name or title, as *Queen Mary*. **2.** a sentence or phrase with a naming function, as *I'm called Joe*. **3.** the relation between a term and its referent. *Cp.* **signification** (def. 1). *adj.* **appellative**.

applied linguistics the application of linguistic theory, methods, and findings to language or language-related problems, as literacy instruction, second-language instruction, etc.

applied research formal research or study designed primarily to produce practical applications rather than theoretical knowledge. See also **action research**. *Cp.* **basic research**.

appositive *n.* a word or phrase that restates or modifies an immediately preceding nominal, as *Enrico* in *My son Enrico is 12 years old* or *my favorite flowers* in *Violets, my favorite flowers, grew wild in the valley. Note*: An appositive is often useful as a context clue for determining or refining the meaning of the word(s) to which it refers. *Cp.* **parenthesis** (def. 1). *n.* **apposition**.

appropriateness *n.* in sociolinguistics, an indicator for determining if a speech act or utterance is suitable or permissible in a particular social situation, as using a contraction such as *I've* in informal conversations. See also **felicity conditions**.

approximation and correction a term used to describe goal-oriented learning behavior as a pattern of educated guesses as contrasted to the randomness suggested by the term *trial and error. Cp.* **trial-and-error learning**.

aptitude test a test used to predict future performance in a given activity, "intended to predict success in some occupation or training course" (Cronbach, 1984). *Cp.* **achievement test**.

aptitude-treatment interaction the effect of a treatment or program that varies depending on student characteristics as, for example, the observation that visual learners do better in a reading instruction program that emphasizes graphics.

archetypal criticism *n.* the study of apparently perennial images, themes, symbols, stories, and myths in literature, including narratives that unite the seasons with literary genres. *Note*: Apart from its association with anthropology, religion, and psychoanalysis, archetypal criticism is best known through the work of Northrop Frye (*Anatomy of Criticism*, 1957). Such criticism favors mythic and religious figures over realistic and naturalistic characters. The nature of the archetypes themselves remains open to substantial dispute.

argot *n.* originally, the specialized vocabulary of the underworld, used to conceal meaning from outsiders, but now applied to vocabularies of other specific groups. See also **cant**; **jargon**; **slang**.

argumentation *n.* a type of discourse in speech or writing that develops or debates a topic in a logical or persuasive way. *Cp.* **description**; **exposition** (def. 1); **narration** (def. 1). *adj.* **argumentative**.

arteriosclerosis *n.* a thickening and hardening of the walls of small and terminal arteries, believed to contribute to some language difficulties. *adj.* **arteriosclerotic**.

article *n.* **1.** an essay or prose composition of nonfiction material. **2.** a grammatical marker of a noun, as the definite article *the* and the indefinite articles *a* and *an*. See also **determiner**.

articulate 1. *v.* to modify the air flow from the lungs to produce speech sounds. **2.** *v.* to enunciate with great clarity. **3.** *v.* to use clear, expressive language. **4.** *adj.* able to produce speech. **5.** *adj.* spoken with clear enunciation. **6.** *adj.* capable of using clear, expressive language. **7.** *adj.* organized into an integrated whole, as an articulated language arts program.

articulation *n.* **1.** in phonetics, the physiological process of producing speech sounds in the throat or mouth. **2.** the act of producing comprehensible speech. **3.** the organization of ideas in a meaningful way, as *An effective curriculum requires the articulation of important concepts.* **4.** the development of a complete test battery to provide comparable test scores. *adj.* **articulatory.**

articulatory defect inaccurate speech sound production, commonly omissions, substitutions, and distortions.

articulatory phonetics the study and classification of speech sounds based on their method of production by the vocal organs. *Cp.* **acoustic phonetics**; **auditory phonetics**; **phonetics.**

artificial concept an abstract idea with well-defined borders and unique defining features that distinguish it from other concepts, as *centimeter.*

artificial language 1. an invented language intended for special use, as an international language, as Esperanto, or as a fictional language, as Klingon in the *Star Trek* television series. **2.** a code system composed of abstract symbols, signs, or numbers, as the computer programming languages COBOL, FORTRAN. *Cp.* **auxiliary language.**

aspect *n.* a grammatical category that describes an action of a verb as either continuing or completed. *Note*: English contains two aspects of verbs: perfect, indicating a completed action; and progressive, indicating a continuing action. See also the box "Types of Aspect" in the next column; **tense.**

aspirate 1. *n.* an unvoiced speech sound produced by a puff of air, as /h/ in *hat.* **2.** *v.* to produce such a sound.

aspirated stop a stop consonant sound released with a puff of air, as /k/, /p/, and /t/ at the beginning of a word.

aspiration *n.* **1.** the release of a puff of air in pronouncing some consonant sounds. **2.** the act

of breathing. **3.** a goal or objective set by the learner. See also **level of aspiration.**

Types of *Aspect*
Perfect
past perfect (also pluperfect):
    Joan *had read* the book.
present perfect: Joan *has read*
    the book.
future perfect: Joan *will have*
    read the book.

Progressive
past progressive: Joan *was read-*
    ing the book
present progressive: Joan *is read-*
    ing the book.
future progressive: Joan *will be*
    reading the book.

---

assessment *n.* the act or process of gathering data in order to better understand the strengths and weaknesses of student learning, as by observation, testing, interviews, etc. *Note*: Some writers use the term *assessment* to refer also to the judgments or evaluations made after data are gathered. See also **evaluation** (def. 1). *v.* **assess.**

Types of *Assessment**
alternative
authentic
classroom based
clinical
content referenced
differential
formal
informal
integrated
learner
needs
on demand
performance

---
*Terms are all defined in this dictionary.

---

assessment center a setting in which teachers are evaluated by demonstrating their skills and knowledge under controlled conditions.

assimilation *n.* **1.** the process of incorporating new ideas to make them part of one's present knowledge, as the assimilation of current curriculum theory. **2.** the process of learning something so well that it becomes part of behavior, as the assimilation of handwriting skills. **3.** the psychological process of making new knowledge fit into one's experiential structure to avoid cognitive dissonance. **4.** the process by which members of a group become more like those of a culturally different group, as the assimilation of Puerto Ricans in New York City. **5.** in speech production, the process of making a sound similar to or identical to a neighboring sound, as in pronouncing *grandpa* as /gram' pa/. *Cp.* **dissimilation**; **sandhi**. **6.** in Piagetian theory, a mental activity that incorporates a new experience into an existing cognitive structure, altering the experience in the process but preserving the structure; changing one's representations of the world to fit one's way of thinking. *v.* **assimilate**. *adj.* **assimilative**.

assisted learning any supportive activity that helps a learner complete a task, as supplying a clue to a needed word meaning; aided learning. *Note*: Numerous terms referring to assisted learning of reading exist, as *assisted reading*, *aided reading*, *partner reading*, *echo reading*, *paired reading*, *scaffolding*, etc.

association *n.* the statistic estimation of relationship between two or more variables; correlation coefficient.

assonance *n.* the repetition in words of identical or similar vowel sounds followed by different consonant sounds, as /a/ in *the mad hatter*. *Cp.* **consonance** (def. 1).

assumptive teaching any instruction in which the teacher takes for granted that the students have the prerequisite experiences, skills, and vocabulary to profit from that instruction. *Cp.* **diagnostic teaching**.

asterisk **1.** *n.* a symbol (*) used: **a.** to refer to, as to a footnote, or to indicate an omission, as *Go to ****!* **b.** in general linguistics, to mark a faulty utterance. **c.** in historical linguistics, to indicate a hypothetical or reconstructed form, as Germanic **bōkō* "beech," from which comes *book*. **2.** *v.* to mark with an asterisk.

asthenopia *n.* any general discomfort and fatigue of the eyes, often with headache; eyestrain.

astigmatism *n.* **1.** an irregularity in the cornea or lens of the eye which prevents the clear focus of light rays in one or more axes of the retina. **2.** a defect in vision because of such an aberration. *adj.* **astigmatic**.

asymbolia *n.* a serious impairment in which many types of symbolic behavior are disturbed, including oral language, reading, written language, and mathematics.

at risk referring to a person or group whose prospects for success are marginal or worse.

attention-deficit disorder (ADD) "a developmental disorder involving one or more of the basic cognitive processes relating to orienting, focusing, or maintaining attention" (Bloomingdale et al., 1991). *Cp.* **attention-deficit hyperactivity disorder**.

attention-deficit hyperactivity disorder (ADHD) attention-deficit disorder plus hyperactivity. *Note*: "The basic problems of children with ADHD are primarily inattention, impulsivity, and deficits in rule-governed behavior, not the restlessness or squirminess that have often been the focus of adults' concern.... In addition, ADHD appears to involve problems of motivation" (Kaufmann, 1993). *Cp.* **attention-deficit disorder**.

attenuation *n.* a reduction in the size of a correlation coefficient because of error in the original measures. *v.* **attenuate**.

attitude scale a set of self-report items for measuring one's reactions to some issue, person, or object, as *an attitude scale toward the prospect of achieving worldwide literacy. Cp.* **rating scale**.

attribution *n.* **1.** See **attributive**. **2.** in motivation theory, the assignment of the causes of personal success or failure to factors beyond the control of the individual, either external or internal.

attributive **1.** *n.* an adjective or noun that modifies a noun within a noun phrase, as *sincere* in *the teacher's sincere efforts* or *coffee* in *coffee cup.* **2.** *adj.* expressing a quality or characteristic, especially by an adjective in English, as *first* in *first reader. Cp.* **predicate adjective**.

atypical learner a general term for one who is different from the usual person in aspects of physical, intellectual, social, or emotional development; specifically, in child development, "a child who differs from the norm in mental characteristics, sensory abilities, communication abilities, social behavior, or physical characteristics to the extent that special education services are required for the child to develop to maximum capacity" (Kirk & Gallagher, 1989); exceptional child. *Note*: In the statistical sense, *exceptional* refers to significant deviations from the norm in either direction—for example, both the gifted and the retarded child represent atypical mental functioning. Commonly, however, the term is a euphemism for a person with some deficit or handicap. See also **mainstreaming**; **mental retardation**; **special education**.

audience *n.* **1.** the respondents to such media events as drama, television, visual arts, or written text. **2.** the intended target group of a message, as adolescents for young adult literature.

auding *n.* the processes of perceiving, recognizing, interpreting, and responding to oral language; listening comprehension. *Cp.* **rauding**; **reading comprehension** (def. 1).

audiogram *n.* a graph that shows the air or bone conduction results of an audiometric test.

audiology *n.* the scientific study of hearing and its disorders.

audiometer *n.* an instrument for measuring hearing acuity in decibels for pure tones or speech. See also **pure-tone audiometer**. *n.* **audiometry**. *adj.* **audiometric**.

audiovisual (AV) materials **1.** nonprint materials such as films, audio- or videotapes, compact discs, etc. **2.** See **educational media**.

auditory acuity the keenness or sensitivity of hearing; auditory threshold. *Cp.* **auditory discrimination**.

auditory aphasia difficulty in comprehending words even with unimpaired hearing, as in Wernicke's aphasia; word deafness.

auditory area the region of the cortex involved in hearing and understanding sounds and language. Also **auditory center**. *Note*: If the auditory area is injured, the result is the speaker's use of rapid and nonsensical oral language because the speaker literally cannot hear him- or herself talk.

auditory association the ability to connect several ideas or concepts presented aurally.

auditory blending the ability to fuse discrete phonemes into recognizable words. See also **blend** (def. 1). *Cp.* **auditory closure**.

auditory closure the ability to form meaningful words or utterances from incomplete or distorted sound patterns. See also **closure** (def. 1). *Cp.* **auditory blending**; **visual closure**.

auditory discrimination the ability to hear phonetic likenesses and differences in phonemes and words. See also **visual discrimination**. *Cp.* **auditory acuity**.

auditory-discrimination test a test of the ability to hear likenesses and differences in sounds, usually speech sounds in pairs of words differing in only one phoneme.

auditory feedback the act or process of re-acting to the monitoring of one's own speech, without which it is difficult to learn normal speech.

auditory image the mental representation of something previously heard, either present in memory or activated by a stimulus.

auditory memory the retention, recall, or recognition of what has been heard. *Note*: Auditory memory often allows one to recognize a word in print by saying that word aloud.

auditory memory span "the number of items that can be recalled from oral stimulation" (Myers & Hammill, 1990). *Cp.* **visual memory span**.

auditory phonetics the study of the perceptual responses of listeners as mediated by the hearing organs. See also **acoustic phonetics**; **articulatory phonetics**; **phonetics**.

auditory processing the full range of mental activity involved in reacting to auditory stimuli, especially speech sounds, and in considering their meanings in relation to past experience and to their future use. *Cp.* **visual processing**.

auditory scanning the process of searching among a sequence of sounds, as those of speech, for a designated sound or sound pattern.

auditory-visual integration the association of sound and sight, as phoneme-grapheme associations.

augmented alphabet an alphabet designed to make spelling and reading easier by adding letters to an existing alphabet so that each letter or grapheme represents a different phoneme of the spoken language. *Note*: Augmenting an alphabet to achieve a one-to-one match between phoneme and grapheme has been a common suggestion for spelling reform of the English language since John Hart's *Orthographie*, 1568. See also **initial teaching alphabet**.

aural rehabilitation aid to persons with mild hearing impairments, but not medical aid or the education of deaf and hard-of-hearing persons.

auteur theory in film criticism, the view that the director, not the author of the script or its source, is in fact the creator of the filmed product.

authentic assessment a type of assessment that seeks to address widespread concerns about standardized, norm-referenced testing by representing "literacy behavior of the community and workplace" and reflecting "the actual learning and instructional activities of the classroom and out-of-school worlds" (Hiebert et al., 1994), as with the use of portfolios; naturalistic assessment. See also **alternative assessment**; **assessment**. *Cp.* **classroom-based assessment**.

authentic text 1. text materials representative of the real world; nonacademic text; as bus schedules, directions for assembling a computer, etc. **2.** in student programs, text that has not been altered in form or content, as original publications of children's literature.

author 1. *n.* a writer. **2.** *n.* the creator of any intellectual or artistic work. **3.** *v.* to write; to be the writer of.

authoring cycle **1.** a process-based curriculum framework for the language arts that is built and draws on the social and psychological strategies children use in language learning. **2.** a metaphor for the learning cycle (Harste et al., 1985). *Cp.* **composing strategy**.

authoring system a computer program that allows nearly natural language to be used in writing other computer programs, or that prepares such programs on the basis of choices made from menus by the computer user.

author's chair a special chair in which students are privileged to sit while reading aloud their own writing to other class members.

author's intent the motive or reason for which an author writes, as to entertain, inform, or persuade. Also **author's purpose**.

autistic *adj.* **1.** marked by a severe developmental disorder in which the individual is so self-centered as to be largely or wholly unable to judge reality. *Note*: In extreme autistic behavior, social interaction, especially through language, is minimal or nonexistent. **2.** referring to the perception of the world existing solely to gratify one's desires, as by extreme or psychotic daydreaming, fantasy, or introversion. *n.* **autism**.

automaticity *n.* fluent processing of information that requires little effort or attention, as sight-word recognition. *adj.* **automatic**.

automator *n.* a control system that is self-acting, self-regulating, or able to be operated without attention or conscious effort. *Note*: Skilled readers develop an automator for rapid word identification. *n.* **automation**.

autonomous literacy independent literacy; the individual's ability to make independent judgments of meanings in text. See also the essay "Literacy" on p. 142. *Cp.* **basic literacy**.

auxiliary language a non-native language or dialect adopted by a language community for purposes of communication, trade, education, etc., as English and French for many African communities; lingua franca. *Cp.* **artificial language**.

auxiliary verb a verb that precedes another verb to express time, aspect, mood, or voice, as *has* in *has been* or *will* in *will do*. *Cp.* **modal auxiliary**.

average **1.** *n.* a typical amount, rate, quality, etc. See also **norm** (def. 1). **2.** *n.* the arithmetic mean. See **mean** (def. 3). **3.** *n.* a general term applied to measures of central tendency in distributions of numerical values. See also **mean** (def. 3); **median** (def. 1); **mode**[1] (def. 1). **4.** *v.* to find an average value for. **5. on the average**, usually; typically. **6.** *adj.* referring to an average, as average weight. **7.** *adj.* ordinary; common.

B̄

babbling *n.* a stage in early language acquisition, usually beginning about the fourth or fifth month, in which an infant engages in vocal play with vowel and consonant sounds, including some not in its language environment. *v.* **babble**.

back-formation *n.* the process of deleting a word's affix to form a new, shorter word that usually functions as a verb, as *edit* from *editor*.

balanced bilingualism a presumed equal proficiency in the use of two languages in all social settings.

ballad *n.* **1.** a narrative poem, frequently of unknown authorship, composed of short verses intended to be sung or recited. *Note*: "In Scotland, Hungary, and elsewhere in Europe, the ballad is a very old type of poem that contains elements of the epic, lyric, and drama, and is often tragic in tone" (Adamik-Jászó, 1994). **2.** a popular type of folksong, as Mexican "Corridos."

bar graph a chart in which the length of parallel rectangular bars indicates the frequency of data represented.

basal (mental) age the highest age level at which, and assumedly below which, a subject has passed all tests on the Stanford–Binet Intelligence Scale. *Note*: Partial age credits (in months) for tests passed above the basal age are added to the basal age in computing mental age on this scale. *Cp.* **mental age**.

basal reading program a collection of student texts and workbooks, teacher's manuals, and supplemental materials for developmental reading and sometimes writing instruction, used chiefly in the elementary and middle school grades. Also **basal reading scheme** (*Brit.*). See also **reading program**.

base component in transformational-generative grammar, the set of phrase structure rules and lexicon that generates basic sentence patterns.

base word a word to which affixes may be added to create related words, as *teach* in *reteach* or *teaching*. Also **base**; **base form**. See also **stem**. *Cp.* **root** (defs. 1, 2).

basic literacy communicative competence in an oral culture that does not have a writing system. See also **literacy**. *Cp.* **autonomous literacy**.

basic research in education, research or study designed to generate knowledge or to validate a theoretical proposition which may or may not have direct application to curriculum and instruction in the schools. *Cp.* **action research**; **applied research**; **teacher research**.

basic skills a general term referring primarily to cognitive and language-related skills such as speaking, listening, reading, writing, and mathematics, which are needed for many school learning tasks.

bathos *n.* **1.** in literature, an anticlimax that abruptly shifts the written style from the lofty to the commonplace. **2.** an insincere and overly sentimental expression, as *My dear, you look simply too, too divine!*

battledore *n.* **1.** a paddle made of wood or cardboard that was used as a substitute for the hornbook; battledore book. *Cp.* **hornbook**. **2.** an ABC book.

Bayesian statistical inference a statistical procedure in which an estimate of an expected distribution of values is made before data are collected and which then serves to modify the estimate.

beast tale a story in which animals play the roles of human beings in human settings.

behavioral objective a statement of the nature and degree of measurable performance that is expected for a specified instructional outcome, as setting a goal of writing a short essay without spelling errors.

behavior disorder disruptive conduct without an organic basis that often interferes with learning or social adjustment.

behaviorism *n.* the view that psychological study should be limited to observable behavior. *Cp.* **cognitive psychology**.

behavior modification **1.** a technique to change behaviors by systematically rewarding desirable behaviors and either disregarding or punishing undesirable behaviors. **2.** the application of this technique in remedial education.

behavior problem **1.** negative behavior that is less severe than a behavior disorder, as a temper tantrum. **2.** one who exhibits negative or disruptive behaviors.

beta risk in statistics, the possibility of accepting as true something that is false or unacceptable; the chance of making a Type II error. *Note*: If, for example, it is important that no one who *might* fail a course be allowed to enroll in that course, the beta risk will be made small by using a tight acceptance level. See also **power**. *Cp.* **alpha risk**.

bibliophile *n.* a lover of books.

bibliotherapy *n.* the use of selected writings to help the reader grow in self-awareness or solve personal problems.

bidialectalism *n.* the relatively equal ability to communicate in several dialects of a language. See also **communicative competence**; **register** (def. 1). *adj.* **bidialectal**.

big book an enlarged version of a beginning reading book, usually illustrated and with very large type, generally used by a group of students to read together and learn about concepts of print and various reading strategies. Also **blown-up book** (*N.Z.*).

bilateral transfer the shifting of a skill learned with one side of the body to the other, as in being able to read Braille with the right hand after having learned to read it with the left.

bilingual education the use of two languages as the media of instruction in part or all of an instructional program. *Note*: Several types of bilingual educational programs exist, including **a. transitional bilingual programs**, in which the primary language of the students is used for instructional support until some prescribed level of proficiency in the second language is reached. **b. maintenance bilingual programs**, in which the primary language of the students is first used, with a gradual transition toward the use of the primary language in some subjects and the use of the second language in others. **c. immersion programs**, in which the second language is the medium for all instruction in a supportive environment that includes teachers who speak the primary language of the students.

bilingualism *n.* the ability to speak or understand with some degree of proficiency a language besides one's native language. *Note*: The ability to read and write the second language may or may not be associated with bilingualism. See also **functional bilingualism**. *Cp.* **biliteracy**; **multilingualism**. *n., adj.* **bilingual**.

biliteracy *n.* the ability to read and write in more than one language. *Cp.* **bilingualism**. *adj.* **biliterate**.

bimodal distribution a frequency distribution with two modes or high points.

binary feature in phonology, a phonetic property that has two mutually distinct possible classifications, as voiced and unvoiced sounds.

binaural *adj.* **1.** having to do with both ears, as *binaural hearing*. **2.** having to do with sound transmitted from two sources, as stereophonic recordings.

binding *n.* **1.** in government/binding theory, a relationship between noun phrases in a sentence such that their respective interpretations are inseparably linked or bound together, as *her* being "bound" to *Carrie* but not to *Connie* in *Carrie asked Connie to call her.* **2.** the covers and spine that hold together and protect the pages of a book, periodical, or other material.

Binet Scale one of the earliest series of standardized individual tests of mental ability arranged on an age scale of increasing difficulty, first developed by Binet and published with Simon in 1905, with revisions in 1908 and 1911. Also **Binet–Simon Scale**. See also **Stanford–Binet Intelligence Scale**; **Wechsler Intelligence Scale**.

binocular fusion the blending into a single image of the separate images from each eye.

binocular vision the coordinated use of both eyes to produce a single visual impression.

biolinguistics *n.* the study of language in relation to humans' biological characteristics, especially anatomical and physiological. *Cp.* **neurolinguistics**.

biserial correlation a correlation between two variables, both assumed to be continuous and normal in distribution, one of which has been divided into two classes, as a correlation between IQ scores and pass-fail in school. *Cp.* **point-biserial correlation**; **tetrachloric correlation**.

bivariate analysis statistical analysis applied to two variables only, as in biserial correlation. *Cp.* **multivariate analysis**.

black comedy comedy that substitutes morbid, unfunny, situations for pleasant, funny, carefree ones. See also **theater of the absurd**.

Black English Vernacular (BEV) a variety of American English spoken by many African Americans, especially by those at lower socio-economic levels or in urban areas. *Note*: *Black English Vernacular* has long been a controversial term, chiefly because of its suggestion that all black Americans use this variety and because of social stereotypes associated with its use. BEV is spoken in geographic areas as widespread as Los Angeles, Chicago, Washington, D.C., New York City, and rural Mississippi (though most closely identified with urban settings). It is highly structured and logical and has characteristic lexical, phonological, and intonational patterns as well as distinctive syntactic features. Among the latter are the use of the double negative, *be* to indicate habitual action, deletions rather than standard contractions (as *I go* for *I'm going*), and the lack of possessive forms of nouns. Not all such features are necessarily present to the same extent in all BEV speakers. See also **nonstandard dialect**; **sociolect**.

blank verse unrhymed verse, especially unrhymed iambic pentameter.

blend **1.** *v.* to combine the sounds represented by letters to pronounce a word; sound out. See also **auditory blending**. **2.** *n.* the joining of the sounds represented by two or more letters with minimal change in those sounds, as /gr/ in *grow*, /spl/ in *splash*; consonant cluster. *Cp.* **digraph** (def. 1); **cluster** (def. 2). **3.** *n.* a word made by combining elements of other words, as in combining /br/ in *breakfast* with /unch/ in *lunch* to make *brunch*. See also **portmanteau word**.

blindness *n.* profound visual disability; lack or loss of useful sight. *Note*: *Legal blindness* is visual acuity of 20/200 or less in the better eye after correction, or reduction of the visual field to 20 degrees or less; *absolute blindness* is lack of all perception of light. *n., adj.* **blind**.

blind spot *n.* **1.** the light-insensitive point at which the optic nerve enters the retina. **2.** any small, irregular, light-insensitive area of the retina; scotoma. **3.** something about which one is uninformed, prejudiced, or insensitive.

Blue-Back(-ed) Speller a popular name for Noah Webster's spelling book derived from the color of its cover. *Note*: The book was first published in 1783 as *The Grammatical Institute, Part I*, retitled *The American Spelling Book* in 1787, and revised as *The Elementary Spelling Book* in 1829. This spelling book, actually a reader and speller, was most widely used in the United States with an estimated 100,000,000 copies sold.

board book a book printed on heavyweight cardboard and sturdily bound, as the first books offered to infants.

book **1.** *n.* a written or printed composition gathered into successive pages and bound together in a volume. **2.** *n.* blank pages assembled for writing, drawing, recording data, etc., as *a composition book*, *a sketch book*. **3.** *n.* a major division of a literary work, as *Book I* of Homer's *Iliad*. **4.** *n.* the text or libretto of an opera, musical play, etc. **5.** *n.* the script of a play. **6. the (Good) Book**, the Bible. **7.** *adj.* referring to book(s), as *a book catalog*. **8.** *adj.* learned chiefly from books, as *book knowledge*. **9. by the book**, in the proper form or manner, as *exercise by the book*. **10. closed book**, something one cannot or prefers not to reveal, as *The protagonist in F. Scott Fitzgerald's* The Great Gatsby *kept his past a closed book*.

book banning preventing people from reading books thought by others to be unfit to read, either by declaring them so or by destroying them. See also **censorship** and the essay "Censorship" on pp. 29–30.

book club **1.** a commercial organization within the publishing industry designed to: **a.** encourage students to buy selected titles in low-cost paperback form. **b.** sell books at a discount to adults. **2.** an informal organization in a school, class, or library established to encourage reading by its members. **3.** an instructional group in which students read, discuss, and write about a common book.

book fair a book exhibit designed to encourage the reading habit, especially in young readers, by providing an opportunity to browse, ask questions, etc.

Book Flood the use of children's books as the main source of instructional materials in which many books are brought in to "flood" a classroom. *Note*: This movement is identified with Warwick Elley of New Zealand, whose initial Book Flood project brought a large amount of reading to Fiji and had a profound effect on literacy throughout the South Pacific.

booklist *n.* a collection of book titles, often those recommended by some group and sometimes including annotations.

book nook a special place in a library or classroom for quiet, comfortable reading; reading corner. Also **book corner**.

bookplate *n.* a label pasted inside the front cover of a book on which the owner's name appears.

book report an oral or written reaction to a book, usually intended to stimulate thoughtful discussion of the book, made in classrooms, adult reading groups, etc.

Books in Print a series of comprehensive annual guides to currently available books, listed in separate volumes by author, title, and subject. *Note*: A specialized *Children's Books in Print* also exists.

book talk a discussion of one or more books by a teacher, librarian, or student to introduce books and to induce others to read them.

bookworm *n.* one devoted to reading.

borrowing *n.* a word or phrase introduced into a language from another language, as *chaise lounge* into English from the French *chaise longue*. See also **loan word**. *v.* **borrow**.

boundary *n.* in linguistics, a division between units of a language, as between: **a.** words, as *my book* (word boundary). **b.** word parts, as *un-kind-ly* (stem or affix boundary). **c.** syllables, as *knowl-edge* (syllable boundary).

bound morpheme a morpheme that cannot stand alone as an independent word, as *re-*, *-tain*, and *-er* in *retainer*; formative. *Cp.* **affix**; **free morpheme**; **root** (def. 2).

boustrophedon *n.* a method of writing in which the direction of each line of a text is alternately reversed, and in some instances also the directional shapes of the letters. *Note*: The term derives from the Greek, meaning "as the ox turns in plowing." Early Greek writing followed this practice, but gave way to writing left to right by the classical period.

THISISANEXAMPLEOFWRITINGIN
.DOHTEMNODEHPORTSUOBEHT

bowdlerize *v.* to remove from any piece of writing that which a censor feels is offensive or indecent; expurgate. *Note*: The term comes from Thomas Bowdler, an English physician, who removed such words from his edition of Shakespeare in the early 1800s. *Cp.* **censorship**; **expurgate**.

Braille **1.** *n.* a system of written language, including letters, numbers, punctuation, abbreviations, and prepositions, using embossed patterns of one to six raised dots to allow the blind to read by touch. *Note*: Braille may be written on a computer, a special typewriter, or by hand with a stylus and appropriate slate. **2.** *adj.* referring to Braille. Also **braille**. *Cp.* **Moon type**.

brainstorm **1.** See **brainstorming**. **2.** *n.* a suddenly conceived clever idea.

brainstorming *n.* a learning technique involving open group discussion intended to expand the range of available ideas, as to solve a problem, clarify a concept, etc. *Cp.* **clustering**. *v.* **brainstorm**.

branching program a kind of programmed instruction or computer program that provides alternate pathways through presented material depending on choices made at each response point. *Note*: Branching programs are designed to adjust to individual differences in interests or learning style or rate. Branching books, for example, read differently depending on choices made by the reader, each choice sending him or her to a different page. *Cp.* **linear program**.

Breakthrough to Literacy a reading-writing scheme in England that encourages the early composition of sentences by children.

breve *n.* an orthographic symbol (˘) sometimes placed directly above a vowel to indicate that it has short duration or lax pronunciation, as /ă/ in *cat*, or a weak stress in a metrical foot, as /me trĭ kəl/. *Cp.* **accent** (def. 2d).

broad-field curriculum a curriculum in which subject areas are synthesized into a new field of study, as the subjects of history, geography, economics, etc., into the social studies.

bulletin board **1.** a surface for displaying messages, graphics, etc., as *a bulletin board for posting student artwork*. **2.** a central location in an e-mail network for leaving messages for other computer network users.

burlesque 1. *n.* writing or acting that ridicules its subject by absurd exaggeration for comic effect. *Cp.* **caricature**; **lampoon** (def. 1); **parody**; **travesty** (def. 1). **2.** *v.* to act, write, or illustrate in such ways. 3. *n.* a variety show with bawdy humor, slapstick, and often a striptease act. Also **burlesk**.

cacography *n.* **1.** poor handwriting or penmanship. *Cp.* **calligraphy**. **2.** poor spelling. *Cp.* **orthography** (def. 2). *adj.* **cacographic(-ical)**.

caesura *n., pl.* **-ras, -rae 1.** in modern usage, a break in the rhythm of language, especially a natural pause in a line of verse, marked in prosody by a double vertical line. **2.** in classical Greek and Roman poetry, a pause within a metrical foot. Also **cesura**.

calligraphy *n.* the artful production of handwritten script, as Chinese characters, alphabet letters, etc.; penmanship. *Cp.* **cacography**. *adj.* **calligraphic**.

calque *n.* a borrowing of the meaning of a word or phrase from another language, as the English *beer garden* from the German *Biergarten*; loan translation.

canon *n.* in literature, the body of major works that a culture considers important at a given time; i.e., works that express cultural values and artistic excellence. *adj.* **canonic(-al)**.

cant *n.* **1.** a specialized vocabulary of a social or occupational group, often including the use of stock phrases; jargon. See also **argot**.

canto *n.* a main section or a major division of a long poem.

capacity test a test that presumably measures one's potential for something. *Note*: "Much misuse or misinterpretation of mental tests arises simply from the labels 'intelligence' or 'capacity' as they suggest that inborn capacity is being measured" (Cronbach, 1970). "Only in the sense that a present behavior sample can be used as an indicator of future behavior can we speak of a test measuring capacity. No psychological test can do more than measure behavior" (Anastasi, 1976). *Cp.* **intelligence test**.

captioning *n.* the addition of information through subtitles, sign language, etc., to a movie or television program to allow persons with limited hearing to follow the dialogue or to help viewers understand the dialogue in a language they do not know. Closed captioned television requires the use of a special decoder. *adj.* **captioned**.

caretaker speech a distinctive form of speech used by mothers and other caregivers when talking to young children; motherese; baby talk. *Note*: Caretaker speech is characterized by the use of simplified grammar, exaggerated intonation, diminutives, etc., which are presumed to make speech more understandable to the child. See also **child-directed speech**; **telegraphic speech** (def. 1).

caricature *n.* **1.** an exaggeration or distortion of characteristics or defects of a person or thing, either in a picture or in words. *Cp.* **burlesque** (def. 1). **2.** the process of producing such an exaggeration or distortion. **3.** an extremely poor imitation; travesty. *n.* **caricaturist**.

cartography *n.* the making of maps or charts. *n.* **cartographer**. *adj.* **cartographic**.

cartoon 1. *n.* a drawing intended to amuse. **2.** See **comic book**; **comic strip**. **3.** *n.* an animated series of comic drawings viewed in motion, as in film or television presentations. **4.** *n.* a satirical drawing, as that of a political figure or event. **5.** *v.* to create such drawings, books, strips, or animations.

cartouche *n.* an oval or oblong figure used in ancient Egyptian writing to enclose characters representing a royal or divine name. Also **cartouch**. See also the illustration "Cartouche of King Tutankhamen" on p. 27.

case *n.* a grammatical category that indicates the syntactic/semantic role of a noun phrase in a sentence. *Note*: In inflected languages such as German, Russian, Sanskrit, Finnish, Latin, and Old English, word endings are used to indicate

Cartouche of King Tutankhamen

cases such as nominative, accusative, genitive, dative, etc. (See these terms.) Present-day English relies primarily on word order (as *the boy hit the ball* vs. *the ball hit the boy*) and prepositions (*the boy was hit* by *the ball*) to perform case functions. Case is exhibited in English in pronouns and in possessive forms, as *girl's* vs. *girls*. *Cp.* **declension**.

case grammar an approach to grammatical analysis developed within generative grammar by Charles Fillmore (1968) in which syntactic constructions are generated and studied in terms of the semantic relation of noun phrases to verbs.

case history in remedial education, a formal, comprehensive report on an individual's learning problem of more than usual severity. Also **case study**. *Note*: A case history usually contains both qualitative and quantitative descriptions of the nature of the individual's problem, including diagnostic data, remedial procedures implemented and their results, and suggestions

for further remedial efforts. Specialized personnel are usually involved in preparing case histories of students with particularly pronounced problems. Case histories may be reviewed by interested parties in a case conference.

casual speech the informal style of discourse used when talking with friends, acquaintances, and others with whom there are no social barriers. Also **casual style**. *Note*: Casual speech is marked by: **a.** the omission or ellipsis of background information. **b.** the use of slang or jargon. See also **communicative competence**; **register** (def. 1); **style of discourse**.

cataphora *n.* the process by which a word or group of words refers to a forthcoming word or group of words; forward reference; as *Here* in *Here is a list of things to do*. See also **reference** (def. 5). *Cp.* **anaphora** (def. 1); **endophora**; **exophora**. *adj.* **cataphoric**.

cataract *n.* a clouding of the crystalline lens of the eye or its capsule that leads to decreased vision.

causal network theory the premise that the structure of knowledge, as in a narrative, may be revealed by an analysis of the organization of the chain of events or states. *Note*: In this theory, a state or event is designated as a *node*, and the relationship between nodes as a *consequence* (Graisser et al., 1990).

cause-effect relationship a stated or implied association between an outcome and the conditions which brought it about, often an organizing principle in narrative and expository text, as *TV violence causes crime*.

cedilla *n.* an orthographic symbol (ڈ) placed below a letter to indicate some distinction in pronunciation from the unmarked letter, as the French or Spanish *ç* to indicate /s/, as in the French *français* or Spanish *Curaçao*.

ceiling *n.* **1.** an actual or assumed upper limit. **2.** the highest possible score on a test. See also **ceiling effect**.

ceiling effect the failure of a test to identify fully the performance of the most competent because of a limited number of difficult test items.

censorship *n.* **1.** any attempt to limit access to ideas, however presented; especially, to limit the opportunity of others to read certain books or magazines or to see certain films or plays or portions of them. *Cp.* **book banning**; **bowdlerize**; **expurgate**. **2.** the acts of an official responsible for examining books, films, plays, etc., to see whether they contain objectionable features. See also the essay "Censorship" on pp. 29–30. *v.* **censor**.

centile *n.* any of the 100 parts of a percentile distribution of scores, or its rank order. *Cp.* **decile**; **percentile**.

central auditory processing disorders hearing difficulties due to fundamental deficiencies in cognitive processing as well as to deficits in auditory perceptual processes.

central tendency a single central value used to summarize a distribution of scores. See also **mean** (def. 3); **median** (def. 1); **mode**[1].

centration *n.* in Piagetian theory, the tendency, particularly in young children, to attend to a single feature of an object or event, neglecting other features. *Cp.* **decentration**.

cerebral dominance the superiority of one hemisphere of the brain over the other in cortical functions; lateral dominance. *Cp.* **mixed cerebral dominance**.

cerebral localization **1.** the mapping of specific functional areas of the cerebral cortex, as those involved in speech, reading, and writing. **2.** attempts to determine the cause and location of defective brain functioning by surgical or noninvasive procedures.

chapter book a book long enough to be divided into chapters but not long or complex enough to be considered a novel, as books in Cynthia Rylant's Henry and Mudge series.

character *n.* **1.** in writing, printing, and computer work, an orthographic symbol used to represent a unit of language. *Note*: In an *alphabetic* writing system, characters include letters, numbers, and spaces, as well as symbols such as # or £. In a *nonalphabetic* writing system, characters represent larger units of language, as syllables, words, phrases, and sentences. See also **writing system**; **hieroglyphic**; **ideograph**; **letter**; **logograph**; **phonogram**; **pictograph**. **2.** a graphic symbol used in transcribing sounds, as in the International Phonetic Alphabet. **3.** a person represented in or acting in story, drama, etc.

characterization *n.* the way in which an author presents a character in imaginative writing, as by description, by what the character says, thinks, and does, or by what other characters say, think, or do about the character. *v.* **characterize**.

charity school a late 18th- to early 19th-century publicly supported school in the urban United States intended to socialize and prepare children for industrious roles in society. *Note*: In charity schools teaching focused on poor children's moral development in the belief that they came from weak family structures where moral training was inadequate. *Cp.* **common school**.

checked *adj.* **1.** of a syllable, ending with a consonant sound, as *of* with /v/, *off* with /f/. *Cp.* **closed syllable**. **2.** of a vowel, a vowel sound in a checked syllable, as /o/ in *Bob*. See also **closed vowel**; **short vowel**.

checklist *n.* in assessment, a list of specific skills or behaviors to be marked off by an observer as a student performs them.

Censorship: Rage and Outrage

In some respects the life of a censor is more exhilarating than that of an emperor. The best the emperor can do is to snip off the heads of men and women, who are mere mortals. The censor can decapitate ideas which but for him might have lived forever.

Heywood Broun, *Pieces of Hate and Other Enthusiasms* (1922)

Andrea Harte's parents have come to the school to protest an English assignment for students to read any one story by Edgar Allan Poe. Andrea had chosen "The Tell-Tale Heart," which appeared in the school library's anthology of American short stories and which the media specialist had recommended. According to the Andrea's parents, "The story is too violent for a 14-year-old to read. Besides, there is enough violence in the world without having young people read horror stories by such an immoral person as Poe. We would like the assignment to be canceled and more time to be spent in teaching literature and basics that provide inspiration and hope for young people." Mr. and Mrs. Harte claim they are speaking for several parents, and they have presented the principal with a petition signed by 12 parents of students in Andrea's class.

In another school, media specialist Nick Drake has decided not to order many books recommended by an education association, including ones written by such notable young adult authors as Judy Blume, Richard Peck, Harry Mazer, Norma Fox Mazer, Robert Cormier, Ron Koertge, Anne Snyder, Joan Lowery Nixon, and Jerry Spinelli. He read in a newspaper article that several of the titles had caused a stir in nearby school districts, so he is going to be cautious. The fact that the books have received very good reviews and their authors have been honored by local, state, and national organizations is irrelevant. Mr. Drake states, "I don't want parents to come marching in here to complain about books like they did in those other districts. In fact, I don't want any books that are controversial. I have enough to do without going through all those hearings and everything."

These two examples are not exaggerations of what is happening in schools and libraries throughout the United States and in many other countries today. There is hardly a book in print that someone or some group can't find a reason to object to. Some groups are so well organized in their challenging of texts that they intimidate school personnel: in many cases, the principal, teacher, and media specialist meet and resolve the problem by canceling assignments and removing books.

At one time books were attacked primarily if they included profanity or sex. Now there are many more reasons for banning books: the characters use drugs and alcohol; the characters are not good role models for students; the stories raise issues of right and wrong, which can lead to questioning of morality, confusion, and maybe juvenile delinquency; the books describe ghosts, witches, and spirits, which are satanic forces; the books do not adequately represent members of particular groups or cultures. The list of objections could easily be extended.

In responding to censorship, one should first recognize that teachers are professionals who develop curricula based on sound judgments and select print and nonprint teaching materials that will enable them to do their best to teach every child. While input from the community might be desirable, final decisions about selection of methods and materials to be used should lie with professionals. The selection criteria should be available for anyone to see at any time, however, and teachers, media

(continued)

Censorship: Rage and Outrage (cont'd.)

specialists, administrators, and school board members should work to develop a carefully planned policy statement on these criteria and on how challenges will be addressed. When a challenge is made, for any reason, the complainant must present it in writing. A special review committee, consisting of teachers, administrators, media specialists, and parents, should examine the complaint thoroughly. If there is a way to resolve the conflict in an amiable manner, then this is clearly desirable, but nothing should be changed in the curriculum until the review committee makes its report.

No teacher or school media specialist should have to face a challenge alone. In almost all cases, a professional and responsible decision was made to use the methods and materials under challenge, and the entire educational community should respond together when attempts at censorship arise. Many teachers and media specialists have wilted at the first sign of an objection. Educators need to support one another and let the public know that *they* know what they are doing, and that they have good reasons for doing it in the way they have chosen.

M. Jerry Weiss

child-authored message a communication in a child's emergent literacy phase that is planned and executed by the child and that may include letters, pictures, and other marks intended to convey information to others.

child-centered *adj.* referring to a curricular approach in which teaching and learning experiences are selected from and organized around a child's own intellectual, social, and emotional needs and interests. *Note*: A basic tenet underlying child-centered curricula is the belief that true growth occurs when children are free to develop intrinsic interests naturally. See also **activity curriculum**; **curriculum**. *Cp.* **subject centered**.

child-directed speech (CDS) speech adjustments made by adults when talking with children which are intended to meet the language and cognitive levels of the listeners. *Cp.* **caretaker speech**; **telegraphic speech** (def. 1).

children's literature writings specifically intended for children, or that children have made their own. *Cp.* **young adult literature**.

children's theater a formal play complete with costumes and scenes, presented by adults for an audience of young people. *Note*: Children's theater is based on a theme of interest to children or, more often, on a book for children.

child-study team a specialized group representing different specialties and working together to make a multidisciplinary evaluation of a student's academic or emotional problems.

Chi-square *n.* a statistical formula for determining whether differences between theoretical and obtained frequencies in various categories of a distribution can be considered to differ because of chance variation in sampling.

choral reading group reading aloud. *Note*: Choral reading may be used with a group to develop oral fluency or to make a presentation to an audience. It may also be used by two people, one of whom usually is a better reader and serves as a model during the reading.

chronological age (CA) the age of a person counted from birth measured by standard units, as months or years. See also **intelligence quotient**. Cp. **mental age**.

chunk 1. n. a unit of text longer than a sentence and shorter than a paragraph that forms a discrete syntactical unit. **2.** v. to integrate or otherwise organize details of information or bits of discrete data into larger units. See also **chunking**.

chunking n. in short-term memory, the process or result of grouping or reorganizing smaller units into larger, more meaningful ones.

cinquain n. a stanza of five lines; specifically, one that has successive lines of two, four, six, eight, and two syllables.

cipher 1. n. in some theories of reading, a systematic, internalized code for mapping printed words onto spoken ones, and vice versa. Also **orthographic cipher**. **2.** n. a system for writing a message in a secret code. **3.** n. a key to such a code. **4.** v. to write in such a code.

cipher sight-word reading in beginning reading instruction, "the process of reading sight words by setting up connections in memory between entire letter sequences and phonemic constituents in pronouncing words" (Ehri, 1992). See also **amalgamation theory**. Cp. **phonetic-cue reading**; **visual-cue reading**.

circle graph a graph in which a circle represents a whole unit divisible into parts, thus showing the relative size of the parts and their relationship to the whole unit; pie graph; pie chart.

circumflex n. an orthographic symbol (^) placed above a vowel to indicate pronunciation, as French *papier-mâché*. See also **accent** (def. 2b); **diacritic mark**.

citation form 1. the form of a lexical unit that, regardless of its variant inflections, is used as the referent in linguistic discussions and dictionary entries, as the citation form *be* can include *am, are, was, were, be, been, being*. **2.** the spoken form of a word in isolation from its pronunciation in running speech. Cp. **lexical item**.

citizenship schools in the United States, adult education programs organized by Miles Horton between the 1950s and 1970s in Tennessee and the Sea Islands to help disadvantaged rural blacks gain political power and control over their daily lives, especially through knowledge of documents relating to voting rights and privileges. See also **volunteer literacy programs**.

class n. **1.** a group of things with some property in common; category. **2.** a group of students organized for instructional purposes. **3.** a group of persons of similar socioeconomic, educational, and cultural level or status; social class. **4.** an interval in a frequency distribution, which, without overlapping, has the same range of scores or values as each other interval. *Note*: The use of classes in the analysis of data may simplify data processing. Cp. **rank order**. **5.** See **form class**. **6.** a topic of study, as *a biology class*.

class inclusion in Piagetian theory, the determination of what members belong to a given class; specifically, a developmental problem: when a class of things (B) is composed of two parts (A and A^1) of unequal size (A > A^1), the understanding is that A is not greater than B; i.e., in a school class where there are more girls than boys, a young child without class inclusion might agree that there are more girls than children.

class interval the range of scores in a class; the size of an interval in a frequency distribution.

classicism standards of literary taste and artistic expression based on the achievements of ancient Greece and Rome. *Note*: The Renaissance and the Neoclassic Period especially admired Greco-Roman writings. Whenever found, classicism tries to capture the theory and practice of some version of antiquity.

classroom-based assessment assessment of student learning and progress while participating in a normal school learning situation. *Cp.* **alternative assessment**; **authentic assessment**.

classroom climate the affective consequences of the interaction of students, teacher, and the physical attributes of the classroom; ecology of the classroom.

classroom language the language used in instructional settings that differs in form and function from language used in other settings. *Note*: Since language is a social instrument, classroom language is shaped by the social roles played by its participants. For example, if the teaching role is that of a questioner and evaluator, the students' role will be that of respondents.

classroom library a specially selected collection of books for classroom use, often changed periodically.

classroom literate a person competent in reading, writing, and speaking the language of the academic world, but not necessarily that of the "real world."

clause *n.* a group of words with a subject and a predicate, used to form either a part of or a whole sentence. See also the box "Types of Clause" in the next column. *Cp.* **phrase** (def. 1). *adj.* **clausal**.

cleft sentence a two-part sentence in which each part contains a verb used for meaning em-

---

Types of *Clause*
comparative
conditional
coordinate
dependent
independent
nonrestrictive
relative
restrictive

*Terms are all defined this dictionary.

---

phasis, as *It's a great essay that Melissa wrote* vs. *Melissa wrote a great essay*. *Note*: Cleft sentences generally begin with *It* and a form of *to be*. *Cp.* **pseudocleft sentence**.

clinical assessment an appraisal process involving both the administration of formal tests and the observation of behaviors.

clinical method **1.** an in-depth, structured study of individuals, using systematic diagnostic and treatment procedures. **2.** the procedure(s) used in a clinical setting. **3.** a. in Piaget's early work, an interview procedure for exploring children's cognitive processes. b. in his later work, a combination of interview and experimental procedures called *critical exploration*.

clipping *n.* the shortening of a word to a new form with the same meaning, as *lab* for *laboratory*, *bus* for *omnibus*. *Cp.* **shortening**.

clitic *n.* a grammatical form that cannot stand by itself in an utterance, as *n't* for *not* in *shouldn't*, *'m* for *am* in *I'm*.

closed class a grammatical class of words, the primary function of which is grammatical rather than substantive, as conjunctions, prepositions, articles, etc. *Note*: Closed-class words are relatively few in number and new ones are seldom added to a language. *Cp.* **open class** (def. 1).

---

closed syllable a syllable ending with one or more consonants, as in *mat*, *hand*; blocked syllable; checked syllable. *Cp.* **open syllable**.

closed vowel a vowel in a syllable or morpheme that precedes one or more consonants, as /a/ in *hat*, *hand*; checked vowel; blocked vowel. *Cp.* **open vowel** (def. 2).

close observation **1.** in writing, detailed attention to or documentation of situations, scenes, etc. **2.** the detailed or "thick" descriptions characteristic of ethnological methodologies in pedagogical and literacy research.

close vowel a vowel sound made with the tongue in the highest position in the mouth close to the palate or velum, as /ē/ and /o͞o/ in *read* and *hoot*; high vowel. *Cp.* **open vowel** (def. 1).

closure *n.* **1.** the tendency to perceive things as wholes, even if parts are missing or there are gaps in continuity, as the ability to interpret pictures from seeing only the parts, or the ability to detect a spoken word even though only parts are heard. See also **auditory closure**; **visual closure**. **2.** the temporary blocking of the air stream in voice production, as /b/ in *book*. **3.** the completion of a task.

cloze procedure **1.** any of several ways of measuring a person's ability to restore omitted portions of an oral or written message by reading its remaining context, as in the Degrees of Reading Progress tests. **2.** the completion of incomplete utterances as an instructional strategy to develop reading or listening comprehension with respect to sensitivity to style, attention during extended passages, etc. **3.** in second-language instruction, focusing attention on specific grammatical features by careful selection of omitted words.

cluster **1.** *n.* a linguistic sequence: **a.** of sounds, as the consonant cluster /sp/ in *spell*. **b.** of parts

of speech, as the verb cluster *might have been*. **2.** *n.* a group of languages or dialects whose common features may be explained geographically. **3.** *n.* a subgroup of highly correlated variables. **4.** *v.* to group or be grouped in some way.

cluster analysis any of several statistical procedures for detecting a group of highly correlated variables in a correlation matrix.

clustering *n.* a content field technique or strategy to help students freely associate ideas in their experience with a keyword proposed by the teacher, thus forming a group of related concepts; a teaching process of "relating a target word to a set of synonyms and other word associations" (May, 1994). *Note*: Clustering can be used to stimulate the recall of related ideas in reading and writing, especially in prewriting. *Cp.* **brainstorming**. *n.*, *v.* cluster.

cluster phonics a phonics instructional approach that emphasizes the identification of phonograms, as *ate* in *mate*. *Cp.* **letter phonics**; **whole-word phonics**.

cluttering *n.* rapid, incomplete speech that is often jerky, slurred, spoken in bursts, and difficult to understand; "nervous" speech.

cocktail party phenomenon a person's ability to attend selectively to a particular conversation while other conversations are simultaneously going on; selective listening.

code **1.** *n.* the storable information that enables one to send or understand messages. **2.** *n.* in computer work, **a.** a set of conventions, or keys, for converting one sign system into another; **b.** a computer program. **3.** *n.* a system of signals for transmitting a message, as *Morse code*, *sign language*, etc. **4.** *v.* to change information into a code. *Cp.* **decode** (def. 2); **encode** (def. 1); **recode** (def. 1). **5.** in sociolinguistics, any system of linguistic communication, as a dialect or language. *Cp.* **elaborated code**; **restricted code**. **6.** *v.* in semiotics, a set of normative or prescriptive rules, either linguistic or nonlinguistic, for governing one's actions. **7.** *n.* a system of oral or graphic symbols used in transmitting messages requiring secrecy; secret code.

code mixing   the use of linguistic elements of two languages in an utterance. *Cp.* **code switching**.

code switching   a person's change from one language or language variety to another during spoken or written communication, as from Spanish to English in a bilingual setting, or from a formal to casual style of speech. *Cp.* **code mixing**.

coefficient alpha   a formula for determining test reliability by analysis of the internal consistency of responses to the test items of a single form, especially useful where partial credit is awarded on a test item; alpha. *Cp.* **Kuder–Richardson formulas**.

coefficient of alienation (k)   a statistical measure that shows the degree to which two or more variables are unrelated. *Cp.* **coefficient of correlation**.

coefficient of concordance (w)   a statistical measure of the degree of agreement among several rankings.

coefficient of correlation   any one of several statistical measures that show the degree to which two or more variables are related. See also **reliability coefficient**. *Cp.* **coefficient of alienation**.

cognate   **1.** *n.* a language with the same historical source as another language or languages, as the Romance languages, which are each derived from Latin. **2.** *n.* a word related in meaning and form to a word in another language or languages

because the languages have the same ultimate source, as *mother* (English), *moeder* (Dutch), *moder* (Danish), *mater* (Latin), *matr* (Sanskrit), etc. *Cp.* **etymon**. **3.** *adj.* referring to languages or words with common historical sources.

cognate object   a syntactic construction in which a noun and verb are traditionally related, as *tell a tale*, *run a race*, etc. *Cp.* **collocation**.

cognition   *n.* the process or result of recognizing, interpreting, judging, and reasoning; knowing. *Note*: Perception is considered a part of cognition by some psychologists, but not by others. *Cp.* **perception** (def. 1); **thinking**.

cognitive clarity   in language processing, the understanding that text represents real language that has a communicative function. See also **linguistic awareness**; **metalinguistic awareness**.

cognitive code   the transformation of the physical stimulation represented by language symbols into meaningful schema.

cognitive deficit   a perceptual, memory, or conceptual difficulty that interferes with learning.

cognitive dissonance   a motivational state of tension resulting from an inconsistency in one's attitudes, beliefs, perceived behaviors, etc.

cognitive domain   the psychological field of intellectual activity. *Cp.* **affective domain**; **psychomotor domain**.

cognitive entry   in reading a literary work, the ability to participate actively in and relate to one's experience the cognitive behaviors of knowing, comprehending, applying, analyzing, synthesizing, and evaluating. *Cp.* **imaginative entry**.

cognitive map   a hypothetical mental scheme that functions to preserve and organize information about events that occur in a learning situation in a systematic way. *Note*: The term was first hypothesized by Tolman (1932) to explain how rats learn to run a maze.

cognitive psychology a view of psychology that encompasses "all processes by which sensory input is transformed, reduced, elaborated, stored, recovered, and used" (Neisser, 1967). *Note*: This view of psychology has stimulated research into covert mental processes, significantly advancing the understanding of reading, writing, and other language processes. *Cp.* **behaviorism**.

cognitive strategy a mental plan of operation for studying, solving a problem, coping with a situation, etc.

cognitive structure the organization of thinking into a consistent system, as in schema theory.

cognitive style a preferred way of perceiving and organizing information and of responding to stimulation; learning style. *Note*: Cognitive styles vary, as from analytic to thematic or from impulsive to reflective.

coherence of text the subjective interpretation by the reader of the extent to which ideas in text appear to "hang together" in a clear, unified pattern. *Cp.* **cohesiveness in text**.

cohesion a set of meaning relationships among grammatical or lexical components of text, as between pronouns and their antecedents. *Note*: "Cohesion does not concern what a text means; it concerns how the text is constructed as a semantic edifice" (Halliday & Hasan, 1976). *Cp.* **anaphora**.

cohesiveness in text the links or ties that connect text elements to provide unity and clarity within or between sentences and contribute to the reader's impression of text coherence. *Cp.* **coherence of text**.

collaborative learning learning by working together in small groups, as to understand new information or to create a common product. *Note*: There are many variations of collaborative learning, from exploration of a topic to its mastery and from the beginning to final stages of product development. This term does not specify roles or responsibilities of members and groups, and the practices it describes include little to intensive group interaction. In collaborative writing, for example, group interaction may be designed to help improve the writing of each group member; in collaborative reading, group interaction may promote sharing ideas to lead to a better understanding of a text. *Cp.* **cooperative learning**.

collective noun a noun that denotes a group of persons, animals, or things. *Note*: Collective nouns may be interpreted as a single entity, as *the faculty is angry*, as a collection of entities, as *the faculty are angry*, or as a plural, as *the faculties of the English and psychology departments are angry*.

collocation *n.* **1.** in linguistics, the habitual association or co-occurrence of words within some grammatical structure, as *submit a proposal*, *pen and ink*. **2.** the habitual co-occurrence of words in certain genres, as *decedent*, *will*, and *heir* in legal discourse about the inheritance of a deceased person's property. *Cp.* **cognate object**. *v.* **collocate**.

colloquial *adj.* **1.** referring to an expression or language use that is appropriate in informal situations but not in formal ones. **2.** referring to an expression or style that is considered old-fashioned or folksy, as *Aw, shucks*. *n.* **colloquialism**.

combinatorial reasoning in Piaget's construct of formal operational thought, the intellectual process that enables the individual to combine factors logically in all possible combinations.

combining form a bound base or root designed to be combined with another combining form or word to form a new word, as *bio-* and *-graphy* of *biography*. *Note*: Combining forms are most commonly found in words derived from Latin and Greek. Through the linguistic process of clipping, some combining forms become words in themselves, as *bio*, *metro*, and *porno*.

comedy of manners drama that satirizes the manners and customs of a highly sophisticated society or social class, often focusing especially on their amorous affairs, as Oscar Wilde's *The Importance of Being Earnest*.

comic book a book or magazine in which stories, often of adventure and fantasy but sometimes dealing with serious themes, are told primarily through a sequence of drawings and dialogue, as in *Superman*.

comic strip a sequence of drawings and dialogue, usually appearing in newspapers, that tell an amusing incident or story, as *Peanuts*; comics; funnies. *Note*: Though the term suggests lightness and humor, some comic strips deal forthrightly with realistic problems and are often devoid of humor.

comma fault the improper use of a comma between two independent clauses not connected by a conjunction, as *My dog came running, he was glad to see me*. Also **comma splice**. See also **run-on sentence**.

commentary *n.* **1.** a series of remarks on a text; annotations. **2.** an explanatory essay.

common noun a noun denoting a class or class member rather than a unique thing, as *mountain* vs. *Mount Fuji*. *Cp.* **proper noun**.

common school in the early to mid-19th century United States, a public school attended by children regardless of social class and religious background in which a curriculum with common content and political and social ideology was provided for all. *Note*: The common school movement established state agencies to control local schools and aimed to use public schools as instruments of government policy to solve social problems. *Cp.* **charity school**.

communality *n.* **1.** that part of the variance of a single test that is shared with another test. **2.** the sum or average of the communalities of single tests.

communication *n.* **1.** the sharing of information or ideas. *Note*: Communication is a central concept in the study of language, as in sociolinguistics, psycholinguistics, etc. **2.** the process or results of conveying information. *Note*: Communication may take place between social units such as persons or groups, between persons and mechanisms such as computers, or between such mechanisms. **3.** the transmission and reception of information by means of gestures, words, or other symbols. **4.** information which has been, is being, or is to be transmitted, as the content of a telegram. **5.** a dynamic interdependence or relationship between individuals. **6.** **communications** the study of media production and use. *Cp.* **information theory**. *v.* **communicate**. *adj.* **communicative**.

communication arts **1.** aspects of the curriculum that emphasize verbal, nonverbal, and visual processes for conveying meaning, as in radio, television, drama, and dance. **2.** language arts.

communication disorder an impairment in the ability to receive, send, process, and comprehend concepts or verbal, nonverbal, and graphic symbol systems. *Note*: "A communication disorder may be evident in the processes of hearing, language, and/or speech. A communication disorder may range in severity from mild to profound. It may be developmental or acquired. Individuals may demonstrate one or any combination of communication disorders. A communication disorder may result in a primary disability or it may be secondary to other disabilities" (Guideline of the American Speech-Language-Hearing Association, 1993).

communicative competence　the ability to use any form of language appropriate to the demands of social situations. *Note*: The components of communicative competence include linguistic knowledge, cultural knowledge, and interaction skills. *Cp.* **productive competence**; **receptive competence**.

community language **1.** language representative of an identifiable group of persons with similar traits, backgrounds, or interests. **2.** (*Austral., Brit.*) the language of immigrant groups.

community literacy reading, other than that done in school, "associated with participation in neighborhood activities and in government, church, and social organizations" (Arthur & Greany, 1991), as the reading of signs, documents, regulations, etc. *Cp.* **recreational reading**.

comparative clause a dependent clause in a complex sentence that provides a comparison with someone or something referred to in an independent clause. *Note*: Comparative clauses usually begin with *as* or *than*, as *Rhonda doesn't read as well as Rita* or *Tina is taller than Toni*.

comparative literature a field or course of study that examines the interrelationships of literature from two or more cultures or languages.

comparison *n.* **1.** the change of an adjective or an adverb to show greater or lesser degree, as *sad, sadder, saddest, most sad, least sad.* **2.** a literary technique of placing together like characters, situations, or ideas to show common or contrasting features. *v.* **compare.** *adj.* **comparative.**

compensatory education educational programs designed to help children compensate for the negative effects of social and economic deterents to academic and social growth.

compensatory reading (*Brit.*) remedial reading.

competence *n.* a person's internalized "knowledge of the rules of a language" (Chomsky, 1957). See also **communicative competence**; **universal grammar**. *Cp.* **performance** (def. 5; see *Note*).

competency-based education **1.** a type of education "deriving from the specification, learning, and demonstration of the knowledge, skills, behaviour, and attitudes required for a given role, profession or career" (UNESCO, 1978). **2.** education programs that emphasize performance, as in the ability to apply learning to specified tasks.

complement **1.** *n.* the word or words that completes the action of a verb in the predicate of a sentence, as *a policeman* in *Tom is a policeman*; verb phrase. **2.** *v.* to so complete a grammatical construction. *adj.* **complementary.**

complementarity *n.* a state of relationship between words with contradictory meanings, as *man-woman, bachelor-husband*. Note: Complementarities are characterized by a lack of gradation of meaning between them. In contrast, in antonymy words have opposite meanings, each of which can nevertheless be graded, as *big-small, bigger-smaller, biggest-smallest*.

complementary distribution a pattern of two or more phonetic variations of a phoneme or speech sound that do not occur in the same position within a word in a language, as the voiced /l/ in *lip* cannot replace the voiceless /l/ in *play* in English. *Cp.* **free variation**.

complete predicate the verb in a syntactical construction along with all its modifiers, complements, or subordinate parts, as *is going home* in *Lassie is going home*.

complete subject the principal noun in a syntactical construction which, with all its modifiers, determines the number of the verb, as *Still waters* in *Still waters run deep. Cp.* **subject** (def. 3).

completion item a test item in which the omitted part(s) must be filled in. *Cp.* **cloze procedure** (def. 1).

complex sentence a sentence with one independent clause and one or more dependent clauses, as *I knew* (independent clause) *when you came in* (dependent clause).

composing strategy in teaching writing, any of a number of activities designed to stimulate inventive thinking and discussion to advance students' writing efforts, as brainstorming, memory prompts, etc.

composite score a single score representing one's performance on several different measures; technically, the sum or average of different measures, often weighted, of the same individual or object. *Note*: The regression equation is a means of combining different measures of the same object in order to derive a composite score.

composition *n.* **1.** the structure or organization of a work of art, music, or literature. **2.** in writing, the process or result of arranging ideas to form a clear and unified impression in order to create an effective message. *Note*: The four major forms of composition are *argumentation*, *description*, *exposition*, and *narration*. See these terms. *Cp.* **writing** (def. 3). **3.** a short school essay. **4.** the arrangement of type for printing. *v.* **compose**.

compound bilingualism in bilingualism, having a single mental representation, or meaning, of something that has different names in the languages involved. *Cp.* **coordinate bilingualism**.

compound-complex sentence a compound sentence with one or more dependent clauses, as *Teachers speak and students listen* (compound independent clauses) *when both are motivated* (dependent clause). *Cp.* **compound sentence**.

compound noun a group of two or more nouns treated as a meaning unit, as *student teacher*, *tree farm. Cp.* **compound word**.

compound phonogram in phonics, two or more letters that represent a sound unit but do not make a word, as *gr, aw, ing*.

compound predicate a predicate consisting of two or more verb phrases, as in *Charlie enjoys swimming daily and diving occasionally. Cp.* **simple predicate**.

compound sentence a sentence with two or more coordinate independent clauses but no dependent clause, as *George talked, and Harry listened. Cp.* **compound-complex sentence**.

compound subject the complete subject, or noun phrase, formed by two or more simple subjects, as *men* and *women* in *Men and women chatted together*.

compound word a combination of two or more words that functions as a single unit of meaning; compound. *Note*: Compound words are written as a single word (*booklist*), hyphenated words (*books-on-demand*), or separately (*book report*).

comprehension *n. Note*: Comprehension, "the essence of reading" (Durkin, 1993), is often taken to mean *reading* comprehension in the literacy literature unless restricted specifically or by inference from its context. **1.** the reconstruction of the intended meaning of a communication; accurately understanding what is written or said. *Note*: The presumption here is that meaning resides in the message awaiting interpretation, and that the message received is congruent with the message sent. **2.** the construction of the meaning of a written or spoken communication through a reciprocal, holistic interchange of ideas between the interpreter and the message in a particular communicative context. *Note*: The presumption here is that meaning resides in the intentional problem-solving, thinking processes of the interpreter during such an interchange, that the content of meaning is influenced by that person's prior knowledge and experience, and that the message so constructed by the receiver may or may not be congruent with the message sent. "Comprehension is a process in which the reader constructs meaning [in] interacting with text...through a combination of prior knowledge and previous experience; information available in text; the stance [taken] in relationship to the text; and immediate, remembered or anticipated social interactions and communications" (Ruddell et al., 1994). "The meanings of words cannot be 'added up' to give the meaning of the whole. The click of comprehension occurs only when the reader evolves a schema that explains the whole message" (Anderson, 1993). *Cp.* **comprehension strategy**; **reading**; **reading-writing relationships**; **transactional theory**. **3.** See **reading comprehension**. **4.** all that a word or concept implies; connotation; as *one's comprehension of* literacy. **5.** the symbolic meaning or sign of an experienced event. See also **symbol** (def. 1). *v.* **comprehend**.

comprehension monitoring   in the act of reading, the noting of one's successes and failures in developing or attaining meaning, usually with reference to an emerging conception of the meaning of the text as a whole, and adjusting one's reading processes accordingly. See also **metacognitive awareness**.

comprehension processes any of the perceptual-cognitive ways by which one attains meaning. See also **cognitive psychology**.

comprehension strategy *Note*: There is little consensus in the research literature on what constitutes a comprehension strategy. **1.** in reading, a systematic sequence of steps for understanding text, as in the SQ3R study method (Robinson, 1946). **2.** (*pl.*) **a.** any of these steps used singly or in combination to attain comprehension. **b.** teaching techniques such as mapping, tree diagramming, etc., used to help students become strategic readers.

A General Reading
Comprehension Strategy*
Before reading: preview text; link to prior knowledge; set purposes
During reading: paraphrase text; monitor comprehension; integrate ideas; adjust purposes
After reading: summarize text; evaluate ideas; apply ideas
Note: These steps are not discrete; several may function together.

---

*After Flood & Lapp, 1991.

---

comprehensive school a secondary school with courses of study in many areas, as academic, technical, commercial, and trade curricula.

compressed speech an audiotape from which very short portions of the original signal have been randomly omitted. *Note*: Such compression does not hinder but often improves listening comprehension. Time-compressed tapes are widely used by the blind.

computer-assisted instruction (CAI) **1.** an automated learning program presented step by step by a computer with responses from the learner evaluated and indicated as correct or not, and with options for the learner to follow. **2.** a computer program that gives individualized lessons, tests, periodic reports, etc. *Cp.* **computer-based instruction**.

computer-based instruction teaching that relies heavily on computer-assisted instruction. Also **computer-managed instruction**. *Note*: Computer-based instruction implies a system in which the results of student learning, whether accomplished by computer or not, are evaluated by computer, and in which summaries of results, sometimes with suggestions for further or remedial work, are presented to students or the teacher.

computer literacy possession of the skills and knowledge necessary for operating a computer.

concatenation *n.* the process by which syntactic elements are linked to form phrases, clauses, etc., as *the + girl + s + play + ed + soccer = the girls played soccer.*

conceit *n.* **1.** a fanciful and often witty notion or idea, especially in poetic images, as "And the sabbath rang slowly / In the pebbles of the holy streams" (Dylan Thomas, "Fern Hill"). **2.** a far-fetched, overly elaborate metaphor, as "Our eye-beams twisted, and did thread / Our eyes upon one double string" (John Donne, "The Extasie"). *adj.* **conceited**.

concept book a book in which examples and comparisons are used to present abstract ideas in concrete, understandable ways.

concept cluster a group of terms organized to show their relationship graphically to a key concept, as in a semantic web.

concept formation **1.** the process of or stages in the development of understanding of an abstract idea. **2.** a cognitive system for integrat-

ing and organizing information based on common relationships.

concept load **1.** the proportion of different ideas presented in a text in relation to the text's length. **2.** a factor incorporated into some early readability estimates determined by examining the number of abstract words, the degree of abstractness of the words or ideas presented, or the proportion of items of information in relation to the length of the passage. Also **concept density**. *Cp.* **vocabulary burden**.

concept matrix a table for relating two or more sets of ideas, especially valuable in organizing ideas for expository writing, as in a listing of key ideas with corresponding examples.

conceptual frame(work) a scheme used to form hypotheses, models, etc. See also **model** (def. 3).

concrete noun a noun with a material referent, as *house*, *book*. *Cp.* **abstract noun**.

concrete operations in Piagetian theory, the first organized system of logical thought in mental development, usually occurring from about 7 to 11 years, that is dependent upon direct interaction with the real, concrete world. *Note*: A child who can develop a hierarchy of classes of objects that he can see, but cannot do so for absent objects, is using concrete operations. See also **infralogical operations**; **operations**; **preoperational thought**. *Cp.* **formal operations**; **stage** (def. 2).

concrete poetry poetry in which the physical arrangements of words are used to help suggest the author's meaning or theme, as in some poetry of Dylan Thomas and e.e. cummings.

concrete reasoning **1.** in Piaget's theory of intellectual development, a level of reasoning in which conservation is present. **2.** a form of thinking found to a marked degree in some brain-injured persons that is characterized by such symptoms as inability to shift a mental set, form gestalts, plan for the future, etc. Also **concrete thinking**. *Cp.* **abstract reasoning**.

concretism *n.* **1.** using specific examples of things and experiences in real life to illustrate abstract concepts and qualities. **2.** the theory and practice of concrete poetry.

concurrent validity evidence of validity gained by correlating test scores with performance at approximately the same time on some external criterion, as correlating test scores with cumulative grade point average for the same students.

conditional clause a clause that expresses a supposition, usually introduced by *if* as in *If I were king....* or *unless* as in *Unless you stop that....*

conditional knowledge knowledge that is dependent on further knowledge or information, as "This is true if..."

conditioning *n.* the process or result of linking a stimulus with a response originally caused by a different stimulus. *Note*: There are three major types of conditioning: **a. classical conditioning**, linking a response to a stimulus that would not ordinarily produce that response by pairing it with a stimulus that does produce the response; Pavlovian conditioning. **b. instrumental conditioning**, linking a response to a stimulus that would not ordinarily produce that response by following that stimulus with a second stimulus that is then followed by reinforcement. **c. operant conditioning**, varying the reward rate to produce rapid or sustained response to an instrumental conditioning connection.

conduction deafness impaired hearing because of a defect in the mechanical conduction of sound. *Cp.* **sensorineural deafness**.

cone *n.* any of the light-sensitive cells in the retina needed especially for fine visual discrimination and for color vision. *Cp.* **rod**.

conference *n.* a discussion, as about student work between a teacher and student or a teacher and parent.

confidence interval the limits in a sample distribution between which one expects with a particular degree of confidence that the population value will lie; specifically, the distance in standard deviation units from the mean that determines such limits.

confidence level the percentage of times that a sample would be expected to fall by chance outside the confidence interval; risk level. *At the .05 confidence level, only 5 percent of the time would a person's score fall by chance outside the confidence interval. Cp.* **statistical significance**.

configuration clue a shape or outline that aids in word identification; especially, the pattern the letters make above and below the main body of the word, as in jolly , general , reading . See also **visual cue**.

confirmation *n.* **1.** in reading or listening, the verification of predictions through information revealed later about the writer's or speaker's meaning or use of language. *Ant.* disconfirmation. **2.** See **tag**.

confirmatory factor analysis factor analysis conducted to test a stated hypothesis about the number or kind of factors measured by a given set of tests.

conjoin *v.* to connect two or more parallel syntactic units with one or more coordinating conjunctions to form compound predicates, etc., as *but* acts to conjoin the syntactic units in *We came not to play but to work. Cp.* **conjunction** (def. 2).

conjugation *n.* **1.** the inflection of verbs. **2.** the complete set of all possible inflected forms of a verb, as *sing*, *sings*, *singing*, *sang*, *sung* for the verb *to sing*. **3.** a class of verbs with the same inflection markers. See also **paradigm** (def. 2). *v.* **conjugate**.

conjunction *n.* **1.** a word used to connect words, phrases, clauses, or sentences; connective; as *and* in *she and I* or *When* in *When you are ready, we will go*. *Note*: A *coordinating* conjunction, as *and*, *or*, *but*, etc., connects two equivalent grammatical elements. When used in pairs, as *either...or*, they are called *correlative* conjunctions. A *subordinating* conjunction, as *because*, *when*, *unless*, etc., introduces a dependent clause, connecting it to an independent clause. **2.** the process or result of so connecting. *Cp.* **conjoin**.

conjunctive adverb an adverb, as *however*, *nonetheless*, *therefore*, used to introduce or connect independent clauses.

conjunctive thought a form of thinking in which logical relations are identified. *Cp.* **disjunctive thought**; **relational thought**.

connected text two or more words that convey meaning. *Both this definition and the greeting "Hi, there!" are connected text. Cp.* **collocation**.

connotation *n.* the emotional association(s) suggested by the primary meaning of a lexical unit, which affects its interpretations; affective meaning; emotive meaning. *Cp.* **denotation**. *v.* **connote**. *adj.* **connotative**.

conservation *n.* in Piagetian theory, the logical thinking ability to keep an invariant property of something in mind under changing perceptual conditions. *Note*: Piaget conducted several famous experiments in conservation, as by pouring the same quantity of water in markedly different-shaped containers and asking children whether the quantity changed. *Cp.* **nonconservation**.

considerate text text that the writer has made easily comprehensible, as by clarity of organization, appropriate vocabulary, and supplemental explanatory features. *Cp.* **reader-friendly writing**.

consonance *n.* **1.** the repetition of the final consonant sound in words with different vowels; consonant rhyme; as *ham-hum*, *stick-stake-steak*. *Cp.* **assonance**. **2.** agreement or unity. *adj.* **consonant**.

consonant **1.** *n.* a speech sound made by partial or complete closure of part of the vocal tract, which obstructs air flow and causes audible friction in varying amounts. **2.** *n.* an alphabet letter used in representing any of these sounds. **3.** *adj.* referring to such a sound or letter. *adj.* **consonantal**.

consonant cluster in a syllable, a sequence of two or more distinguishable consonant sounds before or after a vowel sound, as /skr/ and /mz/ in *screams*. Also **consonant blend**. *Note*: The term refers only to sounds, not to letters representing sounds. *Cp.* **blend** (def. 2).

consonant digraph a combination of two consonant letters representing a single speech sound, as *gn* for /n/ in *gnat*, or *gh* for /f/ in *rough*. *Cp.* **blend** (def. 2).

consonant substitution a word-identification technique in which a known consonant sound, usually in the initial or final position, is combined with a known phonogram to facilitate pronunciation of unknown words, as replacing /h/ of *hole* with /r/, /p/, /m/, or /s/ to identify *role*, *pole*, *mole*, or *sole*.

consonant-vowel-consonant (CVC) **sequence** one of the commonest sequences of sounds in syllables, as in *cat*, *red*, *dog*.

constant error a consistent error in one direction. See also **error** (def. 5).

constituent *n.* any identifiable unit in a linguistic construction.

constraint *n.* a restriction or limitation placed on language production or use, as the constraint in Black English Vernacular against forms of the type *I don't have any,* using instead *I don't have none.* See also **contextual constraint**. *v.* **constrain**.

construct *n.* a theoretical concept based on observable phenomena that aid researchers in analyzing and understanding some aspect of study, as *the construct of status* in sociolinguistics.

constructed response a student-created response to a test item, as an essay response.

construction *n.* **1.** an arrangement of two or more forms that make up a grammatical unit, as morphemes, constituent words, or word phrases, constituent clauses, etc. *Note: Bookmark* is a construction of the morphemes *book* and *mark*; *The cat ate the rat* is a construction of a subject and a predicate. **2.** a group of words or morphemes governed by a grammatical rule. *v.* **construct**. *adj.* **constructive**.

constructive cue system **1.** in reading, relevant linguistic data that a reader can use in creating meaning from text. **2.** in speaking, acoustic and articulatory information used in creating meaning from speech.

constructivism *n.* **1.** a philosophical perspective derived from the work of Immanuel Kant which views reality as existing mainly in the mind, constructed or interpreted in terms of one's own perceptions. *Note:* In this perspective, an individual's prior experiences, mental structures, and beliefs bear upon how experiences are interpreted. Constructivism focuses on the process of how knowledge is built rather than on its product or object. *Cp.* **social constructivism**; **transactional theory**. **2.** Piaget's view that "the

child must make and remake the basic concepts and logical thought forms that constitute his intelligence" (Gruber & Voneche, 1977).

construct validity evidence of validity gained by showing the relationship(s) between a theoretical construct and tests that propose to measure the construct.

consultative speech the informal style of discourse commonly used when speaking to others who do not have the background of shared experiences required for casual speech. Also **consultative style**. *Note:* Consultative speech is marked by a speaker's supplying background information and the listener's full participation in the discourse. See also **communicative competence**; **register** (def. 1); **style of discourse**. *Cp.* **casual speech**.

content analysis a systematic procedure for determining the extent to which printed materials present specific aspects of content, as in determining which of three newspapers presents the most local news. *Cp.* **text analysis**.

content field an organized body of knowledge; discipline. Also **content area**. *Note:* Content fields often have their own technical vocabularies. Literacy instruction cuts across all content fields and is ordinarily not itself considered a content field.

content plane in semiotics, a term coined by Louis Hjelmslev for the object or content aspect of a sign. See also **signified**.

content-referenced assessment the use of items reflecting specific behaviors in a content domain to improve content validity. *Cp.* **curriculum-based assessment**.

content validity evidence of validity gained by showing that the test content is representative of a specified behavior domain. *Cp.* **curriculum validity**; **instructional validity**.

content word a word that refers to a thing, state, action, or quality; lexical meaning; contentive. *Cp.* **function word**.

context *n.* **1.** the sounds, words, or phrases adjacent to a spoken or written language unit; linguistic environment. See also **context clue**. **2.** the social or cultural situation in which a spoken or written message occurs. *adj.* **contextual**.

context bound in phrase-structure grammar, referring to the dependence of the content of phrases or phrase elements on the surrounding context. Also **context sensitive**. *Cp.* **context free**.

context clue information from the immediate textual setting that helps identify a word or word group, as by words, phrases, sentences, illustrations, syntax, typography, etc.

context free in phrase-structure grammar, referring to the independence of phrases or phrase elements from the surrounding context, such that rewrite rules can be freely applied. *Cp.* **context bound**.

context of situation the meaning of a word, phrase, etc., in terms of both linguistic and situational contexts.

contextual analysis **1.** the search for the meaning of an unknown word through an examination of its context. **2.** the study of the broader context to determine as exactly as possible what the author means, as in literary criticism. **3.** the use of a larger linguistic unit to determine the meaning of a smaller unit.

contextual constraint any limitation placed on the nature and amount of information available in spoken or written communication due to linguistic, social, cultural, situational factors, etc.; textual constraint. See also **constraint**.

contextualized *adj.* **1.** literally, "kept in context," as in reading a full text rather than an excerpt from it. **2.** referring to language that can be easily assimilated into an existing schema. **3.** in reader response theory, referring to the broader social and psychological context in which a literary response is viewed. *Note*: "Not only what the reader brings to the transaction from past experience with life and language, but also the socially molded circumstances and purpose of the reading provide the setting for the act of symbolization. The reading event should be seen in its total matrix" (Rosenblatt, 1985). *Cp.* **de-contextualized**. *n.* **contextualization**.

contextual meaning **1.** the interpretation of a linguistic unit as affected by the text in which it occurs, as the meaning of a sentence within a larger discourse. **2.** the interpretation of a linguistic unit in terms of the social context in which it is used, as in an informal social interaction, a religious ceremony, etc.

contingency table a classification table with different levels on each of two or more variables, forming cells into which numbers may be entered to show frequency of occurrence.

continuant *n.* a speech sound produced as an uninterrupted air flow, as vowels and some consonants in English, as /s/, /z/. *Cp.* **stop** (def. 2).

continuous progress plan a curriculum plan in which students advance at their own rate rather than at a rate set by age or grade standards.

contraction *n.* **1.** the shortening of a written or spoken expression by the omission of one or more letters or sounds, as *can't* for *cannot*. See also **aphesis**; **apocope**; **syncope** (defs. 1, 2). **2.** a Braille sign representing a word or part of a word. *v.* **contract**. *adj.* **contractive**; **contractible**.

control group in an experimental design, a comparison group of subjects that is as like the experimental group as possible and receives the same treatment conditions save that of the experimental variable. *Cp.* **experimental group**; **matched group**.

controlled reading reading done under any of a wide variety of conditions designed to guide eye movements, fixations, or rate, as in the use of a reading pacer.

convention *n.* **1.** an accepted practice in a spoken or written language. **2.** an accepted way of creating an effect, as the soliloquy in drama, the flashback in fiction. **3.** a set of rules for group behavior; custom. *adj.* **conventional**.

convergence *n.* **1.** a coming together of ideas, objects, events, behaviors, etc., so as to focus on one thing or to produce a common result. **2.** the bending of light rays to a focus as they pass through the crystalline lens of the eye or through a convex lens. **3.** the turning in of the lines of sight by both eyes from far to near points so that, with accommodation, images of nearby objects fall on corresponding parts of the foveal areas of the retinas to permit binocular fusion. *Cp.* **accommodation** (def. 4); **divergence**. *v.* **converge**. *adj.* **convergent**.

convergence insufficiency failure to achieve binocular fusion at nearpoint distances, a condition that may contribute to reading difficulties.

convergent thinking the process of analyzing and integrating ideas in order to infer reasonable conclusions or specific solutions from given information. *Cp.* **divergent thinking**.

convergent validity the process or result of finding that two or more indicators thought to assess the same variable correlate with each other. *Cp.* **construct validity**; **discriminant validity**.

conversational analysis the study of the structure and conventions of spoken or written exchanges, usually in natural, informal settings.

conversational babble a form of babbling in early language development that is accompanied by eye contact, gestures, and intonation features, but which lacks meaning; expressive jargon; modulated babble. *Note*: Infants engaged in conversational babbling appear to have a sense of the social nature of speech, and adults may respond with neutral comments such as "Really" or "You don't say." See also **babbling**.

conversational maxim an unstated but understood rule or norm that guides spoken interaction. *Note*: As proposed by Grice (1975), conversations proceed on the assumption that four maxims are in operation: **a.** *quality*—speakers' contributions to conversations are true. **b.** *quantity*—appropriate amounts of information are provided by speakers. **c.** *relevance*—speakers' contributions are purpose related. **d.** *manner*—speakers' contributions are clear and brief. The term *conversational implicature* is applied to the meanings conveyed by the use of these maxims, while the tacit agreement between speakers to use these maxims is termed the *cooperative principle*.

converted hand dominance preference for the use of a hand other than that originally preferred, usually a shift in preference from left-handedness to right-handedness.

co-occurrence *n.* a necessary or customary relationship between or constrained by different parts of a sentence, as the noun-verb relationship in subject-predicate or the article-noun relationship. *v.* **co-occur**. *adj.* **co-occurrent**.

cooperative learning any pattern of classroom organization that allows students to work together to achieve their individual goals. *Cp.* **collaborative learning**.

coordinate bilingualism having two different mental representations for words in the languages used. *Note*: In some views of bilingualism, the circumstances in which the languages are learned accounts for the differences between *coordinate bilingualism* and *compound bilingualism*. When two languages are separately learned, coordinate bilingualism results; when they are simultaneously learned, as often occurs when a child lives in a bilingual household, compound bilingualism results. *Cp.* **compound bilingualism**.

coordinate clause any of two or more independent clauses joined by a conjunction, as *Julie jogged, and Ruth ran.*

copula *n.* a verb that connects a subject and a complement so that the complement describes the subject; linking verb; as *is* in *Linda is a leader.*

copybook *n.* a book with models of penmanship for doing exercises in handwriting, once used in early British and U.S. schools.

core curriculum **1.** a curriculum organized on the basis of subjects deemed essential for all students to study regardless of other subjects taken, as English, mathematics, science, and social studies in U.S. high schools to meet college admission requirements; subject-centered curriculum. **2.** a curriculum organized on the basis of students' problems or societal needs and which draws on the content of subjects that can contribute to understanding or resolving them. *Cp.* **correlated curriculum**.

core grammar grammatical statements that hold for a high proportion of languages but are not universal, as, for example, the observation that "in over 99% of languages whose word order has been studied, grammatical subjects precede objects" (Crystal, 1987). See also **universal grammar**.

core vocabulary the basic words and meanings needed to understand a special field, textbook, topic, etc.

corneal-reflection method a technique for studying eye movements by observing or photographing light reflected from the clear part of the outer layer of the eyeball in front of the iris and lens. See also **eye-movement camera**.

coronal *adj.* referring to sounds produced with the tongue tip close to or touching the alveolar ridge, as /t/ in *tip* and /ch/ in *chip*.

corpus *n., pl.* **-pora** **1.** a body; collection; as in *the corpus of word entries in this dictionary.* **2.** a set of data representing a sample of any type of linguistic material for a given language, usually collected for purposes of analysis.

correction for attenuation a statistical correction that increases the size of a correlation coefficient between two variables by removing the effects of measurement error in the variables. See also **attenuation**.

correction strategy the use of a reader's or speaker's knowledge of language and the context in which it is used to correct self-produced language errors; self-correction.

corrective reading supplemental, selective instruction for minor reading difficulties that is more specific than developmental reading but less intensive than remedial reading and is often provided within a regular classroom by the regular teacher, an aide, or a peer tutor. *Cp.* **remedial reading**.

correctness *n.* language usage that meets an accepted standard. *Note*: Language correctness is usually related to prescriptive views of language use.

correlated curriculum a curriculum organized to show relationships in the content of two or more areas of study while retaining the identities of the respective subjects.

correlation *n.* **1.** a statistical procedure for analyzing the extent to which two or more variables tend to vary together and which yields a coefficient expressing the degree of relationship. **2.** See **coefficient of correlation**. **3.** See **correlated curriculum**.

Types of *Correlation**
biserial correlation
intercorrelation
multiple correlation
partial correlation
point-biserial correlation
product-moment correlation
rank-order correlation
tetrachloric correlation

*Terms are all defined in this dictionary.

---

correlational research research designed to examine through the statistical process of correlation the extent to which two or more variables tend to vary together.

correlative **1.** *n.* a pair of coordinating conjunctions, as *either-or*, *neither-nor*. **2.** *adj.* referring to such a pair.

cortical blindness the inability to see, despite intact peripheral visual apparatus, due to lesions of the cerebral cortex.

cortical deafness the inability to hear, despite intact peripheral auditory apparatus, due to lesions of the cerebral cortex.

counting book an early childhood book for developing number concepts by pairing numerical characters, usually 1 to 10, with a like number of pictures of objects. *Cp.* **alphabet book**.

count noun a noun that refers to things that can be counted, as *apple*, *book*. *Cp.* **mass noun**.

couplet *n.* a stanza of two rhyming lines; especially, such lines of the same length, as "The learn'd is happy nature to explore, / The fool is happy that he knows no more" (Alexander Pope, *An Essay on Man*).

covariance *n.* in statistics, the tendency for one variable to change in the same direction as another.

craft literacy in Western cultures, the increasing prominence, beginning around A.D. 1300, of the use of the everyday vernacular of the craftsman in lieu of the Latin used by professional classes.

creative dramatics **1.** informal dramatization of a story using simple staging and few, if any, sets and costumes. **2.** creation of an original story idea through dramatic play, usually in an informal setting.

creative thinking **1.** thought processes characterized by unique powers of problem identification, hypothesis formation, and solution evaluation. *Cp.* **critical thinking** (def. 1). **2.** divergent thinking.

creative writing prose and poetic forms of writing that express the writer's thoughts and feelings imaginatively, primarily through metaphorical language and relational thought. *Note*: Presumably, creative writing does not require the factual accuracy and logical progression of ideas characteristic of expository writing. *Cp.* **exposition** (defs. 1, 2).

creole *n.* **1.** a pidgin language developed from two or more languages that eventually comes to be used as a native language. *Cp.* **patois** (def. 2); **pidgin**. **2.** (*cap.*) a patois, principally French, spoken chiefly in parts of Louisiana and the West Indies, especially Haiti. *Note*: A creole language is a fully developed language with a number of varieties: *acrolect*, the highest form in social status, educational achievement, and success because it most nearly approximates the standard language to which it is related; *basilect*, the variety that carries the least prestige; and *mesolect*, midway between these extremes. **3.** (*cap.*) a person born in the West Indies or Latin America but of European ancestry, usually Spanish. **4.** a person of mixed Spanish and Negro or French and Negro ancestry. See also **dialect**; **sociolect**. *v.* **creolize**. *adj.* **creole**; **Creole**.

criterial feature a standard of judgment used in such cognitive tasks as literary criticism, logical proof, etc.

criterion level the score which a person must achieve on a test to meet a predetermined standard of performance; cut(-ting) score.

criterion-referenced measurement the assessment of performance on a test in terms of the kind of behavior expected of a person with a given score. *Note*: "During most of the history of psychological testing, test specialists have emphasized norms, but criterion reference and norm reference are both useful. The former tells what a person is able to do; the latter tells how he compares with others. The former is useful in judging him as an isolated individual; the latter in judging his ability to compete" (Cronbach, 1970). *Cp.* **norm-referenced measurement**.

criterion score a specific score or score range on a measurement used to indicate a particular criterion level; cut(-ting) score. *Note*: A criterion score is often used as a dependent variable in research.

criterion variable in a predictive validity study, a variable whose value is used as a standard to distinguish what is predicted (criterion variable) from what is doing the predicting (predictor variable). See also **predictor variable**.

critical analysis a study of a literary or other artistic work according to formal principles and standards of criticism. See also **literary criticism** (def. 1).

critical evaluation the process of arriving at a judgment about the value or impact of a text by examining its quality in terms of form, style, and rhetorical features, the credibility of the author, and the consistency between ideas it presents and the reader's experience, including: **a. internal evaluation**, the process or result of arriving at a judgment of the worth of a selection by examining the extent to which its content, form, and style achieve the author's desired purpose. **b. external evaluation**, the process or result of judging the worth of a selection by comparing it to other selections that are similar in purpose and of known quality. See also **critical reading**.

critical linguistics examination of the use of language in relation to broader social, cultural, and political processes. *Note*: Critical linguistics draws on critical theory in the social sciences to examine how language reflects, sustains, or transforms relations of power and dominance.

critical literacy **1.** "the use of language in all of its forms, as in thinking, solving problems, communicating, etc." (Venezky, 1994). **2.** "the ability not only to read and write but to assess texts in order to understand the relationships between power and domination that underlie and inform them" (Hull, 1993). *Note*: Critical literacy in this sense leads to the attainment of *emancipatory literacy* that "illuminate[s] the power relationships in society and teaches the learner how to participate in and change those power structures" (Freire, cited in Newman & Beverstock, 1990). Many writers have addressed the nature and significance of critical literacy. For example, Bhola (1979) regarded the expanded definition of a literate person in UNESCO (1978)—one who can "use reading, writing, and calculation for his own and the community's development"—as a significant departure from previous UNESCO definitions of literacy. Street (1984) declared that literacy is not "a neutral 'thing' to be used in social practices when required, but it is itself the set of socially constructed practices involving reading and writing which are shaped by wider social processes and are responsible for reinforcing or challenging values, traditions, patterns of power found with social settings.... [It] is a shorthand for the social practices and conceptions of reading and writing; it has political and ideological significance and cannot be separated from that significance and treated as though it were an 'autonomous' thing." See also **critical theory**.

critical pedagogy 1. the study of schools in both historical and sociopolitical contexts. See also **critical theory**. **2.** the art or science of teaching as viewed by advocates of social change. *Note*: Giroux, a leading advocate of critical theory as applied to education, views critical pedagogy as "the reconstruction of social imagination in the service of human freedom" (1985). It involves both "the practices students and teachers engage in and the cultural politics such practices support.... [It is] a pedagogy whose standards and achievement objectives are determined in relation to goals of [Marxist] critique and the enhancement of human capacities and social possibilities" (1983). Hull (1993) writes that "for students, the chief goal of critical pedagogy is to help them develop analytical skills and moral initiative to transform, not just serve, the dominant social order." The concept of critical pedagogy also provides specific interpretations of such terms as *empowerment* and introduces such concepts as *deskilling* and *hidden curriculum*. (See these terms.)

critical ratio (CR) a test of the level of significance of a particular statistic; specifically, the statistic divided by its own standard error.

critical reading 1. the process or result of making judgments in reading, of "evaluating relevancy and adequacy of what is read" (Betts, cited in Smith, 1965). **2.** reading in which a questioning attitude, logical analysis, and inference are used to judge the worth of text according to an established standard. *Note*: "Critical reading is the judgment of validity, or worth of what is read, based on sound criteria or standards developed through previous experiences" (Robinson, 1970). Drawing on Betts's work, Gray, Russell, and others endorsed the critical function in reading based on the belief that reading and thinking processes form an integral unit. Critical reading came to be thought of as an extension of reading beyond the literal and interpretative levels to include an evaluative aspect. Among the skills of critical reading are those having to do with ascertaining the author's credibility, intent, or purpose; assessing the accuracy, logic, reliability, and authenticity of the writing; and identifying literary forms, components, and devices through literary analysis. See also **critical evaluation**.

critical theory an ongoing sociological examination of the ideas and influence of Karl Marx, especially as they apply to the values and institutions of capitalist societies and to the role of an ideology designed to foster economic, political, and social change. *Note*: In Eisner's (1992) words, critical theory is "an approach to the study of schools and society that has as its main function the revelation of tacit values that underlie the enterprise." A fundamental assumption of critical theory dialectics is that the individual and society "are inextricably interwoven, so that reference to one must by implication mean reference to the other...[in focusing] simultaneously on both sides of a social contradiction" (McLaren, 1989). In relation to literacy, this implies that the production and interpretation of spoken and written discourse must be subjective since it is not possible to construct meaning outside the context of social and political reality. The basic tenets of critical theory are revealed in two closely related concepts: *critical literacy* and *critical pedagogy*. See these terms. See also **politics of literacy**; **reading the word**; **reading the world**; **sociology**.

critical thinking   **1.** the logical thought processes characteristic of the scientific method. *Cp.* **thinking** (def. 3). **2.** the thought processes characteristic of creativity and criticism in literature and other arts; divergent thinking. *Note*: Heath (1991) observed, "Educators do not, in general, equate either inventive thinking or literary and other artistic criticism with logical, reflective, critical thinking. Instead they tend to link critical thinking with problem-solving heuristics that characterize science."

cross-age tutoring   instruction of a student by a knowledgeable student of another age group, usually older.

cross-cultural research   the scientific study of the effects a particular environmental situation has on persons in two or more cultures, as in a study of early formal reading instruction in the United States and England.

crossed dominance   visual-motor or other motor preferences not controlled by the same cerebral hemisphere, as in being right-handed but left-footed. *Note*: "Such preferences represent a developmental feature of brain organization that is no longer considered a cause of reading disability and other developmental disabilities" (Duane, 1994). *Cp.* **cerebral dominance**.

cross-sectional research   a way of studying behavior or development by taking a large-scale, representative measure on one or more variables at same time or age. Also **cross-section research**. *Cp.* **longitudinal research**.

cross-validation   *n.* the application of a prediction formula or composite scoring rule devel-

oped on the data for one sample to the data for another sample.

cued recall   recall that is aided or prompted. See also **recall** (def. 1).

cued speech   a manual system of hand signals used to make English phonemes visible for a speech-reading deaf person. See also **speech reading**.

cue reduction   a process by which the perception of fewer and fewer aspects of a stimulus are needed to set off a learned response.

cuing system   any of the various sources of information that may aid identification of a word unrecognized at first glance, as phonics, structural analysis, and semantic and syntactical information.

cultural criticism   the practice of extending the techniques of literary analysis to include nonliterary texts and issues. *Note*: Cultural criticism examines the political meaning of art, typically producing a sociology of literature and taste. Race, class, and gender recur as major concerns in judging cultural products.

cultural literacy   **1.** literacy that reflects knowledge of significant ideas, events, values, etc., of a society, as in advanced literacy. **2.** according to Hirsch (1987), "[the possession of] the basic information needed to thrive in the modern world." **3.** according to Freire and Macedo (1987), "familiarity with selected literary works and historical information deemed necessary for informed participation in a nation or culture." See also **literacy**.

cultured literacy   literacy of the more highly educated, as that possessed by "those who read Faulkner and Wittgenstein" (Asheim, 1987); advanced literacy; high literacy. See also **literacy**.

culture-fair test a test that attempts to be as free as possible from specific cultural or class bias. *Note*: While the term *culture free* is sometimes used as a synonym for *culture fair*, no test is completely free of cultural bias.

cumulative frequency curve a curve showing the summed number or percentage of scores or values falling at and below or at and above each plotted point. Also **cumulative frequency distribution**. *Note*: For a normal distribution, the cumulative frequency curve is a flattened s-shape, or ogive.

cumulative spelling spelling a word by adding each syllable cumulatively to the preceding syllable, as in "a-d *ad*, m-i *mi*, admi, r-a *ra*, admira, t-i-o-n *shun*, *admiration*" (Barnard, 1863). *Cp*. **alphabet method** (def. 1).

cumulative tale a story with many details repeated until the climax, as in "The House That Jack Built"; predictable text.

cuneiform *n.* a script that takes the form of wedge-shaped marks pressed into clay, as in ancient Sumerian and Ugaritic.

Sun   Man

Cuneiform characters
(Assyrian, *c.* 700 B.C.)

curriculum *n., pl.* **-la, -lums** *Note*: Definitions of *curriculum* vary widely because of alternative perceptions held by theorists about the nature and organization of formal schooling. **1.** an overall plan or design of institutionalized education. **2.** the actual opportunities for learning provided at a particular place and time. **3.** the vehicle for bringing about behavioral changes in students as a result of planned activities in an educational institution. **4.** the total program of formal studies offered by a school. **5.** all the educational experiences planned for and provided by a school. **6.** a particular part of the program of studies of a school, as *the English curriculum*, *the reading curriculum*, etc. **7.** in critical pedagogy, "the introduction to a particular form of life that partly serves to prepare students for dominant and subordinate positions in the existing society" (McLaren, 1989). *adj.* **curricular**.

curriculum-based assessment the appraisal of student progress by using materials and procedures directly from the curriculum taught. *Cp*. **content-referenced assessment**.

curriculum guide a written plan describing the general academic curriculum of a school, school system, or program of study. *Note*: Curriculum guides vary in scope and detail but usually give the philosophy, specific objectives, and ways of carrying out the curriculum.

curriculum laboratory an instructional materials center for teacher use; resource center.

curriculum validity evidence of the validity of a test gained by showing that the test content is representative of the behavior domains of the curriculum. *Cp*. **content validity**; **instructional validity**.

cursive writing handwriting in which all or most letters are joined within each word; longhand writing. *Cp*. **manuscript writing**.

This is cursive writing.

cutaneous sense the sense of touch on which the blind rely in reading Braille.

cut score a score on one or more tests that divides subjects into different groups, as pass-fail, qualified-unqualified, selected-rejected. Also **cutting score**.

cybernetics *n.* the study of communications and of the control of communication processes in people, in machines, and in the interactions between people and machines. *Note*: The term was coined by Wiener (1948) to refer to the regulation of behavior by messages. See also **information theory**. *adj.* **cybernetic**.

Cyrillic alphabet the alphabetic writing system used in Russian and certain other Slavonic languages. *Note*: The Cyrillic alphabet was developed by Cyril, a Greek Christian missionary, in the 9th century A.D. for use among the Slavs of Central Europe and was based on old Greek letters.

Cyrillic alphabet

D

dactylology *n.* communication of ideas by finger movements that stand for letters or letter combinations in conventional spelling, as in the manual alphabets of the deaf; finger spelling. *Cp.* **sign** (def. 3); **sign language**.

Dale–Chall readability formula a method of estimating the difficulty level of reading material based on the percentage of words not on the *Dale List of 3,000 Familiar Words* and on the average number of words in sample sentences. *Note*: This method, developed by Dale and Chall, predicts 50 percent comprehension, with a table yielding corrected reading grade levels. A considerable number of modifications, extensions, and special uses of the formula have been suggested since the formula's first publication in 1948, but it continues to be used primarily as originally published. See also **readability**; **readability formula**. *Cp.* **Flesch readability formula**; **Fry readability graph**; **Spache readability formula**.

dame school up to the early 19th century in Great Britain and the United States, an informal private school for children from three to six in a woman's home. *Note*: The "dame" taught the alphabet and the rudiments of reading.

dangling modifier most commonly, a participle or participial phrase which, as it is placed, modifies the wrong object, as *Dangling in midair, the volcano was viewed by the balloonist.* Also **dangling participle**; **unattached modifier**; **unattached participle**.

dative case 1. the case of a noun or noun phrase that expresses an indirect object relationship, indicated by word order, or, in inflected languages, by a change in word form. See also **indirect object**. **2.** in case grammar, the case of the noun or noun phrase affected by a verb action or state, as *The kitten* in *The kitten was given away.*

dead language a language that is no longer spoken and exists only in historical records, as Hittite, or is spoken only by language specialists or in rituals, as Latin or Sanskrit. *Ant.* **living language**.

dead metaphor a metaphor so common and habitual that it is no longer thought of as a metaphor, as *the face of a clock*. See also **metaphor**.

deafness *n.* the inability to hear; hearing loss of at least 70 db that causes speech communication problems even with amplification. See also **hard of hearing**; **hearing loss**.

Types of *Deafness**
conduction
cortical
nerve**
sensorineural
tone
word

---

*Terms are all defined in this dictionary.
Term is defined under **sensorineural deafness.

---

décalage (*Fr.*) *n.* in Piagetian theory, a time lag that occurs in the intellectual growth of a child: **a. horizontal *décalage***, the lag within a developmental stage between a child's having the ability to apply a cognitive scheme or structure to one aspect of an object or event and the ability to apply it to another. **b. vertical *décalage***, the lag across stages between being able to complete a simple and a complex intellectual task, as the difference in the ability of a child in the pre-operational stage to find his way around a room and the ability in the later concrete operations stage to draw a map of the room.

decentration *n.* in Piagetian theory, the ability to take account of several aspects of an object or event at the same time. *Cp.* **centration**.

decibel (dB) *n.* the standard unit for measuring sound loudness or intensity in audiometric testing. *Note*: Hearing loss expressed in decibels indicates the difference between the expected normal hearing level and the intensity needed for the sound to be heard by the subject.

decile *n.* **1.** the points dividing a distribution of scores into parts each containing ¹⁄₁₀ of the scores. *Cp.* **centile**; **percentile**. **2.** any of these ten parts that indicate a decile rank.

declarative knowledge factual knowledge available to a person for use.

declension *n.* **1.** in certain languages, the inflections of nouns, pronouns, and adjectives for case. **2.** a word class with the same inflection forms. See also **case**. *v.* **decline**.

decode *v.* **1.** to analyze spoken or graphic symbols of a familiar language to ascertain their intended meaning. *Note*: To learn to read, one must learn the conventional code in which something is written in order to decode the written message. In reading practice, the term is used primarily to refer to word identification rather than to identification of higher units of meaning. See also **encode** (def. 1); **recode** (def. 1). **2.** to change communication signals into messages, as *to decode Morse code signals*, *to decode body language*. **3.** to translate an unfamiliar code of symbols into a familiar one, as *to decode a secret message*.

deconstruction *n.* a philosophical method influential in literary criticism that demonstrates the inherently ambiguous and unavoidably repressive nature of language. *Note*: Opposed to structuralism, deconstruction dismantles Western tradition by showing that language does not correspond to nature or the external world. It also argues that all literary texts contain contradictions. By revealing what texts assume, suppress, and ignore, it produces skeptical responses to major works, freeing the reader to substitute personal for public meaning. See also **poststructuralism**; **structuralism**.

decontextualized *adj.* **1.** literally, "taken out of context," as in the content of many workbook exercises. **2.** referring to language that is not easily assimilated into an existing schema. **3.** in reader response theory, referring to the extent to which the broader psychological and social context is neglected in viewing a literary response. *Cp.* **contextualized**. *n.* **decontextualization**.

deduction *n.* **1.** the process of logical reasoning from principles to specific instances; reasoning from wholes to parts. **2.** a conclusion drawn or inferred from something known. **3.** in semiotics, the process by which necessary consequences are drawn from hypotheses. **4.** the result of such a process. *Cp.* **abduction**; **induction**. *v.* **deduce**. *adj.* **deductive**.

deductive method a teaching-learning method in which a generalization or rule is first considered and then applied to specific examples. *Cp.* **inductive method**.

deep cognitive processing converting the apparent or surface structure of meaning into its underlying or deep-structure meaning. See also **deep structure**.

deep structure in transformational-generative grammar, the meaning to which a spoken or written sentence refers; the result of deep cognitive processing; deep meaning. *Note*: The meaning of a sentence may not be apparent from its surface structure until verified by sentence transformation. For example, while the surface structure of *John is eager to please* and *John is easy to please* is the same, the deep structure or meaning is different. *Cp.* **surface structure**.

degree *n.* one of three forms of adverbs and adjectives that show difference in quality, quantity, or intensity.

Types of *Degree*		
	adjective	*adverb*
positive	easy	likely
comparative	easier	more (less) likely
superlative	easiest	most (least) likely

degrees of freedom (df) the number of observations or statistical values that are free to vary; usually, the total number of values minus the fixed constraints. *Given a sample of readers and nonreaders, there is only one degree of freedom beyond the category of readers—the category of nonreaders.*

deixis in linguistics, a term used to indicate words and phrases that relate an utterance to personal, temporal, or locational aspects of the situation in which the utterance occurs, as *I, you, now, then, there, over there, etc. Cp.* **demonstrative**. *adj.* **deictic**.

delayed recall remembering material at some point in time after study. *Cp.* **immediate recall**.

delayed speech the later than normal acquisition of spoken language due to one or more developmental factors, as maturation, experience deprivation, psychological or physiological difficulties, etc.

demonstrative 1. *n.* a word that points out something specific, as the pronouns *this, those, such.* 2. *adj.* referring to such a word.

demotic script *n.* an ancient Egyptian cursive script used for everyday secular purposes. See the illustration in the next column. *Cp.* **hieretic script; hieroglyphic**.

denotation *n.* the relationship between a linguistic event and its referent, as *book* denotes the object "book"; referential meaning; denotative meaning; cognitive meaning. *Cp.* **connotation**. *adj.* **denotative**.

Demotic script

dependent clause a clause that modifies a main or independent clause to which it is joined; subordinate clause; as *until you leave* in *I will wait until you leave. Cp.* **independent clause**.

dependent variable the response variables in an experiment that are affected by the manipulation of the independent variable(s). See also **intervening variable**. *Cp.* **independent variable**.

depth perception 1. the detection of relative distance. 2. the detection of three-dimensional aspects of space and its objects; space perception; stereopsis. *Note*: Depth perception is a complex act which may involve binocular vision and motion parallax as well as shadow, perspective, and especially occlusion.

derivation *n.* 1. the use of affixes to build new words from a root or base word, often with a change in the grammatical class of a word, as *predict → prediction*. 2. See **etymology**. 3. in transformational-generative grammar, the process of ascertaining the surface structure of a sentence from an underlying deep structure. *v.* **derive**. *adj.* **derivational**.

derivational affix a prefix or suffix added to a root or stem to form another word, as *un-* in *unread*, *-ness* in *likeness*. *Note*: A derivational suffix changes the word to which it is added into another part of speech, as *-ness* forms nouns from adjectives. *Cp.* **inflectional suffix**.

derivational morpheme a word created by the addition of affixes to a base word, as *de-* + *-con-* + *-ion* to the base *-struct-* to make *deconstruction*.

derivational morphology a branch of morphology concerning the formation of words from other words by adding affixes to roots and stems to form derivational morphemes. See also **derivation** (def. 1); **derivational affix**; **derivational morpheme**. *Cp.* **inflectional morphology**.

derivative *n.* a word formed by adding an affix to a root or stem; derived form; as adding *pre-* before *fix* to make *prefix*.

derived meaning **1.** an acquired meaning of a base word or stem when a prefix or suffix has been added. *Cp.* **word formation** (def. 1). **2.** an acquired meaning of a term applied in a situation other than the one in which it is usually used, as *I must get my bearings amid all this paperwork. Cp.* **etymology**.

derived score a unit into which a score, usually a raw score, is changed, as standard scores, mental age, or percentile rank. *Cp.* **raw score**.

derived sentence in early transformational-generative grammar, a sentence produced by applying transformational rules to a kernel or base sentence. See also **kernel sentence**; **transformation** (def. 2); **transformation rule**.

description *n.* a composition in writing or speech that gives a verbal picture of character and event, including the setting in which they occur. *Cp.* **argumentation**; **exposition** (def. 1); **narration** (def. 1).

descriptive *adj.* **1.** referring to an adjective or other modifier that expresses the quality of

something, as *good* in *a good writer*. **2.** nonlimiting with reference to a modifying clause; nonrestrictive; as *whoever he was* in *The man, whoever he was, took our picture*.

descriptive grammar a grammatical system based on usage rather than on prescription. *Cp.* **prescriptive grammar**.

descriptive linguistics **1.** language study that describes the structure and function of aspects of a single language at a certain stage of its development disregarding changes over time; synchronic linguistics. **2.** American structural linguistics prior to the rise of transformational-generative linguistics in the late 1950s. See also **structural linguistics**.

descriptive research an investigation, often of a survey type, that attempts to describe accurately and factually a subject or an area.

deskilling *v.* in critical pedagogy, the removal of teachers' responsibility and control over the goals and methods of instruction and reliance instead on technical materials such as teachers' manuals and basal textbooks as sources of instructional control. *Note*: "In this view, technology rather than the teacher is seen as the teaching agent in the production of literate students" (Shannon, 1989). *v.* **deskill**.

desktop publishing use of computer programs designed to assist in the layout and printing of text and graphics.

determinative *n.* an auxiliary sign used to aid the reader in correctly determining the meaning of a logograph, as in Chinese writing; semantic indicator; radical.

determiner *n.* a grammatical unit that occurs in conjunction with nouns and serves to point out certain semantic features such as quantity, number, or possession, as *the, those, her, some,* *first*, etc. See also **article** (def. 2); **demonstrative** (def. 1).

determining letter any letter that provides a visual clue to word identification, as initial consonants, ascending or descending letters, or double letters. *Note*: Overuse of determining letters in instruction may cause problems in students' identification of words of similar form.

developmental *adj.* **1.** in psychology, referring to changes in the complexity and organization of behavorial processes and structures relating to growth over the course of the life span. **2.** in learning disability, referring to a defective neurological condition, proven or presumed, that delays the emergence of an ability or the development of a skill, as *developmental dyslexia*.

developmental age level of growth or development, either specific or general, stated as an age equivalent, as *social age*.

developmental lag a delay in the maturity of one or more, but not all, areas of normal growth; developmental imbalance. *Note*: The term implies that the delay is temporary.

developmental reading **1.** reading instruction, except remedial, for students at all levels. **2.** reading instruction, except remedial, for all students beyond the elementary school level. *Note*: According to Smith (1965), this is the earliest meaning of the term in the reading literature. **3.** a comprehensive school program of remedial and nonremedial reading instruction for all students.

developmental testing the tryout of instructional methods and materials to determine which parts need revision.

deviation *n.* **1.** any departure from a standard or norm. **2.** in statistics, the difference between one set of values and some reference point, usually the mean.

deviation IQ a standard score in the measurement of intelligence in which the mean is taken as 100 and the standard deviation as approximately 15. See also **intelligence quotient**.

dextral **1.** *adj.* having to do with the right side; moving from the left to the right. *Note*: Written English, French, Spanish, etc. are *dextral languages*. **2.** *n.* a person who consistently chooses to use the right side, right hand, etc. *Ant.* **sinistral**. *n.* **dextrality**.

diachronic linguistics the study of changes in a language over time, as in its phonology, grammar, and the forms and meanings of words. See also **historical linguistics**. *Cp.* **synchronic linguistics**.

diacritic mark a mark added to a graphic character in a writing system to indicate a specific pronunciation. Also **diacritical mark**. *Note*: Diacritic marks are generally used to augment an alphabet in one of these ways: **a.** to make a unique symbol available for each phoneme in a particular language. **b.** to describe the preferred or existing pronunciations of words in a nontechnical but clear fashion, as in a dictionary. **c.** to make a unique symbol available for each distinct speech sound in a phonetic alphabet. *Cp.* **accent** (def. 2).

Types of *Diacritic Marks*

acute accent*
apostrophe
caret
cedilla*
circumflex*
dieresis*
grave accent*
macron*
tilde*
umlaut*

---

*Term is defined in this dictionary, with example of mark.

diagnosis *n.* **1.** the act, process, or result of identifying the nature of a disorder or disability through observation and examination. *Note*: Technically, *diagnosis* means only the identification and labeling of a disorder. As the term is used in education, however, it often includes the planning of instruction and an assessment of the strengths and weaknesses of the student. **2.** the classification of people or things into established categories. **3. negative diagnosis**, the indication of a disorder by the recognition of what it is not. *Note*: A diagnosis of dyslexia is usually a negative diagnosis because there is no alternative explanation of the reading difficulty. **4. positive diagnosis**, an indication of a disorder that is confirmed by evidence. *adj.* **diagnostic**.

diagnostic teaching the use of the results of student performance on current tasks to plan future learning activities; instruction in which diagnosis and instruction are fused into a single ongoing process. *Cp.* **assumptive teaching**.

diagnostic test a test designed to analyze strengths and weaknesses in content-oriented skills. *Note*: "Diagnostic tests may permit comparison among several subabilities of the same individuals and sometimes comparisons of strong and weak points of a group or class.... Available instruments for the diagnosis of reading difficulties vary widely in the thoroughness of analysis they permit and in the specific procedures followed. Among the most common weaknesses of diagnostic reading tests are inadequate reliabilities coupled with high intercorrelations of the subtests from which separate scores are derived" (Anastasi, 1976). *Cp.* **survey test**.

diagramming *n.* **1.** a process of analyzing sentence structure by making a linear chart to help learners visualize the relationships of sentence components, as sometimes used in teaching traditional grammar. **2.** See **tree diagram** (def. 1). *Cp.* **parsing**.

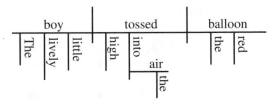

The lively little boy tossed the red balloon high into the air.

Diagramming

dialect *n.* a social or regional variety of a particular language with phonological, grammatical, and lexical patterns that distinguish it from other varieties. *adj.* **dialectal**.

Terms Related to *Dialect**
accent
creole
idiolect
nonstandard dialect
patois
prestige dialect
regional dialect
sociolect

*Terms are all defined in this dictionary.

dialectology *n.* the study of regional, social, and temporal varieties of a language to determine how these varieties differ in pronunciation, grammar, and vocabulary in terms of their geographical distribution.

dialogue *n.* **1.** conversation between two or more persons or between a person and something else, as a computer. **2.** a literary work written as conversation, as Plato's *Dialogues*. **3.** conversation used as an oral technique in teaching English as a second language or in foreign language instruction. Also **dialog**.

dialogue journal written conversations in which students exchange ideas, including responses to literary works, with peers and teachers.

dichotic listening the simultaneous stimulation of both ears with different words or tones in each, to determine the lateralization of auditory function. *Note*: Such lateralization is regarded as a characteristic of cerebral dominance and is used by some researchers to study developmental language and reading disability.

dictation *n.* **1.** a message spoken for transcription. **2.** a transcribed spoken message. **3.** in school practice, the message spoken by the teacher for students to copy; *dictée (Fr.)*. *Note*: Dictation is often used in the teaching of foreign languages to verify the accuracy of spellings, diacritic marks, etc. *v.* **dictate**.

diction *n.* **1.** clarity of speech; enunciation. **2.** the careful choice of words in speaking or writing in order to communicate clearly.

dieresis *n., pl.* **-ses 1.** the graphic symbol sometimes placed above the second of adjoining vowel letters to indicate a separate syllable, as *ë* in *aërial*. Also **diaeresis**. *Note*: There is a diminishing use of dieresis in American spellings in favor of hyphens or omission of any punctuation or diacritic marks. *Cp.* **umlaut** (def. 3). **2.** the separation of adjoining vowels to make two syllables, as *po'et*. **3.** a pause, or caesura, in a line of verse when a word ends a metrical foot.

differential assessment the adaptation of the means of appraisal to the individual student.

differential diagnosis diagnosis that attempts to distinguish among symptoms with similar characteristics.

differential item functioning inconsistency in the performance of two or more groups on a test item after accounting for differences in overall performance on the knowledge, skill, or ability being measured.

differential reading instruction the provision of varied learning situations, as whole-class, small-group, or individual instruction, to meet the needs of students at different levels of reading competence.

differential validity the degree to which a classification battery of tests yields a set of scores that predict in which of two situations a person will perform better.

diglossia *n.* the use of two varieties of language, one for formal use in writing and in restricted speech situations and one for colloquial or informal use, as in Greek, Arabic, and some varieties of German. *adj.* **diglossic**.

digraph *n.* **1.** two letters that represent one speech sound, as *ch* for /ch/ in *chin* or *ea* for /e/ in *bread*. *Cp.* **blend** (def. 2). **2.** a grapheme resulting from the fusion of two letters into one, as *œ*, *Æ*; ligature. *Cp.* **trigraph** (def. 1). *adj.* **digraphic**.

dilemma tale a story that ends in a quandary rather than a conclusion, as Frank Stockton's *The Lady or the Tiger*. Dilemma tales are one of the basic oral traditions used in many parts of the world to challenge children's thinking ability.

diminutive *n.* an affix used to describe something small, youthful, fragile, feminine, etc., as *-let* in *booklet*, *-ette* in *kitchenette*.

dinomia *n.* in sociolinguistics, "the coexistence and complementary use within the society of two cultural systems, one of which is dominant" (Saville-Troike, 1989).

diopter *n.* the standard unit for expressing the refractive power of a lens in which one diopter represents the power of a lens that will focus parallel light rays at a distance of one meter.

diphthong *n.* **1.** a vowel sound produced when the tongue moves or glides from one vowel sound toward another vowel or semivowel sound in the same syllable, as /ī/ in *buy* and the vowel sounds in *bee*, *bay*, *boo*, *boy*, and *bough*. *Note*: In the Thai language, the change of vowel sound can be extended to three vowels; see **triphthong**. See also **falling diphthong**; **monophthong**; **rising diphthong**. **2.** a graphic symbol of two adjacent letters in brackets used in phonetics to represent diphthongs, as [ay]. *Cp.* **vowel digraph**.

diplopia *n.* seeing two objects when only one is present; double vision.

direct discourse an exact quotation of speech or writing. Also **direct speech**. *Cp.* **indirect discourse**.

directed reading activity (DRA) **1.** a step-by-step process for presenting a reading lesson; developmental reading lesson, especially in the content fields. **2.** a reading lesson plan involving: **a.** preparation and motivation for reading. **b.** silent reading. **c.** vocabulary and skills development. **d.** silent or oral rereading. **e.** follow-up or culminating activities. *Note*: The directed reading activity can take various forms, but the underlying concept remains the same. A further step in the process is the *directed reading-thinking activity (DRTA)* in which the chief elements are prediction and verification (Stauffer, 1969). In the prereading stage, students set their own purposes for reading by making predictions; during reading they verify their predictions; and in the postreading discussion stage they check their verifications.

directional confusion a weak or nonexistent ability to perceive spatial orientation accurately, as in uncertainty or inconsistency in perceiving the orientation of English from left to right. *Cp.* **directionality**.

directionality *n.* the ability to perceive spatial orientation accurately; directional orientation. *Cp.* **directional confusion**.

direct object the person or thing that receives the action or is affected by the action of a transitive verb in a sentence, as *John* in *Tom hit John*. *Cp.* **indirect object**.

discourse 1. *n.* conversation. **2.** *v.* to converse. **3.** *n.* the act or result of making a formal written or spoken presentation on a subject, as *a learned discourse on literacy*. **4.** *n.* in linguistics, any form of oral or written communication more extensive than a sentence.

discourse analysis the study of meaningful language units larger than a sentence. *Cp.* **rhetoric** (def. 3); **text linguistics**.

discriminant validity a type of construct validation; specifically, the process or result of finding that two or more indicators thought to assess different variables do not correlate significantly with each other. *Cp.* **convergent validity**.

discriminator *n.* a distinctive orthographic feature of a letter, word, or phrase that aids identification, as the use of italics or boldface for emphasis in a text.

disjunctive thought a form of logical thinking in which logical but unrelated elements are identified, as opposites, distinctive features, etc. *Cp.* **conjunctive thought**; **relational thought**.

dispersion *n.* the extent to which observations or events vary among themselves or deviate from some reference point, as from the mean. *The standard deviation is a statistical measure of dispersion*. *v.* **disperse**.

dissertation *n.* **1.** any formal scholarly presentation, usually in writing. **2.** a formal paper or essay reporting on one's own research. *Cp.* **thesis** (def. 1).

dissimilation *n.* the process or result by which a speech sound becomes phonetically less like a neighboring speech sound, usually for ease of pronunciation, as the *l* in *marble* replaced the *r* in the word as derived from the French *marbre*. *Cp.* **assimilation** (def. 5). *v.* **dissimilate**.

distance education education, as by telecommunications and computers, that "provides systematic instruction to learners who are physically separated from teachers" (Ely & Foley, 1992). *Note*: An early form of distance education was the correspondence course.

distance vision the ability to see objects that are far away rather than near, usually measured by having the subject identify the smallest possible target at a distance of six meters or more.

distinctive feature 1. a distinguishing characteristic of an object or field; salient feature; especially, a characteristic that contrasts noticeably with another perceived characteristic. *Note*: Many current theories of reading hold that some type of distinctive feature analysis occurs in the beginning stages of processing text. **2.** any aspect of speech sound description used to differentiate one phoneme from another, as /b/ from /p/ due to voicing of /b/. **3.** any theoretical system in which features of speech sounds are compared for purposes of identifying generalizable relationships among sounds of a language, as vocalic vs. nonvocalic, strident vs. mellow, syllabic vs. nonsyllabic, etc. *Note*: Distinctive features may be based on acoustical, articulatory, or perceptual data.

distribution *n.* **1.** the act or result of grouping elements into classes. **2.** the result of grouping data into classes or categories. **3.** the set of positions in which a particular linguistic unit of a language, such as a phoneme or morpheme, can occur, as /zh/ in *treasure* and *mirage* never occurs at the beginning of an English word. See also **complementary distribution**. *v.* **distribute**. *adj.* **distributing**.

disyllable *n.* a word with two syllables. Also **dissyllable**. *adj.* **disyllabic**; **dissyllabic**.

divergence *n.* **1.** a difference or separation in ideas, objects, events, behaviors, etc.; deviation. **2.** the bending of light rays away from one another as they pass through a concave lens. **3.** the normal turning out of the eyes as the distance to their point of fixation increases. **4.** the abnormal turning out of one eye relative to the other. *Cp.* **convergence**. *v.* **diverge**. *adj.* **divergent**.

divergent thinking the process of elaborating on ideas in order to generate new ideas or alternative interpretations of given information. *Cp.* **convergent thinking**; **creative thinking**.

document center a facility for the organized collection and distribution of documents, often specialized.

document processing in the electronic sense, the creation, editing, tagging, encoding, storing, searching, and transmission of documents.

doggerel 1. *n.* a form of verse, often trivial and sentimental, usually of irregular rhythm, and sometimes comic or burlesque in intent, as "She kissed the hairbrush / By mistake / She thought it was / Her husband Jake" (advertisement for Burma Shave). **2.** *adj.* referring to such verse or its characteristics.

domain-referenced measurement the assessment of learning based on a sample of measurable behavior in a specific domain, as the vocabulary of first grade students.

domain-specific knowledge knowledge restricted to a particular field of action, knowledge, or influence.

dominant letter a letter in a word that is easy to distinguish and aids word identification, usually because it extends above or below the average height of most lowercase letters, as *jeopardy* has the dominant letters *j*, *p*, *d*, and *y*. See also **configuration clue**.

doublespeak *n.* language that is intended to be evasive or ambiguous; doubletalk. *Note:* Four types of doublespeak are: **a.** euphemisms. **b.** jargon. **c.** gobbledygook; bureaucratese. **d.** inflated language.

doublet *n.* one of two or more words in a contemporary language derived from the same origin, as *grammar* and *glamour*, *aptitude* and *attitude*, *treasure* and *thesaurus*, etc.

doubletalk **1.** *n.* a rapid, meaningless mix of real and nonsense words. **2.** *n.* the intentional use of ambiguous language; doublespeak. **3.** *v.* to engage in or influence by doubletalk.

drafting *n.* the process or result of putting ideas into writing in a rough form, often edited later for publication. *n.*, *v.*, *adj.* **draft**.

drama *n.* a play; a story in dramatic form, typically emphasizing conflict in key characters and written to be performed by actors.

dramatic irony a situation in which a character says or does something, the full meaning of which the character does not understand but which the audience does. See also **irony** (def. 2).

dramatic play play as a child's creative expression. *Note:* "In drama—i.e., doing and struggling—the child discovers life and self through emotional and physical attempt, and then through repetitive practice, which is dramatic play" (Slade, 1975).

dramatic poetry the use of one or more techniques of drama, such as characters, dialogue, conflict, etc., in poetry.

dual curriculum a program of teaching and learning based on the assumption that every ac-

tivity is an opportunity for both linguistic and cognitive development.

duality of structure in linguistics, the notion that language has two abstract organizational levels, a phonological level which lacks meaning and a morphemic level (morphemes and words) which includes meaning.

dual texts the notion that each reader builds a personal text parallel to the external text that is being read.

duration of fixation the length of time that the eyes pause during visual inspection, commonly about ⅕ of a second during reading. See also **eye-movement pattern**.

dysfluency *n.* repetitious, hesitant speech. *adj.* **dysfluent**.

dysgraphia *n.* difficulty in producing handwriting because of disease of or injury to the brain. *Cp.* **dysorthographia**.

dyslexia *n.* a developmental reading disability, presumably congenital and perhaps heredity, that may vary in degree from mild to severe. *Note:* Dyslexia, originally called *word blindness*, occurs in persons who have adequate vision, hearing, intelligence, and general language functioning. Dyslexics frequently have difficulty in spelling and in acquiring a second language, suggesting that dyslexia is a part of a broad type of language disability. See also the essay "Dyslexia" on pp. 64–65; **alexia**; **aphasia**; **learning disability**; **legasthenia**; **word blindness**. *n.*, *adj.* **dyslexic**.

dysnomia *n.* difficulty in recalling words, as the names of objects, people, events, etc.

dysorthographia *n.* spelling difficulty that reflects defective cognitive processing of language rather than motor incoordination. *Cp.* **dysgraphia**.

Dyslexia

Dyslexia means generally an inability or partial inability to read. Originally it referred to the loss of ability to read following central nervous system damage or dysfunction, but it is now used to refer to a congenital or hereditary condition that interferes with the acquisition of reading skills and is often a part of a broader language problem. It is not due to sensory impairment, mental retardation, emotional disorders, lack of motivation, or faulty instruction; rather, the problem seems to be intrinsic.

Over the years, many theories regarding the fundamental nature of dyslexia have emerged. The earliest derived from studies of brain-behavior relationships and the symptoms associated with *acquired dyslexia*. Yet many physicians, diagnosticians, and educators recognized differences between acquired and congenital reading problems and distinguished the two by using the term *developmental dyslexia* for the latter. Others, however, objected to medically oriented labels and preferred *specific reading disability*. Currently *dyslexia* is used by some, but not all, reading professionals.

With the development of brain imaging techniques, more evidence for studying the biological bases for reading disabilities has become available. In addition, studies of familial dyslexia indicate possible hereditary factors, and several investigators have reported a high incidence of poor readers in families. Other researchers have focused on the behavioral, linguistic, and cognitive aspects of dyslexia to determine whether certain characteristics are more prominent or pervasive in dyslexics than in other groups of poor readers or normal achievers. For example, some theorists have suggested that dyslexics may suffer from visual perceptual deficits because of their tendency to reverse letters. Because reading involves both auditory and visual processes, other investigators have hypothesized and found some evidence for intersensory or crossmodal deficits. Others refuted these findings on methodological grounds. Several clinicians and researchers, often those working in the field of neuropsychology, have found evidence for possible subtypes of dyslexia, each perhaps rooted in a different deficit. Needless to say, the subtypes that emerge through research vary with the test instruments used, as well as with the age of the subjects.

Many professionals have studied dyslexia from a psycholinguistic perspective. These researchers explore the acquisition of multiple-rules systems and the integration of spoken and written language. In recent years, numerous studies have indicated that the core problem in dyslexia is related to phonological coding and a lack of linguistic awareness, particularly phonemic awareness. Some theorists have identified deficits in higher order verbal skills including morphology, syntax, and comprehension. In forming their conclusions, however, a great deal depends on the researchers' definitions of reading and the measures of reading used in their studies. Other researchers use paradigms from cognitive psychology, concentrating on information processing, lexical decision making, working memory, and other factors that contribute to reading disabilities. Still others use developmental perspectives and ask whether dyslexics simply acquire skills at a slower rate or in a different way from normally achieving readers. In recent years, the emphasis has been on verbal coding, particularly phonological coding, and numerous studies support the hypothesis that dyslexia may stem from deficits in this area.

(continued)

Clearly, many causes of dyslexia have been posited over the years, and we have yet to arrive at a conclusive explanation for the problem. It seems that we must continue to investigate broader language and conceptual problems, possibly through more large collaborative studies aimed at determining whether there are distinct patterns of problems among dyslexics. However, it is probably true that no single problem can account for all disabilities. Even in families with histories of dyslexia, the symptoms are not always the same.

Dyslexics are similar because they all have reading problems and verbal deficits of some type. The core problem for those with word-recognition difficulty appears to involve phonological coding and phonemic awareness, but others have higher order problems. We cannot ignore the fact that visual processing is required for reading and that students must integrate spoken language with print. However, we also need to acknowledge the complexity of the reading process and the many different ways that individuals respond to instruction.

In diagnosing any reading disability, the assessment should be comprehensive so that appropriate intervention can be provided. Certain students can compensate for minor weaknesses because of strengths in other areas. For many years, educators in both regular and special education have argued for the teaching of multiple reading strategies and for ensuring balance in programs. In order to be competent readers, students need to use many strategies, including sight-word recognition, morphological analysis, phonetic analysis, and contextual cues; they also need a good background of knowledge and oral language skills. Therefore, when working with dyslexics, we need to evaluate their use of many types of strategies across various reading tasks to determine which skills are intact or deficient, and then conduct more research to determine the most successful intervention procedures.

As we conduct research in the future, we must remember that not every poor reader is deficient in phonological awareness: we cannot ignore the many students who can "recode" without comprehension. In recent years, considerable emphasis has been given to problems of adult literacy and dyslexia. Adults with persistent, severe reading disabilities frequently have global language disorders that involve far more than decoding. Detailed studies of their disabilities may provide data that can be used for prevention of reading problems in early childhood. When we set up our studies, we must also be aware that long-term, follow-up research indicates that even with excellent help, many problems persist among dyslexics. Even though students make progress, they often have residual problems in decoding, reading speed, spelling, and written language. (The latter might be expected since writing is the highest form of language and typically requires more skills than reading.)

One final suggestion for future research: in any new study, whatever terminology is used, researchers should specify the characteristics of the population. It is not enough to know whether subjects are good or poor readers. When examining a complex problem such as dyslexia, we must also know about subjects' intellectual levels, cognitive processes, language use, and other symbolic behavior.

Doris Johnson

Ɛ

early childhood education (ECE) infant school, preschool, daycare, nursery school, and other educational programs ordinarily for children prior to entrance to the primary grades.

early reader a student who is able to read before entering school. *Cp.* **emergent reading**; **fluent reader**.

easy reader a trade book with a limited vocabulary and a storyline interesting to children who are ready to move beyond picture books for their independent reading. *Cp.* **chapter book**.

echolalia *n.* in early language development, the imitation of words, phrases, or sentences spoken by others without understanding of their meanings, usually occurring in children at 18–24 months; echophrasia. *Note*: In some analyses of the early stages of language development, *echolalia* refers to an infant's normal repetition of vocal sounds made by others.

eclectic methodology a way of introducing children to reading that provides them with opportunities "(a) to learn words as wholes; (b) to learn the sounds that letters record so that sounds can eventually be blended to form words; and (c) to learn to write words" (Durkin, 1993). *Cp.* **whole-word methodology**; **word method**.

eclectic reader any of several series of readers of the mid-19th century that introduced varied content to replace the earlier religious and patriotic emphases in American readers; (*Hung.*) encyclopedic reader. *Note*: *Eclectic* was a popular catchword in the mid-19th century United States and was used in connection with textbooks in other subjects.

edit *v.* **1.** to prepare materials for publication or presentation. **2.** in the writing process, to revise or correct a manuscript. *Note*: As practiced in many school writing programs, *edit* more narrowly refers to the correction of mechanical features of writing, as spelling, punctuation, capitalization, etc., while *revise* refers to making structural and content changes in a manuscript. **3.** to omit; take out.

educable mentally retarded (EMR) a person with an IQ between 2 and 3 standard deviations below the mean, usually between 55 and 70, who is able to learn sufficiently to maintain him- or herself socially and economically in the community; educable mentally handicapped. See also **mental retardation**; **trainable mentally retarded**.

education 1. *n.* the changes in a person caused by teaching and self-directed learning. *Note*: *Nwoman ye kanea* ("Education is light in our path") is an evocative metaphor in the Twi language that captures this meaning of the word (Asiamah, 1993). **2.** *n.* in a broad sense, the processes used in teaching and learning to produce the knowledge and highly generalizable skills needed to reason, make judgments, and develop aesthetic appreciation. **3.** *n.* in a narrow sense, the processes used in teaching and learning to gain specific practical skills; training. **4.** *n.* a level or degree of schooling. **5.** *n.* teaching; pedagogy. **6.** *adj.* having to do with teacher preparation, as *an education student*. *v.* **educate**. *adj.* **educational**.

educational measurement the act or result of assessing school learning and its effects usually with a view to improving instructional practices, as the National Assessment of Educational Progress in the United States.

educational media the various means of communicating instructional material, such as motion pictures, filmstrips, photographs, recordings, television, printed materials, graphics, CD-ROMs, computer-based instruction, etc.; audiovisual aids; audiovisual materials.

educational psychology a branch of psychology devoted to the study of educational problems, procedures, and practices in order to improve educational effectiveness.

Educational Resources Information Center (ERIC) any one of several federally supported agencies in the United States that examine, evaluate, collect, and distribute information related to research in educational theory and practice, as The Center for Reading and Communicating Skills (ERIC/RCS) or The Center for Language and Linguistics. *Note*: The centers are important storehouses of such materials as speeches and pamphlets that otherwise might be lost.

educational technology the body of educational methods and resources used in instruction. *Note*: Beyond media hardware and software, educational technology involves the design, development, and management of learning processes through instructional systems.

effects of reading the influences of reading on the reader brought about by his or her motivations to read and the extent that these motivations are satisfied by what is read. Also **functions of reading**. *Note*: "Any effects of reading imply interaction between the reader's predispositions and the content of the publication" (Waples et al., 1940). Waples et al. identified five primary effects of reading: **a. aesthetic effect**, appreciating the beauty of the author's ideas and style of expression. **b. instrumental effect**, adding to knowledge, often in a practical way. **c. prestige effect**, reducing feelings of inferiority. **d. reinforcement effect**, strengthening a presently held attitude. **e. respite effect**, finding relief from tensions.

efferent reading a type of reading in which "the attention is focused on abstracting out, analyzing, and structuring what is to be retained after the reading, as, e.g., information, logical argument, or instructions for action" (Rosenblatt, 1991). See also **effects of reading**. *Cp.* **aesthetic reading**.

egocentric language in Piagetian theory, speech that is unadapted to the point of view of others or is not specifically directed to others, as children's monologues and songs while playing. Also **egocentric speech**.

egocentric logic in Piagetian theory, a mode of thinking that is more intuitive than deductive, with little value attached to proving or checking propositions. See also **syncretism** (def. 2).

egocentrism *n.* **1.** the characteristic of being self-centered or indifferent to others. **2.** in Piagetian theory, a child's inability to take another's point of view. *Note*: With respect to the child, *egocentrism* is not a pejorative term because the child *cannot* take another's point of view, while an egocentric adult is able to but does not.

eidetic image a vivid and detailed mental picture of something previously seen, as a page of a text, an illustration, etc.; the ability to so picture. *Note*: An eidetic image is clearer and more accurate than a memory image. It may be projected like an afterimage, but it remains constant to permit the viewer to examine different parts of it. Some believe that the ability to picture these images is common in children but decreases with age. *Cp.* **memory image**.

elaborated code a term coined by the British sociologist Basil Bernstein in the 1970s to describe the structurally complex language used by speakers in relatively formal, educated settings; public language. *Note*: The user of an elaborated code employs a range of syntactic patterns, vocabulary, etc., to express meaning rather than relying on a common context or experiential background among those addressed. Bernstein's notions provoked controversy because they became linked to social class differences and educational success and thus to a deficit view of language and learning to which Bernstein has responded (1990). See also **formal speech**. *Cp.* **restricted code**.

elementary school in the United States and most of Canada, the school that most children of 5 or 6 to 11 or 12 years attend; grade school. *Note*: The elementary school may include kindergarten and extend through grades 4, 6, or even 8. See also **middle school**; **secondary school**.

elision *n.* **1.** the omission of a sound or syllable in a word in pronunciation, as in *I'll, doesn't*. **2.** in verse, the dropping of a vowel for a metrical purpose, as "And 'mid this tumult Kubla heard from far…" (Samuel Taylor Coleridge, *Kubla Khan*). **3.** omission of a passage in a written work. *v.* **elide**.

e-mail the sending and receiving of messages between computers. Also **electronic mail**.

emancipatory literacy the use of reading and writing to "illuminate the power relationships in society and teach the learner how to participate in and change those power structures" (Freire, cited in Newman & Beverstock, 1990).

embedding *n.* a sentence-combining process in which one clause or phrase is contained inside another; nesting; as *E.J. Gaines's book won an award* may be embedded with *The book was a novel* to form *E.J. Gaines's book that won an award was a novel. Cp.* **recursiveness** (def. 2).

emergent literacy development of the association of print with meaning that begins early in a child's life and continues until the child reaches the stage of conventional reading and writing; "the reading and writing concepts and behaviors of young children that precede and develop into conventional literacy" (Sulzby, cited in Barr et al., 1991). See also the essay "Emergent Literacy" on pp. 71–72.

emergent reading the course of a child's early interaction with books and other print, as from pretend reading to genuine efforts to understand the nature and meaning of print. See also **pretend reading**.

emmetropia *n.* normal vision; specifically, the ideal refractive condition in which, without accommodation, an object six meters or more away is focused clearly on the retina. *Cp.* **astigmatism**; **hyperopia**; **myopia**. *n.* **emmetrope**. *adj.* **emmetropic**.

empirical validity validity established by observed facts or experience.

empowerment *n.* **1.** in general educational practice, giving authority to teachers and students to act responsibly in their teaching and learning, as in the selection of learning materials, modes of learning, etc. **2.** in critical pedagogy, enabling students "to understand and engage the world around them as well as to exercise the courage needed to change the social order when necessary" (McLaren, 1989). *v.* **empower**.

empowerment evaluation the design, implementation, and interpretation of program evaluation controlled by participants, as in the California Self-Study and Program Quality Review.

encode *v.* **1.** to change a message into symbols, as *encode oral language into writing*, *encode an idea into words*, *encode a physical law into mathematical symbols*. See also **decode** (def. 1); **recode** (def. 1). **2.** to give a deep structure to a message. *n.* **encoding**.

endocentric *adj.* referring to a group of syntactically related words that have the same function as a head term, as the noun phrase *bright red sunset* for the head *sunset*. See also **head**. *Cp.* **exocentric**.

endophora *n.* a linguistic expression whose referential meaning is identifiable from its surrounding text, as *Hotsuho* in *My friend's name is Hotsuho*. See also **reference** (def. 5). *Cp.* **anaphora** (def. 1); **cataphora**; **exophora**. *adj.* **endophoric**.

Emergent Literacy

Only relatively recently has the concept of emergent literacy come to be a widely accepted theoretical and instructional perspective on young children's written language development. During the late 1970s and early 1980s, the work of a number of researchers coalesced to the point where it was clear that applying the traditional reading readiness perspective on early literacy was no longer adequate. In the mid-1980s, Elizabeth Sulzby and I tried to capture the essence of this new way of thinking about young children's reading and writing development by bringing together in an edited volume the work of many of the leading researchers in the area at the time. We chose to use the term *emergent literacy* to describe this body of work relating to how reading and writing concepts, behaviors, and dispositions precede and develop into conventional literacy. In 1987, *emergent literacy* appeared as an ERIC descriptor for the first time, signaling that the concept was having an impact on the field. Currently, it is fair to say that emergent literacy is the lens that most researchers and educators use to focus on early reading and writing development.

To me, the essence of what is new and better about an emergent literacy perspective (as opposed to reading readiness, which used to be the most widely accepted way of conceptualizing early literacy) is that it views reading and writing development from the child's point of view. Emergent literacy examines changes over time in how the child thinks about literacy and in the strategies the child uses in attempts to comprehend or produce written language. Often children's concepts and strategies are different from those of mature readers, but there is a consistent underlying logic to what they are trying to do to solve the reading-writing puzzle. Understanding this logic helps us plan instruction that fosters young children's development along the path toward conventional reading and writing.

Emergent Literacy Instruction

Instruction built on an emergent literacy paradigm is based on these principles:

Involve children in reading and writing from the first day of school.

Create a print-rich environment by including a wide variety of written language (e.g., children's literature, signs and labels, children's writings, and writing equipment such as paper, pens, markers, and computers).

Make written language a functional and important part of the classroom.

Involve children in play and lesson activities in which written language functions to achieve a wide variety of goals.

Key instructional practices characteristic of an emergent literacy classroom include the following.

Group storybook readings or lap readings. The teacher reads aloud to the whole class, small groups, or individuals daily. A wide variety of quality children's literature is used, and the readings involve considerable discussion among teacher and children.

(continued)

Storybook readings by children. Young children's "pretend readings" of books that have been read to them are critical experiences for emergent literacy. Classroom reading corners serve as places where children have access to children's literature and can engage in these readings.

Embedding written language in everyday classroom activities. Signs, lists, charts, calendars, notes, and other items are read and written by children as part of their routine activities in the classroom.

Response-to-literature activities. Children respond to books that have been read aloud to them through discussion, writing, art, music, and dramatic re-enactments.

Writing. Each day the teacher demonstrates the process of writing, and the children write their own meaningful messages of different types (e.g., stories, notes, messages, invitations). To demonstrate writing, the teacher may conduct an activity such as Morning Message: as the children watch, she or he writes a brief message on the chalkboard about something the children will do that day, reading aloud what is being written and getting the children to participate. This helps young children learn about aspects of writing ranging from directionality to phoneme-grapheme correspondences. When the children write themselves, they may draw pictures, scribble, use random letters, or use invented or conventional spelling.

Phonemic awareness development. Through nursery rhymes, poetry, language play, and a variety of oral language games, children hear the constituent sounds that make up the language.

Letter and letter-sound activities. Children learn the letters of the alphabet and the sounds associated with them, especially in the context of the activities described previously.

Issues in Emergent Literacy Research and Instruction

There are still many issues related to emergent literacy that need further research and development. Three of the most critical at this time are as follows.

Transition to conventional literacy. What happens during the critical and relatively brief period when a child is at the point of making the transition from emergent reading and writing to conventional reading and writing? What "clicks" into place for the child? What strategies and knowledge that weren't there before does the child come to control?

Assessment of emergent literacy. Many contend that formal testing of young children's literacy learning is especially problematic. Considerable efforts have been aimed at developing observational, informal, performance-based measures to evaluate early literacy learning that are as natural a part of classroom instruction as possible, but much remains to be done in this area.

The effectiveness of an emergent literacy instructional paradigm. Relatively few studies have directly examined the effectiveness of an emergent literacy curriculum. More research that employs a combination of qualitative and quantitative methodologies for examining this topic needs to be conducted.

William H. Teale

end rhyme the rhyming of ends of lines of verse, the most typical place for rhyme in English verse.

engagement *n.* the emotional involvement of the reader in the process of responding to the content of reading, as occurs in a total absorption in a story or play. *v.* **engage**.

English as a foreign language (EFL) a program for teaching English language skills in a non–English-speaking community or country to a student whose first language is not English. *Cp.* **English as a second language**.

English as a second language (ESL) a program for teaching English language skills in an English-speaking community or country to students whose first language is not English. *Note*: The term *English for/to speakers of other languages* (*ESOL*) is increasingly used instead of ESL to acknowledge that learners may be acquiring English as a third, fourth, fifth, etc., language. See also **teaching English as a second language**. *Cp.* **English as a foreign language**.

English school a form of secondary education provided in England and the United States in the 18th and early 19th century for students who needed a practical and vocational education rather than a classical one. *Note*: In the United States, English schools provided an alternative to the classical curriculum of grammar schools. Reading, spelling, writing, arithmetic, and, to some extent, geography and history were offered. *Cp.* **Latin grammar school**.

enrichment *n.* "the provision of some form of additional educational experience which supplements regular classroom activities" (Vernon, 1978), as special provisions for the disadvantaged and the gifted as well as such activities as supplementary reading in the classroom. *Note*: Enrichment is sometimes applied only to activities that expand skills or knowledge after competence is reached, thus excluding drill or review activities. *v.* **enrich**. *adj.* **enriched**.

entering behavior a description of the skills and concepts needed to begin a learning activity.

entropy *n.* **1.** a measure of randomness. **2.** in information theory, uncertainty.

environmentalist theory the belief that the totality of external things, conditions, and influences, including instruction, can facilitate literacy development. *Cp.* **maturationist theory**.

environmental print print and other graphic symbols, in addition to books, that are found in the physical environment, as street signs, billboards, television commercials, building signs, etc. *Note*: Environmental print affords opportunities for learners in early phases of emerging literacy to discover and explore the nature and functions of graphic symbols as conveyors of meaning, even when they are not able to read in a formal sense. Also **environmental text**.

epenthesis *n.* the insertion of a sound or sounds in the middle of a word, as /ath´ ə lēt/ for *athlete*. See also **intrusion**. *Cp.* **metathesis**; **syneresis**; **tmesis**.

epic **1.** *n.* a long narrative poem, usually about the great deeds of a folk hero, stated in lofty, elevated language, as Homer's *Iliad*. *Cp.* **saga** (def. 1). **2.** *n.* a similar long narrative poem, more sophisticated in literary style and less heroic in content, as Vergil's *Aeneid* and Milton's *Paradise Lost*. **3.** *adj.* referring to an epic. *adj.* **epical**.

epigram *n.* **1.** a brief saying, usually witty and pointed. **2.** a short poem, often with a satirical twist, related historically to the epitaph, as "Underneath this stone doth lie / As much beauty as could die; / Which in life did harbour give / To more virtue than doth live"

(Ben Jonson, *Epigrams*). *adj.* **epigrammatic**; **epigrammatical**.

epigraphy *n.* a field of study aimed at deciphering and interpreting ancient inscriptions, as runic and cuneiform writing, on monuments, etc. *Cp.* **paleography**.

episodic *adj.* a style of narrative or storytelling that describes a chain of incidents.

episodic memory memory that is "autobiographical, personal, and sensitive to the effects of context" (Best, 1989), a type of memory especially important in the creative writing of poetry and narratives. *Cp.* **semantic memory**.

epistle *n.* **1.** a letter, generally written in formal and sometimes didactic style. **2.** (*cap.*) one of the books in the New Testament, or a section from it, written as a letter by an apostle.

epitaph *n.* a brief memorial statement for a dead person, often inscribed on a tombstone or found in literary works.

epithet *n.* **1.** any word or brief phrase used to characterize a person or thing, as *The Roughrider* for American president Theodore Roosevelt. **2.** an expression of contempt or abuse.

equilibration *n.* in Piagetian theory, a principle referring to the dynamic balance between accommodation and assimilation in the process of mental development. *Note*: Along with heredity, environment, and social transmission, equilibration makes possible the acquisition of more complex mental structures. *v.* **equilibrate**.

equilibrium *n.* **1.** a balance between opposing forces in the body, as the physiological condition of homeostasis, or evenness in emotional mood. **2.** the balanced, upright posture that is aided by the semicircular canals of the inner ear. **3.** in Piagetian theory, the coordination and cog-

nitive balance of factors related to heredity, environment, and social transmission in intellectual development. *Note*: In this sense, equilibrium is mobile and dynamic, fleeting for the elementary cognitive functions such as perception and more stable for the higher mental functions.

equivalency test a test presumed to certify competence, as the General Educational Development test (GED) in the United States, considered the equivalent of high school subject mastery. *Note*: Equivalency tests are a major tool in adult literacy programs for ensuring that students obtain recognition for their life and work experiences as well as for school learning.

error *n.* **1.** a mistake. **2.** a mistaken opinion or belief, as an error of faith. **3.** a belief in something not true. **4.** a wrong doing. **5.** deviation from a true score or value. See also **constant error**; **standard error**. **6.** in an experiment, any uncontrolled quantitative variation caused by the experimenter or experimental conditions. *v.* **err**.

Types of *Error* [*]

constant error
error of estimate [**]
error of measurement
probable error
sampling error
standard error
standard error of estimate
standard error of mean
standard error of measurement
systematic error
Type I error
Type II error

---

[*]Terms are all defined in this dictionary.
[**]Term is defined under **standard error of estimate**.

---

error of measurement in classical testing theory, an estimate of the difference between a hypothetical true score and an actual score due to inconsistency (or lack of reliability) associated with the observer, the measurement instrument, or the testing occasion. *Cp.* **generalizability**.

essay **1.** *n.* a relatively brief literary composition, usually in prose, giving the author's views on a particular topic. *Note*: The essay has so many varieties that it defies more specific definition. It has been an important form and force in literature since Michel Eyguem de Montaigne first used the term to describe the written expression of his views in the 16th century. **2.** *v.* to try; attempt.

essay examination a test requiring a written response, usually of some length, to one or more questions or topics. Also **essay test**. *Note*: The evaluation of essay examinations is often regarded as highly subjective. Numerous studies have shown, however, that a relatively high degree of objectivity may be achieved by proper construction of test items and by the training of test scorers. *Cp.* **objective test**.

ethnographic research in education, the on-site, naturalistic study of classroom teaching-learning situations; observational research.

ethnography *n.* **1.** in anthropology, the scientific study of individual cultures. **2.** loosely, the study of human groups through first-hand observation. *adj.* **ethnographic**.

ethnography of communication the study of language as it is perceived and used by speakers and writers within societal and cultural contexts, with emphasis on describing the linguistic interaction that occurs, as in Shirley Brice Heath's (1983) *Ways with Words*; ethnography of speaking; ethnolinguistics. See also **adjacency pair**; **communicative competence**; **ethnographic research**; **ethnomethodology**.

ethnolinguistic minority group a subcultural group that uses a language distinct from that of the dominant culture, as the Cajuns in the United States.

ethnology *n.* in anthropology, the study of the differences and similarities among cultures in terms of their historical development.

ethnomethodology *n.* **1.** in anthropology, the study of the rules and rituals that underlie social activities and interactions. **2.** the study of "the underlying processes which speakers of a language utilize to produce and interpret communicative experiences, including the unstated assumptions which are shared cultural knowledge and understandings" (Heath, 1989).

etiology *n.* the study or assignment of the causes of diseases or disabilities. *adj.* **etiological**.

etymological spelling the respelling of a word so as to indicate its language of origin, as respelling Middle English *dette* as *debt*, after the Latin *debitum*.

etymology *n.* the study of the history and development of the structures and meanings of words; derivation. See also **folk etymology**. *Cp.* **derived meaning**; **word history**. *adj.* **etymological**.

etymon *n.* the ultimate historical source of a word in a language or of related words in other languages, as English *father* and Spanish *padre* are traced to the Indo-European etymon *pəter-*. *Cp.* **cognate** (def. 2).

euphemism *n.* **1.** a socially acceptable word or expression used to replace unacceptable or taboo language, as words or expressions for bodily functions. **2.** a substitution for straightforward language that tactfully conceals or, in the extreme, falsifies the meaning of that which it replaces. See also **doublespeak**. *adj.* **euphemistic**.

euphony *n.* **1.** a pleasing sound effect, especially in combinations of speech sounds. **2.** the changing of speech sounds to simplify pronunciation, as /wŏŏs´ tər/ for *Worcester. adj.* **euphonic**.

evaluation *n.* **1.** judgment of performance as process or product of change. *Note*: Evaluation is an attempt to understand a process that is sometimes guided by preset objectives but at other times involves objectives added during the evaluation process. **2.** the process of testing, appraising, and judging achievement, growth, product, process, or changes in these, frequently through the use of formal and informal tests and techniques. *Note*: The process of evaluation is global in conception and application. It represents a broad concept that may be distinguished from the concerns of measurement, appraisal, and assessment in that the latter operations can form the basis for evaluation, but not the reverse. **3.** a synthesis of appraisals as by test scores, interviews, etc., in a case study. See also **assessment**; and the essay "Evaluation in Education" on pp. 77–78. *v.* **evaluate.** *adj.* **evaluative**.

Types of *Evaluation* [*]
critical evaluation
empowerment evaluation
formative evaluation
summative evaluation
teacher evaluation

---

[*]Terms are all defined in this dictionary.

---

every-pupil response approach any of several classroom techniques that ensure that each student resopnds to every question posed by the teacher, as asking for a show of hands; i.e., the student need not know the correct answer, but must be attentive.

evocation *n.* in Rosenblatt's transactional theory of reading, an initial and continuing phase of the reading process in which the reader "responds to the verbal signs [in text] and constructs or organizes his responses into an experienced meaning which for him is 'the work'.... [It is] the lived-through process of building up the work under the guidance of the text" (Rosenblatt, 1978). See also the essay "Reader Response" on pp. 209–210; **transactional theory**. *Cp.* **interpretation** (def. 1); **reflection** (def. 3). *v.* **evoke**.

examination **1.** *n.* the act of testing. **2.** *n.* a test. **3.** *n.* an inquiry; investigation. **4.** *n.* subjected to testing, as a *physical examination*. **5.** *adj.* referring to a test, as *an examination question. n.* **examiner.** *v.* **examine**.

exclamation *n.* a grammatical construction expressing strong opinion or emotion, often punctuated by an exclamation point or marked by intonation, as *What a fantastic play!* Also **exclamatory.** *adj.* **exclamative; exclamatory**.

existentialism *n.* a set of philosophic ideas that assume that each person is a uniquely important, free, and responsible individual. *Note*: Existentialism has been expressed in various forms, especially in literature by Jean-Paul Sartre and in religion by Sören Kierkegaard. Although many playwrights and novelists have emphasized the loneliness and despair of free man in a hostile world, the existential writings of theologians elaborate the positive nature of freedom of choice. In teaching, an existential point of view leads a teacher or clinician to adopt the role of a reality mirror, showing students the implications and probable consequences of their behavior but allowing them to make their own decisions. *Cp.* **phenomenology.** *adj.* **existential**.

existential sentence a type of sentence structure that expresses the location or existence of something, as *There are the books.*

Evaluation in Education

Evaluation, which means literally "fixing value," is a complex human activity. Like assessment and testing, it entails collecting and weighing evidence for decision making. A parent assesses neighborhood schools, a jobhunter weighs employment prospects, a car buyer ponders the showroom. In literacy, evaluation arises in judgments of student achievement, student placement, and textbook selection, among other things. This essay focuses on evaluation of programs and teachers, significant areas in literacy for both practitioners and researchers. Unfortunately, the two domains are usually separated by contexts and methods. Program evaluation appears in the 1960s' First Grade Reading Study or the 1990s' examination of compensatory education in the United States; teacher evaluation arises when a new teacher is tenured or an experienced teacher is reviewed for mentorship. Program evaluation employs the experimental control paradigm (an innovative technique compared with the usual lack of rigor in comparing educational programs); teacher evaluation uses observations to gauge compliance with predetermined standards.

Evaluation concepts and methods have changed substantially in recent decades, shifting toward reconceptualization as applied research with validity as the essential criterion and informed argument as the primary outcome. *Construct validity*, the trustworthy interpretation of evidence in support of an argument, has displaced *predictive validity*. Regarding this change, Messick (1989) notes that "validity is now considered an integrated evaluative judgment of the degree to which empirical evidence and theoretical rationales support the adequacy and appropriateness of inferences and actions based...on assessment through scientific inquiry." In the realm of program evaluation, Tyler (1991) distinguishes programs from underlying principles: "Principles can be generalized since they have been developed by observations of a variety of practices that revealed similarities among the diversities. Programs cannot be easily generalized since teachers and other professionals, consciously or unconsciously, modify programs as they interact with students or other clients." A trustworthy interpretation is generalizable across a range of variables: time, situations, clients, instruments, observers.

Suppose a study shows statistically higher test scores of students in Program *X* than of those in regular instruction. Earlier views of evaluation ask about test reliability, program implementation, and sampling adequacy. Newer views also ask, "Is authentic reading taught and tested? Do students read more? Do they like reading more? Do effects last over time and situations? Can others reproduce the results? Do effects hold up across teachers, schools, districts, language and ethnic groups?" But even when evaluation methods are unreproachable, the eventual task, according to Cronbach (1982) is effectively informing the clients: "The mission [of educational evaluation] is to facilitate a democratic, pluralistic process by enlightening all participants."

Teacher evaluation arises when a teacher seeks certification as an accomplished professional. In the United States, this kind of evaluation typically relies on observations made and checklists completed by harried administrators regarding tenure candidates who have completed two years on the job; subsequent evaluation is usually pro forma. There are changes coming in this area, too, however. Mirroring the types of questions now being asked in program evaluation, the National Board of Professional Teaching Standards (NBPTS) in their evaluations asks, "Is authentic teaching

(continued)

Evaluation in Education (cont'd.)

being assessed? Can the teacher rationalize practice? Are observed practices typical over time, students, and settings? Do different observers and different assessment techniques yield similar portrayals?"

Contemporary evaluations rely on argument along with method, balance quantitative with qualitative techniques, and value critical judgment over mechanistic techniques. Reports lay out strengths and weaknesses: no program is perfect, and every teacher has room for improvement. Effective reports clarify constructs and enhance practice. Exemplary program evaluations describe shortcomings as well as accomplishments and open the door to improvement. NBPTS procedures for teacher evaluation lead to certification decision, but the teachers themselves also report benefits from the assessment.

Finally, new evaluation concepts, in parallel with new testing methods, attempt to bridge the "internal-external" gap by sharing responsibility among parties to achieve *empowerment evaluation*. Self-evaluation is a challenge both conceptually and practically; California's Program Quality Review exemplifies a strategy designed to meet this challenge in both program and teacher evaluation. If current trends continue, in the coming years even greater emphasis will be placed on client-centered evaluation, with implications for program entrepreneurs and classroom teachers, for advocates of whole language and Reading Recovery, for quantitatively oriented psychologists and qualitatively oriented ethnographers. From this perspective, evaluation as applied research connects the rigor of the social scientist with the pragmatic reality of the classroom teacher.

Robert C. Calfee

---

exocentric *adj.* referring to a group of syntactically related words in which there is no discernable head, as *Tonya slipped. Cp.* **endocentric**.

exophora *n.* a word or word group that requires reference to something outside the text in order to be understood, as *That* in *That book is rare.* See also **deixis**; **reference** (def. 5). *Cp.* **anaphora** (def. 1); **cataphora**; **endophora**. *adj.* **exophoric**.

expansion rule in transformational-generative grammar, a rule that enables a single symbol, as VP (verb phrase), to be rewritten into a string of symbols showing its constituent parts, as VP →V + NP. See also **phrase structure rule**.

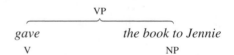

expected response in miscue analysis, an accurate oral reading of a text.

experience approach an instructional program based on student needs and interests rather than on preplanned curriculum materials. See also **writing approach to reading**.

experience chart text that is dictated by students about a common experience and then transcribed by a teacher, often used later for instruction.

experiential learning learning acquired in the workplace or in everyday situations rather than through formal schooling.

experimental design the plan for conducting a specific piece of research; specifically, the plan for selecting subjects, manipulating dependent variables, and collecting and analyzing data.

experimental group in an experimental design, a group of subjects, matched as closely as possible on specified characteristics to a control group, that receives the experimental or independent variable treatment. *Cp.* **control group**; **matched group**.

expert processes **1.** in writing, any of several strategies adopted by writers who are aware of audience needs and use appropriate planning and revising processes. **2.** in reading, the flexible use of perceptual resources and cognitive strategies by the reader to attain comprehension. *Note*: The study of expert processes in both writing and reading provides insightful contrast with those processes used by beginners. *Cp.* **naive processes**.

expletive *n.* **1.** an interjection of frustration or anger, commonly a swear word. **2.** a substitute or added word or phrase used in a sentence, as *It* in *It is his duty to go* instead of *His duty is to go*.

explication de texte (*Fr., pl.* **explications de texte**) **1.** a very close and detailed method of analyzing literature, developed first in France. **2.** an approach to literary criticism that uses such a method.

explicit memory memory used to reorganize or recall presented materials.

exploratory talk in language acquisition, the early efforts of children to develop a strategy of communication and engage in conversation.

exposition *n.* **1.** one of the four traditional forms of composition in speech and writing, intended to set forth or explain. *Note*: Good exposition is clear in conception, well organized, and understandable. It may include limited amounts of argumentation, description, and narration to achieve this purpose. *Cp.* **argumentation**; **description**; **narration** (def. 1); **transactional writing**. **2.** the act of explaining or setting forth. **3.** a display, as in a public exhibition. *adj.* **expository**.

expression *n.* **1.** the act or result of setting forth something in words; utterance; writing. **2.** a particular manner of wording, as *I don't believe it—you lie*. *Cp.* **idiom** (defs. 1, 2). **3.** modulation and pacing in speech to convey meaning. **4.** the quality of feeling shown, as *read aloud with forceful expression*. **5.** an act representative of an organism, as *Thinking is an expression of the higher mental process*. **6.** a symbolic representation, as *the mathematical expression x = y*. *v.* **express**. *adj.* **expressive**.

expressionism *n.* an early 20th century intellectual and artistic movement originating in Germany that rejects objective reality in favor of the inner life. *Note*: By encouraging the artist to convey strong feelings, expressionism emphasizes highly subjective experiences at the expense of objectivity. *Cp.* **impressionism**. *adj.* **expressionistic**.

expressive aphasia **1.** difficulty in producing syntactic speech and often writing because of brain injury or disease. **2.** difficulty in recalling the sequence of words needed to say what one wishes to say, as in Broca's aphasia.

expressive language **1.** the use of language to convey feelings or attitudes. **2.** vivid and colorful language. **3.** the conveyance of a message orally or graphically. *Cp.* **receptive language** (def. 3).

expressive vocabulary the vocabulary used to communicate in speaking and writing. *Cp.* **receptive vocabulary**.

expressive writing highly personal writing, as in diaries, personal letters, autobiographies, etc. *Cp.* **poetic writing**; **transactional writing**.

expurgate *v.* to censor; "cleanse" by removing objectionable, erroneous, or obscene parts of material before presentation or publication. *Cp.* **bowdlerize**; **censorship**.

extension *n.* in logic, the class of things to which a term applies. See also **denotation** (def. 2). *Cp.* **intension**.

extralinguistic *adj.* referring to nonlanguage aspects of a message that contribute to its meaning, as gestures, facial expressions, etc. *Cp.* **paralanguage**.

extraposition *n.* the process of moving some element of a sentence to another position, as *To read* The Giver *is an emotional experience* vs. *It is an emotional experience to read* The Giver.

extrinsic method a teaching-learning approach in which goals and rewards come from the teacher, not the student. *Cp.* **intrinsic method**.

extrinsic phonics phonics taught as a supplemental learning aid rather than as an integral part of the program of reading instruction, often in separate workbooks during special time periods. *Cp.* **intrinsic phonics**.

eye dialect written language spelled according to regional or social dialect and intended to convey such dialect, as "'We's safe, Huck, we's safe! Jump up and crack yo' heels! Dat's de good ole Cairo at las', I jis knows it is!'" (Mark Twain, *Adventures of Huckleberry Finn*).

eye dominance in normal vision, the consistent use of or preference for one eye in a sighting or visual motor task, as in alternating vision.

eye-movement camera an instrument for photographing eye movements, especially while reading. *Note*: For many years, a corneal reflection method was used to record eye movements photographically. Later, heat-sensitive paper and electric pens allowed a direct printout of such movements, bypassing the need to develop film. More recently, TV cameras, computer analysis of movements, and electromyograms have been used in the study of eye movements. See also **corneal-reflection method**; **eye-movement pattern**.

eye-movement pattern the characteristic way the eyes move during reading, as the number and duration of fixations, saccades, regressions. See also **eye-movement camera**; **eye-movement record**.

eye-movement record any record of eye movements during reading or other visual inspection tasks. See also **eye-movement camera**; **eye-movement pattern**.

eye-voice span (EVS) **1.** the average number of words by which the eye is ahead of the voice in oral reading. *Note*: Good oral readers have a wide eye-voice span that allows them to anticipate meaning, phrase in thought units, adjust intonation and breathing, and check pronunciation before speaking. **2.** "the amount of text that can be read in one second which is an indication that material already perceived is stored in short-term memory until a vocal response is made" (Geyer, 1968).

fable **1.** *n.* a short tale in prose or verse that teaches a moral, usually with animals and inanimate objects as characters. *Cp.* **allegory**. **2.** *n.* a myth or a legend. **3.** *n.* a lie or falsehood.

face validity the degree to which a test appears reasonable and usable; test content that is valid superficially but not necessarily technically. *Note*: Face validity refers only to user acceptability, not to content validity. For this reason a test with face validity alone is a poor test, but one with high face validity and content validity may be very good and widely used.

factor analysis any of several methods for analyzing the intercorrelations of tests; a type of multivariate analysis. *Note*: When a factor is located in factor analysis, it is interpreted as a source of communality that is often given a name. *Rate of reading* is a factor found in many different factor analyses and is therefore understood to exist independently of the particular reading test used.

factorial design any experimental design that involves the systematic variation, or possible combination, of two or more independent variables in relation to the dependent variable, as a study of the effect of phonic skills and vocabulary knowledge on rate of comprehension.

factor loading the relationship between a factor and a test, expressed as a correlation in multivariate analysis. *Note*: The higher the factor loading, the more adequately the factor accounts for scores on the test, and vice versa.

factor score in multivariate analysis, the weighted sum of scores on the tests, designed to give a score maximally correlated with the underlying factor.

fairytale **1.** a folk story about real-life problems, usually with imaginary characters and magical events. **2.** a story involving wee folk such as fairies or leprechauns. Also **fairy tale**. *Cp.* **folktale**; **legend** (def. 1); **myth**.

falling diphthong a diphthong in which the first element of the diphthong is stressed, as in the first part of /ou/ in *loud*. *Note*: In English, falling diphthongs are primarily used. *Cp.* **rising diphthong**.

false cognate a word in one language similar in form to that in another but with a different meaning; *faux ami*; false friend; as the English *library* and the Spanish *liberia* (bookstore).

family literacy literacy efforts or activities involving more than one generation. *Note*: A family literacy program generally has three components—literacy for children (including study skills), literacy for parents (e.g., GED instruction), and instruction for adults on how to foster literacy in their children or other young relatives. *Cp.* **intergenerational literacy**.

fantasy *n.* a highly imaginative story about characters, places, and events that, while sometimes believable, do not exist. Also **phantasy**. *Cp.* **realistic fiction**. *v.* **fantasize**. *adj.* **fantastic**.

farce **1.** *n.* a light, humorous play emphasizing improbable situations rather than characterization, as Georges Feydeau's *A Flea in Her Ear*. **2.** *n.* humor of the type found in such plays. *Note*: Historically, farce was the injection of jokes and gags into a play. **3.** *n.* a sham; mockery. *adj.* **farcical**.

far point a distance of about 20 feet (6 meters), real or simulated by projection, for measuring visual acuity and distance vision. *Cp.* **near point**.

feature *n.* in linguistics, a distinctive speech sound, grammatical structure, or semantic characteristic used in linguistic analysis. *Cp.* **distinctive feature** (defs. 1, 2).

feature analysis a method of analysis that describes qualities of linguistic components, as the "voiced" vs. "voiceless" characteristics of consonants.

feedback loop the pathway by which information about the results of a process is sent back to modify or control the process.

feedback marker a signal of assent or dissent, verbal or nonverbal, given by one speaker to another during a conversation, as a smile, headshake, "Yeah," "OK," etc.

felicity condition in the study of speech acts, any of the criteria or conditions that must be satisfied if a particular type of speech act is to be successful, as in making a statement, giving a command, asking a question, etc. *Note*: For example, in giving a command, two conditions must be present: **a.** the person addressed is able to execute the task. **b.** any objects involved can be identified. "Go fly a kite" could satisfy these felicity conditions in certain circumstances but not in others. See also **appropriateness**.

feminist (literary) criticism literary criticism that opposes male writing and thinking in order to create a female consciousness. *Note*: Feminist criticism frees women from Western paternalism by expanding the human experience, by recovering works of women writers often ignored, and by encouraging new literature by women.

feminist literature **1.** writings by and about women. **2.** a reappraisal by women of the historical, sociological, and psychological status and role of women that was analyzed initially by men. *Note*: Much of this literature expresses points of view about the stereotyping of women and is especially directed toward removing sexism in language, in occupational and educational opportunity, and in the home. **3.** writings from the feminist movement advocating social, economic, and political rights for women equal to those of men.

feral children children who, in their formative years, are raised in environments deprived, or largely so, of contact with other humans, especially adults. *Note*: Feral children are of special interest to psycholinguists because they provide opportunities to study the effects of linguistic deprivation on language development during the early, critical period of life.

Fernald(–Keller) method a technique for learning to identify printed words, also called *VAKT* because it involves looking at a word (*v*isual) while saying it (*a*uditory) and tracing it (*k*inesthetic, *t*actile), described at length in Grace Fernald's *Remedial Techniques in Basic School Subjects*. *Note*: The technique, or variations of it, is usually one part of a more comprehensive instructional program, often in remedial settings. *Cp*. **Gillingham method**; **visual-motor method**.

fiction *n.* imaginative narrative in any form of presentation that is designed to entertain, as distinguished from that which is designed primarily to explain, argue, or merely describe; specifically, a type of literature, especially prose, as novels and short stories, but also including plays and narrative poetry. *Note*: Fiction, or a fictional element, is found in many literary forms, such as historical fiction, fables, fairytales, folklore, legends, and picture books. Elements of fiction may also be found in some biographies, autobiographies, and other forms of nonfiction. *Cp*. **nonfiction.** *adj.* **fictional**.

fictionalized biography the life story of a person, based partly on fact and partly on the imagination of the writer, as Jean Lee Letham's many fictionalized biographies for young readers.

field of discourse the nature or type of subject matter upon which discourse is based, as science, history, religion, etc. See also **mode of discourse**; **tenor of discourse**.

field research research that, unlike laboratory research, takes place in natural and less controlled settings. Also **field study**. *Cp.* **laboratory research**.

field work in the discipline of education, any type of off-campus work, usually of a practical nature, sponsored by a school or college. Also **fieldwork**.

figura (*Lat.*) *n.* letter shape; one of the three characteristics of each letter of the alphabet recognized by early grammarians, the others being *nomen* (name) and *potentes* (power).

figurative knowledge in Piagetian theory, perceptual and symbolic knowing attained directly from language, gesture, mental imagery, and perceptual recognition; static concepts representing external or figural aspects of objects and events, as in learning to identify and write letters and words. *Cp.* **operativity**.

figurative language language enriched by word images and figures of speech. See also **figure of speech**; **image** (def. 4).

figure-ground *n.* the perception or awareness of a distinctive form (figure) on a relatively formless background (ground), as the perception of an embedded figure or the awareness of a familiar voice in a noisy room. *Note*: Figure and ground interact, one influencing the other and sometimes becoming the other, as in a reversible figure. See also the illustration "Reversible figure" in the next column.

figure of speech the expressive, nonliteral use of language for special effects, usually through images, as in metaphor and personification. *Cp.* **figurative language**.

final e silent e; the spelling pattern in English in which *e* is the last letter in a word, does not represent a final sound, and often signals a long vowel sound for the preceding vowel letter, as *e* in *hate*, *kite*, *robe*. See also **silent letter**.

fine motor coordination the control of small

Rubin's ambiguous figure, the "Peter-Paul Goblet"
Reversible figure

sets of voluntary muscles, as those used in writing or in eye movements.

finite verb a verb form that is capable of indicating person, number, mood, and tense, as *opens* in *She opens the door. Cp.* **infinitive**.

first person **1.** See **person**. **2.** a passage written from the point of view of the main character.

fixation *n.* **1.** the observable stops in eye movements, as when viewing a picture, looking around the environment, or reading. *Note*: Visual perception occurs during, not between, fixations. See also **duration of fixation**; **eye-movement pattern**. *Cp.* **saccade**. **2.** the adjustments internally and in the position of the eyes to achieve clear vision. **3.** a preoccupation to the point of obsession with some idea or action. **4.** in psychoanalytic theory, a strong and lasting emotional attachment that prevents or greatly hinders the making of new relationships or new response patterns. **5.** a habit that has outlived its usefulness, as washing dishes thoroughly before putting them into an automatic dishwasher. **6.** the strengthening of a motor behavior or memory through practice and review. *v.* **fixate**.

fixation disparity a condition in which the visual axis of one eye is slightly misaligned with respect to the other, yet objects are still seen as single rather than double. *Note*: The presence of fixation disparity may indicate a fusional disorder with symptoms of visual discomfort.

fixation point in reading, where the eyes are focused at a given moment in the reading act. *Note*: Fixation points are separated by saccades. *Cp*. **saccade**.

flannelboard *n.* a stiff display board covered with felt or flannel for displaying pictures, symbols, cutouts, etc., for instructional purposes; feltboard.

flashback *n.* the technique of disrupting the chronology of a narrative by shifting to an earlier time in order to introduce information.

flashcard *n.* **1.** a teaching tool of cards on which numbers, letters, words, etc., are written and are displayed for viewing by a student for a brief moment. **2.** any short exposure device that displays cards or slides for a predetermined amount of time, often a fraction of a second; tachistoscope. Also **flash device**. *Note*: The use of flashcards is thought to focus attention and to increase recognition of written material.

Flesch readability formula a method of estimating the difficulty level of adult reading material developed by Flesch and published in 1943, originally based on sentence length in words, the number of affixes, and the number of personal references in 100-word samples of material. *Note*: The formula has undergone several revisions. A 1948 revision called the *Reading Ease formula*, based on number of syllables per 100 words and sentence length in words, has been widely used. See also **readability**; **readability formula**. *Cp*. **Dale–Chall readability formula**; **Fry readability graph**; **Spache readability formula**.

flexible grouping allowing students to work in differently mixed groups depending on the goal of the learning task at hand. *Note*: Flexible grouping is sometimes used in classes in which students are ordinarily organized on the basis of ability.

flipchart *n.* a group of sheets, usually of paper or plastic, that are hinged at the top for displaying instructional material one page at a time, often used to show children's stories and art.

fluency *n.* **1.** the clear, easy, written or spoken expression of ideas. **2.** freedom from word-identification problems that might hinder comprehension in silent reading or the expression of ideas in oral reading; automaticity. **3.** the ability to produce words or larger language units in a limited time interval. *Note*: This type of fluency is often tested in a comprehensive reading diagnosis. **4.** the ability to execute motor movements smoothly, easily, and readily. *adj*. **fluent**.

fluent reader **1.** a reader whose performance exceeds normal expectation with respect to age and ability; independent reader. **2.** any person who reads smoothly, without hesitation and with comprehension.

focus *pl.* **-cuses**, **-ci** **1.** *n.* a center of interest or attention. **2.** *v.* to direct attention to. **3.** *n.* the site of origin or major concentration of a disease or injury. **4.** *n.* the point at which rays, as light, heat, sound, etc., meet or appear to meet after refraction or reflection; focal point, as of a lens. **5.** *v.* to adjust the focal distance of the eye, a lens, etc., in order to produce a clear image.

focused freewriting freewriting that is restricted by time. *Cp*. **freewriting**.

focus group a small group selected from a wider population from which opinions and suggestions are sought through open discussion about some topic or (potential) product. *Note*:

Focus groups are now commonly used by educational publishers in preparing texts and other instructional materials.

folk etymology the modification of a word or expression based on a false understanding of its origin, as *hangnail* for *angnæl* (literally "painful nail" in Middle English).

folklore *n.* the traditions and beliefs of a people that have been passed down from generation to generation orally or as written tales. *Note*: To about 1850, folklore was called *popular antiquities*.

folktale *n.* a narrative form, as an epic, legend, myth, fable, etc., that is or had been retold within a culture for generations and is well known through repeated storytelling, as *an Anansi tale* (see this term). Also **folk tale; folk story**. *Cp.* **fairytale; tale**.

foot *n., pl.* **feet** a unit of rhythm in verse, usually with one stressed syllable and one or more unstressed syllables; metrical unit.

forced-choice item a test item containing several plausible choices to which one must respond, as those often used in personality inventories.

foreign accent the result of carrying over phonetic characteristics of a native language to another language later acquired.

foreigner talk a type of speech used by a native or fluent speaker of a language when speaking with someone who is not proficient in that language, as *"You lost, yes?" Note*: Foreigner talk is typically: **a.** carefully, slowly, and loudly pronounced. **b.** simple in grammar and vocabulary.

foreignism *n.* a foreign word or expression used in a native language that is generally chosen for effect or to indicate special knowledge, as using in English *panache* (French) or *sashimi* (Japanese).

foreshadowing *n.* the technique of giving clues to coming events in a narrative. *v.* **foreshadow**.

form **1.** *n.* the external features or configuration of a language unit. **2.** *n.* in linguistics, the abstract phonological, grammatical, or lexical properties of language units; linguistic form. **3.** *n.* the expression of language by means of speaking or writing; spoken form; written form. **4.** *n.* an inflectional variant of a word. **5.** *n.* something perceived as a psychological whole; gestalt; as *an ink blot form*. **6.** *n.* the philosophic concept of the underlying structure, pattern, or nature of a thing; essence. **7.** See **literary form**. **8.** *n.* technical style. **9.** *n.* a document to be completed in writing, as *a tax form*. **10.** *v.* to give shape to; arrange; as *form letters in handwriting*.

formal assessment the collection of data using standardized tests or procedures under controlled conditions.

formalism *n.* the study of the inner shape and nature of a work of art without regard to outer meaning. *Cp.* **New Criticism**.

formal operations in Piaget's theory of mental development, an organized system of logical thinking ability that usually appears between about ages 11 and 15, involving abstract reasoning and the setting up and testing of verbal hypotheses. See also **infralogical operations; operations; preoperational thought**. *Cp.* **concrete operations; stage** (def. 2).

formal speech a style of speaking used to inform an audience in impersonal terms, marked by careful attention to organization of content and to grammatical structure and pronunciation, as in professional lectures. Also **formal style**. See also **communicative competence; elaborated code; register** (def. 1); **style of discourse**.

formant *n.* in voice spectrograms, one of several acoustic frequency bands used to identify the characteristic patterns of resonance in vowels and in some consonants.

formative evaluation the continuing study of the process of change in an instructional program as it moves toward its goals and objectives by monitoring the learning progress of its participants. *Cp.* **summative evaluation**.

form class **1.** those words that are used as a group in the same way in all sentences of a language, as nouns, verbs, adjectives, adverbs, etc. See also **part of speech**; **word class**. **2.** those linguistic forms that can fill a given position in a sentence, as *Mary* or *She* in completing the sentence ____ *likes to play basketball.*

form-oriented instruction in writing, instruction focused on teaching students to gain control of specific types of discourse, as narration or exposition.

form perception the perception of shapes, outlines, and wholes, as *word form perception.* See also **visual discrimination**.

formulaic expression an expression of several words that are learned and used as a single unit, as *How do you do?* Also **formulaic language**; **formulaic speech**. *Cp.* **phatic communion**.

formula story a narrative that relates highly predictable events, suggesting the author was following a set of directions, as in the common narrative formulas of love vs. loyalty and boy meets girl; *Cp.* **pattern book.**

foveal vision **1.** normal vision in which the line of sight falls on the fovea, a small area of cones near the center of the retina in which, under well-lighted conditions, vision is sharpest. *Cp.* **peripheral vision**. **2.** vision with maximum clarity and color sensitivity.

fragment *n.* an incomplete grammatical construction.

frame **1.** *n.* a single picture on a filmstrip or motion picture film. **2.** *n.* a single unit of programmed instructional material to which a learner must respond, as *information, response, and feedback frames.* **3.** *n.* in language teaching, each blank in a lesson, as *verb* would fit in the frame *A* ____ *shows a state of being or action.* See also **slot** (def. 2). **4.** *n.* box-like lines to set off printed material on a page. **5.** *v.* to use one's hands to isolate words recognized, as on an experience chart.

frame of reference a cognitive structure or scheme to which ideas, information, etc., may be related; schema.

F **ratio** an index of the significance of the difference between two variances, in which the larger variance is divided by the smaller one. *Note*: The ratio may be interpreted by means of a standard *F*-ratio table based on the degrees of freedom of the two statistics.

free association an unstructured and uncensored flow of ideas, impressions, or words. See also **stream of consciousness**.

free morpheme a morpheme that can stand alone as an independent word, as *cat.* *Cp.* **bound morpheme**.

free recall a memory task in which a subject is given a series of items and is later asked to recall them in any order.

free-response test a test in which one states answers in one's own words rather than by selecting from given responses, as in an essay examination.

free translation a nonliteral, idiomatic translation from one language to another, intended to reflect the communicative function and spirit of the original, as *I'm ten years old* for the strictly literal *I have ten years* in the French *J'ai dix ans*. *Cp.* **literal translation**.

free variation in phonology, the ability of a sound to be substituted for another in the same context without change in meaning or function of a word, as /tə mā′tō/ vs. /tə mä′tō/. *Cp.* **allophone** (def.1); **complementary distribution**.

free verse verse with an irregular metrical pattern and line length that originated in 19th-century France as a movement to free poetry from the strict metrical rules of that time; *vers libre*.

freewriting *n.* writing that is unrestricted in form, style, content, and purpose. *Note*: Like brainstorming, freewriting as a teaching technique is designed to help the student-writer find a personal voice through uninhibited expression. Teachers often find that freewriting is helpful for the student who says, "I can't think of anything to write about." *Cp.* **focused freewriting**.

frequency curve a graphic form of a frequency distribution in which the midpoint frequency of each successive class interval is joined by a continuous line, usually smoothed. See also **frequency distribution; frequency polygon; histogram**.

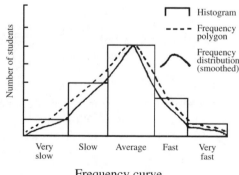

Frequency curve

frequency distribution the number of times each of the possible events occurs in each of the possible categories, as the frequency distribution of student scores at each grade level, often displayed graphically on a frequency curve. See also **frequency curve; frequency polygon**.

frequency polygon a graphic form of a frequency distribution plotted at the midpoint frequency of each class interval. See also **frequency curve; frequency distribution; histogram**.

fricative *n.* a consonant speech sound made by constricting but not stopping the air flow; spirant; as /z/ in *zero*.

frozen style an extremely formal style of speech and writing that is marked by subtlety, gentility, and quality of presentation that reveals fresh meaning and insights in rereading, as in the great classics. Also **frozen speech**. *Note*: "In frozen style the writer who is dedicated can enable the reader to educate himself indefinitely far beyond what the writer put into the text in the first place.... Good frozen style is whatever lures the reader on and on through successive inventive discoveries" (Joos, 1961). See also **communicative competence; register** (def. 1); **style of discourse**.

frustration reading level a readability or grade level of material that is too difficult to be read successfully by a student, even with normal classroom instruction and support. *Note*: Although suggested criteria for determining a student's frustration reading level vary, less than 90 percent accuracy in word identification and less than 50 percent comprehension are often used as standards. See also **independent reading level; informal reading inventory; instructional reading level**.

Fry readability graph a method of estimating the difficulty level of reading material developed by Fry and based on the number of syllables and sentences in 100-word samples, with corresponding grade-level values read from a graph. *Note*: A number of modifications have been proposed since the graph's original publication in 1965, chiefly in extending the values downward to preprimer level and upward to college. Also **Fry readability scale**. See also **readability**; **readability formula**. *Cp.* **Dale–Chall readability formula**; **Flesch readability formula**; **Spache readability formula**.

F test a statistical test for the significance of the difference between the variances of two samples of behavior; *F*; *F* value. *Note*: The *F* test is useful in showing the homogeneity of variance in different samples—i.e., the extent to which the variance of test scores in the samples is stable.

function **1.** *n.* purpose; role. **2.** *n.* in sociolinguistics, the intended use or effect of language. *Note*: "We may exhort, beg, wheedle, needle, order, command, demand, question, assert, and sometimes just plain fool around. We vary the function of language to fit our goal" (DeStefano, 1980). **3.** *n.* the relationship between a linguistic form and other parts of the construction in which it is used, as using a noun as the subject of a sentence. **4.** *adj.* referring to such a role. **5.** *n.* a factor related to or dependent on another factor, as *x is a function of y. adj.* **functional**.

functional adult education educational programs for adults that stress knowledge and skills needed in everyday life.

functional bilingualism the ability to understand, speak, read, and write in both one's native language and a second language. *Cp.* **bilingualism**.

functional grammar an alternative to transformational grammar; specifically, a theory of grammar that adopts "a pragmatic view of language as social interaction, and sets up 'functional units'...within sentence structure" (Crystal, 1987).

functional hearing loss the loss or reduction of hearing acuity without a known organic cause.

functional literacy **1.** a level of reading and writing sufficient for everyday life but not for completely autonomous activity. **2.** the application of the skills and knowledge of reading and writing to adult or near-adult responsibilities in the workplace; adult literacy; functional adult literacy; pragmatic literacy; required literacy. **3.** "the knowledge and skills in reading and writing which enable a person to engage in all those activities in which literacy is normally assumed in his culture or group" (Gray, 1956). *Note*: The genesis of current conceptions of functional literacy may be seen in Gray's reference to engagement in cultural or group activities. This allusion was later extended in UNESCO documents to include both individual and social functions, then to the economics of the workplace (work-oriented literacy), and finally to include personal fulfillment, social progress, and economic development. See also the essay "Functional Literacy" on p. 90; **literacy**.

functional print environmental print specifically intended to convey information, as words on a cereal box.

functional reading **1.** reading for practical purposes, as to get information. **2.** the level of reading skill needed to get along in a society. See also **functional literacy** (defs. 1–3 and essay). **3.** environmental print encountered.

functional shift the extension of the use of a word from one grammatical category to another, as *witness* (verb) from *witness* (noun) in *She witnessed the accident*; conversion.

Functional Literacy

The United Nations Educational, Scientific, and Cultural Organization (1978) defines a literate as one "who can with understanding both read and write a short simple statement on his everyday life." Yet there are many people who are literate in this restricted sense, but who nonetheless suffer serious problems with more complex reading and writing tasks. These are the "functionally illiterate."

To be functionally literate a person must be able to "engage in all those activities in which literacy is required for effective functioning of his group and community and also for enabling him to continue to use reading, writing, and calculation for his own and the community's development" (UNESCO, 1978). Note that functional literacy is a relative measure rather than an absolute one. The same skill level may result in one being considered functionally literate in one context and functionally illiterate in another. Also, *functional* literacy calls for a broader as well as a higher level of basic skills than does literacy because it embraces calculations as well as reading and writing. It is, in effect, a measure of one's capacity to cope with the educational challenges of a given environment.

While there is a tendency to associate functional illiteracy with industrialized countries and "plain, old" illiteracy with the developing countries, this is by no means accurate. There are many illiterates in industrialized countries and, alas, a rapidly growing number of functional illiterates in developing countries.

Yet if we consider the matter more deeply, we realize we are all illiterate in one way or another. We may know English but not French or FORTRAN. We may be able to read a page from a novel with joy but be left in puzzlement before one from a statistics book. We may understand a map of our local bus system but be bewildered by a diagram of the electrical circuits within our own home. The dichotomy of "literate" versus "illiterate" does not suffice to deal with skill levels that run from zero to Shakespeare and vary from utter confusion in one sphere to easy mastery in another. Illiteracy is, thus, not a completely foreign concept to any of us. We have all tasted of it and know that its flavor runs from tart and biting in small sips to downright bitter in deep draughts.

John Ryan

function word a word such as a conjunction, preposition, or article whose primary purpose is to show grammatical relationships in and between sentences; closed-class word; functor; empty word. *Cp.* **content word**; **lexical word**.

fused curriculum a curriculum design in which the content of two or more subjects is integrated into a single area of study, as the fusion of Asian history, literature, and geography into a course on Asian civilization.

fusion *n.* **1.** the merging of separate things into a whole in which the original parts tend to lose their identity. **2. sensory fusion**, the blending of several sensations, as of the images from the two eyes into one sensation. **3. flicker fusion**, the perception of rapidly blinking light as steady. **4.** in linguistics, the merging of large elements, as two vowels to form a diphthong. **5.** in psychoanalysis, the balance between the instinct to live and to die that is present in a normal personality.

fusional vergence reserve sufficient extra oculomotor control to achieve fusion and comfortable vision even when oculomotor imbalance is present.

futhork *n.* an alphabet of angular letters carved in wood or stone developed from the Greek and Roman alphabets in the 2nd or 3rd century, used in Old Scandinavian and other northern European languages; runic alphabet. Also **futhark**. *Note*: The term *futhork* is made up of the phonetic values of the first six letters of this alphabet. See also **rune** (def. 1).

Futhork

gatekeeper *n.* **1.** a controlling influence, as standardized tests to determine who shall receive schooling. **2.** originally, an editor who decides specifically what shall and what shall not be included in a newspaper. *n.* **gatekeeping**.

geminate **1.** *adj.* arranged in pairs. **2.** *n.* the prolonging of the sound represented by doubled consonant letters; doubling; as in *mamma*. **3.** *n.* in orthography, a pair of adjacent identical letters, as *pp* in *happy*. **4.** *n.* the production of the same speech sound twice in succession, as /k/ in *book* and /k/ in *keeper* in *bookkeeper*. **5.** *v.* to produce such a succession of sounds. **6.** *v.* to repeat immediately a word or phrase for emphasis, either in speaking or writing.

gender *n.* a grammatical category used in some languages in which articles, nouns, pronouns adjectives, and sometimes verbs, are specifically indicated, as French *le livre* (masculine) or *la bibliothèque* (feminine) and German *das Buch* (neuter). *Note*: In English, gender markers are generally restricted to third-person singular pronouns.

General Educational Development (GED) **test** a battery of tests taken by individuals who did not graduate from high school that measures the extent to which prior experiences in and out of school are equivalent to the knowledge, understandings, and skills normally acquired in high school. *Note*: Successful test takers are issued certificates of high school equivalency by most state educational agencies. See also **equivalency test**.

general factor (*g*) *n.* **1.** a factor hypothesized by Spearman (1904) to be common to all tests of mental ability; *g* factor. **2.** in factor analysis, a factor common to all tests being analyzed.

generalizability *n.* in testing theory, inferring from "the score on a sample of behaviors to the average of all the observations that could be in the domain" (Cronbach, 1984). *Note*: Generaliz-ability is a theoretical alternative to a true-score concept of error of measurement. "True-score theory speaks as if error variance were all of one kind. Generalizability theory recognizes that there are several kinds of errors and alternative universes of generalization" (Cronbach, 1984). See also **error of measurement**.

generative phonology within transformational-generative grammar, the attempt to determine the phonological rules that govern the sound system of language(s).

generative semantics a grammatical theory, developed in the 1960s and 1970s that attempts to unify syntax and semantics as a single area of study; general semantics. *Note*: In this theory, the semantic structure of a sentence is regarded as the base from which its syntactic structure is derived or generated.

genetic epistemology the philosophical and scientific study of the origin and development of knowledge. *Note*: The term is closely identified with the psychologist, Jean Piaget, who has often been described as a "genetic epistemologist" (McNally, 1974).

genitive *n.* a case form in some inflected languages that indicates relationships such as possession or source. *Note*: In written English, this relationship is marked by the apostrophe, as in *my father's car*, or by the preposition *of* as in *the report of the committee*. See also **possessive** (def. 2).

genre *n.* **1.** a category used to classify literary works, usually by form, technique, or content. *Note*: Classic literary genres are tragedy, comedy, epic, lyric, and pastoral. "Today, the novel, essay, short story, television play, and motion picture scenario are also considered genres" (Holman & Harmon, 1992). Children from an early age prove adept at identifying prototypical genres such as fairytales and mysteries, which makes genre a valuable instructional in-

Genre

The concept of genre is a powerful one. I use it frequently to understand and explain literacy practices. I use my knowledge of the conventions of text genres as a stance to help me understand or construct texts. By perceiving a text as a novel, for example, I know, as Rabinowitz (1987) has noted, that I need to attend to certain salient cues, as titles, endings, key events; to predict story outcomes; to infer prototypical character traits, beliefs, and goals; and to interpret thematic meanings. And, by perceiving a novel as a mystery, I know, with Berger (1992), that the detective is typically more competent than the bungling police, is eccentric or unusual, is able to sort out clues and red herrings, is often setting a trap for the criminal, and is able to explain the criminal's motives at the end. When texts deviate from my genre expectations, I learn to revise or readjust those expectations, a process that can be challenging but aesthetically enjoyable. In constructing texts, I employ certain features conventionally associated with the genre in which I am writing.

I originally wrote this essay as a more formal expository text. In revising it to make it more personal, I needed to consider the differences between the conventions of formal expository writing and those of more informal discourse. All of this raises crucial questions for educators: How do students acquire these conventions? Do they simply absorb them by osmosis from reading, or can they be taught as a set of abstract conventions? If I do teach these conventions in the abstract, will students understand what they mean without having read a number of examples of the genre under consideration? There is considerable debate, particularly that in Australia (Reid, 1988), between advocates of direct, formalist instruction in genre conventions versus whole language advocates who argue that students acquire conventions through active reading and writing. My own position is that students need both instructional approaches. They not only need ample experience with texts in order to understand the abstract concepts, but also information about the abstract concepts that can provide them with insights into their experiences.

A related issue is whether students are motivated to learn certain genres which have appeal not only because they are reassuringly predictable but also because they fulfill certain psychological needs. For example, intermediate elementary or middle school students often have a strong interest in adventure, animal, fantasy, detective, and romance novels, exhibiting "binge" reading of certain romance or mystery genre series. By imagining themselves as the heroes or heroines depicted, students perceive themselves as competent individuals successfully coping with problems (Appleyard, 1990). This suggests that teachers should select genre texts that are related to students' own developmental needs.

At the same time, educators must examine the ways in which genres perpetuate cultural attitudes and stereotypes. Take, for example, the "James Bond phenomenon" described by Bennett and Woollacott (1987). From experience with the James Bond novels, movies, and related publicity at the height of their popularity in the 1960s, readers learned to adopt the "subject position" constituted by traditional masculine, pro-Western, anti-Communist attitudes. Similarly, Christian-Smith (1990) has demonstrated that the young adult romance novel often perpetuates patriarchal attitudes toward women. By critically examining the assumptions underlying genre storylines, students may recognize how genres both mirror and shape cultural attitudes.

(continued)

Genre (cont'd.)

More recently, the scope of genre theory has been broadened by Bahktin (1986) and by Berkenkotter and Huckin (1993) to include the social uses of language, or "speech genres." This includes the genres of everyday social exchanges, negotiations, sermons, lectures, letters of recommendation, eulogies, user manuals, bargaining, formal invitations, scientific reports, etc. Each of these genres, according to Lemke (1990), involves certain language styles (formal versus informal), appropriate speech acts, and discourse such as "science talk." For example, young children's often playful language games, what Daiute (1993) describes as "youth genres," involve their own figurative use of language and speech acts such as teasing or mimicking adults' talk. Older children learn to use the conventions of what Gee (1992) describes as "school discourse" genres associated with being good students. (In relation to this last example, we must be aware that students from middle- and upper-class homes often acquire social practices that are compatible with the school discourse genres.) However, many students from lower socioeconomic backgrounds often have quite different social practices that may conflict with the school discourse genre. Educators must recognize and accommodate the inevitable tensions between the school discourse genre and genres of students from all backgrounds.

Richard Beach

---

strument. **2.** any type of discourse that possesses typified, distinguishable conventions of form, style, or content in recurring contexts. *Note*: "Genre is a class of communicative events [in which] the critical feature is some set of shared communicative events" (Swales, 1990). Recent theory, as Freedman (1993) notes, has reconceived genre as social action by studying the social and psychological purposes that it may serve as well as its cultural effects. By shifting the emphasis from formal textual features as in literary analysis to the communicative purpose of any form of "typified rhetorical action based on recurrent situations" (Miller, 1984), theorists have altered not only the focus but the range of application of genre, thus creating difficulty in defining the term. **3. complex genre**, two or more related genres, as in a prose poem or a discourse event such as a church service.

gerund *n.* a word derived from a verb that is used as a noun; in English, a word formed by adding *-ing* to a basic verb, as *reading* in *reading is fun*. See also **participle**; **verbal** (def. 4).

gesture *n.* body movement used to communicate; specifically, "spontaneous movements of the hands and arms [that are] closely synchronized with the flow of speech" (McNeill, 1992). *Note*: Believing that "speech and gesture must cooperate to express [a] person's meaning," McNeill identified five types of gesture: **a. iconic**, having a "close formal relationship to the semantic content of speech," as throwing a ball. **b. metaphorical**, presenting an abstract idea similar to a concept, as rubbing one's stomach to indicate hunger. **c. beat**, a rhythmic stroke, as in marking time. **d. cohesive**, a pattern of gestures that indicates continuing action, as in demonstrating the steps in operating a machine. **e. deictic**, a pointing gesture.

gibberish *n.* talk or writing that is perceived as unintelligible, meaningless, or nonsensical; flummery; humbug.

gifted *adj.* **1.** having special talents or skills. **2.** having superior intellectual functioning or potential. **3.** having so much demonstrated or potential talent as to need distinctive educational programs or services. *Note*: Opinions vary about how superior one needs be to be called "gifted"; for example, the lower limit for the gifted may be considered the top 10 percent, the top 2 percent, more than 2 standard deviations above mean, or at some specific IQ score (sometimes as low as 130). Often overlooked are the artistic and leadership aspects of giftedness.

Gillingham method a synthetic phonics system reinforced by intensive writing and spelling practice. Also **Orton–Gillingham method**. *Cp.* **Fernald(–Keller) method**.

gingerbread method a 17th- and 18th-century practice in England, more written about than used, in which the letters of the alphabet were made of gingerbread, so that the child presumably could eat the letters when able to name them. "And that the Child may learn the better, / As he can name, he eats the letter; / Proceeding thus with Vast Delight / He spells, and gnaws from Left to Right" (Matthew Prior, *Alma*, as cited in Smith, 1965).

global method **1.** an approach to emergent literacy teaching that emphasizes reading-writing relationships through the use of children's written efforts as materials for reading (Freinet, 1977, 1979). Also **global approach**. *Note*: The global method, especially popular in European and Latin American countries, has many parallels to the language experience and whole language approaches (Temple et al., 1993). **2.** an

early term for the look-and-say approach; reading instruction that emphasizes the immediate recognition of whole words, not analysis of word parts. *Note*: Occasionally, the term refers to the sentence method and the story method.

gloss **1.** *n.* a brief explanation of printed text, usually in the margin or in an appendix but sometimes between the lines, as in an interlinear gloss. **2.** *v.* to make such an explanation. **3.** *n.* a study strategy of making interpretive comments on a text that aids in selecting and rephrasing significant information. **4. gloss over**, to make intentionally an explanation that is beside the point, as *gloss over careless thinking with a flurry of words*. **5.** *n.* a glossary.

glottal stop the stopping and quick release of the air flow made by closing the opening between the vocal folds in the larynx, as in the transition between the first and second syllables of the negative *unh-uh*.

gobbledygook *n.* language marked by jargon and circumlocution, as in many governmental publications. Also **gobbledegook**.

goodness-of-fit test any of several statistical measures that test the degree to which obtained scores agree with a theoretical set of expected values.

Gothic novel **1.** a style of novel, especially popular in the late 18th and early 19th centuries, characterized by mysterious settings, an atmosphere of gloom and terror, supernatural happenings, and often violence and horror, as Mary Shelley's *Frankenstein*. **2.** a modern story written in that style.

government *n.* **1.** in traditional grammar, the relationship between two or more grammatical elements such that one controls or imposes some requirement on the form of the other(s), as between nouns and verbs, prepositions and nouns.

2. in government/binding theory, the relationships among elements of a sentence.

government/binding theory (GB) a theory of language developed by Chomsky (1982) from generative grammar that seeks to explain the principles and conditions of a universal grammar. See also **universal grammar**.

Main Subcategories of
Government/Binding Theory

• _Binding theory_ describes the referential relationships among noun phrases in a sentence.

• _Bounding theory_ describes the rules that restrict the movement of sentence constituents.

• _Case theory_ describes the assignment of cases, or functions, to noun phrases in a sentence.

• _Theta theory_ assigns semantic roles to elements of a sentence.

• _X-bar theory_ describes phrase structures.

---

governor _n._ in government/binding theory, a sentence element that influences, or governs, another element.

graded word list a list of words ranked by grade level, reader level, or other level of difficulty or complexity, often used to assess competence in word identification, word-meaning knowledge, and spelling.

grade equivalent a type of derived score based on the grade at which an average person from a test-standardized population earns a given score. _Note_: Most test authorities and professional organizations such as the International Reading Association strongly condemn the use of the grade equivalent as well as the age equivalent in educational practice, chiefly on two grounds: because the individual is compared to members of another group from whom he or she may be very different, and because such comparisons have led to unfortunate educational policy decisions. See also **grade norm**. _Cp._ **age equivalent**.

grade level **1.** successive levels of an educational program into which students are divided according to age or achievement; grade. **2.** achievement in relation to assigned level in an educational program. **3.** a designated level of text difficulty determined by a readability formula. **4.** level of reading performance on a standardized reading test as compared to the level reached by a norming population.

grade norm typically, the median score obtained by students in a particular grade at a given time of year. See also **grade equivalent**.

grade point average (GPA) the average of numerical values assigned to letter grades, often A = 4, B = 3, etc., used widely in the United States (and to a lesser degree elsewhere) to reflect scholastic performance and serve as a criterion measure for admission to further schooling.

gradient _n._ **1.** a change in the sound pattern of response, from high to low or vice versa. **2.** a change in motivational strength resulting from a change in stimulation.

graffiti _n. pl._ writing or drawings made in public places. _sing._ **graffito**.

grammar _n._ **1.** "a linguistic description of some language—a set of statements saying how a language works" (Langacker, 1973). _Note_: In this usage, _grammar_ includes the phonological, morphological, syntactic, and semantic description of both the language's structure at a given time and its evolution over time. **2.** the morphology and syntax of a language. **3.** the descriptive study of a language or languages. **4.** what one knows about the structure and use of one's own language that leads to its creative and communicative use.

grammarian *n.* one who studies or specializes in grammar.

grammar school **1.** (*Brit.*) a public eight-year secondary school. **2.** (*Brit.*) after 1580, a secondary school with a classical curriculum. **3.** See **Latin grammar school**. **4.** (*archaic*) in the United States, an elementary school.

grammaticality *n.* the degree to which a written or spoken utterance follows the grammatical rules of the language to which the utterance belongs; grammaticalness. *Note*: The grammaticality of a certain sentence can be controversial, as in *Drive slow*. Grammaticality is often considered to be correctness in language usage according to prescriptive grammar (see the essay "Grammar and Grammatical" on pp. 99–100) although linguists tend to support that usage favored by a majority.

Grammar and Grammatical

By *grammar* and *grammatical* we can mean one of three things: (1) conformity to certain structural aspects of speech and writing that we judge acceptable, (2) descriptions of those aspects of structure, or (3) aspects of the mental competence that lets us speak and write at all.

"Good" and "Bad" Grammar

The meaning of *grammar* and *grammatical* familiar to most of us refers to "good" and "bad" usage: we have often heard that it is bad grammar to begin a sentence with *and* or end it with a preposition; it is good grammar to avoid splitting infinitives, and so on. In this sense, *good grammar* means those forms of speech that conform to a small set of prescriptions that many schooled speakers and writers know about but that most do not unself-consciously observe. A second common meaning of *good grammar* focuses on the more systematic differences that distinguish a standard language from other social dialects. In English, these include distinctions such as the presence or absence of the verb *is* (*He's in the house* versus *He in the house*), double versus single negatives (*I don't have any money* vs. *I don't have no money*), and forms of verbs (*brought* vs. *bringed*). While speakers of standard English might unself-consciously split an infinitive, they are unlikely to use a double negative or the verb form *bringed* because these patterns are more systematic.

When most linguists analyze grammatical differences, they avoid describing them as "correct" or "incorrect" or "good" or "bad" for two reasons: first, when they describe a language, they study not how teachers, editors, and textbook writers think we *should* speak and write, but how we *do* speak and write; second, they have discovered that "nonstandard" dialects often have a structure as logical and regular as that of standard language. For example, linguists acknowledge that nonstandard English is likely to be rejected by those who speak and write standard English, and so in that sense most would agree that nonstandard English can be inappropriate when the *social* context calls for standard English. But linguists assume that if they can see in a language patterns that are regular and predictable, then those patterns are evidence of a grammar that exists in the minds

(continued)

of speakers (see the discussion under "Grammar and Competence," following) and are therefore not "ungrammatical."

When linguists do use the terms *grammatical* and *ungrammatical,* they are usually referring to patterns fundamental to a dialect and from which speakers of that dialect rarely knowingly deviate unless they are seeking some special effect, as in poetry or jokes. When linguists think about such deviations, they include those as extreme as *Dog the found bone a* or as subtle as *Fortunately, where are your going?*

Grammar as Description of Patterns of Language

The most familiar systematic grammar is the one most of us learned in grade school: a noun is a person, place, or thing; a verb shows action; a sentence expresses a single thought. Many of the elements in this kind of description can be traced back to grammars of Latin and Greek. Modern linguists have discovered so many fundamental complexities in human languages, however, that they have had to develop a more abstract, almost mathematical, way to construct grammars. But more important, many linguists now seek to describe not just a language itself, but that mental competence

(see the next subsection) that allows us to produce sentences at all. In their descriptions, they include terms for parts of words (*prefix, suffix, inflection, root, stem,* etc.) and for the mental system that lets us assemble those elements into words; they include terms for different kinds of words (*noun, verb, article, adjective*), terms for relationships among those words in phrases, clauses, and sentences (*subject, predicate, object, modifier*), and descriptions of the mental system, or "rules," that let us assemble those phrases, clauses, and sentences.

In this sense, a grammar describes not just the patterns we can see in sentences before us, but those mental competencies that all humans possess. Linguists often use the term *rule* to describe these competencies, a usage that confuses many who think of rule as something like "Don't split infinitives." By *rule*, linguists mean only that aspect of our abstract mental competence that we apply systematically and predictably, and the specific written-out description of that element of our competence.

Grammar as Competence

In this sense of the term, we all have a "grammar" somewhere in our minds as well as a sense of "good" grammar. Because we and professional linguists use the terms *grammar* and *grammatical* in so many different ways, we often fall into disputes over what we should call "grammatical." When linguists say that *He don't got no money* is "grammatical," they do not mean that we should accept it in the same way we accept *He doesn't have any money,* particularly when a speaker is in a social context that calls for standard English. Indeed, they would probably reject it in the writing of their own students. But linguists go on to point out that such nonstandard sentences nevertheless have a regular, describable structure, a "grammar" that is as logical and consistent as its parallel structure in standard language and which requires mental competence for its development and use.

Joseph M. Williams

grammatical meaning meaning that depends on syntactical relationships, as the meaning of the subject or object of a sentence. *Cp.* **lexical meaning**.

grammatic closure the tendency to fill in missing or unclear syntactical or grammatical information to comprehend a message, often enabling a listener to anticipate the next word of a speaker.

graph *n.* **1.** any graphic symbol. **2.** in orthography, one of the possible forms or shapes a grapheme may take in writing, as b, *B*, b, *B*, etc. See also **allograph** (def. 1). **3.** a diagram or pictorial device that displays relationships, as between sets of numbers, etc. See also **bar graph**; **circle graph**; **line graph**.

grapheme *n.* a written or printed representation of a phoneme, as *b* for /b/ and *oy* for /oi/ in *boy*. *Note*: In English, a grapheme may be a single letter or a group of letters. It includes all the ways in which the phoneme may be written or printed. *Cp.* **allograph** (def. 1). *adj.* **graphemic**.

grapheme-phoneme correspondence the relationship between a grapheme and the phoneme(s) it represents; letter-sound correspondence, as *c* representing /k/ in *cat* and /s/ in *cent*. *Note*: Technically, grapheme-phoneme correspondence refers to how letters correspond to sounds, not vice versa. Phonics as a teaching device in reading instruction concerns grapheme-phoneme correspondences—that is, how to pronounce words seen in print. *Cp.* **phoneme-grapheme correspondence**.

graphemics *n.* (*with sing. v.*) the study of the use of orthographic signs in a writing system; graphology. *Cp.* **graphetics**; **orthography**.

graphetics *n.* (*with sing. v.*) the study of the general function and shape of orthographic symbols irrespective of their particular use in a writing system. *Cp.* **graphemics**.

graphology *n.* **1.** See **graphemics**. **2.** the study of handwriting, especially for the purpose of discovering the character and personality of the writer. *adj.* **graphological**.

graphophonic *adj.* referring to the sound relationships between the orthography and phonology of a language.

graphotactics *n.* **1.** *pl.*, the permissible arrangements of orthographic symbols in forming morphemes and words of languages. **2.** *sing.*, the study of such arrangements. *adj.* **graphotactic**.

grave accent **1.** a graphic mark (`) placed directly above a vowel to indicate that the vowel sound is falling in pitch (Greek), open or lax (French), or secondarily stressed (English), as in *Súndày*. **2.** in English, a mark placed above a normally unpronounced *e* to indicate that it is to be pronounced as the vowel /e/, as *hallowèd*. See also **accent** (def. 2); **diacritic mark**.

Great (English) Vowel Shift a change in certain vowel sounds in late Middle English, as from Middle English *hus* to the present *house*. *Note*: "These vowels took a clockwise turn in the height dimension: low vowels became mid, mid vowels became high, and high vowels became low" (Schane, 1973).

Greek alphabet an alphabet developed by the Ancient Greeks that extended the Semitic alphabet by adding vowel letters and served as the source for the Roman, Coptic, and Cyrillic alphabets as well as for various symbols used in mathematics, linguistics, etc.

grouping *n.* the division of students into classes for instruction, as by age, ability, or achievement, or within classes, as by reading ability or interests. *Note*: The many varieties of grouping include cross-age cross-class grouping. See also (*Brit.*) **streaming**; **flexible grouping**. **2.** *pl.*, in Piagetian theory, a set of inferred logical structures—closure, reversibility, associativity, identity, and repetition—that underlie and make possible the concrete logical operations; often (*Fr.*) **groupements**.

groups *n. pl.* in Piagetian theory, logical models that represent the classificatory and relational thinking of children in the concrete operations period.

group test a test designed to be administered to groups varying in size from a few to a hundred or more. *Note*: In educational practice, most tests, as standardized tests, are group tests that require special care in their administration. *Cp.* **individual test**.

guided imagery a reading technique advocated by Samples (1977) that encourages students to daydream about a concept or activity as a means of motivation, organizing prior knowledge, stimulating discussion, etc.

guided reading reading instruction in which the teacher provides the structure and purpose for reading and for responding to the material read. *Note*: Most basal reading programs have guided reading lessons. See also **directed reading activity**.

gymnasium *n., pl.* **-siums**, **-sia** a classical school in continental Europe, especially Germany, that prepares students for university.

gynocriticism *n.* a version of feminist literary criticism that promotes female values in literature and its evaluation.

haiku *n., pl.* **-ku** **1.** a major type of Japanese poetry; specifically, a form of verse written in seventeen syllables with three lines of five, seven, and five syllables, respectively, to express a single thought and intended to call forth a specific response. **2.** a poem written in this manner.

handbook *n.* an instructional guide, manual, or reference tool, usually small and designed for quick and easy use.

handedness *n.* a consistent preference for either the left or right hand from which cerebral dominance may be inferred. *Note:* Similarly, cerebral dominance may be inferred by preference for either foot, or *footedness.*

handicapped **1.** *n.* a person who because of one or more types of disability has difficulty, but not complete inability, in the performance of specific tasks, as in schooling or employment; disabled. *Note:* Definitions of particular types of handicapped, as *perceptually handicapped,* are given under the describing term. See also **multiply handicapped**. **2.** *adj.* referring to such a person or condition. **3.** *adj.* referring to a limitation imposed by the environment on a person with a disability, as *handicapped by lack of access to a facility.* **4. the handicapped** (*with pl. v.*), the disabled, as a group. *Note:* The use of this term has fallen into some disfavor because of its implication that those with handicaps suffer a deficit and so are of less worth than those without. *n., v.* **handicap**.

handwriting scale an ordered scaled set of handwriting specimens used for judging the legibility of handwriting. *Note:* Since handwriting varies from person to person in terms of size, slant, and letter formation, and because of possible rater bias for a particular style of handwriting, exact judgments of handwriting legibility are difficult.

Hangul *n.* the Korean alphabetic writing system, consisting of 14 consonant and 10 vowel letters. Also **Han'gul**. *Note:* Hangul letters are written in syllable-sized perceptual groups, as in a syllabary, unlike the linear writing of letters in other alphabetic scripts.

Letter	Transcription	Letter	Transcription
Pure vowels:			
ㅣ	/i/	ㅡ	/ŭ/
ㅔ	/e/	ㅓ	/ə/
ㅐ	/æ/	ㅏ	/a/
ㅟ	/ü/	ㅜ	/u/
ㅚ	/ö/	ㅗ	/o/
Consonants:			
ㄱ	/k/	ㅇ	/ŋ/
ㄴ	/n/	ㅈ	/c/
ㄷ	/t/	ㅊ	/cʰ/
ㄹ	/l/	ㅋ	/kʰ/
ㅁ	/m/	ㅌ	/tʰ/
ㅂ	/p/	ㅍ	/pʰ/
ㅅ	/s/	ㅎ	/h/

harangue **1.** *n.* a long, impassioned speech, especially one delivered in public. **2.** *n.* lengthy sermonizing in writing or speech. **3.** *n.* a verbal attack; scolding. **4.** *v.* to so speak or write.

hard c in phonics, the /k/ sound represented by the letter *c* in *cake, ascot.* Cp. **soft c**.

hard consonant in phonics, a voiced consonant produced by the vibration of the vocal cords, as /d/ and /g/ in *dog.* Cp. **soft consonant**.

hard g the /g/ sound represented by the letter *g* in *gate, again.* Cp. **soft g**.

hard of hearing a person with measurable hearing loss who is still able to communicate aurally and orally, with or without a hearing aid; any partial hearing loss.

Hawthorne effect an increase in effort because of the motivating effect of receiving special attention. *Note*: This effect was first observed in an experiment to increase productivity in the Hawthorne industrial plant of the Western Electric Company in the United States. Control groups now routinely used in experimental situations provide information to offset a possible Hawthorne effect.

head **1.** *n.* in grammar, a word in a phrase that determines the syntactic classification of the entire phrase, as *car* in *older cars* (noun) or *tired* in *unusually tired* (adjective); head term. **2.** *adj.* referring to such a word or phrase.

Head Start a federally funded educational program in the United States designed to stimulate the intellectual, physical, and emotional development primarily of low-income pupils of ages four, five, and six, with the intent to improve their later performance in school.

hearing disorder the result of impaired auditory sensitivity of the physiological auditory system. *Note*: "A hearing disorder may limit the development, comprehension, production, and/or maintenance of speech and/or language. Hearing disorders are classified according to difficulties in detection, recognition, discrimination, comprehension, and perception of auditory information" (American Speech-Language-Hearing Association, 1993).

hearing impaired a person with any degree of hearing loss.

hearing loss a reduction in auditory acuity. *Note*: Hearing loss is measured in decibels of loss from normal hearing. One contemporary scale measures hearing loss as: **a. mild**, 21–40 dB. **b. moderate**, 41–60 dB. **c. severe**, 61–80 dB. **d. profound**, 81 dB+. See also **conduction deafness**; **mixed hearing loss**; **sensorineural deafness**.

hearing test an audiometric examination to determine the hearing threshold for pure tones or speech.

hearing threshold **1.** the lowest intensity in decibels at which a tone can be distinguished from silence during audiometric examination. **2.** the lowest intensity at which speech sounds or words can be accurately identified 50 percent of the time.

hemianopia *n.* full or partial blindness in one half of the visual field of one or both eyes. Also **hemianopsia**.

heritage language in Canada, the language, other than English and French, of a minority group, whether indigenous or not, as Ojibwa or Italian.

hermeneutics *n.* **1.** the science and method of the interpretation of meaning. **2.** a view in literary criticism, stemming from the study of sacred texts, that objective meaning as well as the author's intentions can be recovered from a work if sufficiently rigorous techniques are used. **3.** in speech activity, inferences and predictions about what is conveyed, based on interpretations made of an ongoing conversation measured against one's prior experience. *adj.* **hermenuetic**.

heroic couplet a pair of lines of iambic pentameter poetry, as "What dire offense from amorous causes springs! / What mighty contests rise from trivial things!" (Alexander Pope, *The Rape of the Lock*).

hesitation phenomenon the habitual insertion of neutral sounds and silent breaks between words in natural speech; pausing; as *um...um, er, mmm....*

heterogeneous grouping the organization for instruction of students of differing levels of intelligence or achievement in one or more skills or subjects, either within or across classes. *Cp.* **ability grouping**; **homogeneous grouping**.

heterograph *n.* a word with variant spellings, as *inquiry* vs. *enquiry*, *catalog* vs. *catalogue*.

heterography *n.* **1.** in an alphabetic writing system, the representation of different sounds by the same letter or group of letters, as *ough* in *bough*, *though*, *thought*, *tough*, *through*. *Cp.* **one-to-one correspondence** (def. 2). **2.** any nonstandard spelling, as *nite* for *night*. *adj.* **heterographic**.

heteronym *n.* **1.** a homograph. **2.** in popular usage, a word with the same spelling as another word, but with a different pronunciation and meaning, as *lead* pronounced /led/ or /lēd/. *Cp.* **homonym**. *n.* **heteronymy**.

heterophoria *n.* a general term for oculomotor imbalance, the tendency for the eyes to deviate from one another in their line of sight; phoria. *Note*: Heterophoria may cause fusion to be broken and thus double vision. Efforts to restore binocular vision may create fatigue, discomfort, and eye strain.

heterotropia *n.* a general term for the deviation of one eye from the point of fixation of the other; muscular imbalance. *Note*: Heterotropia refers to all such eye conditions in any direction, whether caused by refractive, muscular, neurological, or hysterical conditions, and whether permanent or occasional.

heuristic **1.** *adj.* helpful in leading to further investigation. *Theoretical models of the reading process have heuristic value.* **2.** *adj.* encouraging the student to learn for himself, as in the Socratic method of questioning. **3.** *n.* a process of conscious inquiry. *Learning to write abstracts is a practical heuristic.*

hiatus *n.*, *pl.* **-tuses**, **-tus** **1.** the pause in speech between two words when the vowel at the end of the first word and the vowel at the beginning of the second are both carefully enunciated, as in *be eager*. **2.** any gap or interruption in knowledge, series of events, etc.

hidden curriculum in the politics of education, the assumption that below the surface in any schooling is the goal of socializing students to the particular political and economic systems in power at that time; the covert agenda of formal educational systems; "the subtextual contours of instruction" (McLaren, 1989).

hieretic script *n.* a simplified cursive form of hieroglyphic writing in ancient Egypt (approximately 1900–200 B.C.), used mainly by priests and government officials. *Note*: Hieretic script (literally "priest" writing) was primarily written on papyrus or similar surfaces, unlike hieroglyphic script. Demotic script (approximately 400–100 B.C.) evolved from hieretic script for common use, although it was still mainly reserved for use by the privileged class. *Cp.* **demotic script**; **hieroglyph**.

Hieretic script

hieroglyph *n.* a graphic symbol used in ancient Egyptian writing in which conventionalized pictures represent ideas, words, and syllables. See the illustration on p. 107. *Cp.* **ideograph** (def. 1); **logograph**.

Hieroglyphics

hieroglyphic(-al) *adj.* **1.** written in or referring to the graphic symbols used in the ancient Egyptian writing system. See also **hieroglyphics**. *Cp.* **demotic**; **hieretic**. **2.** hard to read or decipher.

hieroglyphics **1.** *n.* a writing system, as ancient Egyptian, Hittite, or Mayan, in which pictures of objects represented words, ideas, or syllables; literally "sacred carved letters." *Cp.* **ideography**; **logography**; **logosyllabic writing**; **pictography**; **syllabary** (defs. 1, 3). **2.** See **hieroglyph**.

higher education education beyond the secondary school, as in colleges and universities.

higher mental processes **1.** a form of complex thinking, especially of a logical or abstract-type. Also **higher mental functions**. **2.** mental functions that "require voluntary self-regulation, conscious realization, and the use of signs for mediation" (Vygotsky, 1986).

higher order structure **1.** a topic or heading under which related information is grouped. **2.** in structural grammar, a level of increasing abstraction. *A phoneme is a higher order structure than a phone.*

high-frequency loss a hearing loss for frequencies above 2000 Hz. *Note*: The sounds of sibilants, as /s/, and fricatives, as /f/, may not be heard in high-frequency loss.

high-frequency word a word that appears many more times than most other words in spoken or written language. *Note*: Basic word lists generally provide words ranked in order of their frequency of occurrence as calculated from a sample of written or spoken text suitable for the level of intended use. See also **word-frequency count**.

high interest–low load referring to stories of demonstrated appeal to most readers that are written at low levels of textual difficulty for use by poorer readers. Also **hi(gh)-lo(w)**.

high literacy an advanced level of literacy; higher literacy; cultured literacy. See the essay "Literacy" on p. 142.

hiragana *n., pl.* **-na**, **-nas** **1.** the Japanese cursive syllabary used to represent affixes, grammatical words, and content words not represented by Chinese characters or kanji. **2.** a character of this writing system. *Cp.* **katakana**.

い	ろ	は	に	ほ	へ	と	ち	り	ぬ
i	*ro*	*ha*	*ni*	*ho*	*he*	*to*	*chi*	*ri*	*nu*
る	を	わ	か	よ	た	れ	そ	つ	ね
ru	*o*	*wa*	*ka*	*yo*	*ta*	*re*	*so*	*tsu*	*ne*
な	ら	む	う	ゐ	の	お	く	や	ま
na	*ra*	*mu*	*u*	*i*	*no*	*o*	*ku*	*ya*	*ma*
け	ふ	こ	え	て	あ	さ	き	ゆ	め
ke	*hu*	*ko*	*e*	*te*	*a*	*sa*	*ki*	*yu*	*me*
み	し	ゑ	ひ	も	せ	す			
mi	*shi*	*e*	*hi*	*mo*	*se*	*su*			

Hiragana

histogram *n.* a graphic form of a frequency distribution that uses rectangular bars the width of the class interval to show the height of the frequency of each class interval. See illustration under **frequency curve**. See also **frequency distribution**; **frequency polygon**.

historical fiction a long narrative of past events and characters, partly historical but largely imaginative, as *The Three Musketeers* by Alexandre Dumas (père). *Note*: Determining what is historical fact and what is imagination is sometimes a problem for the reader. Conversations between Queen Elizabeth I and Sir Francis Drake appearing in a modern novel, for example, may be based on fact, but the conversation itself comes, of course, from the imagination of the author.

historical linguistics the study of language change over time, as by comparing related languages at different points in their development and by examining the internal structure of the language as it exists today; diachronic linguistics.

historical method the methods used by researchers to reconstruct and interpret the past as contrasted with experimental and qualitative methods. *Cp*. **historical research**; **qualitative research**; **quantitative research**.

historical research the techniques used by historians to reconstruct and interpret the past. *Note*: The data for historical research are the spoken, written, and printed sources or other material originating from those who participated in or witnessed the events studied. The historian must evaluate these data for authenticity, bias, and generalizability, and draw conclusions from them. *Cp*. **historical method**.

holistic *adj*. **1.** referring to a psychological premise that the whole is different from and greater than its parts; gestalt. **2.** in word recognition, referring to the recognition of a word as a single unit apart from its letter components. *n*. **holism**.

holistic approach **1.** teaching in which subject matter is kept intact rather than separated

into parts for instructional purposes, as the integration of speaking, listening, writing, and reading into a unified approach to literacy instruction. *Note*: In terms of literacy instruction, a holistic approach is often referred to as *integrated language arts*, *whole language*, *functional literacy instruction*, or the like, depending on the age of the students and the preferences of the people running the program. **2.** whole-part-whole teaching; providing an overview before details are covered, then recapitulating how the parts fit into the whole. **3.** instruction that attempts to make conscious the connection between the student's emotional and personal life and the materials being presented.

holistic scoring in writing assessment, the assignment of a single score to writing samples on the basis of the adequacy of the overall coverage and presentation. *Note*: Holistic scoring applies criterion-referenced measurement in the use of "anchor" papers selected from the entire population sample to represent a range of performance levels. *Cp*. **analytic scoring**.

holograph *n*. a piece of writing entirely in the handwriting of one person.

holophrase *n*. a single word used to express the meaning of a phrase or sentence; holophrastic speech. *Note*: The term is usually used to characterize an early stage of language acquisition during which, for example, a child may say, "Shoe," for "I want my shoes" or "Where are my shoes?" etc. *adj*. **holophrastic**.

homeschooling *n*. the assumption of parental responsibility for educating children and adolescents at home rather than in an institutionalized education system.

homogeneous grouping the placement of students across or within classes according to one or more selected criteria, as age, ability, achievement, interests, etc. See also (*Brit*.) **streaming**. *Cp*. **heterogeneous grouping**.

homograph *n.* a word with the same spelling as another word, whether or not pronounced alike, as *pen* (a writing instrument) vs. *pen* (an enclosure), or *bow* (and arrow) vs. *bow* (of a ship). *Cp.* **homophone**. *n.* **homography**.

homonym *n.* **1.** a word with different origin and meaning but the same oral or written form as one or more other words, as *bear* (an animal) vs. *bear* (to support) vs. *bare* (exposed), or *row* (to propel a boat) vs. *row* (a line) vs. *row* (a brawl). *Note*: In this sense, homonym includes homophones and homographs. The different spellings or pronunciations of homonyms are due to differing origins of these words. **2.** in popular usage, a word with the same pronunciation and spelling as another word but different in meaning, as *bay* (a body of water) vs. *bay* (part of a window). *Cp.* **heteronym**. *n.* **homonymy**.

homophone *n.* **1.** a word with different origin and meaning but the same pronunciation as another word, whether or not spelled alike, as *hare* and *hair*, or *scale* (of a fish) and *scale* (a ladder). **2.** in popular usage, two or more different graphemes that represent the same sound, as /k/ spelled *c* in *candy*, *k* in *king*, *ch* in *school*. *Cp.* **homograph**.

Horatio Alger story a story with a rags-to-riches theme. *Note*: Horatio Alger was an early author of a long series of such books.

hornbook *n.* a single page fastened to a small hand-held paddle, used from the mid-15th through the mid-18th century in England and in the American colonies to introduce children to reading and to Christian prayers. *Note*: The term is derived from a transparent sheet of horn that originally protected the text. The page regularly consisted of a Christ-cross-row (the alphabet preceded by a cross), part of the syllabarium, the invocation, and the Our Father. The hornbook was the child's first text along "the ordinary road of the hornbook, primer, Psalter, Testament, and

Bible" (John Locke, *Some Thoughts Concerning Education*, 1693). See also ABC **book**; **abecedarium**. *Cp.* **battledore** (def. 1).

hybrid word a word formed from morphemes derived from more than one language, as *television* from (*Gr.*) *tele-* + (*Lat.*) *-vision*. *n.* **hybridization**. *v.* **hybridize**.

hygiene of reading the study of the physical factors that affect the legibility of texts and may cause reading fatigue. *Note*: Such factors include type size and style; spacing between letters and lines; line length; book size; quality and level of illumination; reading posture and distance.

hyperactivity *n.* **1.** chronic distractibility, instability, and excessive motion, usually with a low tolerance for frustration; hyperkinesis. **2.** an unusual or excessive degree of activity. See also **attention-deficit hyperactivity disorder**. **3.** in ordinary use, the normal fast-paced exploration, investigations, and activity-changing behavior of young children. *Cp.* **hypoactivity**. *adj.* **hyperactive**.

hyperbole *n.* an intentionally exaggerated figure of speech, as *I have told you a million times*.

hypercorrection *n.* **1.** the use of a word, pronunciation, inflectional pattern, or grammatical construction mistakenly assumed to be more correct than that which it replaces; overcorrection; as *Whom* for *Who* in *Whom do you think you are?* *Note*: Hypercorrection most commonly occurs among speakers of nonstandard dialects who seek to use a standard dialect, speakers who are engaged in second-language learning, and children in the early formative stages of language development. **2.** the overcorrected usage.

hypernym *n.* in semantics, a term denoting a general class that encompasses subcategories of linguistic items within the class, as *flower* is a hypernym of *rose*, *dahlia*, *tulip*, etc.; superordinate. See also **hyponomy**. *Cp.* **hyponym**.

hyperopia *n.* farsightedness; hypermetropia; specifically, a refractive condition in which the principal focus of retinal images is not clearly on the retina so that objects appear unclear, either because the light rays do not converge sufficiently or because the eye itself is too short from front to back. *Note*: Persons with uncorrected hyperopia may experience difficulty in distance seeing as well as in reading comfortably at the near point. *Cp.* **emmetropia**; **myopia**. *n.* **hyperope**. *adj.* **hyperopic**.

hypertext *n.* in computer use, a sophisticated branching program that allows the user to move among or relate text, graphics, and sound data in new patterns in any desired order.

hypoactivity *n.* **1.** a less than normal level of activity; hypokinesis. **2.** a chronic state of inaction, lethargy, and apathy. *Cp.* **hyperactivity**. *adj.* **hypoactive**.

hyponomy *n.* the semantic relationship among specific and general terms when the former are embodied in the latter. *Note*: Hyponomy is a relational notion that concerns the meaning links between a general semantic class and its members. For example, *red*, *green*, *blue*, and *yellow* are members of the larger class *color*. See also **hyponym**; **hypernym**.

hyponym *n.* in semantics, a term for a linguistic item that is a subcategory of a more general or wider semantic class, as *boys* and *girls* are hyponyms of *children*. *Cp.* **hypernym**. See also **hyponomy**.

I

icon *n.* **1.** an image, picture, or representation of something; iconic sign; as a picture of a dog to signify "a dog." **2.** in some religions, a picture or representation of a sacred person. **3.** a pictographic orthographic character. *Note*: In number usage, the Roman numeral *II* is an icon, but *2* and *two* are symbolic. **4.** an image that controls a computer operation. See also **pictograph**; **symbol** (def. 1). *Cp.* **ideograph**; **logograph**. *n.* **iconicity**. *adj.* **iconic**.

identification book a book in which pictures are accompanied by appropriate labels; information book; "a naming book at its simplest level" (Huck, 1976).

identity *n.* in Piagetian theory, the recognition that an object remains basically the same object across transformations.

ideograph *n.* **1.** a graphic symbol that represents an idea or object rather than a speech sound or word. **2.** a conventionalized graphic symbol that conveys by association the idea, object, or event represented, as the international symbol Ø, usually in red, for "no entry." *Note*: Ideographs rely on common cultural experiences or understanding for meaning. **3.** any graphic symbol representing an idea, word, or morpheme; logograph. Also **ideogram**. *Cp.* **pictograph**. *adj.* **ideographic**.

ideography *n.* **1.** a writing system that uses ideographs. *Cp.* **pasigraphy**. **2.** a writing system based on the use of ideographs, as Chinese or Japanese Kanji. See also **ideograph** (def. 1); **writing system**. *Cp.* **alphabetic writing**; **logography**; **logosyllabic writing**; **pictography**; **syllabary** (defs. 1, 3).

idioglossia *n.* **1.** an invented, private form of speech used by a child or by children in close association, as twins. **2.** a pathologically based form of speech, which is unintelligible to others.

idiolect *n.* an individual's unique speech habits, including pronunciation, grammar, and vocabulary; personal dialect. *Cp.* **dialect** (def. 1).

idiom *n.* **1.** an expression that does not mean what it literally says, as *to have the upper hand* has nothing to do with hands. *Note*: Idioms are peculiar to a given language and usually cannot be translated literally. For this reason, languages especially rich in idioms, as English, French, German, and Russian, are difficult to translate. **2.** a language, dialect, or style of speaking peculiar to a people, as *New England idiom*. *Cp.* **expression**. **3.** a distinctive, individual style or character, especially in music and art. **5.** a password; secret signal. *adj.* **idiomatic**.

idyll *n.* **1.** a short poem or prose narrative describing simple life and times in a romantic and sometimes pastoral way, as Christopher Marlowe's *The Passionate Shepherd to His Love*. See also **pastoral** (def. 1). **2.** a long narrative poem idealized in subject, tone, and mood, as Alfred Tennyson's *Idylls of the King*. Also **idyl**. *adj.* **idyllic**.

illiteracy *n.* **1.** the inability to read or write a language; specifically, "the inability to use reading and writing with facility in daily life" (UNESCO, 1988). *Note*: The 1988 UNESCO proclamation also stated that "widespread illiteracy hampers economic and social development; it is also a gross violation of the basic human right to learn, know, and communicate." In English, the negative term *illiteracy* preceded its positive counterpart *literacy* by over 200 years. This is paralleled in other languages, as in Brazilian Portuguese, in which the terms *analfabeto* and *anafalbetismo* appeared much earlier than *alfobetismo* and *letremento* (Soares, 1992). See also the essays "Functional Literacy" (p. 90) and "Literacy" (p. 142). **2.** lack of education. **3.** a mistake in the expected use of language; solecism. *Cp.* **literacy**.

illiterate 1. *adj.* unable to read. **2.** *adj.* unable to read and write, as referring to: **a.** "those lacking totally in reading/writing knowledge" (Venezky et al., 1990). See also the essay "Literacy" on p. 142. *Cp.* **illiteracy. b.** a person "who cannot with understanding both read and write a short, simple statement on his everyday life" (UNESCO, 1978). **c.** a person "who cannot engage in all those activities in which literacy is required for effective functioning of his group and community and also for enabling him to continue to use reading, writing, and calculation for his own and the community's development" (UNESCO, 1978). See also the essay "Functional Literacy" on p. 90. **3.** *adj.* not meeting the educational expectations of a social group, usually the dominant group; unschooled. **4.** *adj.* uncultured; unread (especially in literature). **5.** *adj.* without competence in any content field. **6.** *n.* a person who cannot read and write. *Cp.* **literate.**

illiterate E a variation of the Snellen chart used to test visual acuity in the illiterate or the very young in which the capital *E* is shown with its open side (arms) pointing in different directions and the subject is asked to identify which way the arms point; tumbling E.

illocutionary act a speech act in which what is said performs a function, as the act of making a promise when one says, "I promise…" *Cp.* **locutionary act; perlocutionary act.**

image *Note*: *Image* is a general term with many shades of meaning but usually implying a physical or mental resemblance. An image may be concrete or abstract. It may be based on experience or imagination. It may refer to sensory experiences, especially visual ones, or to any physical or ideational representation of such experiences. **1.** *n.* a mental representation of something, usually incomplete; impression. **2.** *n.* a physical likeness or representation. **3.** *n.* a description in speech or writing. **4.** *n.* a figure of speech, especially a simile or metaphor. **5.** *n.* an optical representation formed by refraction or reflection. **6.** *v.* to conceive, represent, visualize, etc. *adj.* **imaginal.**

> **Types of *Image****
> afterimage
> auditory image
> eidetic image
> memory image
> mental image
> retinal image
> _____
> *Terms are all defined in this dictionary.

imagery *n.* **1.** the process or result of forming mental images while reading or listening to a story, perceiving, etc. **2.** the use of language to create sensory impressions, as the imagery of the phrase *such sweet sorrow*. **3.** collectively, the figurative language in a work. **4.** the study of image patterns in literature for clues to the author's deeper meaning.

imaginative entry the ability to relate to, or empathize with, the vicarious experience of characters, situations, and mood of a literary work by finding parallels in one's own experience. *Note*: "All students are capable of imaginative entry into vicarious experiences merely because they are human and have had many experiences" (Burton, 1964). *Cp.* **cognitive entry.**

imaginative expression "the writing of poems, fictional narrations, and plays; improvisational classroom drama; and the performing of texts of literary works" (Wagner, 1991).

imaginative literature literary creations formed and ordered through the minds of their authors.

immediate recall remembering material very soon after studying it. *Cp.* **delayed recall.**

immersion *n.* in the teaching of foreign languages, the practice of communicating only in the language being taught.

immunization *n.* in studies of the effects of persuasive reading materials on reader attitudes, the use of selections designed to make the reader less likely to change an attitude, as in reading an article on the contributions of labor to industry before reading one on labor strikes.

implication *n.* any of the conclusions, inferences, expectancies, etc., that may be logically determined from the author's argument in a text or utterance, but are not directly stated. *Note*: Reading for implications is useful for testing the adequacy of an author's conclusions by logically projecting what would happen if those conclusions were carried out.

implicit memory memory without awareness; specifically, that which "occurs when information that was encoded during a particular episode is subsequently expressed without conscious or deliberate recollection" (Schacter, 1987).

implicit speech internal or silent speech; covert symbolic language activity inferred from reports of the mental rehearsal of ideas; inner-speech. *Cp.* **subvocalization**.

implied meaning a meaning intended or suggested rather than directly stated by an author.

impressionism *n.* a movement originating in 19th-century French painting and English criticism that concentrates on the way art and the world affect the senses. Also **Impressionism**. *Note*: In literary criticism, impressionism describes the effect of a work on the emotions, feelings, imagination, taste, and intuitions of the reader or consumer. *Cp.* **expressionism**. *adj.* **impressionistic**.

imprinting *n.* learning that takes place quickly and early in life, usually through association with a parent or other role model, and remains difficult to extinguish or to forget. *v.* **imprint**.

improvisational drama informal classroom drama; "a type of oral imaginative expression through which students work together in a fictive enterprise" (Wagner, 1991).

inanimate noun a noun that refers to other than living things. *Cp.* **animate noun**.

inarticulate *adj.* not uttered clearly.

incidental learning change in behavior that is not directly taught or sought. *Cp.* **intentional learning**.

inclusion *n.* **1.** in education, the placement of students of all abilities in a classroom. *Note*: The aim of inclusion is to educate all handicapped children, no matter how severe their disabilities, in ordinary classrooms, usually a goal to be attained rather than a widely accepted practice. *Cp.* **mainstreaming**. **2.** See **inclusive**.

inclusive *adj.* referring to the use of the first person plural pronoun to include those spoken to as well as the speaker, as *we* for *you and me*. *Note*: The contrasting *exclusive* is used when the person spoken to is excluded as part of the reference.

incremental repetition the repeating, with variation, of a refrain or other part of a poem, especially in popular ballads, as *O what will you leave to your father dear? / The silver-shod steed that brought me here. / What will you leave to your mother dear? / My velvet pail and my silken gear.* *Note*: In this ballad of unknown authorship, the incremental repetition refers to the way in which successive dialogue patterns reflect earlier ones. *Cp.* **parallel repetition**.

indefinite pronoun a pronoun without a specific referent, as *whoever, anybody. Cp.* **definite pronoun**.

independent clause a clause containing a complete subject and a complete predicate that stands alone as a complete grammatical construction; main clause. *Note*: An independent clause may be introduced by a coordinating conjunction as *but* or *therefore*, but not by a subordinating conjunction as *when* or *since. Cp.* **dependent clause**.

independent groups design an experimental design with separate control and experimental groups in which each subject gets only one treatment; independent sample design. *Cp.* **repeated measures design**.

independent reading level the readability or grade level of material that is easy for a student to read with few word-identification problems and high comprehension. *Note*: Although suggested criteria vary, better than 99 percent word-identification accuracy and better than 90 percent comprehension are often used as standards in judging if a reader is reading at this level. See also **frustration reading level**; **informal reading inventory**; **instructional reading level**.

independent school a private school.

independent study **1.** an arrangement by which a student works on a paper or project on his or her own as a part of or instead of a formal school course, conferring with one or more faculty members for suggestions and guidance. **2.** learning on one's own, often to seek formal recognition, as in distance education.

independent variable the stimulus variable(s) manipulated in an experiment to observe the effect upon one or more dependent variables. See also **intervening variable**. *Cp.* **dependent variable**.

indirect discourse a paraphrase of speech or writing, as *He is believed to have said "No." Cp.* **direct discourse**; **indirect speech**.

indirect object in sentences with transitive verbs, the person or thing to or for whom an action is done, as *his friend* in *Hua gave a book to his friend.* See also **dative case**. *Cp.* **direct object**.

indirect speech **1.** a report of something said or written as conveyed by the reporter, as *Fanta said that she won't go and she means it.* **2.** See **whimperative**.

individualization *n.* the adjustment of teaching-learning activities to meet student needs, either on an individual or group basis. *v.* **individualize**. *adj.* **individualized**.

Individualized Educational Plan (IEP) a specific instructional plan to meet the specific needs of individual students. *Note*: IEPs, an example of the "least restrictive environment" philosophy in education, are often required in the United States if federal or state funding is being sought. See also **least restrictive environment**.

individualized reading an approach to reading instruction, developed in the 1950s as an alternative to basal reading programs, that emphasizes student selection of reading materials (largely trade books) and self-pacing in reading, with the teacher adjusting instruction to student needs in small-group work and in individual conferences. *Note*: The specific application of the term to one instructional approach has caused confusion. For a more general and widely used concept of individualizing reading instruction, see **individualization**.

individually prescribed instruction (IPI) a series of lessons planned for an individual based on that person's responses in a diagnostic testing program.

individual test a test designed to be administered to one person at a time by a trained examiner, as the Stanford–Binet Intelligence Scale. *Cp.* **group test**.

Indo-European languages a large family of languages spoken by about half of the world's population. *Note*: The Indo-European family of languages is traced back to a hypothetical parent language, Proto-Indo-European, that is assumed to have spread from an area in the north of eastern Europe around 3000 B.C.

induction *n.* **1.** the process of determining principles by logic or observation from data; reasoning from part to whole. **2.** in semiotics, the process by which hypotheses are tested. **3.** the result of such a process; a conclusion. *Cp.* **abduction**; **deduction**. *adj.* **inductive**.

inductive method a teaching-learning method in which specific examples are first examined to identify a common characteristic and then used to develop a generalization or rule. *Note*: A phonics approach that gives many examples of a phonic pattern before arriving at the phonic generalization is an inductive method. *Cp.* **deductive method**.

infant school (*Brit.*) a school for children aged five to seven years, sometimes with nursery classes for three- and four-year-olds.

infant reader (*N. Z.*) a beginning reading book.

infinitive *n.* the uninflected or base form of the verb, as *to go*. *Note*: An infinitive may be used with an auxiliary, as *go* in *He may go*, or with the infinitive marker *to*, as *To err* in *"To err is human"* (Alexander Pope, *An Essay on Criticism*). *Cp.* **finite verb**.

inflected form **1.** a suffix that changes the form or function of a word but not its basic meaning, as *-ed* in *sprayed*, *-ing* in *following*.

2. a root, stem, or compound that takes an inflectional ending to mark the plural, tense, case, etc., as *toast + s* in *toasts*. See also **inflection** (defs. 1, 2).

inflection *n.* **1.** the process or result of changing the form of a word to express a syntactic function without changing the word's grammatical class, as *run* to *ran* or *run* to *runs*. **2.** the affix added to a base in inflection, as *-s* in *run + s = runs*. **3.** change in voice tone or pitch. *v.* **inflect**.

inflectional morphology a branch of morphology concerning the part of word formation that deals with grammar-related affixes, as plurality, verb tenses, etc. *Cp.* **accidence**; **derivational morphology**.

inflectional suffix in English, a suffix that expresses plurality or possession when added to a noun, tense when added to a verb, and comparison when added to an adjective and some adverbs. See also **suffix**. *Cp.* **derivational affix**.

informal assessment appraisal by casual observation or by other nonstandardized procedures. *Cp.* **formal assessment**; **integrated assessment**.

informal reading inventory (IRI) **1.** the use of a graded series of passages of increasing difficulty to determine students' strengths, weaknesses, and strategies in word identification and comprehension. *Note*: This technique was first described at some length by Betts (1946) as a way of identifying students' independent, instructional, and frustration reading levels. The technique is adaptable to the rough assessment of oral reading skills and comprehension, as well as of silent reading. In addition, if passages are read to the student, some indication of level of listening comprehension may be gained. **2.** any casual but sensitive observation of reading behaviors. See also **frustration reading level**; **independent reading level**; **instructional**

reading level; miscue analyses; reading miscue inventory.

information *n.* **1.** knowledge gained through instruction, study, or research, etc. **2.** in perception, that aspect of stimulation that specifies the properties of things and events. **3.** in information theory, an indication of the number of possible alternative messages that may be sent or received. See also **entropy** (def. 2). **4.** in communications theory, the content of something transmitted from source to receiver which is new, unexpected, and nonredundant. *v.* **inform**. *adj.* **informative**.

information book a nonfiction book of facts and concepts about a subject or subjects.

information processing **1.** the act of organizing and handling data, either by the human mind or by mechanical or electronic means. **2.** the study of such an act; informatics.

information retrieval **1.** the process of recovering data either from human memory or from mechanical or electronic storage, as from a library or computer bank. **2.** the study of such a process.

information science the study of the storage and use of information.

information theory the study of communications; especially, the application of probability estimates to the encoding, transmission, and reception of communications, most fully developed by Shannon and Weaver (1949); cybernetics. *Cp.* **communication** (def. 6).

infralogical operations in Piagetian theory, operations such as distance, time, rate, action, space, geometry, movement, speed, and causality that are parallel to and synchronous with concrete and formal operations. See also **concrete**

operations; **formal operations**; **operations**; **preoperational thought**.

initial blend **1.** the joining of two or more consonant sounds, represented by letters, that begin a word without losing the identity of the sounds, as /bl/ in *black*, /skr/ in *scramble*. **2.** the joining of the first consonant and vowel sounds in a word, as /b/ and /a/ in *baby*. *Note*: This process is regarded by some to be a crucial step in learning phonics.

initialism *n.* a single letter, combination of letters, or abbreviation standing for the names of persons, as *G.B.S.* for George Bernard Shaw, organizations, as *YWCA*, etc. *Note*: Initialisms are not usually pronounced as words and may or may not be punctuated or spaced. *Cp.* **acronym**. *v.* **initialize**.

initial teaching alphabet (i.t.a. *or* **i/t/a/)** **1.** an alphabet developed in the 1950s by Sir James Pitman and others that uses additional graphemes and diacritic marks to increase the correspondence between sound and print for beginning readers. **2.** programs or materials that use such an augmented alphabet. *Note*: i.t.a. is one of several augmented alphabets that have been developed to aid beginning reading in English. The premise underlying augmented alphabets assumes that the disparity between the number of alphabet letters (26) and English phonemes (44, as determined by i.t.a. developers) is a basic cause of reading and spelling difficulties. Hence, the 26 letters are augmented and altered to provide a distinct letter for each phoneme. See also **augmented alphabet**.

in medias res (*Lat.*) literally, "in the middle of things"; the technique of opening a story or play in the middle of the action, with flashbacks later to earlier events.

inner speech **1.** See **implicit speech**. **2.** according to Vygotsky, the "mental shorthand" seen in childhood that is imitative in nature and represents "thinking without words" (cited in Seifert & Hoffman, 1991).

insertion *n.* **1.** the addition of one or more words in the oral reading of text; one of several types of oral reading errors commonly recorded in testing oral reading. See also **mispronunciation**; **substitution** (def. 2). *Cp.* **omission**. **2.** that which is added to oral or written expression. *n., v.* **insert**.

inservice education education for employed teachers, often offered by a school district.

instantiation *n.* a concrete representation of some abstract idea.

instructional framework the conceptual structure used to design and analyze teaching.

instructional materials center (IMC) a place in a school that includes the educational media center and usually the library, containing materials and equipment that permit a variety of individual and group learning experiences. *Cp.* **media center**; **resource center**.

instructional reading level the reading ability or grade level of material that is challenging, but not frustrating for the student to read successfully with normal classroom instruction and support. *Note*: Although suggested criteria vary, better than 95 percent word-identification accuracy and better than 75 percent comprehension are often used as standards in judging whether a student is reading at this level. See also **frustration reading level**; **independent reading level**; **informal reading inventory**.

instructional validity evidence of a test's validity gained by showing that the test content is representative of what is actually taught in the classroom. *Cp.* **content validity**; **curriculum validity**.

instrumentation *n.* the array of tests, observations, interviews, surveys, and other data-collection devices and procedures employed in an evaluation.

integrated assessment the holistic appraisal of a broad sample of subject-matter performance. *Cp.* **informal assessment**.

integrated curriculum a curricular organization intended to bring into close relationship the concepts, skills, and values of separately taught subjects to make them mutually reinforcing, as for example, *integrated language arts* in which students study and use the language components of speaking, listening, reading, and writing as a unified core of concepts and activities. See also the essay "Whole Language" on pp. 279–281.

integrated method an instructional approach in which reading is viewed as "a tool in furthering the interests and activities of the children, and both reading and the other subjects are drawn upon as they are needed and as they enter naturally into the children's in-school and out-of-school enterprises" (Smith, 1965). *Cp.* **whole language**.

integrated text text that is especially coherent because of the author's careful cohesion of grammatical structure and meaning. *Cp.* **involved text**.

intellectual realism in Piagetian theory, a child's egocentric representation of the environment as it is thought to be rather than as it is directly perceived. *Note*: For example, a child would reveal intellectual realism in drawing a person by representing the food inside his or her stomach.

intelligence *n. Note*: Intelligence, long studied by psychologists, remains an elusive concept largely because of differing assumptions about its nature and differing methods of investigating it. Binet's (1905) global concept of intelligence, for example, was based on observations of differences between mentally retarded and normal subjects (*Cp.* **Binet Scale**), whereas more recent investigations have employed highly sophisticated statistical techniques. For the most part, methods of investigation have focused on the internal world of the individual, endeavoring to tease out those factors and processes that characterize the active mind at work. Two major approaches have been used to map the workings of the mind: (a) *factor analysis*, a powerful statistical method used to identify both specific and general factors in intelligence, as in Spearman's (1904) general and specific factors and in Thurstone's (1938) seven primary abilities; and (b) *computer modeling* to study by analogy how individuals process information in solving problems. While both approaches have their limitations, in recent years investigations emphasizing processes over factors have been highly favored. **1.** the skills and abilities needed to process information. **2.** general mental ability; brightness; scholastic aptitude; capacity to learn. **3.** purposeful behavior that is "goal directed and adaptive" (Sternberg & Salter, 1982). *Note*: Sternberg (1988), in proposing a new triadic theory of intelligence, states that two factors of intelligence beyond the internal world of the individual should be recognized: (a) that of the *external world*, which refers to the contextual theory that intelligence is determined in part by cultural values; and (b) that of *individual experience* with specific reference to Piaget's developmental theories that biological maturation leads to differences in intellectual functioning, and to Vygotsky, whose conception of intelligence emphasizes the internalization of social processes. See also **multiple intelligences**.

intelligence quotient (IQ) the ratio between mental age and chronological age multiplied by 100. *Note*: IQ was first used in the 1916 Stanford–Binet Intelligence Scale as an index of intellectual potential based on the assumption of a constant rate of intellectual development. Although the assumption has proven to be faulty, IQ has a firm hold in psychological and educational practice and in the minds of laymen. "According to a popular misconception, the IQ is an index of innate intellectual potential and represents a fixed property of the organism.... This view is neither theoretically defensible nor supported by empirical data" (Anastasi, 1976). *Cp.* **deviation IQ**.

intelligence test a series of tests, either group or individual, for assessing general mental ability or scholastic aptitude. *Note*: The use of standardized intelligence tests assumes that each subject has had the same exposure to schooling and culture as the standardization population, and therefore that the test measures how much the subject has profited from the potential opportunity to learn and how much has been remembered from such learning. As a result of this assumption, many individuals may be kept out of educational programs rather than given the opportunity to demonstrate their ability to learn what is directly taught. See also **intelligence quotient**. *Cp.* **capacity test**.

intensifier *n.* an adverb of degree that emphasizes the meaning of a word, as *completely* in *completely exhausted*.

intension *n.* in logic, the set of attributes that determine the applicability of a term, as *"Anything that is canine is a dog"* (Lyons, 1977). See also **connotation**. *Cp.* **extension**.

intentional fallacy in literary criticism, the error of judging a literary work primarily by the author's stated purpose. *Cp.* **affective fallacy**; **pathetic fallacy**.

intentionality *n.* in Piagetian theory, a quality of adaptive behavior in infancy that is purposeful, goal oriented, and indicative of the beginnings of sensorimotor intelligence.

intentional learning change in behavior that is consciously directed and is goal oriented. *Cp.* **incidental learning**.

interaction *n.* **1.** any mutual influence or reciprocal effect of a general nature, as between audience and performers during presentation of a play. **2.** in reading comprehension, the interplay between the reader and the text. *Note:* Since interaction may connote "separate, completely defined entities acting upon one another" (Rosenblatt, 1991), some, as Rosenblatt, prefer the term *transaction. Cp.* **transaction**. **3.** in statistical analysis, the combined influence of two factors or variables that is distinct from their individual effects. *v.* **interact**.

interactive *adj.* **1.** having an interaction either between persons or between persons and some medium. **2.** in computer use, having two-way communication between a data source and a user with the latter controlling input or access to data. **3.** in television, allowing users to respond by direct, electronic means to programming.

interactive-compensatory hypothesis a hypothesis advanced by Stanovich (1984) to explain individual differences in reading; namely, that in an interactive model of reading in which there is a "synthesis of information from all levels of analysis—syntactic, semantic, lexical, and orthographic...a process at any level can compensate for deficiencies at any other level" (Yeu & Goetz, 1994). *Cp.* **text processing**.

interactive processing **1.** See **text processing**. **2.** in information processing, the interplay between parallel processing codes, as semantic or syntactic codes.

intercorrelation *n.* the results of correlating several tests with one another, usually expressed in a table. See also **correlation**. *v.* **intercorrelate**.

interdisciplinary *adj.* involving two or more fields of study.

interest inventory **1.** an informal list of options to which an individual responds, used to explore reading preferences, work and play interests, radio and TV habits, etc. **2.** a formal questionnaire designed to explore the strength and direction of an individual's interests.

interference *n.* **1.** hindrance; obstruction. **2.** a conflict in motives, desires, etc. **3.** the inhibiting effect of previous learning on new learning. **4.** in multilingualism, any negative influence of a first language on a later one; negative transfer. *v.* **interfere**.

intergenerational literacy the efforts of second- and third-generation (etc.) adults in a family (usually an extended family) to help themselves or others in the family learn to read and write. See also **family literacy**.

interiorization *n.* in Piagetian theory, the process or product of the mental representation of actions. *v.* **interiorize**.

interior monologue **1.** the literary clues in stream of consciousness writing that reveal a character's thoughts. **2.** in motion pictures and television, the voicing of a character's thoughts on a soundtrack while the character appears silent on screen.

interjection *n.* a word or phrase expressing sudden or strong emotion, as *Ugh!* in *Ugh! That tasted awful! v.* **interject**.

interlanguage *n.* **1.** in second-language learning, the transitional language used by the novice en route to mastery. **2.** a language created for use in international communication, as Esperanto, or in a region, as Pidgin English in East Africa.

intermediate grades in schools in the United States, usually grades 4–6.

intermediate school in the United States, usually a grade 5–8 school organization plan. *Note*: The intermediate school concept was originally proposed as an attempt to meet the needs of 10- to 14-year-old children (Curtis, 1968) as a variant of the middle school movement.

internal consistency **1.** the extent to which the items of a test are homogeneous. **2.** a comparison of scores on two equivalent halves of a test. See also **splithalf reliability coefficient**.

internalize *v.* **1.** to make external values and ideas part of oneself through learning and socialization. **2.** in Piagetian theory, to represent actions mentally; interiorize. See also **interiorization**.

internal reconstruction in historical linguistics, a method of determining the structure and rules of an earlier form of a language by studying the contemporary structural patterns, irregularities, and variants of that language and deducing its probable earlier construction. See also **protolanguage**.

internal rhyme a rhyme that occurs within a line of verse, as *dreary* and *weary* in "Once upon a midnight dreary, while I pondered, weak and weary" (Edgar Allan Poe, "The Raven").

international language **1.** a language used worldwide by speakers of different languages, as written English in scientific research. **2.** a worldwide symbolic system, as mathematical or musical notation. See also **artificial language** (def. 2).

International Literacy Day September 8, the day designated since 1990 by the United Nations to recognize the worldwide importance of literacy.

International Phonetic Alphabet (IPA) a standardized, widely used set of graphic sym-

CONSONANTS

	Bilabial	Labiodental	Dental	Alveolar	Postalveolar	Retroflex	Palatal	Velar	Uvular	Pharyngeal	Glottal
Plosive	p b			t d		ʈ ɖ	c ɟ	k ɡ	q ɢ		ʔ
Nasal	m	ɱ		n		ɳ	ɲ	ŋ	ɴ		
Trill	ʙ			r					ʀ		
Tap or Flap				ɾ		ɽ					
Fricative	ɸ β	f v	θ ð	s z	ʃ ʒ	ʂ ʐ	ç ʝ	x ɣ	χ ʁ	ħ ʕ	h ɦ
Lateral fricative				ɬ ɮ							
Approximant		ʋ		ɹ		ɻ	j	ɰ			
Lateral approximant				l		ɭ	ʎ	ʟ			
Ejective stop	pʼ			tʼ		ʈʼ	cʼ	kʼ	qʼ		
Implosive	ƥ ɓ			ƭ ɗ			ƈ ʄ	ƙ ɠ	ʠ ʛ		

Where symbols appear in pairs, the one to the right represents a voiced consonant. Shaded areas denote articulations judged impossible.

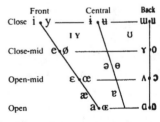

VOWELS

Where symbols appear in pairs, the one to the right represents a rounded vowel.

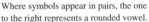

The IPA and other phonetic symbols are described in the *Phonetic Symbol Guide* (Pullum & Ladusaw, University of Chicago Press, 1986).

The International Phonetic Alphabet (revised to 1989).
Reprinted by permission of the International Phonetic Association.

bols for transcribing speech sounds in any language. *Cp.* **phonetic alphabet**; **phonetic spelling**; **phonetic transcription**.

interpretant *n.* in semiotics, the inherent meaning of a sign before it is interpreted. *Cp.* **interpreter**; **object** (def. 3); **sign** (def. 6).

interpretation *n.* **1.** the process of inferring beyond the literal meaning of a communication; "reading between the lines." *Note*: "Interpretation is the thinking side of comprehension" (Tinker & McCullough, 1968). *Cp.* **evocation**; **reflection** (def. 3). **2.** the analysis of the meaning of a communication. *Note*: In this context, interpretation involves both grammatical and semantic analysis and the interplay between them. **3.** a performance, usually artistic, to which the performer gives distinctive meaning. **4.** a translation from another language. *v.* **interpret**. *adj.* **interpretative**; **interpretive**; **interpretable**.

interpreter *n.* **1.** a person who translates one language into another. **2.** in semiotics, one who engages in the process of making sense out of a sign to determine its meaning. *Cp.* **interpretant**.

interpsychological plane a theoretical concept to describe learning that takes place between people and precedes intrapersonal learning (Vygotsky, 1986). Also **intermental plane**. *Cp.* **intrapsychological plane**.

interrogative pronoun a pronoun used to form a question, as *What is your name? Which is your house? etc.* See **pronoun**.

interrogative word a word that marks a clause or sentence as a question. See also **wh-word**.

intersensory integration the combining of information received via two or more sensory channels at the same time; crossmodal integration; as in the Fernald(–Keller) method.

intertextuality *n.* the construct that "meaning derives from readers' transaction(s) with the text in which [they] apply their knowledge of literary and social convention to that text" (Beach et al., 1994). See also essay on **genre**; **transaction**. *adj.* **intertextual**.

interval scale a scale in which numerically equal distances represent empirically established equal distances for the property being measured; equal-unit scale. *Cp.* **ratio scale**.

intervening variable the inferred, hypothetical variable(s) involved in the relationship between an independent and a dependent variable, as between causes and results. Fatigue is an intervening variable between the number of hours of continuous reading and the ability to maintain clearly focused fixations on the page. See also **dependent variable**; **independent variable**.

intervention program any educational program designed to supplement or substitute for an existing situation; specifically any one of several projects, usually with government funding, intended to give children of low socioeconomic backgrounds added cognitive stimulation, as Head Start in the United States.

intimate speech the informal style of discourse between persons who are closely related by family or by social level in which meaning is shared without the use of elaborate linguistic forms. Also **intimate style**. See also **communicative competence**; **register** (def. 1); **restricted code**; **style of discourse**.

intonation the distinctive patterns of pitch that contribute to the meanings of spoken phrases and sentences, as between commands and questions such as "*Go now!*" and "*Go now?*"; intonation pattern. See also **pitch**. *Cp.* **tone** (def. 5).

intransitive verb a verb that does not take an object, as *grow, appear. Cp.* **transitive verb**.

intrapsychological plane a theoretical concept to describe learning that takes place within the person and follows interpersonal learning (Vygotsky, 1986). Also **intramental plane**. *Cp.* **interpsychological plane**.

intrinsic method a teaching-learning approach in which goals and rewards come from student self-direction and satisfaction rather than from the teacher. *Cp.* **extrinsic method**.

intrinsic phonics phonics instruction and materials that form an integral part of a reading instruction program. *Cp.* **extrinsic phonics**.

intrusion *n.* the insertion of additional speech sounds into connected speech that do not normally appear when words are pronounced in isolation, as /r/ in *India(r) and China*. See also **epenthesis**.

intuition *n.* **1.** the process or result of perception or cognition that is immediate and direct rather than subjected to reflective thought. **2.** in Piagetian theory, a characteristic of preoperational thought in which percepts are internalized directly as representational images rather than transformed and manipulated in logical thought. *adj.* **intuitive**.

intuitive correspondence in Piagetian theory, a relationship that is wholly learned, recalled, and used as a percept, as knowing that bananas and oranges have different shapes. *Cp.* **operational correspondence**.

invented spelling the result of an attempt to spell a word whose spelling is not already known, based on a writer's knowledge of the spelling system and how it works. *Note*: Invented spellings, beginning with the pioneer work of Read (1971), are used both to study young writers' emerging awareness of conventional spelling patterns and as an instructional strategy in beginning writing as the child moves toward controlled use of conventional spelling of words.

invention-discovery *n.* in Piagetian theory, the construction of a mental scheme or operation in ideational thought to achieve a goal, as forming a hypothesis.

inventory *n.* a questionnaire for assessing behaviors, interests, personality characteristics, etc.

Types of *Inventory**
adjustment inventory
informal reading inventory
interest inventory
personality inventory
reading inventory
study-habits inventory

---

*Terms are all defined in this dictionary.

---

inversion *n.* the process or result of reversing the order of elements in a sentence to change its grammatical function, as changing *It is time to leave* to *Is it time to leave? v.* **invert**.

involved text text that lacks unity, emphasis, and coherence of ideas. *Cp.* **integrated text**.

irony *n.* **1.** a figure of speech in which the literal meaning of the words is the opposite of their intended meaning, as in *I could care less*. See also **sarcasm**; **satire**. **2.** a literary technique for implying, through plot or character, that the actual situation is quite different from that presented. See also **dramatic irony**. **3.** an incongruity or discrepancy between an anticipated and realized outcome. *adj.* **ironic**.

irregularity *n.* an exception to a linguistic pattern or rule, as *good, better, best* are exceptions to the usual *-er, -est* pattern of comparatives and superlatives in English. See also **grammaticality**. *adj.* **irregular**.

irregular verb a verb that does not follow the normal patterns of inflectional changes of tense, as *go*, *went*, *gone* as forms of *to go*; strong verb. *Cp.* **regular verb**.

isomorphism *n.* in linguistics, a one-to-one correspondence: **a.** between the sounds and spellings in a language, as in Finnish orthography. **b.** between words or word meanings between two languages. **c.** between linguistic elements and structures in two periods of a language's history. *adj.* **isomorphic**.

item analysis an examination of item difficulty, item discrimination, and an analysis of performance on the various item response options.

item bias a form of bias in testing that refers to the differential difficulty of individual test items for groups with dissimilar cultural or experiential backgrounds (Anastasi, 1988). *Cp.* **differential item functioning**.

item difficulty the average performance of a group of examinees on a test item, usually the percent answering correctly. See also **item analysis**; **item response theory**.

item discrimination the consistency of any test item with the standard measured by the whole set of test items.

item response theory (IRT) statistical models for relating item difficulty to an underlying "ability" scale representing what is being measured, and in which item and person statistics are estimated from empirically observed item responses. *Note*: "Essentially, IRT models are used to establish a uniform, sample-free scale of measurement, which is applicable to individuals and groups of widely varying ability levels and to test content of widely varying difficulty levels" (Anastasi, 1988). See also **item difficulty**.

J

Jack tale any of the stories of the Appalachian mountain people in which the hero, Jack, overcomes all opponents and all difficulties through his quick wit. *Note*: These stories are American variations of folktales brought from the British Isles by early settlers.

Jacotot method a way of teaching reading in which the student memorizes an entire book by hearing it read and then memorizes or reads sentences, recognizes the words in the sentences, and then learns the letters and their sounds within the words. *Note*: The term derives from the French mathematician and teacher Jean Joseph Jacotot (1770–1840) who advocated a "universal" method in education. In American adaptations, the sentence and eventually the word became the starting point, as described in "On Teaching to Read According to the Method of Jacotot" (*American Journal of Education*, 1834). *Cp.* **analytic method**; **story method**.

Jaeger rating an estimate of visual acuity at the near-point based on a subject's identification of words and phrases printed in different sizes of type.

jargon *n.* cant. *Media center*, *student stations*, and *open vertical grouping* are educational jargon for *library*, *desks*, and *a group of children of different ages*. See also **cant** (def. 1). *Cp.* **argot** (def. 2); **pedagese**; **slang** (def. 2); **technical word** (def. 1).

jingle *n.* **1.** a short verse or rhyme with a catchy series of sounds, as many nursery rhymes. **2.** such verse with music.

Job Opportunity and Basic Skills (JOBS) a field study report by Sticht and Mikulecky in 1984 describing job-related basic skills actually needed in the workplace in the United States.

joint distribution in scoring tests, the simultaneous distribution of the frequencies at all possible combinations of two or more sets of scores. See also **scatter diagram**.

journal *n.* **1.** a typed or written record usually kept daily. **2.** a chronological relating of events. **3.** a periodical published by a learned society, association, institution, etc. **4.** a newspaper, especially a daily one. **5.** a collection of student writing in response to reading. *Note*: Student journals, widely used in integrated language arts classrooms, provide data for authentic assessment.

juncture *n.* the flow and pauses between sounds in speech production; transition. *Note*: Phoneticians generally recognize three types of juncture: **a. close juncture**, in which transition between sounds is rapid, as between /p/ and /l/ in *play*. **b. open juncture**, in which a slight pause occurs, as in pronouncing *a name* vs. *an aim*. **c. terminal juncture**, in which speech stops for a moment, as on both sides of the appositive *my teacher* when pronouncing *Ms. Ruiz, my teacher, enjoys reading*. See also **suprasegmental**.

junior novel a book written for young adults. Also **junior book**. See also **young adult literature**.

junior school (*Brit.*) a school for children aged 7–11.

juvenile book a book written for children or adolescents. See also **children's literature**; **young adult literature**.

kana *n., pl.* **-na, -nas 1.** the general term for Japanese syllabic writing, which has two sets of 46 characters each plus diacritics, one set being used for foreign words (katakana) and the other for native words (hiragana). **2.** an orthographic character in this writing system. *Cp.* **hiragana**; **katakana**. See also **syllabary**.

kanji *n., pl.* **-ji, -jis 1.** a set of ideographic characters derived from Chinese characters and used in Japanese writing for many content words. *Note*: Kanji perform an important role in Japanese orthography. A Japanese student must master about 2000 characters by completion of high school. **2.** an ideographic character in this writing system. *Cp.* **ideograph** (def. 2).

katakana *n., pl.* **-ana, -nas 1.** the Japanese syllabic characters, square or angular in appearance, traditionally used for learned words, official documents, and proper names, now reserved for foreign words. **2.** a character of this written set. Also **kata-kana**. *Cp.* **hiragana**.

ア	イ	ウ	エ	オ	カ	キ	ク	ケ	コ
a	*i*	*u*	*e*	*o*	*ka*	*ki*	*ku*	*ke*	*ko*
サ	シ	ス	セ	ソ	タ	チ	ツ	テ	ト
sa	*shi*	*su*	*se*	*so*	*ta*	*chi*	*tsu*	*te*	*to*
ナ	ニ	ヌ	ネ	ノ	ハ	ヒ	フ	ヘ	ホ
na	*ni*	*nu*	*ne*	*no*	*ha*	*hi*	*hu*	*he*	*ho*
マ	ミ	ム	メ	モ	ヤ	イ	ユ	エ	ヨ
ma	*mi*	*mu*	*me*	*mo*	*ya*	*i*	*yu*	*e*	*yo*
ラ	リ	ル	レ	ロ	ワ	ヰ	ウ	ヱ	ヲ
ra	*ri*	*ru*	*re*	*ro*	*wa*	*i*	*u*	*e*	*o*
ガ	ギ	グ	ゲ	ゴ	ザ	ジ	ズ	ゼ	ゾ
ga	*gi*	*gu*	*ge*	*go*	*za*	*ji*	*zu*	*ze*	*zo*
ダ	ヂ	ヅ	デ	ド	バ	ビ	ブ	ベ	ボ
da	*ji*	*zu*	*de*	*do*	*ba*	*bi*	*bu*	*be*	*bo*
パ	ピ	プ	ペ	ポ	ヴ	ン			
pa	*pi*	*pu*	*pe*	*po*	*vu*	*n*			

Katakana

keratometer *n.* an instrument for measuring the curvature of the front of the cornea; ophthalmometer.

kernel sentence 1. in early transformational-generative grammar, a simple declarative sentence that can be changed into more complex sentences by transformation rules. **2.** an unmodified subject and predicate, as *man jogged* in *The man jogged slowly*.

key *n.* **1.** a level of formality in speaking, as *Class, you may begin* (formal) vs. *Okay, get started* (informal). *Cp.* **register** (def. 1). **2.** See **style of discourse**. **3.** a list of answers to test items.

keyword method an instructional approach in which the emphasis is on a target concept, identified by a keyword, and the relationship of other concepts to it, as in clustering and brainstorming. *Note*: This method was first used as early as 1531 by Ickelsamer (Adamik-Jászó, 1993).

kidwatching *n.* the close observation of child behavior, especially in language development, by teachers.

kindergarten *n.* **1.** in the United States and Canada, a class, usually for five-year-olds, conducted in public schools, emphasizing the physical, socioemotional, and intellectual aspects of child development. *Note*: Kindergartens were founded by the German educator Friedrich Froebel in 1837. **2.** in the United Kingdom, a private nursery school or class. **3.** in Australia, usually the first year of infant school. **4.** in Germany, a preschool similar to the U.S. nursery school.

kinesics *n.* (*with sing. v.*) **1.** the nonverbal signals used in spoken communication, as facial expressions, eye contact, use of hands, etc. **2.** the study of such nonverbal signals.

kinesthesis *n.* the perception of body movement, position, and weight arising from sense receptors in muscles, tendons, joints, and the inner ear. *Note*: While vision and other externally stimulated senses may provide information about body movement, kinesthesis usually refers to cues arising within the body. See also **Fernald(–Keller) method**; **kinesthetic method**. *Cp.* **tactile** (def. 1). *adj.* **kinesthetic**.

kinesthetic feedback information from muscles, joints, and tendons that helps in repeating a movement or movements, as in articulating words, or from the ear canals that help maintain balance.

kinesthetic method **1.** any method in which learning takes place through the sense of movement, as in the learning of handwriting by the blind. **2.** a method in which learning takes place through a combination of senses including the kinesthetic, as visual-auditory-kinesthetic (VAK) or visual-auditory-kinesthetic-tactile (VAKT) methods. **3.** a method in which the student traces a word to be learned with one or two fingers while at the same time studying the word visually and saying the parts aloud; tracing method; Fernald(–Keller) method. Also **kinesthetic approach**.

knowledge *n.* **1.** literally, something known; information. **2.** a state of general familiarity with facts, principles, ideas, etc.; learning; erudition. **3.** such a state in a special field. *v.* **know**. *adj.* **knowledgeable**.

Kuder–Richardson formulas any of several formulas for determining test reliability by analysis of the internal consistency of binary responses, as right-wrong, to the test items of a single test form. *Note*: Kuder–Richardson formula 20 is the one most commonly used. It corresponds to the coefficient alpha in the case of binary item scores.

kurtosis (Ku) *n.* the relative flatness (*platykurtosis*) or pointedness (*leptokurtosis*) around the mode of a frequency curve as compared to the roundedness (*mesokurtosis*) of the normal frequency curve. *Note*: The term and its variants refer to the closeness to which scores cluster around the mean.

KWL *n.* a strategy developed by Donna Ogle that is especially useful for identifying purposes for reading expository text. *Note*: The term derives from *What I know*, *What I want to learn*, and *What I have learned*. Also **K-W-L**.

Types of *Knowledge**
conditional
declarative
domain specific
prior
procedural
tacit

---

*Terms are all defined in this dictionary.

laboratory research research that takes place under the highly controlled and artificial conditions of the laboratory. *Note*: Laboratory research is usually conducted to test hypotheses or theories. Usually the independent variables are clearly defined, measurement is precise, and unwanted influences are excluded so that relatively sound inferences may be drawn from the research. *Cp.* **field research**.

lacuna *n., pl.* **-nae**, **-nas** a missing part or gap, as in a text.

lallation *n.* **1.** in some analyses of language acquisition, the stage at which distinct vowel sounds are first produced, occurring after the babbling stage at about six months of age. **2.** poor articulation of /l/ and /r/ because of faulty tongue movements. Also **lalling**.

lampoon **1.** *n.* a sharp, often bitter satire that ridicules a person's character or appearance. **2.** *v.* to write such a piece.

Lancastrian method in early–19th-century England and the United States, an instructional system developed by Joseph Lancaster in which student monitors, overseen by a teacher, instructed from 200 to 1000 students in a single room; monitorial school. *Note*: In this system, the teacher initially taught a lesson to the monitors, each of whom in turn taught the lesson and supervised about 10 students. When monitors were teaching, the teacher sat at a raised desk and supervised the process.

language *n. Note*: A problem in defining *language* is that language itself must be the medium of its own description. As a result, a definition of language is conditioned by the theoretical or subjective linguistic views of the definer. The following definitions represent some of the principal historical and current views of the meaning of the term. **1.** "the systematic, conventional use of sounds, signs, or written symbols in a human society for communication and self-expression" (Crystal, 1992). **2.** in descriptive linguistics, "a system of arbitrary oral symbols by means of which a social group interacts" (Lehmann, 1976). **3.** in transformational-generative grammar, "a set of all the sentences a grammar generates" (Langendoen, 1969). **4.** the speech, vocabulary, and grammatical system shared by people of the same nation, region, community, or cultural tradition, as Swedish, Basque, or Cajun. **5.** oral communication through speech with arbitrary, accepted symbols and meanings. **6.** a system of symbols used in communication; language code; "in a broad sense...a system in terms of which something can be presented by one user and understood by another...a system of communication" (Bloomfield, 1933). *Note*: This definition by a noted linguist includes all forms of language, human and nonhuman, technical and common. Another definition, by an equally noted linguist, limits the meaning to human language: "Language is a purely human and noninstinctive method of communicating ideas, emotions, and desires by means of a system of voluntarily produced symbols" (Sapir, 1921). The latter restriction to language as a purely human activity has become a source of controversy. Although language is normally based on an arbitrary linking of semantic content or meaning with syntactic patterns of speech or writing, it may also be based on linking visual or tactile symbols, as letters or Braille dots, or manual symbols, as those of American Sign Language. The noninstinctive nature of language has also become a source of controversy: some believe that there is a basic part of language structure and function that is shared by all languages and is either innate or reflects innate language-learning strategies. Also, it is now believed by others that some language structures, as sentences, are stored in the brain as wholes. **7.** linguistics; specifically, the theoretical study of the nature of language. **8.** any particular system of communication by **a.** special symbols, as the language of mathematics, music, Braille, etc. **b.** gesture or body movement, as sign language. **c.** style, as formal language. **d.** manner of speech, as critical language. **9. abusive language**, swear words; oaths. **10. animal language**, as the language of the whales.

Types of *Language**

affixing language
American Sign Language
analytic language
artificial language
auxiliary language
body language**
community language
dead language
expressive language
figurative language
Indo-European languages
interlanguage
isolating language†
metalanguage
national language
native *or* primary language
natural language
object language
official language
paralanguage
prestige language
productive language
protolanguage
public language††
receptive language
romance language
sign language
spoken language
standard language
synthetic language
target language
tonic language
written language

---

*Terms are all defined in this dictionary.
Term is defined under **kinesics.
†Term is defined under **analytic language**.
††Term is defined under **elaborated code**.

---

language acquisition the process by which competence is obtained in the use of language. *Note*: Contemporary theories and studies of language acquisition, especially by young children, are foundational in current conceptions of literacy development in and out of school. Also **language learning**.

language acquisition device (**LAD**) in language acquisition theory, the developmental cognitive characteristics that enable a child to use the language environment to become a productive language user. *Note*: "Children make use of the information of...underlying structure very early in the acquisition of language. From the first moment of speech, children have the ability to communicate grammatical relationships in a manner understandable to adults. We can overlook what an astonishing fact this is, but it means that the most abstract part of language is the first to appear in development" (McNeill, 1970).

language across the curriculum a movement in England since the mid-1960s, and since adopted elsewhere, to encourage: **a.** students to construct their own understanding of knowledge through the verbal manipulation of information and the processes they use to obtain information. **b.** teachers to consider the developmental nature of language as well as the demands of language used in schools and in specific school subjects, especially in writing.

language arts 1. the school curriculum areas particularly concerned with the development and improvement of reading, writing, speaking, and listening. **2.** communication arts in which language is the common denominator.

language arts approach any way of teaching that emphasizes an integration of several aspects of verbal communication rather than a focus on one component.

language center the areas of the left hemisphere of the brain, singly or collectively, that are intimately involved in the reception, understanding, and production of language.

language development **1.** See **language acquisition**. **2.** changes in the features of a language over time because of contact with other languages, technological advancements, etc., as the growth of technical terms in English after the Industrial Revolution.

language disorder impaired comprehension or use of spoken, written, or other symbol systems. *Note*: "The disorder may involve (1) the form of language (phonology, morphology, syntax), (2) the content of language (semantics), and/or (3) the function of language in communication (pragmatics) in any combination" (American Speech-Language-Hearing Association, 1993).

language experience approach (LEA) **1.** an approach to language learning in which students' oral compositions are transcribed and used as materials of instruction for reading, writing, speaking, and listening; experience approach. See also **writing approach to reading**. **2.** a curriculum that emphasizes the interrelationship of such modes of language experience.

language family any group of languages assumed to have developed from a common source, as the languages of the Indo-European family (see this term). *Note*: The classification of languages into common families is based on both historical reconstructions and structural comparisons, and groupings of languages vary among scholars. Examples of other language families are Uralic, Niger-Congo, Altaic, Khoisan, Afro-Asiatic, and Dravidian, as well as singular languages such as Basque, Japanese, and Korean.

language handicap any systematic deficiency, from mild to severe, in the way people speak, listen, read, write, or sign that interferes with their ability to communicate with their peers (Crystal, 1987).

language laboratory a space equipped with tape recorders, videorecorders, computers, and the like, designed to instruct, test, and keep records of students learning or improving use of a language. *Note*: Language laboratories, traditionally used for second-language instruction, are now also used to improve one's first language.

language maintenance **1.** in bilingual education, a program for developing and sustaining language skills in the native language of the students. **2.** the extent to which an individual or group continues to use a language in a bilingual or multilingual environment, as immigrants to a country where another language is spoken.

language pattern the systematic arrangement of elements of a language based on their regularities and predictable qualities, as the way morphemes are grouped into words in English or the way pitch indicates meaning in Chinese.

language planning the use of governmental or other types of authority to control the structure, use, and status of a language, as that by the Académie Française to control the standard of French used in France.

language universal a linguistic property shared by all existing or possible languages. *Cp.* **universal grammar**.

language variation **1.** the systematic differences of language use determined by regional, social, or situational influences. *Cp.* **dialect**; **idiolect**; **register** (def. 1); **sociolect**. **2.** the systematic varieties of a given language over time. **3.** the evolution of one language into several languages.

langue *n.* in de Saussure's (1916) description of living languages, the abstract system of grammar and vocabulary of a language shared by a language community and passed on from one generation to the next. See also **competence** (def. 2). *Cp.* **parole**.

lap reading reading to a child while he or she sits on one's lap, often among the child's first experiences with books.

latent hyperopia a tendency toward farsightedness.

lateral **1.** *adj.* away from the middle or center. **2.** *adj.* having to do with a side as opposed to a center. **3.** *n.* a consonant speech sound made when the air flow is pushed along one or both sides of the tongue, as /l/.

lateral imbalance an oculomotor imbalance or deviation in which one of the eyes turns in or out. *Cp.* **vertical imbalance**.

Latin alphabet **1.** the writing system used by the ancient Romans, adopted from the Greek alphabet and the source of the English and other modern Western European alphabets. Also **Roman alphabet**. **2.** the modern Western European alphabets.

Latin grammar school in the United States, a secondary school of a form found in England, where boys were taught Latin and some Greek. *Note*: The Latin grammar school was the main kind of secondary education in New England from the period of colonial settlement until after the American Revolution. In theory, boys were admitted only if they already knew how to read. In practice, reading often had to be taught. *Cp.* **English school**.

Latin square a factorial design having as many experimental trials as there are experimental conditions.

law of effect a generalization about the modification of stimulus-response connections in learning proposed by Thorndike (1913): satisfying responses strengthen connections, while annoying responses weaken them. *Note*: Although the law of effect does not have the force of an ex-planatory principle, the concept of effect in learning has received much attention, especially in reinforcement theory. See also **conditioning**.

law of pragnanz a visual perception principle that holds that every stimulus pattern is seen as the simplest possible structure. *Note*: The law of pragnanz has been used to explain why proofreading is a difficult, exacting task.

lax *adj.* **1.** referring to a distinctive feature in the analysis of speech sounds in which the sound is of relatively short duration and lacks clearly defined resonance, as /ă/ in *cat*. *Cp.* **tense** (def. 3). **2.** having relatively little muscle tension in the tongue and vocal tract in making speech sounds.

lazy eye the nonfixating or deviating eye in strabismus, or the weaker or wandering eye in aphoria. *Note*: Vision tends to be suppressed in a lazy eye to avoid double vision.

learner assessment the appraisal of the strengths and weaknesses of student learning; student assessment.

learning *n.* **1.** the process, or result, of change in behavior through practice, instruction, or experience. **2.** the sum of knowledge acquired by an individual; scholarship. See also the box "Types of Learning" on p. 136. *n.* **learner**. *v.* **learn**. *adj.* **learned**.

learning activity package (LAP) a kit for independent learning, including objectives, directions, subject matter, materials, and test items.

learning center **1.** See **media center**. **2.** a location within a classroom with listening, viewing, art, game, and other instructional materials with clearly defined objectives for their use stated for the learner, specific directions for reaching the objectives, provisions for different ability levels, and self-checking evaluations;

learning station. See also **stations approach**. **3.** at the college and university level, a center providing tutoring and study-skill assistance, sometimes only for reading and writing but usually for all subjects.

<u>**Types of *Learning****</u>
assisted
collaborative
cooperative
experiential
incidental
integrated
intentional
language**
mastery
perceptual-motor
rote
strategic[†]
trial-and-error

---

*Terms are all defined in this dictionary.
Term is defined under **language acquisition.
[†]Term is defined under **strategy**.

---

learning contract an extended assignment that a student agrees to complete within an instructional plan designed to encourage self-motivation and self-discipline.

learning curve a graphic representation of success in performance shown against the num-

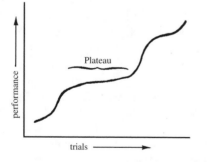

Learning curve

ber of trials needed or the amount of time elapsed. *Note*: Performance is usually plotted on the vertical axis and trials or time on the horizontal axis of the graph. *Cp.* **retention curve**.

learning disability **1.** "a generic term that refers to a heterogeneous group of disorders manifested by significant difficulties in the acquisition and use of listening, speaking, reading, writing, or mathematical abilities. [*Note*:] (Presumably, these disorders are due to central nervous system dysfunction resulting from such factors as anatomical differences, genetics, neuromaturational delay, neurochemical or metabolic imbalance, and severe nutritional deficiency or trauma.) Even though a learning disability may occur concomitantly with other handicapping conditions (e.g., sensory impairment, mental retardation, social and emotional disturbance) or environmental influences (e.g., cultural differences, insufficient/inappropriate instruction, psychogenic factors), it is not the direct result of those conditions or influences" (National Joint Committee on Learning Disabilities, 1980). **2.** in certification for special classes or funding in the United States, "a disorder of one or more of the basic psychological processes involved in understanding or in using language, spoken or written, which...may manifest itself in imperfect ability to listen, think, speak, read, write, spell, or do mathematical calculations. Such disorders include such conditions as perceptual handicaps,...dyslexia, and developmental aphasia. The term does not include...learning problems which are primarily the result of visual, hearing, or motor disturbance, or of environmental disadvantage" (HEW Standard Terminology, 1975). *Note*: Students must have a specified discrepancy between expected and actual achievement in one or more aspects of language use (particularly reading or mathematics) to be so classified. See also **dyslexia**.

learning hierarchy the ordering of skills, habits, etc., from simple learning tasks to progressively more complex ones. *Note*: The assumption here is that learning more complex tasks depends on prior learning of and appropriate ordering of simpler subordinate tasks.

learning log an ongoing record of learning activity kept by students to help them evaluate their progress, think about new learning, and plan further learning.

learning module an organized group of activities and materials designed to help a learner reach a certain objective.

learning rate the speed at which new learning occurs, often plotted as a learning curve on a graph.

learning station **1.** See **learning center** (def. 2). **2.** any of the several locations within a media center.

learning to learn the acquisition of skills and attitudes for their transfer value in making future learning more efficient, as in the development of good study habits that can be generalized to new learning situations. See also **study skills**.

least restrictive environment a school learning setting that is substantially the same for all students, including the disabled, the provision of which is mandated by law in many U.S. states. See also **Individualized Educational Plan**.

Lebenswelt *n.* in semiotics, the world of daily experience. *Note*: A German word that roughly translates as "life world," it refers primarily to the context or environment that is created by human action rather than to human beings themselves. *Cp.* **Umwelt**.

left brain the left cerebral hemisphere, usually the controlling center for language and cal-culation functions as well as for neuromuscular activity on the right side of the body. *Cp.* **right brain**.

legasthenia *n.* literally, "reading weakness"; dyslexia. *Note*: *Legasthenie*, an equivalent term widely used in German-speaking countries, suffers from the same confusion in meaning as does *dyslexia*. Valtin (1992) notes that in Germany today, the term has fallen into disfavor, but in the former East Germany it denoted a "specific reading and spelling disability due to brain dysfunction and with related auditory and articulatory discrimination difficulties." In Austria, *legasthenie* is defined as "a congenital disorder characterized by specific errors in reading and spelling and by a right-left confusion" (Valtin, 1992).

legend *n.* **1.** a traditional, historical tale of a people, handed down first in oral and later in written form. *Cp.* **fairytale**; **folktale**; **myth**. **2.** explanation, as of symbols used in charts, maps, graphs, etc., or of distance on maps. **3.** in Hungary, traditionally a story of the life of a saint (Adamik-Jászó, 1993). *adj.* **legendary**.

leitmotif *n.* **1.** a repeated expression, event, or idea used to unify a literary work. **2.** in music or drama, a theme associated with a particular person, situation, or idea. *Cp.* **motif** (def. 1).

lesson plan a statement of objectives, procedures, and materials for a learning activity.

letter **1.** *n.* one of a set of graphic symbols that forms an alphabet, as A, B, C, etc. **2.** *n.* a graphic symbol used singly or in combination with other letters to represent a phoneme. *Cp.* **character** (def. 1); **grapheme**. **3.** *v.* to print or write with letters. **4.** *n.* a form of written communication. **5.** *pl.*, the alphabet.

letter cluster a sequence of two or more consonants, as *-tt-* in *letter*. *Cp.* **diagraph**.

letter phonics a synthetic phonics approach that emphasizes initially the identification of sounds represented by individual letters. *Cp.* **cluster phonics**; **whole-word phonics**.

level *n.* **1.** in linguistics, any one of several strata or planes of language, as phonology, grammar, semantics, or the subdivisions of each. **2.** a type or style of language in the study of language varieties, as standard versus nonstandard speech. **3.** the degree of loudness of sound.

level of aspiration **1.** the predicted or anticipated degree of success on a particular task under specified conditions. **2.** the degree of success acceptable to or desired by a person; ambition.

level of comprehension **1.** the degree of understanding of a particular passage or set of passages, usually shown in testing as the percent of correct responses to questions about the material. **2.** the degree of ability to understand, often shown in testing as a grade equivalent or as a standard score.

lexical comprehension understanding of word meaning as contrasted to understanding grammar or syntax.

lexical item a linguistic unit with one or more morphemes and with a specific pronunciation and meaning, as a word, word compound, or idiom; lexeme; vocabulary item. *Note*: A lexical item includes its variant inflectional forms, as *talk* includes *talks*, *talked*, *talking*. Derivatives, as *talker*, are considered separate items. An idiom must have a meaning that is unpredictable from the meanings of its components alone to be considered a single lexical item. *Bury the hatchet* is a meaningful noun phrase composed of three lexical items, but as an idiom, has a single meaning, which is not predictable from the lexical meaning of each of its components. *Cp.* **citation form**; **word**.

lexical meaning the denotative or "dictionary" meaning of content words, independent of their syntactical use in linguistic units. *Cp.* **grammatical meaning**.

lexical repetition in expressive language processes, repeating the same word or word unit for emphasis or to develop a rhythmical pattern.

lexical word a word with semantic content, as *book*, *read*, *think*, etc. *Cp.* **function word**.

libretto *n.* the text of an opera or other composition of vocal music.

light verse short lyrical poems that may be witty, joyous, humorous, fanciful, sometimes satiric, and often sophisticated. See also **epigram**; **limerick**; **nonsense verse**; *vers de société*.

limerick *n.* a form of light verse, usually five lines with a rhyme scheme of *aabba*, with the first, second, and fifth lines having three feet, and the third and fourth lines, two feet.

limited English proficiency (LEP) a term used in bilingual education programs specifically to refer to a restricted understanding or use of written and spoken English. *adj.* **limited English proficient** (LEP).

limited English speaking (LES) a term used in bilingual education programs to refer to students who know some English but not enough to participate effectively and actively in a classroom where only English is used in instruction. Also **limited English speaking ability** (LESA).

Linear A an ancient Minoan writing system, around 1600 B.C., still undeciphered.

Linear B an ancient syllabic prototype of a Greek writing system used by Myceneans approximately 1400–1200 B.C.

linear program in programmed instruction, a series of small, planned learning steps whereby the student makes a response and checks its accuracy, moving through the steps one at a time on the way to a desired learning goal. *Cp.* **branching program**.

linear script a writing system, as the English alphabet, that uses nonpictorial characters to represent sound units rather than ideas or words. See also **writing system**. *Cp.* **alphabet** (def. 2); **hieroglyphics** (def. 1); **ideography**; **logography**; **syllabary**.

line graph a diagram showing points connected by lines, dots, dashes, etc., to represent the frequency of relations or connections among data.

lingo *n.* **1.** spoken or written language, often strange or unfamiliar. **2.** cant; jargon. **3.** an individual's peculiar language or speech; idiolect.

linguist *n.* **1.** one who studies the nature of language; one whose field of research is linguistics. *Note*: Linguistic specialization is usually labeled according to the field of study, as *sociolinguist*, *psycholinguist*, etc. See also **linguistics**. **2.** popularly, one who speaks a number of languages or is fluent in the use of language.

linguistic analysis the application of linguistic principles from a defined theory of language structure, function, and change to some aspect of language, as dialect variation or morphological patterning in a specific language.

linguistic atlas an atlas with maps showing the geographic boundaries of the incidence of use of various linguistic features for given dialects of a language.

linguistic awareness "the ability of a speaker-hearer to bring to bear rather deliberately the grammatical and, in particular, the phonological knowledge he does have in the course of reading" (Mattingly, 1972). *Note*: An essential prerequisite to learning to read, linguistic awareness does not need to be conscious, merely available. See also **cognitive clarity**. *Cp.* **metalinguistic awareness**.

linguistic convergence the modification of one's language to conform more nearly to that used by other speakers in a conversation, usually in order to obtain social approval. *Note*: Linguistic *divergence* occurs when a person chooses to be disassociated from other speakers. See also **accommodation** (def. 1).

linguistic geography the study of the regional variety in types of languages and dialects.

linguistic reading program **1.** any approach to the teaching of reading based on linguistic principles. **2.** a beginning reading approach based on highly regular sound-symbol patterns, temporarily substituted for the term "phonic" early in the 1960s; phonic approach.

linguistics *n. (with sing. v.)* **1.** the study of the nature and structure of language and languages. **2.** the study of the nature of language communication. *adj.* **linguistic**.

Areas of *Linguistic Study**
applied linguistics
biolinguistics
critical linguistics
descriptive linguistics
historical linguistics
metalinguistics
neurolinguistics
paralinguistics
(developmental) psycholinguistics
sociolinguistics
structural linguistics
systemic grammar *or* linguistics
text linguistics

---

*Terms are all defined in this dictionary.

lipreading *n.* the observation of the mouth and lips during the speechreading process. *Cp.* **speechreading**.

liquid *n.* a consonant that is articulated without friction and may be prolonged like a vowel, as /l/ in *like* and /r/ in *read*.

listening *n.* **1.** the ability to attend to sound. **2.** the act of understanding speech; listening comprehension; auding.

listening center a place, usually in a media center, library, or classroom, where a student can use a headset to listen to recorded instructional material.

listening comprehension level the highest readability or grade level of material that can be comprehended well when it is read aloud to the student; auding level. *Note*: Listening comprehension level, measured by reading successively more difficult passages to a student, is useful in estimating the student's potential silent reading level. Although the suggested criteria vary, better than 75 percent comprehension is often used as a standard in judging whether a student comprehends material at this level. See also **informal reading inventory**; **listening** (def. 2).

listening vocabulary the number of words a person understands when they are heard in speech; hearing vocabulary. *Cp.* **reading vocabulary**; **speaking vocabulary**; **writing vocabulary**.

literacy *n.* *Note*: Many would agree with Soares's (1992) statement that "consensual agreement on a single definition [of literacy] is quite implausible," although some would qualify this by pointing out that "having argued that a common definition is not feasible...does not imply that there is not need" for one (Cervero, 1985). The complications that arise when seeking a single definition of literacy are many: the

concept of literacy as a continuum; the dual referents of literacy, individual and social; the differing historic, geographic, and linguistic interpretations of the term; the distinctly different yet complementary sets of complex skills and abilities involved in reading and writing; the way it develops differently with respect to such factors as age, sex, and education; and its implication of symbolic language behavior at a level of sophistication far beyond that of ordinary conversation. Soares (1992) observes that "the concept of literacy involves a set of structures ranging from individual skills, abilities, and knowledge, to social practices and functional competencies, to ideological values and political goals." Similarly, Scribner (1984) suggests three metaphors to describe the wide range of concepts of literacy: literacy may be viewed as *adaptation* to societal expectations, *power* to realize one's aspirations and effect social change, or *a state of grace* to be attained by the well-read, cultured person. Because of the breadth of concepts involved in *literacy*, several investigators prefer the use of the plural term *literacies*. **1.** the ability to read. *Note*: "Reading is clearly primary to any definition of literacy and in some sense, the others are secondary. Writing, as a means of recording and communication, presupposes reading; otherwise it is mere copying. Similarly numeracy and document knowledge are supplemental to reading and have no role in the literacy equation without it" (Venezky et al., 1990). **2.** "the basic or primary levels of reading and writing that ...[serve] comparatively over time and across space" (Graff, 1987); a set of "reading and writing practices governed by a conception of what, how, when and why to read and write" (Lankshear, 1987); the ability of a person "who can with understanding both read and write a short, simple statement on his everyday life" (UNESCO, 1951); a continuum of skills, including both reading and writing, applied in a social context (Gray, 1956; UNESCO, 1957) (*Note*: The sources of this last definition are significant for their early description of literacy as a continuum including a dimension of functional, social relevancy); "an outcome of cultural transmission.... Individuals in societies without written systems do not become literate" (Scribner, 1984). **3.** "the possession by an individual of the essential knowledge and skills which enable him or her to engage in all those activities required for effective functioning in his or her group and community and whose attainments in reading, writing, and arithmetic make it possible for him or her to use these skills toward his or her own and the community's development" (UNESCO, 1962); "the ability of a person to engage in all those activities in which literacy is required for effective functioning in his group and community and also for enabling him to continue to use reading, writing, and calculation for his own and the community's development" (UNESCO, 1978). **4.** competence in a special field, as computer literacy. *Note*: The extension of the term *literacy* to competence in virtually all fields of knowledge, as *computer literacy*, and phenomena, as *media literacy*, is relatively recent. **5.** "a strategy of liberation [that] teaches people to read not only the word but also the world" (Freire, 1970); ideological literacy. See also **reading the word**; **reading the world**. Note the evolution of the concept of *literacy* in successive UNESCO definitions. See also **literate**; the essays "Functional Literacy" (p. 90) and "Literacy" (p. 142). *Cp.* **aliterate**; **illiteracy**; **semiliterate**.

literacy event a communication act that represents "any occasion in which a piece of writing is integral to the nature of participants' interactions and their interpretive processes" (Heath, 1978).

literacy fallacy the mistaken assumption that there is an invariant, one-to-one correspondence in the English language between graphemes and phonemes. *Note*: Various phonemes, especially vowels, are symbolized or spelled in several ways in written English, as /ā/ represented by *ay*

Representative Types of *Literacy**

academic literacy
adult literacy
advanced literacy**
autonomous literacy
basic literacy
biliteracy
community literacy
computer literacy
conventional literacy[†]
craft literacy
critical literacy
cultural literacy
cultured literacy
economic literacy[†]
emancipatory literacy
emergent literacy
family literacy
functional literacy
high literacy
ideological literacy[††]
intergenerational literacy
marginal literacy
media literacy
minimal literacy
polyglot literacy
pragmatic literacy
prison literacy
protoliteracy
quantitative literacy
reading literacy
real-world literacy
restricted literacy
scribal literacy
survival literacy
television literacy
vernacular literacy
visual literacy
workplace literacy

---

*Terms are all defined in this dictionary.
Term is defined under **cultured literacy.
[†]Term is defined under **functional literacy**.
[††]Terms is defined under **literacy**.

Literacy

Literacy is a minimal ability to read and write in a designated language, as well as a mindset or way of thinking about the use of reading and writing in everyday life. It differs from simple reading and writing in its assumption of an understanding of the appropriate use of these abilities within a print-based society. Literacy, therefore, requires active, autonomous engagement with print and stresses the role of the individual in generating as well as receiving and assigning independent interpretations to messages. By extension of the basic competence implied by literacy, computer literacy, cultural literacy, economic literacy, and so forth have evolved as designations of minimal competence required in these areas.

Although conceptions of literacy have been based on reading and writing for hundreds of years, recent usage has extended the skill range to include mathematics, under the assumption that the understanding of everyday texts sometimes requires this knowledge. Further extension to include speaking and listening has also been suggested. When used as an adjective, *literacy* tends to have a looser definition, as in the phrase *literacy program*, which refers to a wide range of courses that include instruction in reading, writing, or other basic skills. These directions tend to inflate the significance of *literacy*, making it a cover term for all basic communication and calculation skills required for existing in a modern society.

Literacy derives from the Latin *litteratus*, which, in Cicero's time, meant "a learned person." In the early Middle Ages, the *litteratus* (as opposed to the *illitteratus*) was a person who could read Latin, but after 1300, due to the decline of learning in Europe, it came to signify a minimal ability with Latin. After the Reformation, *literacy* came to mean the ability to read and write in one's native language. According to the *Oxford English Dictionary*, the substantive *literacy* first appeared in English in the early 1880s, formed from the adjective *literate*, which occurred in English writing as early as the middle of the 15th century.

In current usage, the term implies an interaction between social demands and individual competence. Thus, the levels of literacy required for social functioning can and have varied across cultures and across time within the same culture. What was required for literacy in the time of Columbus is assumed to be different from what is required for literacy in industrialized nations today. Nevertheless, these differences may be more quantitative than qualitative. In the past century and well into this century, national emphasis on reduction of illiteracy led to a contrast between literacy and illiteracy, with the concomitant assumption of a sharp division between the two. Today literacy is understood as a continuum, anchored at the bottom by illiteracy. Of equal importance to illiteracy, however, is aliteracy—the unwillingness to use literacy even though the capability is present.

Attempts to define levels of literacy have led to phrases such as *functional literacy, marginal literacy, survival literacy,* and *semiliteracy*. Of these, *functional literacy*, which originated in the 1930s, has the widest currency. Since the UNESCO literacy studies of the 1950s, *functional literacy* has been defined in terms of skills or abilities required to use print to function in everyday life. This form of literacy has also been called *pragmatic* or *conventional literacy*. For marking the higher end of the literacy continuum, *cultured literacy, advanced literacy,* and *high literacy* are used.

Richard L. Venezky

in *day* and *ai* in *aid*. Conversely, a grapheme may represent more than one sound, as *a* in *hat* or *nation*. A teacher who says, "What is the sound of the letter *a*?" makes the literacy fallacy of assuming that the written language, not the spoken one, is the primary language system.

literacy gap the difference between the actual and desired level of literacy.

literacy involvement in reading, the extent to which a person engages in those types of reading activities that meet his or her needs and desires.

literacy laboratory a facility under the direction of a trained teacher in which children are helped to improve their reading and writing skills.

literal comprehension the act or process of understanding what is explicitly stated or clearly implied in text or speech. *Note*: A further assumption of literal comprehension is that it is essentially reproductive, not constructive, in nature. See also **read** (def. 2); **text processing**. *Cp.* **interpretation** (defs. 1, 2).

literal meaning **1.** the explicit sense that is stated or clearly implied in text or speech. See also **literal comprehension**. **2.** See **literal translation**.

literal translation a word-for-word, non-idiomatic translation from one language to another. *Cp.* **free translation**.

literary activity any engagement with a written literary work, as by reading, writing, or speaking it, or by listening to or watching its performance.

literary analysis **1.** the study of a literary work by a critic, student, or scholar. **2.** a careful, detailed reading and report thereof. *Cp.* **literary criticism**.

literary criticism **1.** the analysis and judgment of works of literature. **2.** the body of principles by which the work of writers is judged. *Note*: The principles used in judging a literary work vary from the highly personal and subjective to the relatively objective. They may involve specific consideration of moral values, historical accuracy, literary form and type, etc., and may vary from one literary period to another. See also the essay "Literary Criticism" (pp. 144–145). *Cp.* **literary analysis**.

literary culture **1.** a culture that transmits its values, attitudes, and beliefs primarily through the written language, as most European cultures. **2.** a culture that values the ability to write and read more than the ability to speak effectively. *Cp.* **oral culture**.

literary form **1.** the formal structure or organization of the parts of literary or other artistic work that unifies them and determines their total effect. **2.** the structure used to express literary and other artistic types of content; genre.

literary merit an overall judgment of the quality of a literary work, usually based upon several factors such as style, characterization, unity, etc.

literate **1.** *adj.* able to read and write; especially, referring to "one who could read and write in one's native language, particularly after the Reformation.... In modern usage, literate connotes a lower level of some quality, rather than the more advanced or even average levels" (Venezky et al., 1990). **2.** *adj.* in language use, marked by skillful, clear, and refined expression. **3.** *adj.* acquainted with a field of knowledge, especially of literature; well read. *Note*: The extension of the term to virtually all fields of knowledge is a relatively recent phenomenon. **4.** *adj.* referring to the ability "to use reading and writing as a means of being aware of reality and able to transform it" (Freire, cited in Soares,

Literary Criticism

Unchanged in fundamentals since Plato and Aristotle analyzed poetry and drama in the 4th century B.C., literary criticism evaluates the nature and role of literature. It examines texts and authors in their cultural contexts and throughout history, demonstrating their meaning and significance at different times. Basic questions center on the literary work itself, its connection with literary traditions, its relation to reality or experience, the function of authorship, and the reception of works and writers by a specific public. In the post–World War II period, literary theory or abstract speculation about meaning and language has become increasingly important, often displacing criticism with problems of interpretation pursued more along philosophical than literary lines.

Western literary criticism has undergone varying emphases. From the Greco-Roman period to the late 18th century, critics examined the way literature imitated, copied, reflected, or embodied the external world, natural laws, and permanent truths. Intrinsic to this was a preoccupation with the moral and social effects of art. Such criticism was fairly objective, for it accepted some link between nature and art as well as between ideas and language.

By the time of the American and French revolutions, European romanticism shifted the focus from the world to the mind, from what was portrayed to how it was known and expressed by both artist and reader. This marked the emergence of modern critical theory in the Enlightenment aesthetics of Edmund Burke, Alexander Baumgarten, Immanuel Kant, and Friedrich Schiller. The 19th century moved increasingly toward subjectivism, impressionistic criticism, cultural definition, religious idealism, and aestheticism.

In the 20th century, from Ferdinand de Saussure's linguistic structuralism and infant semiotics to Jacques Derrida's semantic poststructuralism, language became central. Words could not be relied on to convey unequivocal meaning about the world, and they were thought to be arbitrary in nature. Writing came to be viewed not as a way of representing speech and expressing ideas so much as the condition of language or thought itself. This emphasis led away from stable meaning and encouraged multiple interpretations along with individual readings. Language became self-referential. This slant also challenged traditional values in philosophy, religion, politics, and culture.

Before the middle of the 20th century, criticism was basically an act of informed, scholarly, authoritative reading that produced a cultural understanding of the work. One took a bibliographically sound text, clarified allusions, investigated the relevant historical and cultural framework, sorted out the genre, thought about the writer's life, analyzed other works embodied in the text, situated oneself as critic, and judged the art and value of the essentially literary achievement. Today, however, it is usual to think rather self-consciously and philosophically about one's assumptions in approaching literature and to view interpretation as a function of one's theoretical perspective. Literary theory considers how the critic, the reader, and the writer approach the work of literature through general but systematic and inherently ideological principles. All judgments of aesthetic value or cultural significance involved in it are indebted to consciously or unconsciously accepted schemes of interpretation that are fundamentally political. It becomes the task of the literary theorist to analyze these systems of belief and value. Theories and their allied methods frequently loom more important than the literary works they were once intended to clarify or explain.

(continued)

Literary Criticism (cont'd.)

Like philosophy, literary criticism and theory are rich in specialized terminology and intricate techniques. Over the course of the 20th century, various schools of thought have emerged, stressing in turn either the work itself (formalism), the world revealed in it (Marxism), the psyche of the writer (psychoanalytic criticism), the nature of language and rhetoric (structuralism and poststructuralism), the role of the reader-consumer (reader response and reception theory), or the recovery of marginalized writers and traditions (feminism and new historicism). At present, literature as a special category of expression is being replaced by culture criticism, which treats other than exclusively linguistic signs with methods traditionally reserved for literary analysis.

Francis L. Cousens

1993). **5.** *adj.* educated. **6.** *n.* a learned person. See also the essay "Literacy" (p. 142). *Cp.* **illiterate**.

literate culture a learned society, especially one versed in literature.

literate environment a situation that stimulates reading; "an environment in which written language...is meaningful and useful" (Durkin, 1993).

literati *n., pl.; sing.* **-ratus** persons with scholarly interests, especially in literature and the arts; the class of highly educated persons; intelligentsia.

literature-based curriculum a curriculum in which literary works, usually trade books, are the dominant materials for instruction, especially in the language arts.

literature circle that part of a literature-based reading program in which students meet to discuss books they are reading independently. *Note*: The books discussed are usually sets of the same title, sets of different titles by one author, or sets of titles with a common theme.

litotes *n., pl.* **-tes** understatement; especially, the statement of something positive in a negative way, as *She was not ungrateful.* See also **understatement** (def. 1).

loan word a word incorporated both in form and meaning from one language into another, often with an adaptation in pronunciation or spelling, as in the English words *amateur* (French), *patio* (Spanish), *opera* (Italian), or *sabbath* (Hebrew). See also **borrowing**.

local norms the range of test scores that represent the average or usual performance of a restricted sample rather than a local sample. *Note*: If the norming sample is large enough, local norms may be more useful to a school system or district than national norms.

location concept any directional print convention, as left and right or top and bottom of a page, needed by emergent readers.

locative case in case grammar and in some inflected languages, the case that shows place or location.

locutionary act a speech act in which what is said is both meaningful and understood but no consequence results, as this dictionary entry. *Cp.* **illocutionary act**; **perlocutionary act**.

logograph *n.* an orthographic symbol that represents one or more words, as # for *number* or 2 for *two*. Also **logogram**. *Cp.* **ideograph**; **letter** (def. 1); **pictograph**; **symbol** (def. 4). *adj.* **logographic**.

logography *n.* a writing system that uses logographs to represent words or morphemes of a language; word writing. See also **radical**; **writing system**. *Cp.* **alphabetic writing**; **ideography**; **logosyllabic writing**; **pictography**; **syllabary** (defs. 1, 3).

logosyllabic writing a writing system, such as ancient Sumerian or Egyptian, that employs both logographic and syllabic characters; hieroglyphics. See also **writing system**. *Cp.* **alphabetic writing**; **ideography**; **logography**; **pictography**; **syllabary** (defs. 1, 3).

longitudinal research a way of studying behavior or development by taking repeated measures on one or more variables on the same individual or group over an extended period. *Cp.* **cross-sectional research**.

long-term memory (LTM) memory that lasts over an extended period, has great capacity, and patterns information into structures or chunks, as memory of the gist of a story long after it was read. *Note*: LTM is assumed to develop from continued or repeated short-term memory episodes. This process may result in some telescoping or distorting, and thus not entirely accurate recall. *Cp.* **short-term memory**.

long vowel **1.** in teaching practice, the vowel sounds in English that are also the names of the alphabet letters *a, e, i, o, u,* as /ā/ in *halo,* /ē/ in *demon,* /ī/ in *bind,* /ō/ in *told,* /ū/ in *unit. Note*: Technically, long vowel sounds are also represented in spelling by two or more letters, as *ai* in *aim, i-e* in *kite,* etc., the term more accurately referring to the diphthongs that the graphemes represent. See also **diphthong**. **2.** in phonetics, the relatively long duration of time stress of a vowel sound. *Note*: Vowel length is affected by amount of stress and by regional speech habits as well as by context, as *told* in *I told you I was sick! Cp.* **short vowel**.

lowercase letter a letter form, as *a, e, n, b, f,* that is smaller and often different from a capital letter; miniscule. *Cp.* **uppercase letter**.

lyric **1.** *n.* a short poem of personal feelings and emotions, intended to make a single impression on the reader. **2.** *adj.* designating such a poem. **3.** *pl.,* the words of a song. *n.* **lyricism**. *adj.* **lyrical**.

machine translation the act or result of feeding text into a computer programmed to produce text of equivalent meaning in another language, but often with serious limitations in the accuracy and spirit of the machine translation.

macron *n.* **1.** an orthographic symbol (⁻) placed above a vowel to indicate a long vowel sound. **2.** a graphic symbol placed above a syllable in a foot or a line of verse to indicate strong stress. See also **accent** (def. 2d).

macrorule *n.* a principle of writing applied to a whole text rather than to a small part of it.

macrostructure *n.* in text analysis, the topic and general organization of a passage. *Cp.* **microstructure**.

magic realism in literature, a mode of writing in which the supernatural is accepted as real; "an expression of the New World reality which at once combines the rational elements of the European supercivilization and the irrational elements of a primitive American" (Verzasconi, 1965). *Note*: Magic realism is especially prominent in the literature, religion, and art of the Caribbean and other New World cultures. It is featured in John Berendt's novel *Midnight in the Garden of Good and Evil* (1994). Also **magical realism**.

magnet school in the United States, a public school offering specialized programs, as in science or art, to attract students.

main effect an estimate of the contribution of a single variable or experimental treatment taken by itself.

main idea **1.** the gist of a passage; central thought. **2.** the chief topic of a passage expressed or implied in a word or phrase. **3.** the topic sentence of a paragraph. **4.** "a statement in sentence form which gives the stated or implied major topic of a passage and the specific way in which the passage is limited in content or reference" (Harris, 1981). Also **main topic**.

mainstreaming *n.* the placement of special needs students in regular public school settings, often, but not necessarily, in regular classrooms. *Note*: Mainstreaming was mandated in the United States by federal legislation in 1975. See also **special education**; **special needs student(s)**. *Cp.* **inclusion** (def. 1).

malapropism *n.* the substitution of incorrect words for correct words that sound almost alike, usually producing comic meanings, as *derelict* for *dialect* in "*We found it hard to understand his Scottish derelict.*" *Note*: The term is from Mrs. Malaprop, a character in Richard Sheridan's 18th-century play *The Rivals*.

manifesto *n., pl.* **-tos, -toes** a public statement of beliefs, principles, or intentions, written or spoken, as Karl Marx and Friedrich Engels' *Communist Manifesto*.

manner of articulation in the production of speech sounds, the degree of constriction or narrowing at the place of articulation, as a pause with sudden release (/p/ in *pit*) or a closure with slow release (/ch/ in *chart*). *Note*: In phonetics, consonants are conventionally described according to their manner of articulation. See also **consonant**; **vowel**. *Cp.* **place of articulation**.

manual alphabet an alphabet represented by the finger and hand positions used in finger spelling.

manually coded English system any of several communication systems, using English syntax, that have been developed for use in school settings to permit simultaneous signing and speaking. *Note*: These systems are not considered either American Sign Language or English but use features from both for representing English visually.

manual method a means of communicating by the hard of hearing that uses signs, gestures, and manual alphabets. See also **dactylology**; **sign language**. *Cp.* **oralism**; **total communication**.

manuscript writing a type of handwriting in which letter forms that look like ordinary type are wholly or partially unconnected within each word; print-script; printing. *Cp.* **cursive writing**.

This is manuscript writing.

map **1.** *n.* a representation of geographic regions. **2.** *v.* to prepare such a representation. **3.** *v.* to impose one neural pattern or network on another, as to map a visual network on a phonological one. **4. map out**, to plan an approach to a task or problem.

mapping **1.** *n.* instructional activities, particularly graphic ones, that are designed to show the relationships among ideas or topics in text or to plan for writing; cognitive mapping. See also **semantic mapping**; **webbing**. **2.** *n.* the formation of one or more hypotheses or expectations in attempting to solve a problem. **3.** *v.* to relate language to experience. *Note*: "Children become language users by mapping language onto experience" (Newman, 1985). **4.** *v.* to survey material before careful reading to get an overview of its nature and organization. **5.** See **cognitive map**.

mapping principle any of several generalizations governing the relationship between spoken and printed words, with specific attention to the association of particular graphemes with their corresponding phonemes.

marginalized *adj.* in education, referring to students who tend to be left out of traditional academic systems.

marginal literacy literacy that barely meets the functional needs for communication in reading and writing.

Marxist criticism the analysis of a literary work as a representation of its historical, social, and economic context, emphasizing methods and themes derived from the work of Karl Marx. *Note*: Marxist criticism considers how a work is produced and what cultural values are revealed in it. It also examines how history determines the content and shape of a work, and holds that all expression is the result of material factors in uniquely concrete relationships.

masking *n.* **1.** interference with the perception of an auditory signal because of noise, as in a poor telephone connection or in audiometric testing; auditory masking. **2.** interference with or elimination of any sensory process by another, as in the use of white noise to relieve pain.

mass media the chief ways of communicating with large numbers of people, as newspapers, radio, television, etc.

mass noun a noun whose referent is not countable, as *water, earth, happiness*. *Cp.* **count noun**.

mastery learning an instructional approach in which classroom conditions are altered for individual students, as adjusting the amount of learning time, so that most can achieve some established instructional goal. *Note*: Theories of mastery learning stem largely from the work of Benjamin Bloom. He asserts that "most students can attain a high level of learning capacity if instruction is approached sensitively and systematically, if students are helped when and where they have learning difficulty, if they are given time to achieve mastery, and if there is some clear criterion of what constitutes mastery" (Bloom, 1976).

mastery test a test designed to measure the possession, on an all-or-none basis, of a specified level of performance, useful particularly in measuring basic skill performance.

matched group in an experimental design, a group that has been equated on one or more variables with one or more other groups. *Note*: Age and sex are commonly matched variables. However, when matching is done on the basis of test results, the validity of matching is questionable because of test-error factors. Random assignment to groups is the preferred experimental technique in these instances. *Cp.* **control group**; **experimental group**.

matching test a test in which the subject chooses items from one list that correspond to items from another list, as to match pictures of objects with a list of their names.

mathemagenic *adj.* referring to any covert and overt behaviors that lead to learning in an instructional situation. *n.* **mathemagenics**.

matrix *n., pl.* **matrices, matrixes 1.** the environment in which something develops or is molded or embedded; context; as *the matrix of experience*. **2.** a two-dimensional array of numbers, symbols, or events. *Note*: This mathematical concept is used by extension in education, as in the use of a matrix to display variant spellings in a spelling program. **3.** any array of computer components intended to perform a specific function.

matrix sampling a plan for assessing the level of performance in a group of students, in which a large pool of questions is divided into random subsets and each subset is assigned to a random fraction of the students.

maturational lag late development in any aspect of an individual with no apparent organic defect; especially, the theoretical concept of a late development of areas of the brain controlling specific perceptual and motor functions.

maturationist theory the belief that cognitive development, and thus growth of ability needed for reading, is controlled by maturation rather than by environmental factors. *Cp.* **environmentalist theory**.

mature reader a reader who possesses these qualities: "a. unique characteristics...that predispose him to reading. b. a focus, or radix, of interest...which serves as an inner drive or motivating force. c. awareness of himself as a responsible group member.... d. an ever expanding spiral of interests.... e. a high level of competence in reading, which enables him to proceed with reasonable ease and understanding in grasping and interpreting meanings, in reacting rationally to the ideas apprehended, and in applying his ideas with sound judgment and discrimination" (Gray & Rogers, 1956).

McGuffey readers one of the most popular American 19th-century reading series. *Note*: The readers, the first two of which were issued in 1836, were texts for beginning reading instruction that, unlike earlier readers, did not assume that the child using them had already learned to read. The readers helped establish the grade school in the United States. The series is well known for the moralistic nature of its reading selections.

mean 1. *v.* to intend; signify. **2.** *n.* a midpoint between extremes. **3.** *n.* a measure of central tendency; specifically, the arithmetical average (M); the sum of all the values divided by the number of terms. *Cp.* **median** (def. 1); **mode** (def. 1).

meaning *n. Note*: Meaning is "a term whose multiplicity of meanings is so great as to defy summary" (Colapietro, 1993). Following are several definitions that pertain particularly to *meaning* in a language context. **1.** what is signified or intended by a linguistic unit. **2.** See **denotation**. **3.** See **connotation**. **4.** the set of all objects, events, etc., to which a linguistic unit refers, as *vehicle* to refer to *car, bus, truck,* etc.; extensional meaning. **5.** See **contextual meaning**. **6.** See **grammatical meaning**. **7.** the truth inherent in a declarative sentence; propositional meaning. **8.** the way in which emphasis in a sentence is said to influence its meaning, as *Is that* your *watch?* vs. *Is that your* watch*?*; prosodic meaning. **9.** the function of a sentence in some social situation, as *The telephone is ringing* used as a statement or a command; pragmatic meaning.

meaning-emphasis approach a way of teaching beginning reading that emphasizes comprehending, not merely decoding.

meaning vocabulary the number of meanings or concepts a person knows for words. *Note*: Since words often have several meanings, one's meaning vocabulary is generally much larger than the number of words one can recognize.

mean length of utterance (MLU) the average number of words produced in a meaningful sequence or speech act. *Note*: Originally conceived as an indication of language maturity, the MLU does not necessarily reflect either the complexity or maturity of language development.

media *n. pl.* means of communication, especially of mass communication, as books, newspapers, magazines, radio, television, motion pictures, recordings, etc. See also **medium** (def. 1).

media center a place for the storage and use of educational media. *Cp.* **instructional materials center**; **resource center**.

medial *adj.* **1.** referring to the middle or center; specifically, toward the median plane of the body. *Cp.* **lateral** (def. 1). **2.** referring to an arithmetical mean or average. **3.** referring to a sound or letter that neither begins nor ends a syllable or word, as /t/ /a/ /m/ in *stamp* or /a/ in *cat*.

media literacy an understanding of the way in which the instruments of mass communication are used in society. *Cp.* **television literacy**; **visual literacy**.

median (*Md*) **1.** *n.* a measure of central tendency; specifically, the middle value or score in an ordered frequency distribution. *Cp.* **mean** (def. 3); **mode** (def. 1). **2.** *adj.* referring to the middle; medial.

mediated behavior a concept employed by Vygotsky in contradistinction to the behavioral concept of mediation as a link between stimulus and response. *Note*: "What [Vygotsky] did intend to convey by this notion was that in higher forms of human behavior, the individual actively modifies the stimulus situation as a part of the process of responding to it. It was the entire structure of this activity which produced the behavior that Vygotsky attempted to denote by the term 'mediating'" (Cole et al. in Vygotsky, 1978).

mediation *n.* in semiotics, the process or result of bringing together otherwise unconnected things; the function performed by signs; transmediation. *Note*: Mediation is a fundamental concept of semiotics because the term identifies the central role of signs in communication.

mediation theory in learning, a theory that holds that, in thinking, stimuli operate as signs that do not activate responses directly, but only indirectly through complex linking processes.

medium *n., pl.* **-dia 1.** any one of the various vehicles of communication, as books. **2.** a method of communication or expression, as speech, writing, graphic art, etc.

melodrama *n.* **1.** a play characterized by exaggerated plot and characters, suspense often created by a villain, great emotion, and a happy ending, as Agatha Christie's *The Mousetrap*. **2.** actions or events in life and literature with such characteristics. *adj.* **melodramatic**.

memoir *n.* **1.** an account of one's personal experiences and observations; autobiography; often **memoirs**. **2.** a biography. **3.** a record of people and happenings known to the writer, sometimes semiautobiographical, as Marcel Proust's *Remembrance of Things Past.*

memorandum (memo) *n.* **1.** a short note intended to remind. **2.** a longer note written as a record or message.

memory *n.* **1.** the reviving of past impressions and experiences, as through retention, recall, recognition, and learning. *Note*: The role of memory in the relationships among language development, learning, and instruction has been the subject of intense theoretical and practical research in recent years . **2.** a specific recollection. **3.** the sum of all recollections. **4.** the time covered in a recollection. **5.** the storage capacity of a computer. *n.* **memorization**. *v.* **memorize**.

Types of *Memory**
auditory
episodic
explicit
implicit
long-term
rote
semantic
sensory
short-term
state-dependent
visual

*Terms are all defined in this dictionary.

---

memory gem in 19th-century textbooks, a piece of poetry or prose for students to memorize. *Note*: Memory gems were intended to form character, develop appreciation of language, beauty, and nature, provide a common core of knowledge, and stimulate intellect.

memory image the mental reconstruction of an experience, with the awareness that the experience is in the past and that the reconstruction may not be exact. *Cp.* **eidetic image**.

memory reading a reading instructional method that emphasizes comprehension by having a student memorize a selection read aloud before reading it him- or herself. See also **Jacotot method**; **story method**.

memory trace a neural change hypothesized to account for the retention of learned material.

mental ability **1.** the general intellectual power involved in thinking. *Cp.* **intelligence**. **2.** special intellectual power as revealed in mechanical aptitude, musical talent, etc. **3.** scholastic aptitude.

mental age (MA) the chronological age for which the level of performance on a test of mental ability is average. *Note*: A child is said to have a mental age of seven if he or she earns as many points on a test of mental ability as the average seven-year-old. See also **basal (mental) age**; **deviation IQ**; **intelligence quotient**. *Cp.* **chronological age**.

mental image a perceptual representation or ideational picture of a perceptual experience, remembered or imagined.

mental lexicon the number of words, meanings, and knowledge about them retained in the mind; the "human-word store" (Aitchison, 1987); mental dictionary. *Note*: The mental lexicon contains much more information about words than is found in dictionary entries, especially contextual information.

mentally handicapped lacking in normal mental ability. *Note*: The term usually refers to persons who have mild to moderate mental retardation, as the educable mentally retarded.

mental maturity a nontechnical term for: **a.** the relative level of mental development for a given chronological age. *Note*: "Mental maturity is one significant factor in reading readiness" (Betts, 1946). **b.** an adult level of mental development.

mental model in reading comprehension, a scheme for processing text by analyzing the spatial and sequential patterns of keywords to determine their correspondence to the text structure. *Note*: Study of the use of mental models and propositional encoding has greatly advanced knowledge of the intricacies of comprehension and its teaching. *Cp.* **propositional encoding**.

mental retardation a markedly lower mental age than chronological age; "a significant lack of intellectual ability for a given chronological age; significantly subaverage general intellectual functioning existing concurrently with deficits in adaptive behavior and manifested during the developmental period"—American Association on Mental Retardation (Grossman, 1983). *Note*: Mental retardation and mental deficiency have been classified at many levels for different purposes at different times. The *Diagnostic and Statistical Manual of Mental Disorders* (1987, 3rd ed.) defines *mild* mental retardation as an IQ of 50–70, *moderate* as 35–55, *severe* as 20–40, and *profound* as below 25. Common educational usage describes one with an IQ of 75–85 as a *slow learner*. See also **educable mentally retarded**; **intelligence quotient**; **special education**; **special needs student(s)**; **trainable mentally retarded**.

merry-go-sorry *n.* a story or poem that arouses both joy and sorrow.

meta-analysis technique any of several methods, usually statistical, for combining the results from a collection of program evaluations to reach an overall conclusion about program effects, usually expressed as effect size or the average magnitude of the program in standard deviation units.

metacognition *n.* awareness and knowledge of one's mental processes such that one can monitor, regulate, and direct them to a desired end; self-mediation. *Note*: Studies such as those by Paris et al. (1983) suggest that one's attitudes and beliefs are involved in metacognition. *adj.* **metacognitive**.

metacognitive awareness in reading, knowing when what one is reading makes sense by monitoring and controlling one's own comprehension; metacomprehension. *Note*: Good readers appear from an early age to possess metacognitive awareness that allows them to adjust their reading strategies; poor readers do not. See also **comprehension monitoring**.

metalanguage *n.* language used to describe and analyze natural language; language about language. *Note*: A metalanguage (and also an object language) can be a natural language, as Japanese, English, etc., or a formal one, as mathematical or logical notation. *Cp.* **object language**. *adj.* **metalinguistic**.

metalinguistic *adj.* **1.** referring to metalanguage. **2.** referring to language in relation to culture.

metalinguistic awareness a conscious awareness on the part of a language user of language as an object in itself. See also **cognitive clarity**. *Cp.* **linguistic awareness**.

metalinguistics *n.* **1.** the study of metalanguage. **2.** the study of language and its interrelationships with culture.

metaphor *n.* a figure of speech in which a comparison is implied by analogy but is not stated, as *"death is slumber"* (Percy Blysshe Shelley, "Mont Blanc"). *Note*: Metaphors may be uncomplicated or elaborate, as in an extended allegory. See also **dead metaphor**; **mixed metaphor**. *Cp.* **simile**.

metathesis *n., pl.* **-ses** **1.** the change of the order of letters, syllables, or sounds in a word, as in the modern *bird*, derived from the Old English *brid*. **2.** change in usual word order; anastrophe. *Cp.* **epenthesis**; **syneresis**; **tmesis**.

meter *n.* **1.** the rhythmical pattern in verse, made up of stressed and unstressed syllables; foot. **2.** a specific form of such a pattern, depending on the number and kind of feet, as *iambic pentameter*. Also **metre**. See also **prosody** (def. 2). *adj.* **metric**; **metrical**.

method of limits a procedure for determining when a subject first notices differences, either by decreasing discriminable differences until they are no longer differentiated or by increasing nondiscriminable differences until they are differentiated.

metonymy *n.* literally, "change of name"; a figure of speech in which one uses a word or word phrase that is associated with or is suggested by another word, as *the arm of the law* for *the police. n.* **metonym**.

metric **1.** *adj.* having to do with a decimal measurement system. **2.** *n.* any scale of measurement, especially an interval scale, as *a metric to express level of sociability. n.* **meter**.

metrical phonology a set of subtheories of generative phonology that seeks to characterize the properties of stress in terms of its rhythmic structure.

metrics *n. (with sing. v.)* the study of the rhythm or meter in verse; prosody. *adj.* **metric**; **metrical**.

microstructure *n.* in text analysis, the details of a passage. *Cp.* **macrostructure**.

microteaching *n.* a technique in teacher education that uses short, specific episodes of teaching, usually videotaped, for analysis and instruction.

middle school a school usually for grades 5 or 6 through 8. *Cp.* **elementary school**; **intermediate school**; **secondary school**.

midlevel literate **1.** *n.* a functional literate whose skills are insufficient to adjust to changing social and economic conditions. **2.** *adj.* referring to such a level of literacy.

migrant education education for shifting populations, as for agricultural workers and their families who move from place to place.

mindmapping *n.* the application of semantic mapping to notetaking; specifically, at the college level, graphic representation of a key idea with subordinate ideas shown radiating from it and often with descriptive information shown on the connecting lines.

minilesson *n.* **1.** in teacher education, a short teaching demonstration by an aspiring teacher that is viewed, sometimes videotaped, and critiqued by a mentor or professor. **2.** a short, focused segment of a larger curriculum unit.

minimal brain dysfunction (MBD) a hypothetical construct concerning the nature of a learning disability—namely, that subtle brain dysfunction interferes with cognition and learning and is manifest by soft neurologic signs without clear-cut evidence of injury to the nervous system.

minimal literacy the lowest level of functional literacy.

minimal pair two linguistic items, usually words, whose meanings are distinguished by a single phonemic contrast between them, as *book* and *look* are contrasted by /b/ and /l/; minimal contrast.

minimal terminal unit a main clause, with all of its appended modifiers. Also **T-unit**. *Note*: Kellogg Hunt (1965) developed the minimal terminal unit as a more significant measure in calculating syntactic maturity than the conventional measure of sentence length.

minimum competency survey in the United States, a testing movement designed to measure the lowest level of performance acceptable for a high school diploma in specified aspects of the language arts and mathematics. Also **minimum competency testing**. *Note*: The particular skills and the level of acceptable performance vary from state to state. ·

miracle play **1.** a medieval play, usually about the lives and deeds of Christian saints and martyrs, often presented in cycles by trade guild merchants and workers. *Cp.* **morality play**. **2.** See **mystery play**.

mirror method **1.** an informal technique for observing eye movements in which an observer, sitting next to the reader and positioning a small mirror at an angle near the text, watches the reader's eye movements and obtains a rough estimate of the number of fixations made. **2.** in speech therapy, the use of a large mirror in which the student can easily observe the articulation of sounds and words by self and therapist. See also **mirror reading**.

mirror reading a diagnostic technique used to determine if a person can read the mirror-image of a word or text more easily or accurately than the same word or text in normal orientation. *Note*: A mirror is placed facing the word or text, and the person is asked to read what appears in the mirror. Some believe that a better performance with mirror reading indicates a reading disability caused by a neurologic dysfunction. See also **mirror method**.

mirror writing **1.** the unintentional production of letters, numbers, or whole words either upside down or backwards. *Note*: Some mirror writing is normal in young children but becomes a source of concern if it persists. **2.** intentional backward writing, usually done for purposes of privacy or secrecy.

miscue *n.* a term advanced by K.S. Goodman (1965) to describe a deviation from text during oral reading or a shift in comprehension of a passage. *Note*: The assumption is that miscues are not random errors, but are attempts by the reader to make sense of the text. They therefore provide a rich source of information for analyzing language and reading development.

miscue analysis a formal examination of the use of miscues as the basis for determining the strengths and weaknesses in the background experiences and language skills of students as they read.

mispronunciation *n.* the incorrect oral reproduction of a word. *Note*: Mispronunciations are one of several types of errors commonly recorded in testing oral reading accuracy. Variations in pronunciation due to dialect, foreign accent, or speech problems are ordinarily not considered mispronunciations. See also **insertion** (def. 1); **omission**; **substitution** (def. 2). *v.* **mispronounce**.

mixed cerebral dominance a concept based on the inference that mixed laterality of motor or sensory function reflects an anomaly in cerebral development. *Note*: Mixed cerebral dominance may be a correlate of some developmental disorders of speech and language. See also **cerebral dominance**.

mixed hearing loss reduced auditory acuity because of combined conduction and nerve hearing losses.

mixed metaphor a metaphor that makes an inappropriate comparison, as *when the iron is hot, keep the ball rolling.*

mnemonic **1.** *adj.* having to do with memory, especially with strategies to improve memorizing. **2.** *n., pl. (with sing. v.)*, devices and techniques to improve memory.

modal auxiliary a lexical item that gives special shades of meaning when attached to verbs, as *may* in *You may be right, but....* *Note*: A modal auxiliary, also called *modal verb* or *modal auxiliary verb*, displays syntactic characteristics in common with verbs. The question of whether it is a verb is an issue among some linguists. See also **modality** (def. 2). *Cp.* **auxiliary verb**.

modality *n.* **1.** any of the sensory systems of receiving, processing, and responding to sensation. *Note*: The primary modalities involved in literacy development are the *auditory*, *visual*, and *kinesthetic*. **2.** the manner of expressing an attitude in speaking and writing, as in the use of the modal auxiliary *will* in *You will come?* **3.** the categorization of logical propositions as either affirming or denying that they are possible, actual, or necessary.

mode[1] *n.* **1.** a measure of central tendency; specifically, the most common score or value in a distribution. *Note*: In a bimodal distribution, it is possible to have more than one mode in a distribution. *Cp.* **mean** (def. 3); **median** (def. 1). **2.** See **modality** (def. 3). See also **mood[2]** (def. 2). *adj.* **modal**.

mode[2] *n.* **1.** frequently occurring or dominating custom, fashion, or behavior, as *a current mode of speech*. **2.** a way of doing or making something; method.

model **1.** *n.* a standard or example for imitation or comparison. **2.** *v.* to provide such an example. *Cp.* **modeling**. **3.** *adj.* serving, or worthy of serving, as an example. **4.** *n.* a design or description intended to show the flow of an overall process or function, including its constituent processes and their relation to one another and to the process as a whole. *Note*: A publication of the International Reading Association, *Theoretical Models and Processes of Reading* (Ruddell, Ruddell, & Singer, Eds., 4th ed., 1994) provides a number of examples of research-oriented models in reading and literacy. The compilation describes salient aspects of reading processes (language, social context and culture, literacy development, comprehension, reader response, metacognition) and different conceptions of the flow of the reading process taken as a whole ("processing models" of reading and literacy including cognitive, sociocognitive, transactional, transactional sociopsycholinguistic, and attitude influence). It includes a review of process-oriented reading research and suggestions for ways of viewing such processes. *Cp.* **paradigm** (def. 1). **5.** *n.* a design or description showing how something is formed.

modeling *n.* **1.** the act of serving as an example of a behavior. **2.** the imitation of another's behavior, especially as a behavior modification technique.

mode of discourse the medium in which language occurs in a social situation, as speech, writing, sign language, etc. See also **field of discourse**; **register** (def. 1); **tenor of discourse**.

mode of writing any of the major types of writing. See **argumentation**; **description**; **exposition**; **narration**.

modernism *n.* an artistic and literary movement culminating in post–World War I Europe, the United States, and Canada that discovers or creates alternatives to Western values. *Note*: Modernism is inseparable from early 20th-century movements in art, science, philosophy, psychoanalysis, and politics. Typically, it distorts the objective world, responds to quantum relativity, gravitates to the primitive, defines the human condition as irrational, evokes the Freudian unconscious, and reacts to fascism and communism. It emphasizes novelty, eccentricity, and experiment in art and life.

modified alphabet an alphabetic writing system in which existing graphemes are altered or to which graphemes are added to make the number of graphemes correspond to the number of phonemes of the oral language, as the initial teaching alphabet. See also **augmented alphabet**; **spelling reform**.

modifier *n.* a word, phrase, or clause that adds to or qualifies the meaning of another word, phrase, or clause; qualifier; as *several* and *cooperative learning* in *several children in the cooperative learning group*.

monaural *adj.* **1.** referring to one ear; specifically, the reception of sound by only one ear. **2.** referring to the use of a single sound reproducing system.

monograph *n.* **1.** a detailed, well-documented study in one or more volumes of a limited subject or of a limited aspect of a general subject, issued, or planned to be issued, as a unit rather than as a serial. **2.** in literary usage, any writing that is not a serial.

monolog *n.* literally, "speaking alone"; specifically, a lengthy speech by one person that frequently discourages speech in others. Also **monologue**. *Cp.* **soliloquy**.

monophthong *n.* a vowel produced without tongue movement to another position during articulation, as /e/ in *set*; pure vowel. *Cp.* **diphthong**; **triphthong**.

monosyllable *n.* **1.** a word of one syllable, as *book*. **2.** a single vowel sound produced with the speech organs in a fixed position, as /a/ in *bat*; monophthong. *Cp.* **diphthong** (def. 1).

Montessori method a systematized program of individualized education developed by Maria Montessori (1870–1952) in Italy that emphasizes the establishment of a perceptual base for cognitive development through sensory exploration, the development of responsibility in learning, and acquisition of practical life skills of taking care of one's self and managing one's environment. *Note*: In recent years a number of modifications have been made to adapt the method to other curricular approaches. *Cp.* **object method**.

mood[1] *n.* **1.** the emotional state of mind expressed by an author or artist in his or her work. **2.** the emotional atmosphere produced by an artistic work. See also **tone** (def. 7). **3.** the emotional state of a person or group. *adj.* **moody**.

mood[2] *n.* **1.** a meaning signalled by a grammatical verb form that expresses the subject's attitude or intent, as *can* in *Rainbow trout can leap into the air*. See also **modal auxiliary**. **2.** any of several forms of syllogistic reasoning. See also **modality** (def. 3).

moonlight schools in the United States, adult basic education schools established in Kentucky early in the 19th century by Cara Stewart, county superintendent of schools, so named because classes met "on nights when there was enough moonlight to travel to and from class after a day of work" (Newman & Beverstock, 1990). See also **volunteer literacy programs**.

Moon type embossed or raised characters used in a writing system for the blind that require less finger sensitivity than Braille. *Cp.* **Braille**.

morality play a medieval allegorical play in which virtues and vices are characters, and the theme is the struggle between good and evil for man's soul. See also **miracle play**; **mystery play**.

morph *n.* a phonological or orthographic representation of a morpheme, as /book/ and *book*. See also **allomorph**. *Cp.* **morpheme**.

morpheme *n.* a meaningful linguistic unit that cannot be divided into smaller meaningful elements, as the word *book*, or that is a component of a word, as *s* in *books*. See also **bound morpheme**; **free morpheme**. *adj.* **morphemic**.

morphemics *n. (with sing. v.)* **1.** the structure, functions, and relations of morphemes occurring in language. **2.** the study of such characteristics.

morphology *n.* the study of structure and forms of words including derivation, inflection, and compounding. *adj.* **morphological**.

morphophonemics *n. (with sing. v.)* the study of the phonological factors that bear on the forms that morphemes take in speech. Also **morphophonology**. See also **systematic phonemics**.

mother tongue see **native language**.

motif *n.* **1.** the intentional repetition of a word, phrase, event, or idea as a unifying theme, often a dominant feature of a literary or musical work. Also **motive**. *Cp.* **leitmotif**. **2.** a recurring element in a graphic design.

motivation *n.* **1.** the forces within an organism that arouse and direct behavior, as internal sensory stimulation, ego needs, etc.; internal motivation. **2.** the process by which such forces arouse and direct behavior in one direction rather than another; internal motivation. **3.** activity by one person that produces need-goal behavior in another; external motivation. *Note*: The fundamental psychophysiological meaning of motivation is given in defs. 1 and 2. The meaning in def. 3 is a popular extension of this concept. *adj.* **motivational**.

motor area **1.** the area of the cerebral cortex most involved with voluntary movements. **2.** a subcortical area of the brain.

multicultural education educational programs and materials designed to illustrate the likenesses and differences among ethnic groups or among cultural subgroups of the same ethnic origin.

multicultural literature **1.** writing that reflects the customs, beliefs, and experiences of people of differing nationalities and races. **2.** materials designed to reflect the interests, vocabulary, and experiences of students from various cultural or ethnic backgrounds. Also **multiethnic literature**.

multilevel approach the use of reading materials of different levels of difficulty in teaching reading as one way of recognizing individual differences in reading competence.

multilingualism *n.* the ability to speak, with some degree of proficiency, two or more languages in addition to one's native tongue. *Cp.* **bilingualism**. *adj.* **multilingual**.

multimedia *n., pl. (often with sing. v.)* **1.** the combining of several media into a single effort, as in the use of slides, film, sound effects, etc., in a travelogue. **2.** in computer use, the integration of text, sound, full or partial motion video, or graphics.

multiple causation (theory) **1.** the belief that an individual's reading or learning disability arises from a combination of interacting factors. **2.** the belief that there is no single cause of all cases of reading disability, but rather that a number of different factors, singularly or in various combinations, can result in a reading or learning disability, and that these factors can vary from person to person.

multiple-correlation coefficient (*R*) a coefficient expressing the statistical relationship between a criterion variable and a composite of two or more independent variables.

multiple intelligences a theory advanced by Gardner (1983) that there are at least seven distinct "intelligences": verbal/linguistic, logical-mathematical, visual/spatial, kinesthetic, musical, interpersonal, and intrapersonal. *Note*: This theory, which has aroused considerable interest among educators because of its common-sense appeal, has been faulted on technical grounds by Sternberg (1988) as more appropriate to the identification of "talents" than "intelligences."

multiple-regression analysis the statistical process of comparing actual values or scores with predicted ones when a regression line is based on more than one variable.

multiply handicapped **1.** *n.* a person with more than one physical, mental, or social disability. *Note*: The additional handicaps of the multiply handicapped often exclude them from established programs for singly handicapped persons. **2.** *adj.* referring to such disabled person.

multisensory approach an instructional approach that uses a combination of several senses, as the Fernald(–Keller) method.

multivariate analysis statistical analyses involving more than two variables, as in factor analysis. *Cp.* **bivariate analysis**.

mumbo jumbo **1.** ritual, unintelligible speech.

2. nonsensical speech designed to confuse the listener. *Cp.* **gibberish**.

muscular imbalance the inability of the eye muscles to coordinate the two eyes smoothly and easily for normal binocular vision; heterotropia; phoria.

mutation *n.* in phonetics, see **umlaut** (def. 1).

mute **1.** *adj.* not speaking; silent. **2.** *adj.* not capable of speech; dumb. *Note*: The use of *dumb* as a synonym for *mute* is generally considered offensive. See also **mutism** (def. 1). **3.** *adj.* referring to a letter that does not represent a sound in a word, as *e* in *fate*. See also **silent letter**. **4.** *n.* a person unable to speak. See also **mutism**. **5.** *v.* to soften or muffle a sound.

mutism *n.* **1.** lack of speech from either congenital or early developmental causes. **2.** inability to speak because of emotional conflict.

myopia *n.* nearsightedness; specifically, a condition in which the focus of light rays falls in front of the retina so that vision tends to be blurred, especially in distance vision. *Cp.* **emmetropia**; **hyperopia**. *n.* **myope**. *adj.* **myopic**.

mystery play a medieval religious play about the Scriptures. *Note*: Mystery plays later came out from under the influence of the church and were performed by trade guilds. See also **miracle play**. *Cp.* **morality play**.

mystery story a narrative in which the chief element is usually a crime around which the plot is built.

myth *n.* an anonymous, usually primitive, story designed to explain the mysteries of life, generally with larger-than-life characters. *Note*: Every country and culture has its own myths. Bruno Bettelheim (1976) characterizes myths as stories appealing "simultaneously to our conscious and unconscious mind" through stories that are "unique," "awe-inspiring," and "miraculous"; tragic in their ending; and pessimistic in tone. By contrast, fairytales are told in an "ordinary," "casual" way with an optimistic tone and a happy ending. *Cp.* **fairytale**; **folktale**; **legend** (def. 1). *adj.* **mythic**; **mythical**.

N

N the number of observations, subjects, or events in a total population, as *an* N *of 13 students in the study.* Cp. **n**.

n the number of observations, subjects, or events in a subgroup of a total population, as n*s of 5 boys and 8 girls in the study.* Cp. **N**.

naive processes 1. any of several learning behaviors of beginning writers that show they are unaware of audience needs or are unable to deal with them. **2.** written behaviors of beginning readers and writers that are unfocused, inept, and inflexible. Also **novice processes**. *Cp.* **expert processes**.

narration *n.* **1.** a composition in writing or speech that tells a story or gives an account of something, dealing with sequences of events and experiences, though not necessarily in strict order. *Cp.* **argumentation**; **description** (def. 1); **exposition** (def. 1). **2.** the art of telling or narrating. *v.* **narrate**.

narrative *n.* **1.** in general, a story, actual or fictional, expressed orally or in writing. **2.** specifically, "an expression of event-based experiences that are either: a. stored in memory or cognitively constructed, b. selected by the teller/writer to transmit to the audience/reader, or c. organized in knowledge structures that can be anticipated by the audience" (Graesser et al., 1991). *Note*: In this research-oriented definition, the familiar components of character, plot, etc., are considered extraneous. **3.** referring to such a story or set of events and experiences.

narrative chaining a mnemonic device in which keywords identifying facts and concepts to be remembered are woven into a story to provide a meaningful context for their recall. Also **narrative linking**.

narrative poem a poem that tells a story, often at some length. *Cp.* **ballad**; **epic** (defs. 1, 2).

narratology *n.* the examination of narrative text to determine the author's intended meaning; specifically, an exhaustive examination of relations that may be demonstrated or inferred within or in reference to the text. *Note*: Narratology uses sophisticated techniques from linguistics and related disciplines for clues to meaning. Among other things, it examines clues from codes, levels of discourse, and perceived relations among authors—real and implied— and the narrator, as well as clues to author-narrator-audience relations revealed in verb and pronoun use.

narrator the person who relates an account or story, as in a fictional narrative. See also **point of view**.

nasal 1. *adj.* referring to the nose or nasal cavities. **2.** *n.* a speech sound made when all or most of the air passes through the nose so that the nasal cavity acts as a resonator. *Note*: In English, it is usual for nasals to be voiced consonants with no air escaping through the mouth, as /m/, /n/. In languages such as French, on the other hand, nasal consonants and vowels can be formed with air passing out both the nose and the mouth. *Cp.* **oral** (def. 3). *n.* **nasality**. *v.* **nasalize**.

National Adult Literacy Survey (NALS) a 1992 survey in the United States by the Educational Testing Service of the competencies of adults in the comprehension of prose, documentary, and mathematics.

National Assessment of Educational Progress (NAEP) a congressionally mandated project of the National Center for Educational Statistics, U.S. Department of Education, which since 1969 collects and reports information on what American students, in both public and private elementary and secondary schools, know and can do in several subjects including reading, mathematics, science, writing, history, and geography; "the nation's report card." *Note*: The project has recently (1992) extended its coverage to include aspects of adult literacy. For a recent report of the status of reading performance in American schools, see *Reading Report Card for the Nation and States* (Mullis et al., 1993).

National Center on Adult Literacy (NCAL) a United States Department of Education literacy center at the University of Pennsylvania.

National Children's Book Week in the United States, a week in November during which special exhibits and programs sponsored by the Children's Book Council, Inc., are held to stimulate interest in reading, especially in children's trade books.

National Institute of Literacy (NIL) a federal agency in the United States for the integration and coordination of literacy projects and reports.

national language a language designated as the principal language of a country for cultural, ethnic, or political reasons. *Cp.* **official language**.

national norms the range of test scores that represents the average or usual performance in a nationwide sample rather than in a local one. *Note*: National norms vary widely with respect to such factors as sample size and the degree to which they represent the population from which the sample is drawn.

native language **1.** the first language one learns to speak and understand; mother tongue; primary language. *Note*: A native language is generally that which is naturally acquired in childhood, although some speakers may develop native-like control of additional languages. **2.** the primary or oldest language still spoken in a community, district, or country.

nativist theory a theory of language acquisition that holds that children are born with a biological predisposition for primary language learning; innate theory; innateness hypothesis; nativism. Also **nativist hypothesis**. See also **language acquisition device**.

nativization *n.* **1.** the process by which a language that is transplanted into another language community becomes a native language in addition to or instead of the original language, as English in Ireland. **2.** the process by which a pidgin language becomes a creole language, as in Hawaiian creole. **3.** the process by which the pronunciation of a borrowed foreign word is affected by pronunciation patterns of the borrowing language.

naturalism *n.* a view of humanity often expressed in fiction that environment and heredity determine the fate of powerless characters in a universe where even chance is a form of causation. *Cp.* **realism** (def. 3).

natural language a language as used naturally by members of a speech community. *Cp.* **artificial language** (def. 1).

naturalness *n.* in generative phonology, the assumption that some phonological features or rules are innate and universal in all languages.

near point a distance of about 14–18 inches (35–45 cm.) accepted for measuring visual acuity and functioning, at a comfortable reading distance. *Cp.* **far point**.

needs assessment in education, a broad-based appraisal of objectives and conditions in a particular situation as they interrelate; an attempt to relate goals to existing strengths, weaknesses, and feasible changes. *Note*: A needs assessment may examine the goals, assets, limitations, etc., of a particular school system and may lead to specific recommendations for improvement.

negation *n.* **1.** a statement or predicate denying something. **2.** the language devices used to express denial, as *un-*, *not*, etc. *v.* **negate**. *adj.* **negative**.

negative transfer the reduction of the effectiveness of some behavior or learning because of earlier behaviors or prior learning efforts. See also **interference** (def. 4); **proactive inhibition**; **transfer** (def. 1). *Cp.* **positive transfer**.

negotiation *n.* **1.** in transactional theory, the reader's ongoing, internal debate with the author about the meaning of a text. **2.** in the politics of literacy, bargaining for power. *v.* **negotiate**.

neo-Aristotelian criticism the application of the explicit methodology and implicit philosophy of Aristotle's *Poetics* to literary understanding and evaluation. *Note*: Associated with the University of Chicago in the 1930s, neo-Aristotelianism emphasizes plot, character, and thought in literary words. It also examines the way literature affects the reader through catharsis, conveying an insight into the intrinsic or organic wholeness of a successful work.

neologism *n.* **1.** the formation of a new word or saying. **2.** a newly formed word; coined word; root creation.

network *n.* **1.** in sociology, the structures of relations among individuals or social groups. **2.** in computer use: **a.** the interconnection of two or more computers. **b.** the linking together of computer and telecommunication systems to share information. **3.** in neurology, a pattern of neural connections that function as a neurological subsystem, as *a visual network*.

networking *n.* the use of a highly organized system of communication for informative or psychological support.

neural network in brain functioning, a complex of neurons and nerve fibers that permits innumerable interconnections within and between conducting cells of the nervous system.

neurolinguistics *n.* a branch of linguistics that studies the structure and function of the brain in relation to language acquisition, learning, and use. *Cp.* **biolinguistics**.

neutralization *n.* in phonology, the process in which contrasts between phonemes are lost in certain environments, as between /t/ and /d/ in *latter* vs. *ladder*, or the loss of vowel quality differences, as those in *pull* vs. *poor*.

New Criticism a critical approach that concentrates on the purely literary features of a work apart from extrinsic factors, finding artistic meaning in the way content is uniquely shaped by form. *Note*: An American version of formalism, the New Criticism affected the teaching and analysis of literature in the 1940s and 1950s. *Cp.* **formalism**.

New England Primer a textbook designed for reading instruction, which included the alphabet, syllabarium, words up to six syllables, alphabet verses, Lord's Prayer, Apostles' Creed, John Rogers's poem, and a catechism, in print in the United States from 1690 to the early 19th century. *Note*: It was not the first book used for reading instruction in the colonies (John Eliot's *Indian Primer* was), nor was it the most widely used schoolbook from 1790 to 1850 (after about 1790, Noah Webster's *American Spelling Book* was more widely sold).

New England Psalter the Book of Psalms, published in 1640 colonial New England and used for reading and spelling instruction. *Note*: The *Bay Psalm Book*, as it was known, is the oldest extant book printed in colonial America. In revised editions, hymns, the Proverbs, the Sermon on the Mount, and the Apostles' Creed were added. A 1760 edition included a few pages of reading instructional material prefatory to the Psalms. Up to the 1750s, the conventional texts for reading instruction were the hornbook, New England Primer, Psalter, and New Testament.

new historicism a method of studying literature that looks for contradictions in history by examining major and minor texts that resist or expose the traditionally accepted values of a period. *Note*: New historicism shows the influence of Marxism, cultural criticism, and deconstruction.

newspeak *n.* saying one thing while meaning its opposite, especially in an official tone. *Note*: The term was coined by George Orwell in his novel *1984*.

night blindness abnormally poor vision at night or in dim light.

node *n.* **1.** the point at which the branches divide in a tree diagram of the structure of a sentence. See illustration under *tree diagram*. **2.** a junction. See also **causal network theory**. *adj.* **nodal**.

noise *n.* **1.** a complex, inharmonious sound pattern without a specific pitch. **2.** any distortion in the transmission of a communications signal that interferes with the ease or clarity of its reception, as static on a radio, a misprint in a text, "snow" on the television. *adj.* **noisy**.

nomenclature *n.* a set or system of terms used in a particular field, as *the nomenclature of statistics*.

nominal **1.** *n.* a word or expression that functions as a noun, as *To go* in *To go is fun*. See also **noun**. **2.** *adj.* referring to a noun. See also **substantive** (def. 2).

nominalization *n.* **1.** the process or result of forming a noun from another part of speech by adding an affix, as adding *-ation* to *nominalize*

to form *nominalization*. **2.** in transformational-generative grammar, the process or result of deriving a noun phrase from a subordinate clause or verbal construction, as *Frightened people show great strength* for *People show great strength when they are frightened*.

nominal scale a scale in which numbers are assigned to members of a class according to a rule, as 1 = males, and 2 = females. *Note*: A nominal scale is the lowest level of measurement.

nominative case the case form in some inflected languages that indicates that a noun is the subject of a sentence or a predicate noun. *Cp.* **predicate nominative**; **subject** (def. 3).

nonce word a word created for a particular situation or event, as "mileconsuming" in "the wagon beginning to fall into its slow and mileconsuming clatter" (William Faulkner, *The Sound and the Fury*).

nonconservation *n.* in Piagetian theory, the failure in logical thinking ability, particularly in children under seven or eight, to keep an invariant property of something in mind under changing perceptual conditions. *Cp.* **conservation**.

nonfiction *n.* prose designed primarily to explain, argue, or describe rather than to entertain; specifically, a type of prose other than fiction but including biography and autobiography. *Note*: Although its emphasis is factual, fictional elements are sometimes found in the more personal forms of nonfiction. *Cp.* **fiction**.

nonparametric statistics statistical methods appropriate for the analysis of data that are not assumed to be normal in distribution, as the use of Chi-square.

nonphonetic word in teaching practice, a word whose pronunciation may not be accurately predicted from its spelling. *Note*: In linguistic terms, no word is "nonphonetic" in the sense of not being pronounceable. See also **phonetic word**.

nonreader *n.* **1.** a person who is unable to read even after extensive instruction; one who fails to learn to read. **2.** one with an extremely severe reading disability. **3.** an illiterate. **4.** one who knows how to read but chooses not to; an aliterate.

nonrestrictive clause a dependent clause that adds descriptive detail to a noun without limiting or specifying its meaning, as *who likes baseball* in *Charlie, who likes baseball, is a good batter. Note*: In English, a nonrestrictive clause is often set off by commas. *Cp.* **relative clause**; **restrictive clause**.

nonsense syllable a pronounceable combination of graphic characters, usually trigrams, that do not make a word, as *kak, vor, mek* pronounced as English spellings. *Note*: Nonsense syllables are sometimes used in reading to test phonics knowledge and in spelling to test for desired syllabic patterns while avoiding known words.

nonsense verse a form of light verse that defies meaning either by using invented words or by misusing meaningful words in otherwise acceptable grammatical sequences, as in Lewis Carroll's *Jabberwocky*.

nonspontaneous concept in Vygotsky's (1978) theory of cognitive development, a later stage in concept development in which the concept is consciously separated from the object to which it refers. *Cp.* **spontaneous concept**.

nonstandard dialect **1.** a social or regionally limited variety of a standard dialect, as Cockney English. *Note*: Nonstandard dialect is recognized more often in literature than in grammars and dictionaries. They "are not degenerate ver-

sions of a standard dialect; they are not an accumulation of mistakes; they are neither deficient forms nor imperfect copies of the standard dialects. Nonstandard dialects are as highly structured, logical, systematic, and adequate for communication as standard dialect" (Hess, 1974). **2.** a language variety spoken by members of a less powerful or prestigious social group than that using standard dialect. See also **dialect**. *Cp.* **prestige dialect**; **sociolect**.

nonstandard English any variety of English that differs from that used in most textbooks and governmental and media publications, and from the regionally standard varieties of English spoken by members of groups with social, economic, and political power. See also **nonstandard dialect**. *Cp.* **standard language**.

nonverbal *adj.* **1.** non-language, as *noise*. **2.** with little or no use of language. **3.** without skill in language use.

nonverbal ability the ability to understand nonlanguage mental tasks, often tested through representations of pictures or objects, as those used in the nonlanguage portion of the Wechsler Intelligence Scale.

nonverbal communication communication by means other than speech or writing, as by facial expressions, posture, gesture. See also **kinesics** (def. 1); **paralanguage**.

nonverbal IQ the IQ score for non–language-based tasks, as on the Wechsler Intelligence Scale. See also **intelligence quotient**. *Cp.* **verbal IQ**.

nonverbal test a test that requires a response to pictures or objects rather than to words; nonlanguage test. *Cp.* **verbal test**.

noodlehead story a type of story in folk literature in which a foolish character does absurd things, often the right thing at the wrong time; numbskull story.

norm *n.* **1.** usual or average performance. **2.** *pl.*, a range of scores or values that represents an average or a central tendency in a distribution. **3.** a standard, model, or pattern of behavior based on average performance.

normal *adj.* **1.** close to the average. **2.** within the average range. **3.** referring to a range of scores that approximates a random distribution. See **normal frequency distribution**. *Ant.* **abnormal**.

normal (frequency) curve a graphic representation of the normal frequency distribution; bell curve. See also **normal frequency distribution**.

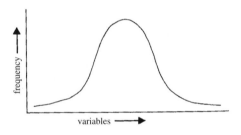

Normal frequency curve

normal frequency distribution the theoretical probability distribution of an infinite, continuous series of values represented by a bell-shaped curve in which the conditions for mean, median, and mode are the same. *Note*: A normal frequency distribution is probable when there are a large number of factors, each contributing a small amount to the variation in scores.

normal hearing the perception of sound within usual expectations of clarity and loudness; specifically, according to commonly accepted standards in audiometric testing, a hearing loss no greater than 25 dB in the 500 Hz–8 kHz range.

normal school a school originating in the 19th century in Europe and the United States for training primary or elementary teachers, originally in a two-year curriculum.

normative *adj.* **1.** referring to norms as standards or values, as *ain't* is a normative usage in some speech communities. **2.** tending to set up a norm, especially by rules.

norming population the group of subjects used to establish test norms or levels of performance by various subgroups.

norm-referenced measurement the assessment of performance in relation to that of the norming group used in the standardization of a test or in relation to locally developed norms. *Cp.* **criterion-referenced measurement**.

notation *n.* **1.** the process or result of representing speech sounds by graphic symbols, as *phonemic notation*, *phonetic notation*. See also **phonemic transcription** (def. 1). **2.** any system of specialized symbols, as those used in phonetics or in music. *adj.* **notational**.

notemaking *n.* the act of writing down reactions, queries, references, etc., in the course of one's reading or listening. *Cp.* **notetaking**.

notetaking *n.* the study skill of outlining or summarizing the important ideas of a lecture, book, or other source of information to aid in the organization and retention of ideas. *Cp.* **notemaking**.

noun *n.* **1.** in traditional grammar, a part of speech that names or denotes persons, places, things, qualities, or acts. **2.** in linguistic analysis, a word with specified grammatical properties: **a.** the subject or object of a verb, as *books* in *Teresa reads books*. **b.** the object complement of a preposition modified by an adjective, as *book* in *in an easy book*. **c.** a word modified by a determiner, as *the book*. See also **nominal** (def. 1); **nominalization**.

Types of *Noun**
abstract
animate
collective
common
compound
concrete
count
inanimate
mass
proper
venereal

---

*Terms are all defined in this dictionary.

---

noun marker a part of speech, as an article or adjective, that identifies or accompanies a noun in a phrase, clause, etc., as *the* in *the library* or *humorous* in *Hans likes humorous poetry*.

noun phrase (NP) in transformational-generative grammar, a construction headed by a noun plus all of its modifiers and articles, as *The tall man* in *The tall man was a suspect*. *Cp.* **head**; **verb phrase** (def. 2).

novel *n.* **1.** an extended fictional prose narrative that allows the author to provide fuller character and plot development than in the short story. **2.** the class of such narratives. *Cp.* **novella**; **short story**.

novelization *n.* a novel based on a screenplay of a motion picture.

novella *n.* **1.** a fictional prose narrative, midway in length between a short story and a novel. **2.** a short novel. *Cp.* **novel**; **short story**.

nucleus *n., pl.* **-clei 1.** See **syllable**. **2.** in phonetics, the most prominent part of a syllable. **3.** a group of nerve cells in the central nervous system. **4.** that central point of a cell containing genetic material or DNA. *adj.* **nuclear**.

null hypothesis a formal statement that no differences exist between variables or samples. *Note*: Rather than the positive assertion that differences will be found, the null hypothesis is usually used in experimentation. The reason for this is that the finding of any significant difference permits the rejection of the null hypothesis, but the finding of a significant difference does not necessarily allow the acceptance of the truth of the positive statement.

number *n.* a grammatical category in which nouns, pronouns, determiners, and verbs are analyzed in terms of their singular, dual, or plural forms. *Cp.* **collective noun**; **mass noun**.

numeracy *n.* fluency in mathematical operations. *Cp.* **literacy**; **oracy**.

nursery rhyme folk verse for very young children, as *Hey, diddle, diddle! / The cat and the fiddle, / The cow jumped over the moon; / The little dog laughed / To see such sport, / And the dish ran away with the spoon*.

nursery school 1. in the United States, a prekindergarten school. See **preschool** (def. 2) **2.** (*Brit.*) a school for children below compulsory school age.

object *n.* **1.** a noun, noun phrase, clause, or pronoun that is affected directly or indirectly by the action of a transitive verb in a sentence or is related by a preposition to some other unit in a sentence. See also **direct object**; **indirect object**. *Cp.* **subject** (def. 3). **2.** in psychology, anything, animate or inanimate, of which a person is aware, has an attitude toward, or responds to. **3.** in semiotics, that which a sign represents; anything that is designated by a sign. *Cp.* **interpretant**; **sign** (def. 6).

object complement the second of two elements in a complement, as *president* in *They elected him president*, *white* in *Bill painted the fence white*, or *to stop* in *They ordered Phyllis to stop*. See also **complement** (def. 1).

objective case **1.** the case of a noun or pronoun that is the direct object of a transitive verb or of a prepositional phrase, as *me* in *She thanked me* and *Give the book to me*. See also **direct object**; **indirect object**; **object** (def. 1). **2.** in case grammar, a noun that is affected by the semantic action of a verb, as *window* in *He broke the window*. **3.** in government/binding theory, any noun phrase governed or controlled by a transitive verb.

objective test a test with high degree of scoring objectivity, as a multiple-choice test. *Cp.* **essay examination**.

objectivity *n.* in testing, "the extent of agreement found when qualified persons score the performance, whether they are dealing with the behavior directly or are dealing with a written record" (Cronbach, 1970).

object language a language that is being described or analyzed. *Note*: In writing, object language is distinguished from metalanguage by typographical means, such as quotation marks or italics. *Cp.* **metalanguage**.

object method in teaching, the use of familiar objects and other materials to establish a perceptual base for presenting concepts. *Note*: Although traditionally associated with Johann Heinrich Pestalozzi (1746–1827), the Swiss educator whose work was familiar to American educators in the 1820s, the object method was not popularized in the U.S. until the 1860s. "This method probably influenced such innovations in reading as the introduction of the word method, the appearance of many pictures in primary readers, and the inclusion of material dealing with objects and experiences familiar to children" (Smith, 1965). *Cp.* **Montessori method**.

object permanence in Piagetian theory, the understanding, usually acquired about age two, that an object exists separate from and independent of the self; i.e., objects are understood to exist independently of their being perceived.

oblique case a case other than the nominative or vocative.

observed response in miscue analysis, the actual oral reading of a text.

occluder *n.* an object placed in front of an eye to block vision or break fusion, often used in visual testing. *v.* **occlude**.

ocular mobility the ease, coordination, and accuracy of eye movements as in following a target, shifting fixations, or making saccades in reading. Also **ocular motility**.

oddity task in studies of phonological awareness, a procedure in which children are asked to identify the discrepant member of a trio of words based on their onset and rime characteristics, as *car* is the odd word among *car*, *duck*, *dog*, and *mail* is odd among *mop*, *mail*, *pop*. See also **onset**; **phonological awareness**; **rime**[2].

ode *n.* an elaborate, formal, and dignified lyrical poem, as John Keats's *Ode on a Grecian Urn*; originally, a Greek verse intended to be sung.

official language a language approved by a government of a country as a medium of communication; especially in the conduct of governmental affairs, business, and schooling, as Hindi and English in India. *Cp.* **national language**.

ogham an ancient alphabetic writing system used by the Celts in the British Isles, with characters made of lines and notches carved into the edges of stones or blocks of wood. Also **ogam**. *Cp.* **rune** (def. 1).

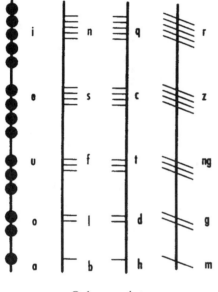

Ogham script

omission *n.* the leaving out of one or more words in the oral reading of text; one of several types of oral reading errors commonly recorded in testing oral reading. See also **insertion** (def. 1); **mispronunciation**; **substitution** (def. 2). *v.* **omit**.

on-demand assessment appraisal of learning, the timing of which is determined by the teacher or administrator rather than being conducted as an integrated, ongoing part of the instructional process.

one-to-one correspondence 1. any relationship in which every member of one set is matched exactly to one different member of a second set. **2.** in an alphabetic writing system, the representation of each phoneme of oral language by one and only one unique grapheme, and vice versa. *Note*: One-to-one correspondence is the chief goal of spelling reform in English. *Cp.* **heterography**.

onomastics *n., pl. (with sing. v.)* the study of the forms and uses of proper names, especially those that name persons. *Cp.* **toponymy**.

onomatopoeia *n.* **1.** the use of words the sound of which suggests their meaning, as *buzz* and *purr*. **2.** a poetic device to produce this effect. *adj.* **onomatopoetic**.

onset *n.* that part of a syllable preceding the syllable peak or nucleus; normally, the consonants preceding the vowel of a syllable, as *str* in *strip. Cp.* **rime**[2].

open class 1. a grammatical class of words to which, in principle, new words can be added without limit to a language, as nouns, verbs, adjectives, adverbs. *Cp.* **closed class**. **2.** in early language acquisition, a grammatical class of words whose members can be used alone or before or after another word in a two-word sentence; as *Daddy* in *Daddy, bye-bye* or *Bye-bye, Daddy. Note*: Open class and pivot class are syntactic concepts introduced in Braine's (1963) *Pivot Grammar*. They have been criticized by some psycholinguists as insufficient to explain children's language knowledge. Contemporary analyses of early language acquisition, such as grammatical development, are now generally given a rich interpretation within the contexts of their use. *Cp.* **pivot class**.

open classroom 1. a classroom, often large and flexibly arranged, that may be divided for instruction into several centers differing in purpose, size, and content. **2.** any decentralized classroom arrangement. **3.** a style of teaching that takes into account curriculum integration, flexible use of space and group size, varieties of learning materials, and student choice of activities.

open-class word a word with a lexical meaning; content word; as *book, house, television. Cp.* **function word.**

open-ended question **1.** a type of question used to explore a person's understanding of what is read or heard and intended to produce a free response rather than a directed one, as *What does the ending of this story suggest to you?* **2.** a question that encourages divergent rather than convergent thinking.

open school **1.** a school with such features as a student-centered curriculum, individualized learning, and flexible grouping. **2.** a school in which classrooms are flexible in size and shape.

open syllable a syllable ending in a vowel sound rather than a consonant sound, as /bā/ and /bē/ in *baby. Cp.* **closed syllable.**

open vowel **1.** a vowel sound made with relatively open lips and jaw and with the tongue away from the palate, as /a/ in *hat* or /o/ in *hot*; low vowel. *Cp.* **close vowel;** **lax** (def. 1). **2.** a vowel sound that is a syllable by itself, as /ā/ in *able*, or is the final sound of a syllable, as /ā/ in *table*.

operational correspondence in Piagetian theory, a relationship that is learned, recalled, and used as a concept. *Cp.* **intuitive correspondence.**

operational definition the act or result of defining a term by showing how it functions or is considered to function, as in defining *reading* as *what a reading test measures.*

operations *n. pl.* in Piagetian theory, internalized actions or thought processes that are reversible and involve some conservation and invariances. *Note*: For Piaget, no operation exists alone; each is related to a system of operations or to a total logical structure. See also **concrete operations; formal operations; infralogical operations; preoperational thought.** *adj.* **operational.**

operativity *n.* in Piagetian theory, the active, generalizable, and structuring aspect of intelligence. *Note*: Operativity implies the ability to construct mentally, transform, incorporate, and logically manipulate ideas. *Cp.* **figurative knowledge.**

ophthalmograph *n.* an early type of eye-movement camera for photographing corneal reflections.

ophthalmology *n.* the branch of medicine having to do with the structure, function, and diseases of the eye; specifically, its diagnosis, medication, surgery, and correction, including the prescription of glasses. *Cp.* **optometry.**

ophthalmoscope *n.* an instrument with adjustable lenses used to inspect closely much of the interior of the eyeball.

opposition *n.* **1.** a phonological difference that permits discrimination of sound, as /b/ and /p/ in *bat* and *pat*. **2.** a grammatical difference that permits discrimination of tense, number, etc., as *present tense* vs. *past tense*. **3.** a semantic difference that represents a paired contrast in meaning, as *big* vs. *small*. Also **contrast.** *v.* **oppose.** *adj.* **opposite.**

optic chiasma *n., pl.* **-mas, -mata** the crossing point at which the optic nerve of each eye joins the other and then separates to form the optic tract, the nasal fibers of each nerve crossing to the opposite side, the temporal fibers remaining on the same side.

optic nerve one of two nerves that carry information from the retina through the optic chiasma to the visual sensory cortex. See also **blind spot**.

optometry *n.* the professional field of the eye specialist whose practice includes examining refractive and other defects of the eye, as well as diagnosing eye diseases, prescribing glasses, and conducting visual therapy programs. *Cp.* **ophthalmology**. *adj.* **optometric**.

oracy *n.* fluency in speaking and listening; oral literacy. *Cp.* **literacy**; **numeracy**; **orality**.

oral 1. *adj.* referring to spoken utterances or to speaking. 2. *adj.* referring to the mouth or oral cavity. 3. *n.* a speech sound made when all the air flow passes through the mouth and none through the nose. *Cp.* **nasal** (def. 2). 4. *adj.* in psychoanalytic theory, referring to the first stage of psychosexual development and its accompanying behaviors and results. *adv.* **orally**.

oral culture 1. a culture whose values, attitudes, and beliefs are transmitted through oral language, as most North American Indian cultures in the 19th century. 2. a culture that values the ability to speak effectively more than the ability to read and write. *Cp.* **literary culture**.

oralism *n.* the philosophy and methods of education for deaf students that stress speech communication, speechreading, and amplification of sound while excluding signing; oral-aural method; oral method. *Cp.* **manual method**; **total communication**.

orality *n.* 1. the spoken language of "an oral culture untouched by writing" (Ong, 1982). 2. the quality of being spoken rather than written, as in an oral tradition or in communication by radio, telephone, etc. *Cp.* **oracy**.

oral reading 1. the process of reading aloud to communicate to another or to an audience. *Note*: Historically, written or printed text was intended to be read orally. Today, in many countries, oral reading is emphasized in beginning reading instruction to help link printed text to speech. 2. the act of oral interpretation, as giving a dramatic reading. See also **read**; **reading**.

oral reading test an individually administered test or inventory for assessing oral reading behaviors, performance, or competence. *Note*: Standardized and informal oral reading tests are usually scored on the basis of word-recognition errors (e.g., mispronunciations, omissions), comprehension, and perhaps reading rate. What constitutes a word recognition error, how comprehension is checked, and what criteria are used to determine adequate word recognition and comprehension vary from test to test. The reader's fluency, task involvement, etc., also may be noted by the examiner. See also **informal reading inventory**; **miscue**; **miscue analysis**.

oral tradition stories, histories, etc., kept alive by the spoken word rather than writing. *Note*: While an oral tradition is characteristic of an oral culture, it may coexist in a writing culture.

oration *n.* a formal public speech, as Abraham Lincoln's Gettysburg Address.

oratory *n.* the art or skill of public speaking.

Orbis Pictus any of various editions and translations of the *Orbis Sensualium Pictus*, the first significant schoolbook with pictures, first published in 1658. *Note*: The Orbis Pictus aimed to present to children the nomenclature for "all the chief things that are in the world." The numbered pictures were identified by numbered words, in parallel columns of Latin and English. An immediate success, its popularity declined in the 18th century. It has often been cited, erroneously, as the first book to advocate the word method of teaching reading.

ordinal scale a scale in which numbers are assigned to a class according to rank order, as in ranking those who finish a contest 1, 2, 3. *Note*: Intervals on an ordinal scale are not assumed to be equal.

orismology 1. the study or practice of defining technical terms. 2. **orismologist**, one who studies or practices orismology, as *T.L. Harris* of *The Literacy Dictionary*. *adj.* **orismologic**.

orthoepy *n.* 1. the study of correct pronunciation; "the art of just pronunciation" (Webster, 1806). 2. accepted or customary pronunciation.

orthogonal *adj.* 1. right angled; perpendicular. 2. statistically independent.

orthographic transcription 1. the representation of language by a standard spelling system. 2. the recording of language by the use of a system of letters. *Cp.* **transcription** (defs. 1, 2). 3. See **orthography** (def. 3).

orthography *n.* 1. the study of the nature and use of symbols in a writing system. *Cp.* **graphemics**. 2. correct or standardized spelling according to established usage in a given language. *Cp.* **cacography** (def. 2). 3. a conventional writing system in a given language. *Cp.* **script** (def. 1); **writing system**. *adj.* **orthographic**.

orthoptics *n. (usually sing.)* the improvement of various visual conditions, such as binocular vision and visual perception, through specialized vision therapy programs; visual training; optometric training. *adj.* **orthoptic**.

ostensive definition a definition of a term made by indicating an example to which the term can be applied.

otitis media an inflammation of the middle ear. *Note*: The inflammation and the fluid it causes temporarily reduce hearing acuity. Chronic otitis media may be one source of reading disability since it occurs most commonly in children at the critical age for making phonemic discriminations and for learning how to process spoken language.

outcome-based education an educational program that relies on performance assessment to determine its effectiveness.

outline 1. *n.* a short verbal sketch that shows in skeleton form the pattern of ideas in text or in a draft prepared for speaking or writing, often with main and subideas highlighted by numbers and letters. 2. *n.* a summary or synopsis. 3. *v.* to prepare an outline. 4. *n.* a graphic line, often without shading, that shows the shape of a figure or object.

out-of-level testing a procedure whereby pupils are given a test at a level determined by their estimated present level of performance rather than by their grade level.

outreach literacy program an alternative literacy program offered in a location that makes it easier for members of the community to attend and encourages attendance of those who tend to resist institutional education.

overextension *n.* in the early acquisition of words and their meanings, the application of a word to include other objects that share common features, as *dog* used to include other animals, *wawa* to include liquids other than water, etc.; overgeneralization; overregularization. *Cp.* **hypercorrection**; **underextension**.

overtone *n.* 1. an additional inferred meaning; connotation. 2. that part of a sound that is higher in frequency than its lowest, or fundamental, tone. *Note*: Most speech sounds have one or more overtones.

ownership *n.* in writing, the personal investment and control a writer maintains throughout the stages of writing.

oxymoron *n., pl.* **-mora** a figure of speech in which contrasting or contradictory words are brought together for emphasis, as *cruel kindness*, *living death*.

P probability.

p **1.** the proportion of a sample that has a specific characteristic. *Cp. q.* **2.** percentile. **3.** the percentage of test takers who get the right answer on a particular item.

pacer *n.* any instrument that controls the rate of reading through the use of light beams, opaque shutters, rapidly changed slides, computer screen changes, etc.; reading accelerator.

pacing *n.* **1.** using a pacer to control rate of reading in connected discourse either mechanically or manually, as by running one's fingers below and across each line of text. **2.** the rate at which material to be learned or read is presented by a teaching machine or through computer-assisted instruction. **3.** setting one's own pace in reading or learning. *Note*: By using a pacing pattern appropriate for the reading task, the reader can be helped to develop a more flexible reading rate. **4.** adjusting the rate at which instruction and instructional materials are provided in order to accommodate differences in learning behavior.

pacing patterns hand movements used to direct the eyes during reading.

paired-associates method an experimental procedure for measuring learning rate and retention of either words or nonsense syllables by using sets of stimuli that are matched with specified responses, as *page—book, ZOC—BAX*.

palatal *n.* referring to a speech sound, usually a consonant, made by touching or nearly touching the hard palate with the tongue, as /ch/ in *chart*, /sh/ in *shoe*, /y/ in *yet*. *n.* **palatization**. *adj.* **palatized**.

paleography *n.* the study of the development and deciphering of ancient writing systems, as found in manuscripts, including their origin and dates. See also **philology**. *Cp.* **epigraphy**. *adj.* **paleographic**.

palindrome *n.* a word, phrase, or number with the same sequence of letters or numbers whether read from right to left or from left to right, as *Anna*; *Madam, I'm Adam*; *1771. Cp.* **anagram**.

panegyric *n.* **1.** a formal statement in praise of someone either living or dead. **2.** overpraise.

paper-hole test an informal test of eyedness in which the subject is asked to sight a distant target through a small opening in a sheet of paper or index card to determine the dominant or preferred eye by noting which eye is used to see the target. *Cp.* **pointing test**.

parable *n.* a simple, rather short story intended to teach a moral lesson; allegorical tale.

paradigm *n.* **1.** a pattern or example intended as a model. See also **model** (def. 3). **2.** in grammar, a set of all the inflected forms of a word, as *read, reader, reader's, readers, readers', reads, reading*.

paradigmatic *adj.* referring to the set of linguistic units that may occupy the same place in a phrase or sentence, as *Francisca reads /widely/, /quickly/, /detective stories/. Cp.* **syntagmatic**.

paradox *n.* **1.** an apparently contradictory statement that suggests a truth, as *Life is but a dream.* **2.** a self-contradictory, illogical statement, as *Include me out* (attributed to Samuel Goldwyn). *adj.* **paradoxical**.

paragraph meaning the content or significance of a paragraph.

paralanguage *n.* voice variations that accompany speech and affect meaning, as voice tone, whispering, giggling, etc. *Note*: In some analyses of paralanguage, gestures, facial expressions, etc., are also included. See also **extralinguistic**; **kinesics** (def. 1); **nonverbal communication**.

paralinguistics *n.* the study of language-associated human behavior, as voice pitch, loudness, or duration, as well as body movements. *Cp.* **paralanguage**.

parallelism *n.* the phrasing of language so as to balance ideas of equal importance; parallel construction; as *"Now if a thousand perfect men were to appear it would not amaze me, / Now if a thousand beautiful forms of women appear'd it would not astonish me"* (Walt Whitman, "Song of the Open Road," *Leaves of Grass*). *Note*: Parallelism may apply to phrases, sentences, paragraphs, or longer passages or whole selections.

parallel processing in the retrieval of information in memory, "the simultaneous transformation of several different cognitive codes" (Best, 1989). *Note*: Evidence of parallel processing in memory retrieval is at odds with an earlier belief that retrieval involved only a single cognitive code.

parallel repetition the repetition of the same words or phrases, especially in or between the stanzas of a poem, as the repeated refrain in some popular ballads. *Cp.* **incremental repetition**.

parameter *n.* **1.** a fixed criterion, limit, or standard used in making judgments. **2.** any statistical value derived from a set of scores, as a mean, believed or designed to estimate a property of a population. **3.** a variable represented by an arbitrary constant in a mathematical formula. **4.** any technique in psychoanalytic therapy other than interpretation. *adj.* **parametric**.

paraphrase *n.* the act or result of restating the meaning of something spoken or written in another form. *v.* **paraphrase**. *adj.* **paraphrastic**.

paraprofessional **1.** *n.* in education, a person trained to assist a professional teacher; aide; parapro. **2.** *adj.* referring to paraprofessionals or to their work.

parenthesis *n., pl.* **-theses 1.** a qualifying or explanatory word or phrase inserted within and set off from some written text, as *a friend of mine* in *John Brown, a friend of mine, won the lottery. Cp.* **appositive**. **2.** an orthographic symbol (( )) used to enclose inessential or tangential words in text. *adj.* **parenthetical**.

parlance *n.* **1.** a particular way of speaking; jargon; vernacular. **2.** formal speech or discussion. **3.** conversation; talk (def. 2).

parody **1.** *n.* a work, often humorous, that imitates another, usually serious, work by burlesque or satire, as Lewis Carroll's *Father William*. **2.** *n.* this class of writing. **3.** *v.* to imitate the work of another by satirizing it.

parole *n.* in de Saussure's (1916) description of living languages, what an individual speaker of a language actually says and writes. See also **performance** (def. 5). *Cp.* **langue**.

parsing *n.* the process of analyzing sentences by grammatical labels as subject, predicate, object, etc. *Note*: Parsing was a common instructional practice in 19th-century schools. *Cp.* **diagramming**. *v.* **parse**.

partial correlation the relationship between two variables when the influence of other variables on the relationship is controlled.

participial phrase a group of words containing a participle. See also **participle**.

participle *n.* a verbal form used as an adjective, as *writing* in the participial phrase *the writing assignment*. See also **participial phrase**. *Cp.* **gerund**; **verbal** (def. 4). *adj.* **participial**.

particle *n.* **1.** an affix. **2.** a word that does not readily fit into a grammatical classification and has functional or relational use, as *to* in English infinitives such as *to read*.

part of speech any of the grammatical classes into which words have traditionally been categorized, as noun, pronoun, verb, adjective, adverb, preposition, conjunction, and interjection. *Note*: Linguists commonly designate these parts of speech as word classes or form classes because of the inexplicit and restricted nature of their traditional definitions.

pasigraphy *n.* **1.** a writing system consisting of signs that represent ideas rather than sound sequences and are interpretable to speakers of any language, as the Arabic numerals 1, 2, 3, etc. *Cp.* **ideography** (def. 1). **2.** an artificial international written language, as Esperanto; international language. *Cp.* **artificial language** (def. 1). *adj.* **pasigraphic**.

pastoral **1.** *n.* a poem dealing with shepherds and rural life, often idealized. See also **idyll** (def. 1). **2.** *adj.* "putting the complex into the simple" (Empson, 1935). *Note*: This use of the term is found in modern literary criticism and is applied to such works as Lewis Carroll's *Alices Adventures in Wonderland* and George Orwell's *Animal Farm*.

path analysis a form of multiple regression analysis intended to identify the variability of an outcome attributable to a specific factor.

pathetic fallacy in literary criticism, the act of giving nature or inanimate objects human characteristics and feelings; especially, emotional descriptions of nature by poets. *Cp.* **affective fallacy**; **intentional fallacy**.

pathos *n.* the quality in literature and other arts that calls forth pity or sorrow in the reader or viewer.

patois *n.* **1.** a regional or social variety of a language, usually without a literary tradition. See also **dialect**; **regional dialect**; **sociolect**. **2.** a mixture of two or more languages. See also **creole**. **3.** jargon; cant.

patter **1.** *n.* rapid, glib speech. **2.** *v.* to speak in this manner; chatter. **3.** *n.* speech of a group, as jargon or cant. **4.** *n.* the stylized speech of auctioneers, etc. *Note*: The term *patter* evolved from *paternoster*, the rapid, mechanical recitation of prayers, and was first applied to chapmen, the itinerant hawkers of cheap books.

pattern **1.** *n.* in linguistics, a set of predictable and describable relations between elements of language, as phonology, word order, or affixation. **2.** *v.* to so identify such relations. **3.** *v.* to arrange in a particular configuration.

pattern analysis **1.** a cluster analysis of test items to determine whether items clustered on the basis of theory or heuristic judgments belong together. **2.** a profile analysis of test scores to determine patterns of profiles that have different degrees of effectiveness in predicting the independent criterion.

pattern book a book with a predictable plot structure and often written in predictable text; predictable book; predictable text. *Cp.* **formula story**.

pattern recognition the perception of ordered stimuli, as a sequence of ideas, a repeated design, a rhythmic beat in music.

pause **1.** *n.* in speech and oral reading, a slight interruption of the voice, as in phrasing, to emphasize meaning or to stress a grammatical relationship. See also **juncture**. **2.** *v.* to make such an interruption of the voice.

pedagese *n.* the complex, abstruse language found in some writing and speaking in the field of education. *Cp.* **jargon**.

pedagogical content knowledge in teacher evaluation, the teacher's ability to describe how to represent subject matter for instructional purposes.

pedagogy of reading the study of the teaching of reading; specifically, an examination of the materials, methods, and problems involved in learning to read and in improving existing reading abilities. *Note*: The pedagogy of reading includes such diverse fields as the history and status of reading, comparative reading, teacher education in reading, literary appreciation, the reading curriculum, and developmental, corrective, and remedial reading.

peephole method an informal technique for directly observing a reader's eye movements by making a small hole in the center of a page of text, then peering through the hole to estimate roughly the number of fixations per line made by the reader. See also **eye-movement pattern**.

peer response in writing, a form of collaborative learning in which students informally discuss, often in small groups, the results of their efforts, the problems they encountered, etc.

penmanship *n.* **1.** the art of handwriting. **2.** a person's style or manner of handwriting.

percentile **1.** *n.* any one of the score points dividing a score distribution into parts each of which contain $\frac{1}{100}$ of the scores. *The 75th percentile is a score that is equal to or better than 75 percent of the scores. Cp.* **centile**; **decile**. **2.** *adj.* referring to such a value.

percept *n.* **1.** the object of perception. **2.** a mental impression of something perceived by one or more senses. *Note*: Some psychologists reject the notion of *percept* in this sense on the ground that perception is a process limited to the processing of sensory stimuli. See **perception**.

perception *n.* **1.** the extraction of information from sensory stimulation. *Note*: Perception is an active, selective process, influenced by a person's attitude and prior experience. In all forms of communication, perception is the crucial link between incoming stimuli and a response that is meaningful. *Cp.* **cognition**. **2.** the result of perceptual processing; comprehension; understanding. **3.** the direct, intuitive recognition of truth, beauty, value, etc., especially in moral or artistic judgments; insight. *Note*: Special types of perception, as *auditory perception*, are defined under the describing terms. *v.* **perceive**. *adj.* **perceptual**.

perceptual analysis the differentiation of a perceptual field into separable component parts, as in identifying correct letter order in a word.

perceptual constancy the tendency for perceived properties of things to remain the same under changing conditions, as in perceiving the size and shape of a chair as constant regardless of the angle from which the chair is viewed. *Cp.* **shape constancy**; **size constancy**.

perceptually handicapped **1.** *n.* a person or group with faulty functioning in one or more aspect of sensory, integrative, expressive, or social perception. **2.** *adj.* referring to such a person or group.

perceptual-motor learning learning characterized by change in overt motor responses that are activated and guided primarily by nonverbal rather than verbal stimuli, as handwriting, typewriting, etc. *Note*: In perceptual-motor learning, someone may give information about the task, but it is mainly learned by matching motor output with perceptual input.

performance *n.* **1.** task-directed activity. **2.** the result of such activity. **3.** entertainment, often dramatic or musical. **4.** the act or manner of providing entertainment. **5.** the "actual use of language in real life" (Chomsky, 1957). *Note*: A speech act may not reflect the speaker's underlying knowledge of or competence in language because of speech errors, distortion of the speech signal, emotional states, and other psychological or environmental circumstances. *Cp.* **competence**.

performance assessment the measurement of educational achievement by tasks that call for the student to produce a response like that required in the instructional environment, as in portfolios or projects; performance-based assessment. *Note*: *Performance assessment* is now commonly used rather than *performance test* to represent a broader domain of achievement. *Cp.* **performance test**.

performance standard **1.** an absolute or relative criterion level for judging the attainment of specified objectives. *Note*: Many reading programs with behavioral objectives use a performance standard of 80–85 percent. **2.** a performance level stated in terms of specific criteria to be achieved, as the mastery of specific handwriting strokes.

performance test **1.** a test composed of tasks that call for nonverbal responses, as the object assembly test in the Wechsler Intelligence Scale. **2.** any test that calls for responses that are an actual sample of work on the activity being measured. *Cp.* **performance assessment**.

perimacular vision vision involving the central area of the retina, including and surrounding the macula; paracentral vision.

peripheral **1.** *adj.* outer. **2.** *adj.* superficial rather than essential. **3.** *adj.* away from the center, especially of the body; external. **4.** *adj.* referring to nerves and nerve ends furthest from the brain and spinal cord. **5.** *n.* any device connected externally to a computer, as a keyboard. *n.* **periphery**.

peripheral field the outer visual field of the retina surrounding the macula or perimacular area.

peripheral vision vision by the stimulation of the peripheral field of the retina, largely in shades of gray and most effective in low light conditions; indirect vision. *Note*: "Word forms indistinctly seen in peripheral vision begin the perceptual process much in advance of direct vision" (Tinker, 1965). *Cp.* **foveal vision** (def. 1).

periphrasis *n.* **1.** circumlocution. **2.** the use of an auxiliary word to indicate a grammatical function or relation rather than the use of an inflected form, as *did* in *her mother did know* for *her mother knew*. *adj.* **periphrastic**.

perlocutionary act the result or effect caused by a speech act, as the listener's response to a command or request made by a speaker. See also **speech act**. *Cp.* **illocutionary act**; **locutionary act**.

perseveration *n.* **1.** the tendency to repeat behavior no longer useful or appropriate or to fail to adapt to change. **2.** stuttering that continues because of failure to break away from a prior mental set. **3.** the continuing of speech habits beyond normal developmental expectancy. *v.* **perseverate**.

person *n.* in many languages, the classification of pronouns in terms of the person(s) speaking, or *first person* (I, we); the person(s) spoken to, or *second person* (you, they); and the person(s) or thing(s) spoken about, or *third person* (he, she, it, they).

personality inventory **1.** a questionnaire designated to reveal the pattern of a person's behavior. **2.** a self-report questionnaire or checklist of one's characteristics.

personal pronoun a pronoun that indicates the speaker, the person spoken to, or something spoken about, as *I, you, it, etc.* See **pronoun**. See also **person**.

personal voice in writing, the distinctive way in which the writer expresses ideas with respect to style, form, content, purpose, etc.; author's voice.

personification *n.* **1.** a metaphorical figure of speech in which animals, ideas, things, etc., are represented as having human qualities. **2.** that which a person, real or imaginary, represents. *v.* **personify**.

peruse *v.* **1.** to read carefully and critically; study. **2.** to look over leisurely and casually. *Note*: Context determines which of these contradictory meanings is intended.

petroglyph *n.* **1.** a carving or inscription on a rock. **2.** a primitive pictograph or set of pictographs cut into rock; petrograph; petrogram. *adj.* **petroglyphic**.

phatic communion a term coined by the anthropologist Bronislaw Malinowski (1923) for stereotyped expressions spoken to establish or maintain social contact rather than for informational purposes, as *Have a nice day. Cp.* **formulaic expression**.

phenomenology *n.* a philosophical and literary movement that isolates mental patterns in awareness and thought by concentrating on the way objects appear to consciousness. *Note*: Phenomenology accompanied the shift to subjective or inner experience in late 19th- and early 20th-century thought and flowered in existentialism in the 1930s and the 1940s. *Cp.* **existentialism**.

phi coefficient (ø) a measure of association between two variables, each of which is divided into two categories.

philology *n.* the study of language through historical written records to understand more fully the interaction of people, language, and the historical-cultural setting, and to clarify texts and word origins. See also **paleography**. *Cp.* **diachronic linguistics**; **etymology**. *n.* **philologist**. *adj.* **philological**.

Phoenician alphabet one of the first alphabets, developed by Phoenicians and other Semites around 1000 B.C., from which Greek, Roman, and other Western alphabets were derived.

phonation *n.* the use of vocal fold vibrations in producing voiced speech sounds; voice production. See also **voicing** (def. 1).

phone *n.* the smallest sound unit identifiable in spoken language and for which phonetic transcription is used.

phoneme *n.* a minimal sound unit of speech that, when contrasted with another phoneme, affects the meaning of words in a language, as /b/ in *book* contrasts with /t/ in *took*, /k/ in *cook*, /h/ in *hook*. *Note*: The phoneme is an abstract concept manifested in actual speech as a phonetic variant, as the allophones of the phoneme /t/ in *top, stop, pot. Cp.* **allophone** (def. 1); **phone**. *adj.* **phonemic**.

phoneme-grapheme correspondence the relationship between a phoneme and its graphemic representation(s), as /s/, spelled *s* in *sit, c* in *city, ss* in *grass. Note*: Technically, *phoneme-grapheme correspondence* refers to encoding speech into writing, not vice versa. *Cp.* **grapheme-phoneme correspondence**.

phonemic alphabet **1.** See **phonemic transcription** (def. 1). **2.** a writing system with a predominant one-to-one correspondence of phonemes with graphemes, and in which other correspondences are predictable by simple rules, as in the Turkish and Finnish alphabets.

phonemic analysis linguistic research designed to identify the number and distribution of speech sounds for a given language. See also **phoneme**.

phonemic awareness See the essay "Phonemic Awareness" on pp. 185–186.

phonemic contrast an identifiable contrast between speech sounds that may occur in words with similar shapes but different meanings, as the difference between /t/ and /d/ in *lit* and *lid*. See also **opposition**.

phonemics *n. (with sing. v.)* **1.** the pattern of relations among phonemes and between phonemes and their allophones. See also **allophone** (def. 1); **phoneme**. **2.** the study of such relations. *Cp.* **phonology** (def. 1).

phonemic transcription **1.** a writing system developed and used by linguists to record speech for later analysis that employs a different graphic symbol for each phoneme of the language being studied; phonemic notation. *Note*: In phonemic transcription, the major distinguishing speech sounds, or phonemes, are recorded rather than discrete phonetic elements. *Cp.* **notation**; **phonetic transcription** (def. 1). **2.** a text or string of words written in such a system.

phonetic **1.** *adj.* referring to the nature, production, and transcription of speech sounds. **2.** *adj.* corresponding to pronunciation. See **phonetic transcription**. **3.** *adj.* agreeing with pronunciation. See **phonetic spelling** (def. 1). **4.** *adj.* referring to the description of nondistinctive elements of a language. **5.** *n.* in Chinese orthography, an element of a character or logogram that indicates sound.

phonetic alphabet **1.** an alphabet containing a distinctive graphic character for each distinguishable speech sound, or phone, of a language, as the International Phonetic Alphabet;

phonetic writing. *Note*: Phonetic alphabets are used by phoneticians and other linguists to record speech sounds on the basis of their articulatory features. Because different languages have different articulatory features, a phonetic alphabet with a uniform symbol for each human speech sound is needed to record language differences uniformly. **2.** a writing system developed for a language in which each speech sound is represented by its own distinctive letter or other graphic symbol. *Note*: Such an alphabet is more properly called a *phonemic alphabet* since a writing system with symbols to record every distinguishable sound would be unwieldy and inefficient. See also **one-to-one correspondence** (def. 2); **phoneme**. *Cp.* **phonemic alphabet** (def. 2).

phonetic analysis **1.** in teaching practice, a misnomer for phonic analysis. **2.** in linguistics, the classifying and recording of individual speech sounds, or phones.

phonetic boundary in speech discrimination, that point at which the perception of one phoneme from another abruptly changes, thus enabling the listener to hear the difference between the two phonemes; juncture.

phonetic-cue reading in beginning reading development, the use of rudimentary phonological cues from printed words, as /d/ in *dog*, or letter names, as /bē/ in *book* (Ehri, 1990). *Cp.* **cipher sight-word reading**; **visual cue reading**.

phonetics the study of speech sounds, generally conducted within one of three branches of investigation: acoustic phonetics, articulatory phonetics, and auditory phonetics. (See these terms.) See also **phonology**.

phonetic spelling **1.** the respelling of entry words in a dictionary or glossary according to a pronunciation key that shows the sounds represented by letters, as *read* (rēd), *read* (rĕd). **2.** the

Phonemic Awareness

Phonemic awareness is the awareness of the sounds (phonemes) that make up spoken words. Such awareness does not appear when young children learn to talk; the ability is not necessary for speaking and understanding spoken language. However, phonemic awareness is important for learning to read. In alphabetic languages, letters (and letter clusters) represent phonemes, and in order to learn the correspondences between letters and sounds, one must have some understanding of the notion that words are made up of phonemes. This insight is not always easily achieved. Phonemes are abstract units, and when one pronounces a word one does not produce a series of discrete phonemes; rather, phonemes are folded into one another and are pronounced as a blend. Although most young children have no difficulty segmenting words into syllables, many find it very difficult to segment at the phoneme level. Indeed, both illiterate adults and adults who are literate in a language like Chinese, whose orthography does not represent phonemes with letters, also find segmenting words into phonemes difficult.

Work in the 1960s by Elkonin (1963) suggested that training in phonemic analysis would be a useful precursor to beginning reading instruction. Since that time, a substantial body of literature has provided evidence of the importance of phonemic awareness. First, correlational studies established that there was a strong relationship between phonemic awareness and reading performance in first and second grades and that phonemic awareness tests in kindergarten predicted later reading skill in the first and second grades. In fact, the phonemic awareness of young prereaders was found to predict success in beginning reading better than did such measures as age, socioeconomic status, and IQ.

The results of these concurrent and predictive correlational studies encouraged the initiation of training studies. Early studies of this type revealed success when phonemic training was incorporated into comprehensive decoding programs. Later studies attempted to isolate the effects of phonemic awareness training per se. It appears that such training does facilitate reading achievement, and spelling, in the early school grades.

How is phonemic awareness measured? Studies have used a variety of tasks ranging from the very simple one of asking students whether two words rhyme, through sound-to-word matching and blending, to more challenging tasks such as isolating individual phonemes, segmenting a word into all its component phonemes, and deleting phonemes ("Say *bird* without the *b*"). One important challenge for the future is for researchers to agree on what measures might be most appropriate for defining the construct, for while it seems justifiable to consider phonemic awareness a *cause* of reading acquisition, it may also be a *consequence* of reading acquisition. Some of the more difficult abilities subsumed under the general label "phonemic awareness" seem to develop only after instruction in word recognition has taken place. A sorting out of these relationships would help the design of instructional programs.

In the classroom, teachers can help children acquire phonemic awareness by providing practice in segmenting spoken words via games based on some of the tasks used to assess phonemic awareness. This is not simply phonics instruction but rather training that enhances concurrent or subsequent phonics instruction or other reading instruction. As part of this concurrent or subsequent

(continued)

Phonemic Awareness (cont'd.)

reading instruction, spelling activities, including the use of invented spellings, are also valuable. In addition, teachers can make sure that children are given literature that focuses on playing with sounds through rhyme, alliteration, and so on.

Joanna Williams

incorrect spelling of a word as though it were phonically regular, as *det* for *debt*. **3.** See **phonetic transcription**. See also **International Phonetic Alphabet**.

phonetic structure the sound patterns of a given language.

phonetic transcription 1. a system of graphic symbols for representing speech sounds or pronunciation; phonetic writing; phonetic notation. See also **International Phonetic Alphabet**. *Cp.* **phonemic transcription**. **2.** the result of such representation.

phonetic word a misnomer for a phonically regular word whose pronunciation may be accurately predicted from its spelling, as *hit* vs. *colonel*. See also **nonphonetic word** (*Note*).

phonic analysis in teaching practice, the identification of words by their sounds. *Note*: The process of phonic analysis involves the association of speech sounds with letters and the blending of these sounds into syllables and words. See also **phonics**.

phonic cue evidence in a word's spelling of the speech sound or sounds represented by a letter or group of letters. *Cp.* **phonic generalization**; **word family** (def. 1).

phonic generalization a statement or rule that indicates under which condition(s) a letter or group of letters represents a particular sound or sounds, as a silent *e* at the end of a word usually indicates that the preceding vowel sound is long, as the *a* in *fate*.

phonics *n.* a way of teaching reading and spelling that stresses symbol-sound relationships, used especially in beginning instruction.

Types of *Phonics*
analytic*
cluster*
deductive**
explicit
extrinsic*
implicit
inductive†
intrinsic*
letter*
synthetic*
whole-word*
*Term is defined in this dictionary.   **Term is defined under **analytic phonics**.   †Term is defined under **synthetic phonics**.

phonogram *n.* **1.** a graphic character or symbol that can represent a phonetic sound, phoneme, or word. *Cp.* **character** (def. 1); **grapheme**; **letter** (def. 2). **2.** in word recognition, a graphic sequence comprised of a vowel grapheme and an ending consonant grapheme, as -ed in *red, bed, fed* or -ake in *bake, cake, lake*. See also **word family** (def. 1).

phonological awareness awareness of the constituent sounds of words in learning to read and spell. *Note*: The constituents of words can be distinguished in three ways: **a.** by syllables, as /bŏŏk/. **b.** by onsets and rimes, as /b/ and /ŏŏk/. **c.** by phonemes, as /b/ and /ŏŏ/ and /k/. *Cp.* **phonemic awareness**.

phonological perception auditory perception applied to speech sounds, as in listening.

phonological rule **1.** a concise account of some aspect of the sound patterns and processes of language or a language. **2.** in generative phonology, a rule that explains how distinct features of sounds are combined and how they vary when used in speech.

phonological system a pattern of phonological elements and rules that is either constructed or hypothesized to account for speech.

phonology *n.* **1.** the study of speech sounds and their functions in a language or languages. **2.** the relation of the surface structure of a sentence to its actual physical representation. See also **generative phonology**.

phonotactics *n. (with sing. v.)* **1.** the permissible arrangements of speech sounds in forming morphemes and words. **2.** the study of such arrangements. *Cp.* **sequential constraint**. *adj.* **phonotactic**.

phonovisual method a synthetic phonics program that uses a pictured keyword for each sound.

photopic vision daylight vision; vision under conditions of bright light; specifically, vision

that relies mostly on the cones in the center of the retina for sharp color vision and for accurate visual discrimination. *Cp.* **scotopic vision**.

phrase **1.** *n.* a grammatical construction without a subject and a predicate: **a.** in traditional grammar, such a group of two or more words. **b.** in transformational-generative grammar, a noun or verb construction consisting of one or more words. See also **noun phrase**; **verb phrase**. *Cp.* **clause**. **2.** *n.* in speech, a word or group of words framed by pauses. **3.** *n.* a saying or expression. **4.** *v.* to use words in a particular way. See also **phrasing** (def. 1).

phrase marker **1.** a syntactic description of the structure of a sentence by a label in brackets or by a tree diagram of its parts. See also **tree diagram**. **2.** a preposition that marks a prepositional phrase.

phrase reading reading in which the unit of meaningful recognition is larger than a word but smaller than a sentence.

phrase-structure grammar a grammar concerned with identifying constituents of grammatical constructions and how they are related.

phrase-structure rule in transformational-generative grammar, an instruction for rewriting a phrase structure; rewrite rule; base rule; as $S \rightarrow NP + VP$ is a phrase structure rule that indicates that *S(entence)* is "rewritten" as a *N(oun) P(hrase)* and a *V(erb) P(hrase)*. See also **co-occurrence**; **expansion rule**; **terminal string**.

phrase word a brief linguistic unit that serves as a type of shorthand label, as *the cost of living, a no-win situation, the bottom line*, etc.

phrasing *n.* **1.** the way in which words are chosen and grouped in speaking or writing. **2.** reading in thought units. **3.** using slashes or extra spaces to mark thought units in material to be read, as *The man walked // into the room.* See also **phrase** (def. 2).

physical abstraction in Piaget's theory of cognitive development, the extraction of information directly from objects themselves, as color, weight, etc. *Cp.* **reflective abstraction**.

physiology of reading **1.** broadly, the study of physiological factors that affect or are affected by the reading process. **2.** specifically, the application of medical, neurological, anatomical, and physiological concepts and techniques to an examination of organic functions and dysfunctions involved in the act of reading. *Note*: The physiology of reading includes the study of vision, speech, and hearing, and may include the study of severe reading disorders, learning disabilities, and other examples of exceptionality.

picaresque *adj.* **1.** referring to an episodic novel originating in Spain, with a rascal hero whose escapades are told in realistic and often humorous detail, as in Miguel de Cervantes' *Don Quixote*. **2.** referring to any fiction dealing with rogues or adventurers.

pictograph *n.* **1.** a picture representing a word or idea, as a pointing hand used to direct the reader to a particular feature of a book; hieroglyph. **2.** one character in a pictographic writing system; pictogram. *Note*: In the view of some analysts, pictographs are directly linked to tangible objects or actions, whereas ideographs represent abstractions. *Cp.* **ideograph**; **logograph**. *adj.* **pictographic**.

pictography *n.* **1.** a graphic system in which pictures are drawn to represent objects, events, ideas, and actions directly. *Cp.* **ideography** (def. 1). **2.** the use of such a system; picture writing; pictorial writing. See also **writing system**. *Cp.* **alphabetic writing**; **hieroglyphics** (def. 1); **logography**; **logosyllabic writing**; **syllabary**.

picture book a book in which the illustrations are as important as the text, both contributing to the telling of the story. Also **picture storybook**. *Note*: Picture books are often among the first books introduced to children and are usually intended to be read *to* them.

pidgin **1.** *n.* a non-native language developed by speakers of different languages when they are placed in close social contact, as traders in the western Pacific. *Note*: A pidgin that becomes a native language is said to have become creolized. *Cp.* **creole** (def. 1). **2.** *adj.* referring to such a language.

Pidgin Sign English a signing variety that mixes American Sign Language and English language structures, reducing the grammatical complexity of either language; pidgin sign language. *Note*: Pidgin Sign English is frequently used by hearing persons to communicate with deaf persons.

pitch *n.* **1.** the rise and fall of the voice when speaking. See **tone** (def. 5); **intonation**. **2.** the perception of the tonal level of sound ranging from high to low depending on the frequency of sound waves. **3.** a standard tonal frequency with which tonal levels of sound may be compared.

pitch discrimination the ability to detect small differences in the tonal level of sounds. *Note*: Pitch discrimination is critical in such tonal languages as Chinese and Thai.

pivot class in early language acquisition, a grammatical class of words that are not used alone or with other pivot-class words but can be used in first or second position in a two-word sentence, as *allgone* in *allgone milk* or *Daddy allgone*. *Cp.* **open class** (def. 2).

place of articulation the physical point in the vocal tract where a speech sound is produced, as the *lips*, *teeth*, *hard palate*, *etc.* (Crystal, 1987). See also **consonant**; *Cp.* **manner of articulation**.

plan **1.** *n.* a purposeful, preconceived scheme for action to reach a specified goal. **2.** *v.* to make such a plan. **3.** *n.* a graphic representation of spatial relations. **4.** *n.* a psychological construct to explain goal-oriented behavior; cognitive map; as a plan for learning how to run a maze.

plateau *n.* in learning, a period of little or no apparent change in performance which, however, may represent periods of consolidation of subordinate types of learning. *Note*: The relatively long, flat parts of a learning curve represent plateaus. See illustration under **learning curve**.

plot **1.** *n.* the structure of the action of a story. *Note*: In conventional stories, plot has three main parts: rising action, climax, and falling action leading to a resolution or denouement. **2.** *v.* to so structure the action of a story. **3.** *n.* a pattern of related episodes. **4.** *v.* to plan or lay out something, as *plot a graph*, *plot a course of work*. **5.** *v.* to make a frequency table or scatter diagram of test scores. **6.** *n.* a scatter diagram.

plural *n.* a grammatical category of number referring to more than one, as *adults* and *children* in *The adults and children played baseball*. See also **number**. *Cp.* **singular**.

plurisyllable *n.* a word with more than one syllable; polysyllabic word. *adj.* **plurisyllabic**.

poem *n.* **1.** a metrical form of composition in which word images are selected and expressed to create powerful, often beautiful impressions in the listener or reader. **2.** such a composition not in metrical form, as *a prose poem*. **3.** something suggestive of the qualities of a poem. See also **poetry** (defs. 1, 2).

poet *n.* **1.** a composer of poetry. **2.** a highly imaginative and creative person with remarkable powers of poetic expression.

poetic justice **1.** the view often found in fiction and drama that the good should be rewarded and the evil punished. **2.** an instance in which a person or character gets, in an unsympathetic and often ironic manner, what is deserved.

poetic license the liberty taken by poets and other writers to depart from convention or logic to attain a desired end by adjustments in rhyme, meter, linguistic structure, etc.

poetic writing a term employed by Britton (1975) and others to describe the use of prose or poetry as an art form; specifically, text in which the sounds of the writer's language, the writer's feelings, and the writer's ideas are patterned in a way that is pleasing to the writer and that likewise may be shared and enjoyed by the reader. See also **expressive writing**; **transactional writing**. *Cp.* **creative writing**.

poetry *n.* **1.** the art of creating poems. *Note*: One function of poetry is to present images concretely (Holman & Harmon, 1992). **2.** literature in metrical form—verse of "high merit"—the major forms of which are epic, dramatic, and lyric poetry. *Note*: While all poetry is verse, verse such as doggerel is not poetry. **3.** the art of recording and transmitting poems. **4.** something that has poetic qualities, as *prose poetry*, *the poetry of ballet*. See also **poem**; **verse**. *adj.* **poetic**; **poetical**.

point-biserial correlation a correlation between two variables, one of which is assumed to be continuous and normal in distribution and the other having only two conditions, as a correlation between grade point average and sex. *Cp.* **biserial correlation**; **tetrachoric correlation**.

pointing test an informal test of eyedness in which the subject points to a distant object with one arm fully extended and both eyes open so that the dominant eye may be determined by noting which eye is in line with the finger and the target. *Cp.* **paper-hole test**.

point of view the way in which an author reveals his or her voice, as in characters, events, and ideas in telling a story. *Note*: With an all-knowing point of view, an author writes as an omniscient narrator, seeing all, hearing all, knowing all. With a limited point of view, a story may be told through one narrator who knows only what he or she sees, hears, feels, or is told. Although this term is usually restricted to fiction, it may be applied to nonfiction when discussing the relative subjectivity or objectivity of a text.

politics of literacy the power struggle in the advocacy and realization of literacy programs: **a.** to enhance the presumed aspirations of all people with respect to command of language, economic well-being, and social status. **b.** to exercise economic and social constraints on literacy education in order to create an elite of the literate with dominance over the illiterate. See also **critical theory**; **literacy**.

polygenesis *n.* **1.** the theory that a myth with origins in several cultures is possible because all persons share common needs and desires. *Cp.* **myth**. **2.** the theory that the world's languages have different origins rather than a common one.

polyglot **1.** *adj.* knowing several languages; multilingual. **2.** *adj.* having, made up of, or in several languages. **3.** *n.* a mixture or confusion of languages. **4.** *n.* a multilingual person. **5.** *n.* a book, notably the Bible, printed in many languages.

polyglot literacy fluency in more than two languages; multilingualism.

polysemy *n.* a term applied to words that have more than one related meaning; multiple meaning. *Note*: The term is used only to refer to the variant meanings of one base word or dictionary entry, as *run*; it does not apply to all meanings of homonyms such as *mood* (feeling) and *mood* (verb form). *adj.* **polysemous**.

polysyllabic *adj.* containing more than one syllable. *n.* **polysyllable**.

portfolio *n.* a selected, usually chronological collection of a student's work that may be used to evaluate learning progress.

portmanteau word a word made by putting together parts of other words, as *motor* and *hotel* to make *motel*. See also **blend** (def. 3). *Cp.* **syncretism** (def. 1).

positive transfer the improvement of the effectiveness of some behavior or learning because of earlier behaviors or of prior learning efforts. See also **transfer** (def. 1). *Cp.* **negative transfer**.

possessive **1.** *adj.* showing ownership or origin. **2.** *n.* a noun or pronoun form indicating ownership, as *boy's* in *boy's journal*, *her* in *her journal*. *Cp.* **genitive**.

possessive pronoun a pronoun that indicates ownership, as *mine*, *your*, *his*, *her*, etc. See **pronoun**.

postliteracy program a program that provides continuing practice in reading and writing after basic literacy acquisition in order to ensure retention of marginal literacy skills as well as to continue literacy growth.

postreading *n.* a discussion, usually between the teacher and students, designed to further comprehension by exploring student reactions to something read.

poststructuralism *n.* an approach to philosophy and literary criticism that rejects the structuralism associated with Ferdinand de Saussure (1916; 1966) and Claude Lévi-Strauss (1963) as too Western. *Note*: Poststructuralism refers to deconstruction and Jacques Derrida's refutation of the tenets of linguistic, anthropological, and philosophical structuralism. It attacks the basic assumptions behind Western culture as well. It can be viewed as a French version of Anglo-American language philosophy. See also **deconstruction**; **structuralism**.

posttest 1. *n.* the assessment of learning at the end of an experiment, a learning task, or an instructional period. **2** *v.* to so assess. *Cp.* **pretest** (def. 1).

potential development level the level of attainment possible within a child's zone of proximal development with appropriate peer or adult guidance (Vygotsky, 1978). See also **zone of proximal development**. *Cp.* **actual developmental level**.

pourquoi story a folktale that explains the "why" (*Fr. pourquoi*) of certain customs, physical events, or animal behavior, as *Why the Bear Is Stumpy-Tailed*.

power 1. *n.* authority; control. **2.** *n.* a specific capacity or skill. **3.** the ability: **a.** of a test to clearly discriminate between individuals or groups. **b.** of a test of significance to reject false null hypotheses. See also **beta risk**.

power test a test with items usually ranging from easy to very difficult, with time limits generous enough to permit all items to be attempted. *Cp.* **speed test**.

practice effect change due to practice; specifically, any change, desirable or otherwise, in test performance.

practicum *n.* the supervised practice of professional skills, as in a teacher-education program, usually conducted in the field.

pragmatic literacy literacy that "varies according to cultural demands and often includes writing, numeracy, and document processing abilities" (Venezky et al., 1990); required literacy; "lower level functional literacy" (Warmald, 1977). See also the essay "Literacy" on p. 142.

pragmatics *n.* in linguistics, the study of the choices of language persons make in social interaction and of the effects of these choices on others (Crystal, 1987). *Note*: Pragmatics overlaps with and draws upon other fields of linguistic inquiry, e.g., stylistics, sociolinguistics, psycholinguistics, etc. *Cp.* **semantics** (def. 1).

predeterminer *n.* a word or group of words in a noun phrase occurring before an article or other determiner, as *all* in *all my children*.

predicate 1. *n.* the part of a sentence that expresses something about the subject; verb phrase; as *is difficult* in *That book is difficult*. *Cp.* **subject** (def. 3). **2.** *adj.* belonging to the predicate. **3.** *n.* that part of a proposition that asserts something about the subject or about an argument. See also **proposition** (defs. 3, 4).

predicate adjective an adjective or adjectival phrase that modifies the subject of a sentence and usually follows a form of the verb *to be* or linking verbs, as *fun* in *Skiing is fun* or *great* in *That CD sounds great! Cp.* **attributive**.

predicate nominative a noun or noun phrase that follows a linking verb; predicate noun; as *a rare book* in *Her gift to John was a rare book*. *Cp.* **nominative case**.

predication *n.* **1.** the act of asserting, as *the predication of a proposition*. **2.** something so asserted. **3.** the relation expressed by a predicate to a subject in a sentence, as that between *rang* and *the telephone* in *The telephone rang*.

predictability *n.* the quality of a narrative that enables the reader to foretell how it will develop and end. *adj.* **predictable**.

prediction strategy a person's use of knowledge about language and the context in which it occurs to anticipate what is coming in writing or speech, as if one reads *prag-* at the end of a line, one prediction strategy might be to expect the word *pragmatic*.

predictive validity the relationship, usually expressed as a correlation coefficient or a regression equation, between scores on a test and later performance as revealed in course grades, job performance, etc. See also **validity** (def. 3); **validity generalization**.

predictor variable in a predictive validity study, a variable used to forecast the outcome on a criterion variable, as predicting college grade point average from rank in high school class. See also **criterion variable**.

prefix *n.* an affix attached before a base word or root, as *re-* in *reprint*. See also **affix**. *Cp.* **suffix**.

prelingually deaf **1.** *n.* a person whose hearing loss precedes the acquisition of language. **2.** *adj.* referring to such a person or class of persons.

preliterate *adj.* **1.** referring to a culture not having or leaving a written record. **2.** referring to a child, usually before entering school or in kindergarten, who has not yet learned to read. *n.* **preliteracy**.

preoperational thought in Piagetian theory, representational rather than logical thought in mental development, usually from about two to seven years, that is characterized by egocen-

trism, centration, syncretism, absence of reversibility, and lack of concern with proof or logical justification. *Cp.* **concrete operations**; **formal operations**; **infralogical operations**; **operations**; **stage** (def. 2).

preposition *n.* a class of function words that precede noun phrases to create prepositional phrases, as *at* in *at school* or *of* in *of your writing*.

prepositional phrase a preposition plus the noun phrase that follows it, as *over the river* and *through the trees*.

preprimer *n.* in a basal reading program, a booklet used before the first reader to introduce students to features in texts and books and sometimes to introduce specific characters found later in the series.

prequel *n.* a narrative in which the action antedates, rather than follows, that in an existing published narrative. *Cp.* **sequel**.

prereading **1.** *adj.* referring to activities designed to develop needed attitudes and skills before formal instruction in reading. **2.** *adj.* referring to activities engaged in immediately before the reading act, as giving the background of a story or having students identify purposes for reading. **3.** *n.* the activities thus referred to.

presbycusis *n.* loss of the ability to perceive or discriminate sounds, commonly associated with aging.

presbyopia *n.* the loss of accommodation power as the crystalline lens of the eye becomes less elastic with age. *n.* **presbyope**. *adj.* **presbyopic**.

preschool **1.** *n.* in the United States, a school or class for children between infancy and entrance to grade one or to kindergarten, usually for three- or four-year-olds. **2.** *adj.* having to do with such a school or class.

prescriptive grammar 1. an approach to language that attempts to establish rules for correct usage. **2.** a grammar based on such an approach; traditional grammar. *Cp.* **descriptive grammar**.

preservice education education, either at the university undergraduate or graduate level, in preparation for employment.

prestige dialect a social or regional variety of a language spoken by a privileged and socially esteemed class. See also **dialect**; **sociolect**. *Cp.* **nonstandard dialect**.

prestige language a language spoken by members of groups who enjoy a certain degree of esteem, power, and social prominence, as French in Haiti.

pretend reading make-believe reading, as turning pages of a book while inventing words; repeating the contents of a book from memory after listening to it before being able to read independently; emergent reading. *v.* **pretend-read**.

preterit *n.* a verb tense form indicating past or completed action; past tense. Also **preterite**.

pretest 1. *n.* a test given before instruction or experiment; specifically: **a.** a test comparable to a posttest but designed to ascertain a level of functioning prior to administration of an experimental treatment or of instruction. **b.** a test designed to help interpret instruction or experimental behavior, as a test of ability. **2.** *v.* to give such a test. **3.** *n.* a practice test.

prewriting *n.* the initial creative stage of writing, prior to drafting, in which the writer formulates ideas, gathers information, and considers ways to organize them; planning.

primacy effect the tendency to remember materials learned early in a series better than those learned later, as initial items on a word list.

primary *adj.* with reference to educational difficulties, having a neurological basis, as a *primary reading disability* might follow a brain injury. *Cp.* **secondary**.

primary accent 1. the vowel or syllable in a word, phrase, or metrical foot with the strongest and loudest emphasis; primary stress. See also **stress** (def. 2). **2.** an orthographic symbol placed above a vowel grapheme or adjacent to a syllable (´) or above a syllable in a line of verse (–) to indicate that the marked vowel or syllable has the stronger emphasis in contrast to some other vowel or syllable. See also **accent** (def. 2a); **diacritic mark**. *Cp.* **secondary accent**.

primary school 1. in the United States, grades 1, 2, and 3 of an elementary school. **2.** in Britain, a school for children aged 5–11. **3.** in Australia, a school that admits children up to 12–13 years.

prime *n.* **1.** in text copy, any mark placed above and to the right of a letter to indicate a letter different from the unmarked version, as in *a'* versus *a''*. **2.** a mark placed above and to the right of a number to indicate a quantity being measured, as *6'* to represent six feet, minutes of arc of an angle, or minutes of time.

primer *n.* **1.** a beginning book for the teaching of reading; specifically, the first formal textbook in a basal reading program, usually preceded by a readiness book and one or more preprimers. **2.** an easy-to-read, introductory book on any subject. **3.** (*Brit.*) from the 14th century, a devotional handbook for laypersons offering the fundamental prayers of Christianity. **4.** a small book for introducing children to reading and to Christianity as in def. 3, but with reading instructional material added in the form of the alphabet, lists of syllables, and words.

primerese *n.* unnatural sounding language characteristic of primer-level texts.

principal parts the set of inflected forms of a grammatical class, as *sing, sang, sung*.

print **1.** *n.* a medium of communication, as books, newspapers, magazines, etc.; a printed publication. **2.** *n.* the process of reproducing impressions by transferring them from an inked surface to a surface such as paper, cloth, plastic, etc.; printing. **3.** *n.* the impressions so produced. **4.** *v.* to so reproduce impressions or cause them to be reproduced; publish. **5.** See **manuscript writing**. **6.** *n.* a positive photographic image. **7.** *v.* to make such a photographic image. **8.** *v.* to publish. **9. in print**, published or available from a publisher. **10. out of print**, no longer available from any publisher. **11. printout**, a record made by a computer. *adj.* **printed**.

print awareness in emergent literacy, a learner's growing recognition of conventions and characteristics of a written language. *Note:* Print awareness includes such features as the recognition of directionality in reading text (left to right and top to bottom in English), that print in the form of words corresponds to speech, that white space marks the boundaries of printed words, etc.

print concept development in emergent literacy, the growing recognition that print needs to be arranged in an orderly way to communicate information in reading and writing.

print convention any of several rules that govern the customary use of print in reading and writing, including location concepts, punctuation, and capitalization. See also **typographical signal**.

print culture the recognition that writing and the printed word constitute a cultural force that dominates economic, social, and educational functions on the international scene.

print-immersion curriculum in emergent literacy, an instructional design that provides a print-rich environment to allow children many opportunities to interact with print in the classroom through such things as a kitchen play area with labeled cans of food, cereal boxes, and named pictures from magazine ads.

prior knowledge knowing that stems from previous experience. *Note:* Prior knowledge is a key component of schema theories of reading comprehension in spite of the redundancy inherent in the term. See also **schema theory**.

prison literacy the literacy that is characteristic of prison inmates. *Note:* "The literacy levels of prison inmates, disproportionately Hispanic and Black in the United States, tend to be low according to the National Adult Literacy Survey" (Kirsch et al., 1993).

proactive inhibition in learning, the interfering effect of information already learned on the later learning of similar material. See also **negative transfer**. *Cp.* **retroactive inhibition**.

probable error an estimate, now seldom used, of the typical size of errors of measurement or statistical estimation, calculated as 0.6745 times the standard error. *Cp.* **standard error**.

problem literature a novel, play, or short story in which the action is focused on difficult choices, as in Charlotte Brontë's *Jane Eyre* or Henrik Ibsen's *An Enemy of the People*.

procedural knowledge **1.** "how-to" knowledge, often revealed in using a skill. **2.** knowledge of the "how," conceived as an instructional strategy and expressed as a series of language production rules by Paris et al. (1983).

processing *n.* **1.** the course of active change in some specific way, especially in psychological activity, as *the processing of text*. See also **text processing**. **2.** the mechanical or electronic handling of data; information processing.

process objective an educational goal that is stated in terms of how it is to be reached, as *To improve word knowledge by voluntary reading*.

process writing a writing instruction model that views writing as an ongoing process and in which students follow a given set of procedures for planning, drafting, revising, editing (proof-reading and correcting), and publishing (sharing by some means) their writing. See also **writing process**.

production rules guides to problem solving: **a.** rules governing observable conditions that must be met. **b.** rules governing actions that conform to the stated conditions. Also **production systems**.

productive competence the ability to produce a wide range of language forms in communication. *Cp.* **communicative competence**; **receptive competence**.

product-moment coefficient (*r*) the coefficient obtained by product-moment, or Pearsonian, correlation. See also **product-moment correlation**.

product-moment correlation a correlation expressed by the coefficient *r* between two or more variables. *Note*: A positive *r* means that two variables change in the same direction; i.e., when one variable increases in value, so does the correlated one. A negative *r* means that the variables change in opposite directions. *Cp.* **rank-order correlation**.

programmed instruction instruction, originally presented in printed form but now primarily by computer, in which a skill or subject matter to be learned is broken up into very small parts to which the learner responds, step by step, and receives immediate information on the accuracy of each response. Also **programmed learning**. See also **branching program**; **linear program**. *Cp.* **computer assisted instruction**.

projective test the use of an unstructured stimulus or task to assess perceptual functioning and personality characteristics as revealed in a person's responses, as word-association and ink-blot tests. Also **projective technique**.

project method a form of group learning in which students work together on an activity directed toward some socially useful end. *Note*: This method was first proposed by W.H. Kilpatrick (1918).

pronominalization *n.* **1.** the process or result of using a pronoun in the place of another part of speech or syntactic structure, as using *she* and *her* to represent *Diane* in *Diane said she would not sell her home*. **2.** in transformational-generative grammar, a syntactic rule that transforms one of two equivalent or identical phrases into a pronoun.

pronoun *n.* a part of speech used as a substitute for a noun or noun phrase. *Note*: The classification of pronouns varies according to the type of grammar used in their analysis. See box for pronouns defined in this dictionary. Also **pronominal**. *adj.* **pronominal**.

Types of *Pronouns**
demonstrative (def. 1)
indefinite
interrogative
personal
possessive
reciprocal
reflexive
relative

---

*Terms are all defined in this dictionary.

pronounceability *n.* the relative ease or difficulty of pronunciation.

pronunciation key the set of graphic symbols used to represent the speech sounds of a language as accurately as possible, as in many dictionaries.

pronunciation symbol **1.** a graphic symbol representing a particular speech sound. See also **graph** (def. 2); **letter** (def. 1). **2.** See **pronunciation key**.

propaganda *n.* **1.** an extreme form of written or spoken persuasion intended to influence the reader or listener strongly, though sometimes subtly, and usually by one-sided rather than objective arguments. **2.** speaking or writing that attempts to persuade listeners or readers to accept a particular point of view, either good or bad depending on the speaker's or writer's intent, as *advertising propaganda to sell mouthwash.*

propaganda analysis a method used to identify half-truths, distortions, and biased approaches found in oral or written communication.

propaganda techniques methods used in creating propaganda, as overgeneralization, guilt by association, etc.

proper noun a noun that names a particular person, place, or thing, as *Mrs. Olson, London, International Reading Association. Cp.* **common noun**.

proposition *n.* **1.** a statement offered as true or for testing for truth. **2.** a plan offered for action. **3.** a unit of thought expressed in an independent or dependent clause, as *I breathe hard / when I run.* **4.** a unit of thought containing a relation, or attribute, and an argument, as *I defend, without fear, my right to speak. adj.* **propositional**.

propositional encoding in reading comprehension, processing text as a series of thought units or propositions. *Cp.* **mental model**.

prose **1.** *n.* written or spoken language that is not verse. **2.** *adj.* referring to nonmetrical language, as fluent prose style. *Cp.* **verse**. *adj.* **prosaic**.

prosodic feature see **prosody** (def. 1).

prosodic sign a graphic mark that denotes a metric feature in poetry or a stress or intonation feature of speech. See also **accent** (def. 2d); **diacritic mark**.

prosody *n.* **1.** the pitch, loudness, tempo, and rhythm patterns of spoken language; suprasegmental prosodic features. See also **accent** (def. 5). **2.** the study of the form and metrical structure of verse. See also **meter**.

protagonist *n.* the central figure in a drama or narrative; hero(-ine). *Cp.* **antagonist**.

protocol *n.* an original, unmodified record of events, experiments, speech, etc., made at the time of occurrence or immediately afterwards.

protolanguage *n.* a hypothetical language postulated to be the ultimate origin of an actual language and related languages, as Proto-Indo-European. *Note*: When written records or several languages known to be related are available, a process of *comparative reconstruction* is used to deduce a protolanguage. See also **internal reconstruction**.

protoliteracy *n.* historically, the earliest form of literacy in a people. See also **literacy**.

proxemics *n. (with sing. v.)* in linguistics, "the study of the way in which the participants in social interaction adjust their posture and relative distance from one another according to the degree of intimacy that obtains between them, their sex, the social roles they are performing, and so on" (Lyons, 1977). *adj.* **proxemic**.

pseudocleft sentence a sentence with a wh-clause used as a subject or complement, as *an economical car is what I want*. *Cp.* **cleft sentence**.

pseudonym *n.* an assumed name used by an author in place of his own name; pen name; nom de plume; anonym.

psychoanalytic criticism a form of literary criticism that draws on the work of Freud and later psychoanalysts in evaluating literature to reveal the hidden meaning of human action.

psycholinguistics *n. (with sing. v.)* the inter-disciplinary field of psychology and linguistics in which language behavior is examined. *Note*: Psycholinguistics includes such areas of inquiry as language acquisition, conversational analysis, and the sequencing of themes and topics in discourse. *adj.* **psycholinguistic**.

psychological novel a type of novel in which characters' motivations are of central importance and are revealed by what they say and do, as in the novels of Henry James.

psychology of reading the application of psychological and linguistic concepts and techniques to an examination of the reading act and its outcomes.

psychometric *adj.* referring to study, practice, or research in psychological measurement; specifically, the development, administration, and interpretation of psychological tests. *n.* **psychometrics**; **psychometry**.

psychomotor domain the psychological field of physical activity. *Cp.* **affective domain**; **cognitive domain**.

public school 1. a school supported by tax dollars and controlled by public officials. **2.** (*Brit.*) a private school.

publishing *n.* the act or process of preparing written material for presentation to an audience, whether informally to classmates, as in part of the writing process, or formally by a publishing house. *v.* **publish**.

pull-out program a remedial program in various subject areas in which children are removed from regular classes for instruction.

pun *n.* **1.** the deliberate and humorous use of a word or phrase to suggest a difference in meaning or use, as the substitution of the slogan *visualize whirled peas* for *visualize world peace*. **2.** a play on words that are the same or similar in sound but different in meaning. See also **shift of meaning**. *Note*: In def. 1, the difference in meaning of the pun may be visual or aural, or may depend on changes in syntax. In def. 2, the pun depends on a change in context.

punctuation mark one of the set of graphic marks used in written phrases and sentences to clarify meaning or to give speech characteristics to written material; punctuation. *Note*: In writing systems based on the Latin alphabet, punctuation marks include those indicating: **a.** a *pause*, as the comma (,), semicolon (;), colon (:), dash (—) and period (.). **b.** a *sentence type*, as the question mark (?) and exclamation mark (!). **c.** a *quotation*, as by quotation marks ("..." and '...'). **d.** an *incidental* or *parenthetical notion*, by brackets or braces ([...], {...},) or by parentheses ((...)). **e.** a *word compound*, by the hyphen (-) or en dash (–). **f.** an *absence of sounds*, by the apostrophe ('). **g.** an *absence of words*, by the ellipsis (...) or dash (—). *Cp.* **diacritic mark**.

pupil[1] *n.* **1.** a school learner, usually young; student. **2.** a person who studies, often individually, with a special teacher or tutor.

pupil[2] *n.* the round opening in the center of the iris that lets light into the eye. *adj.* **pupillary**.

pure-tone audiometer an instrument that sounds tones of selected frequencies at certain volume levels to determine a subject's hearing level, or threshold, for such tones. See also **audiometer**.

purpose for reading **1.** the reason a person reads. **2.** the goal(s) that a reader seeks to attain in each reading experience. **3.** the goal(s) set by the teacher or text for a reading task or experience. *Note*: Purpose for reading is a major determinant of comprehension strategies employed, study modes and materials used, and speed of reading.

Pygmalion effect the influence of teacher expectation on students, especially the belief that high expectations can lead to high performance, as exemplified in George Bernard Shaw's *Pygmalion*.

Q **1.** (*ital.*) See **quartile**. **2.** question. **3.** quarto.

q the proportion of a sample that does not have some specified characteristic. *Cp. **p***.

qualifier *n.* **1.** See **modifier**. **2.** a function word used before an adjective to show the degree of the adjective, as *rather* in *This is rather disappointing*. **3.** an intensifier. **4.** in functional grammar, a word, phrase, or clause that follows a head noun adding to or qualifying its meaning, as *from Tokyo* in *an e-mail message from Tokyo*. *Note*: In functional grammar, *modifier* is restricted to language units performing this function and appearing *before* a head noun.

qualitative research research that is conducted in naturalistic settings in order to make sense of, or interpret, phenomena in terms of the meanings that people bring to them. *Note*: A variety of methodological approaches may be used in the collection of data, including case studies, interviews, observations, introspection, text analysis (including film), among others (Densin & Lincoln, 1994). See also **ethnographic research**. *Cp.* **quantitative research**.

quantifier *n.* a word or phrase, used with a noun, that indicates quantity, as *few*, *several*, etc.

quantitative literacy **1.** fluency in reading and writing computational data. **2.** See **numeracy**.

quantitative research research that measures and describes in numerical terms. *Cp.* **qualitative research**.

quartile (*Q*) *n.* 1 of the 3 points that divide a distribution into 4 equal parts of 25 percent each. *Note*: Q_1 is the lowest of these points, Q_2 the median, and Q_3 the highest.

quasi-experimental design a research design that does not meet the criteria of external validity, in the sense that the design considerably limits the generalizability of any findings, or internal validity, in the sense that the design does not control all but a single variable. *Note*: Because of the complexities of the learning-teaching situation, most educational research is quasi-experimental in design.

quatrain *n.* **1.** a stanza or poem of four lines. **2.** a poem of four verses.

R

R **1.** See **response**. **2.** (*ital.*) See **multiple-correlation coefficient**. **3.** one of the "three Rs" in the phrase "reading, 'riting, and 'rithmetic."

radical *n.* **1.** in logographic writing systems: **a.** that part of a graphic character that assigns the word represented to a particular semantic or lexical class. *Note*: In Chinese, about 220 radicals form the basic semantic classes to which all characters can be assigned. **b.** the component of a graphic character considered to be the basic or first stroke, by which the character is classified in a dictionary or other work; determinative. *Note*: In some Japanese writing primers, kanji are classified by their radicals. See also **logography**. **2.** See **root** (def. 3).

random access the ability, in a person or computer, to retrieve a specific memory without having to go through the entire store of memories in some fixed order.

randomize *v.* to assign subjects, objects, events, etc., in a completely chance manner to experimental treatments.

random sample an experimental sample drawn by chance from a population. *Note*: The use of a random sample helps eliminate systematic bias and strengthens possible inferences to the population from which the sample was drawn.

range of accommodation the distance between the nearest and farthest points at which one can see clearly.

rank order the placement of scores or values according to increasing or decreasing size, as 1, 2, 3, or fast, average, and slow rate of reading. *Cp.* **class** (def. 4).

rank-order correlation a statistical procedure that yields a coefficient expressing the relationship in terms of rank only between two sets of rankings. *Cp.* **product-moment correlation**.

rate of reading how fast a person reads, usually silently; reading speed. *Note*: Rate of reading has been of great interest to reading professionals and to the public especially since schools in the United States began to stress silent reading in the second decade of the 20th century. A formula for expressing the average number of words read per minute was quickly devised, and students were tested for reading speed with no regard to comprehension. Later, separate comprehension scores were given as some arbitrary percent of correct responses to content questions on the text; still later, rate adjustments were introduced in relation to comprehension. Rate of reading scores are so affected by other variables, as purpose for reading, the nature of the content, text format, etc., that comparative studies are difficult. Furthermore, since rate of reading scores are averages, they mask normal and desirable variations in reading speed. See also **speed of comprehension**.

rating scale an instrument, sometimes in graphic form, for recording estimates of the functioning of selected aspects of behavior, as personality traits. *Cp.* **attitude scale**.

ratio scale an interval scale with an absolute zero point. *Cp.* **interval scale**.

rauding *n.* a term introduced by Carver (1977) to refer to the receptive communication skills of reading with comprehension and to draw a parallel to the skills of listening with comprehension, or *auding*. *Cp.* **auding**; **listening** (def. 2).

raw score (x) the number of points earned on a test or the value assigned to an observation before it is transformed to a standard scale. *Cp.* **derived score**.

r-controlled vowel sound the modified sound of a vowel immediately preceding /r/ in the same syllable, as in *care, never, sir, or, curse*, etc. See also **vowel controller**.

reaction time the interval between the stimulus event and the subject's response.

read *Note*: The definitions of *read* are more numerous and tend to be more discrete than those of *reading*. Many are drawn from a long literary heritage and are a catalog of subtle meaning distinctions—often metaphorical extensions of more basic definitions—made by writers and speakers. The chief but not exclusive referent of most definitions of *read* is *silent reading*. **1.** *v.* to engage in silent reading. **2.** See **oral reading** (def. 1). **3.** *v.* to get the literal or stated meaning from something read. See **comprehension** (def. 1); **literal comprehension**; **literal meaning**. **4.** *v.* to transmit meaning; to comprehend text by engaging in an interchange of ideas, or a transaction, between the reader and the text. See **comprehension** (def. 2); **reading** (defs. 10, 11). **5.** *v.* to find an unstated meaning in something read, as *read between the lines*. *Cp.* **interpretation** (def. 1). **6.** *v.* to quickly look over or scan, as *read the newspaper headlines*. **7.** *v.* to react critically to something read. *Cp.* **critical evaluation**; **critical reading**. **8.** *v.* (*chiefly Brit.*) to study, usually at a university, a subject matter field, as *read philosophy*. **9.** *v.* to acquire knowledge about some topic by reading; learn; as *read about dinosaurs*. **10.** *v.* to comprehend the fuller significance of something that is read, as *Can you read Melville's message behind the story of* Moby Dick*?* **11.** *v.* to empathize with characters in imaginative literature, as *read the humor in Don Quixote's many predicaments*. **12.** *v.* to identify the mood, setting, and events of a story or play. **13.** *v.* to accept without hesitation or criticism the point of view and other conditions set by the author in presenting a story or play; to engage in "that willing suspension of disbelief" (Samuel Taylor Coleridge, *Biographia Literaria*). **14.** *v.* to give meaning to nongraphic or nonverbal signs, as *read the signs of spring*, *read a person's mood or character*. **15.** *v.* to discover or explain, as *read the meaning of a riddle*. **16.** *v.* to predict or foresee, as *Carmen could read*

her fate in the cards. **17.** *v.* to understand another graphic or verbal language when reading it, as *read finger spelling*, *read German*. **18.** *v.* to have a certain wording, as *Text A reads "percept" but text B reads "precept."* **19.** *v.* to give directions about, as *read "x" for "y."* **20.** *v.* to examine reading material for mechanical errors or to check the conformity of a copy with its original; proofread. **21.** *n.* the matter read, as *That book is a good read*. **22. read into**, to infer a meaning in something read or experienced. **23.** *v.* to scan or transfer data in the internal operation of a computer or between computers. **24. read in**, to supply information to a computer. **25. read out**, to get information from a computer. See also **comprehension**; **reading**; **reading comprehension**.

readability *n.* **1.** ease of comprehension because of style of writing. *Note*: "Readability, together with accessibility and subject interest, is a major determinant of one's reading" (Waples et al., 1940). Many variables in text may contribute to readability, including format, typography, content, literary form and style, vocabulary difficulty, sentence complexity, concept load or density, cohesiveness, etc. Many variables within the reader also contribute, including motivation, abilities, background knowledge, and interests. Text and reader variables interact in determining the readability of any piece of reading material for any individual reader. **2.** an objective estimate or prediction of reading comprehension of material, usually in terms of reading grade level, based on selected and quantified variables in text, especially some index of vocabulary difficulty and of sentence difficulty. *Note*: In teaching practice, def. 2 may sometimes be accepted as accurately predicting readability, although it is wiser to combine the subjective variables noted in def. 1 with the more objective ones in making such estimates. Similarly, in writing practice, changes in vocabulary and sentence difficulty may sometimes be considered sufficient to produce more readable

Readability

Writing becomes readable, most agree, when variables in a text interact with those in a reader to make the writing easy to understand. Research to date shows that increased reader ability, motivation, and background knowledge of text content rather consistently produce significantly increased comprehension. Research fails, however, to show similar increases when changes are made in language or presentation variables of a text (such as organization, format, and typography). Early research in readability revealed that, in school reading materials, semantic difficulty and syntactic difficulty increased with grade level. These two style variables in text could be counted objectively in one form or another (such as word frequency and sentence length) and became the basis for most so-called readability formulas designed to predict reading difficulty. Other variables, though considered important, have still not been included in most formulas since they cannot be counted objectively.

More than 1000 references to readability can be found in the literature, among them well over 100 different formulas for calculating readability of texts in English and in more than a dozen other languages. Formulas continue to be widely used in educational settings for their intended purpose: the prediction of which materials will be appropriate for particular readers. However, formulas have sometimes also been used in an attempt to make materials more readable—a use for which they were not intended. Making changes to certain text variables, such as cutting sentence length or substituting more common words for less common, may yield better scores on a readability formula without corresponding increases in reader comprehension. Skilled writers, of course, can and do write readably, but improving comprehension through research-based alteration of language and presentation has proved elusive.

Critics, appropriately, label formulas unreliable (if not actually dangerous) when they are used for text-production purposes—and often also when they are used for prediction because they are not perfectly accurate. The following suggestions can help users of formulas to make predictions of readability as accurately as possible.

- Consider your purpose in getting a readability score; cultivating readers calls for more challenging materials than does merely informing or entertaining them.

- Pick a good formula for your intended use, but consider all formulas screening devices and all scores probability statements.

- Choose a formula with two index variables, one semantic and one syntactic, as a desirable minimum.

- Increase the accuracy of your analysis by taking a large random (or numerically spread) sampling of text, both to increase the reliability of your average score and to get an indication of variability.

- Remember that different formulas may give somewhat different grade-level scores.

- Keep in mind that formula scores derive from counts of style variables; they become poorer predictors at higher grade levels where content weighs more heavily.

(continued)

Readability (cont'd.)

- Take into account your readers' ability, motivation, and background knowledge; otherwise scores may over- or underestimate difficulty.

- Do not rely on formulas alone in selecting materials; seek the opinion of experts or get reliable consensus opinions to examine characteristics that formulas cannot predict and to ensure that formulas have not been misused in producing materials.

George R. Klare

---

material, but experienced writers realize that the variables in def. 1 must also be considered. See the essay "Readability" on pp. 204–205. See also **readability formula**. **3.** ease of reading because of the interest value or pleasantness of writing, as *the readability of a good mystery story*. **4.** (*archaic*) legibility of handwriting or typography. *adj.* **readable**.

readability formula any of a number of objective methods of estimating or predicting the difficulty level of reading materials by analyzing samples from them, with results usually expressed as a reading grade level. *Note*: Readability formulas are generally based on vocabulary difficulty, syntactic difficulty, and a number of related factors singly and in combination, usually in terms of a multiple-regression equation. Word length or familiarity and average sentence length in words tend to be the most significant or convenient predictors of the reading difficulty of materials as measured by readability formulas. Estimates of formula validity are usually based on relationships with three types of criteria: **a.** reading comprehension scores. **b.** reading speed or efficiency. **c.** acceptability determined either by readers' or experts' judgments or by reader perseverance. See also **Dale–Chall readability formula; Flesch readability formula; Fry readability graph;**

Spache readability formula; the essay "Readability" on pp. 204–205. *Cp.* **cloze procedure** (def. 1).

reader *n.* **1.** a book used for instruction in reading, as *the McGuffey readers*. **2.** one who reads. *Note*: "There are four kinds of readers. The first is like the hour-glass; and their reading being as the sand, it runs in and runs out, and leaves not a vestige behind. A second is like the sponge, which imbibes everything, and returns it in nearly the same state, only a little dirtier. A third is like a jelly-bag, allowing all that is pure to press away, and retaining only the refuse and dregs. And the fourth is like the slaves in the diamond mines of Golconda, who, casting aside all that is worthless, retain only pure gems" (Samuel Taylor Coleridge, *1811–1812 Lectures on Shakespeare and Milton; Lecture 2*). **3.** a person who reads to an audience; elocutionist. **4.** a person employed to read for some special purpose, as a judge of manuscripts, a teaching assistant who grades papers and examinations, etc. **5.** a collection of short texts, as *An American Reader*.

readerboard *n.* a signboard used to display one or more messages.

reader-friendly writing writing in which the author, viewing a composition as a communica-

---

tion with others, is attentive to the needs of the reader; prose writing that reflects the efforts of authors in preparing and revising texts to take into consideration the background, needs, and interests of an anticipated audience; reader-based writing. *Note*: Writing that fails to reflect a sense of audience is considered **reader-unfriendly writing** or **writer-based reading**.

reader response log a written record of materials read and the reader's personal reactions to them.

reader response (theory) See the essay "Reader Response" on pp. 209–210. See also **transactional theory**.

readership *n.* **1.** those who read a publication. **2.** the particular audience for which a publication is intended. **3.** the habit of regular reading, as in *the promotion of readership*.

Readers Theatre a performance of literature, as a story, play, poetry, etc., read aloud expressively by one or more persons, rather than acted.

readers' workshop that part of a literature-based reading program in which students engage in reading and responding to trade books, including small-group discussions with the teacher to learn or review key concepts about reading and literature. Also **reading workshop**.

readiness *n.* preparedness to cope with a learning task; "the adequacy of existing ability in relation to the demands of the learning task" (Ausubel, 1959). *Note*: Readiness for learning is a holistic concept determined by a complex pattern of intellectual, motivational, maturational, and experiential factors in the individual that may vary depending on time and circumstances. The traditional concept of readiness is based on cross-sectional analyses of the average performance of students, not on the developmental level of individual students.

Thus, if a student does not meet such an average, he or she is considered "unready"—needing either special help or further maturation. See also **reading readiness**.

readiness test a test designed to determine whether the individual possesses the skills and abilities required for a new activity or a new level of performance.

reading *n. Note*: Huey, the first great scholar of the psychology and pedagogy of reading, observed that "to completely analyze what we do when we read would almost be the acme of a psychologist's achievements, for it would be to describe some of the most intricate workings of the human mind" (1908). Silent reading, to which the following group of definitions refers, still remains an elusive concept. Its definition varies with the stage of reading development considered—that of the beginning, intermediate, or mature reader (Spache, 1977)—and with one's point of view toward reading as a visual task, a word-recognition task, a thinking process, or a social event. Most significantly, since reading is a learned process, definitions of *reading* reflect differing assumptions about learning. During the first half of the 20th century, an associational, behavioristic concept of learning dominated definitions. Later, a view of reading as a language-based, developmental process was advanced by scholars drawing largely from cognitive psychology and linguistics. And, as of this writing, views of the reading process have grown increasingly multidisciplinary, especially with respect to sociological, anthropological, and sociolinguistic contributions. As a result, not only have the definitions of *reading* changed over time but so have implications for reading instruction. The evolutionary though somewhat irregular pattern of process-oriented definitions of *reading* is shown particularly in the sequence of defs. 1–13 following. Initially, reading was conceived as an associative perceptual act (defs. 1, 2). Later, this view

---

A Comparison of Behavioral and Cognitive Views of the *Reading* Process

Behavioral	*Cognitive*
• Learning is based on analyses of language skills.	• Learning is based on the learner's state of language development.
• The learner reproduces meaning.	• The learner constructs meaning.
• Learning activated by others is common.	• Learner-activated learning is stressed.
• Motivation tends to be directed by others.	• Motivation is self-directed.
• Learning is text driven.	• Learning is learner driven.
• Learning stresses stimulus-response bonding.	• Learning stresses metacognitive mediation.
• Learning is linear and hierarchical.	• Learning is holistic and patterned.
• Learning features skill development.	• Learning features problem solving.
• Effective comprehension requires automaticity of basic skills.	• Effective comprehension relates learning to prior knowledge and experience.

---

was extended to include comprehension and related thinking processes (defs. 3–6). Toward midcentury, definitions of reading became more and more cognitively oriented (defs. 7–13), thus accentuating the differing theoretical and pragmatic viewpoints that scholars bring to its study. Currently, many scholars also relate reading with the socially directed intentions of language, as seen in Vygotsky's view that use of "language is a highly personal and at the same time a profoundly social process" (John-Steiner & Sauberman, 1978); for example, Harste et al.'s assertion that reading is a "social event" (1984); and Goodman's view that reading is "a transactional socio-psycholinguistic process" (1994). The following sampling of definitions of *reading* amply demonstrate that such definitions need to be seen in the context of the theoretical and pragmatic orientations of the definer. **1.** "distinguishing the separate letters both by the eye and by the ear, in order that, when you later hear them spoken or see them written, you will not be confused by their position" (Plato). **2.** "nothing more than the correlation of a sound image with its corresponding visual image" (Bloomfield, 1938). **3.** "the perception and comprehension of written messages in a man-

ner paralleling that of the corresponding spoken messages" (Carroll, 1964). **4.** "reasoning" (Thorndike, 1922). **5.** "an understanding not only of the literal or sense meaning of a passage but also the meanings implied by the author's mood, his tone, his intent, and himself" (Richards, 1938). **6.** "the central thought process by means of which meaning is put into the symbols appearing on the printed page" (Gray, 1940). **7.** "the reconstruction of the events behind the symbols" (Korzybski, 1941). **8.** "an interaction between the reader and written language, through which the reader attempts to reconstruct a message from the writer" (Goodman, 1968). **9.** "a sampling, selecting, predicting, comparing and confirming activity in which the reader selects a sample of useful graphic cues based on what he sees and what he expects to see" (Goodman, 1975). **10.** "intentional thinking during which meaning is constructed through interactions between text and reader" (Durkin, 1993). **11.** "transacting with a text to create meaning;...bringing meaning to a text in order to create meaning from it" (Galda et al., 1993). **12.** "the recognition of printed or written symbols which serve as stimuli for the recall of meanings built up through past experience, and the construction of new meanings through manipulation of concepts already possessed by the reader. The resulting meanings are organized into thought processes according to the purposes adopted by the reader. Such an organization leads to modified thought and/or behavior, or else leads to new behavior which takes its place, either in personal or in social development" (Tinker & McCullough, 1968). **13.** "a process of translating signs and symbols into meanings and incorporating the new information into existing cognitive and affective structures" (Robeck & Wallace, 1990). **14.** "the process of making discriminative responses...in the broadest sense,...the process of interpreting sense stimuli and of adapting one's behavior with regard to them" (Spencer, cited in Gray & Rogers, 1956). **15.** "part of a communication sequence that begins with the emotional utterances of infants and develops into a complex lexicon of spoken and written English" (Robeck & Wallace, 1990). **16.** any examination and interpretation of symbolic data, as *the reading of test results*. **17.** any material that is read, as *the reading assigned in the course*. **18.** a particular version or form of material to be read, as *a modern reading of the Bible*. **19.** the breadth of knowledge acquired through reading. **20.** *pl.*, a collection of writings of a particular type or from a particular field, often used as supplementary text materials in instruction. See also **comprehension**;**oral reading**; **read**; **reading-writing relationships**.

reading ability **1.** the cognitive processes employed in comprehending and using written text. **2.** See **reading achievement**.

reading achievement the level of reading ability at which an individual is estimated to be functioning. *Note*: Such estimates may be based on: **a.** the person's performance on a standardized or informal reading test. **b.** the level of basal reader being used for reading instruction. **c.** teacher judgment. **d.** the reading group in which a student is placed. **e.** the nature and number of trade books read by the student. **f.** some combination of these features.

reading age an outmoded type of age-equivalent score based on the age in the test-standardization population at which the average person earns a given reading score.

reading center a place, usually in a school, where students may get help to improve their reading. *Cp.* **reading clinic**.

reading clinic a place where individuals with relatively severe reading problems may receive help from specially trained personnel; (*Brit.*) remedial centre. *Cp.* **reading center**.

reading comprehension **1.** the act or result of applying comprehension processes to attain the meaning of a graphic communication; rauding. See also **comprehension** (defs. 1, 2); **comprehension strategy**. *Cp.* **auding**. **2.** one or more of several levels of a presumed hierarchy of reading comprehension processes: **a.** getting the literal meaning. See **literal comprehension**. **b.** getting the interpretive or suggested meaning in reading. See **interpretation** (defs. 1, 2). **c.** evaluating what is read in a critical way. See **critical evaluation**; **critical reading**.

reading development the course of change in an individual's reading processes from their emergence to the more mature skills and abilities of the competent reader. *Note*: Jansen (1993) notes the following terms used in Denmark for identified levels of reading development: **a. rebus reading**, the first phase, in which the visual appearance of the text forms the starting point. **b. transition reading**, the second phase, in which the work of the reader is facilitated or blocked by the language of the text, according to the degree to which the linguistic competence of the reader is met. **c. content reading**, the third phase, in which the contents are the decisive factor. *Cp.* **reading to learn**.

Reader Response

Reader response theory maintains that reader and literary text must *transact*. This intermingling of reader and text is a creative act. In the words of Rosenblatt (1983), reading is thus a "performing art," the transaction unique and "never to be duplicated." The implication is to emphasize each reader's subjectivity, albeit with verification.

The reader response model suggests immediate application even though theorists may not agree on labels or perspective. First, the reader must be encouraged to surrender to the literary work, to "live through" the reading of it, to experience it fully without future purpose in mind. This is a stage of *evocation*, which avid readers will immediately recognize. Second, the reader broadens the transaction, examining *alternatives* based on other points of view suggested by the text, by other readers, and by comparison with other works. Third, the reader considers application of the experience to his or her own life: What is the ultimate effect of the transaction? This is a stage of *reflective thinking* and *evaluation*. The teacher's job, then, is to encourage and guide students through this model without imposing an interpretation or stock response on them.

A contrast exists between the transactional approach and common practice. In common practice, evocation often is supplanted by right-answer questions and text-based activity framed by someone other than the reader. Literary elements and comprehension factors take precedence over the search for alternative responses. "Let's find the author's theme" blocks reflective thinking to derive personal meaning from the transaction. To point out this contrast, Rosenblatt (1978) has described two stances of the reader, the aesthetic and the efferent, one denoting the "living through" evocation and reflective thinking of a reader unimpeded by other direction, the other denoting the "carrying away" of information to be used for some specified purpose. Both stances are desirable, depending on circumstances. They offer a continuum. For instance, a reader may "live through" reading about a dream house or dream boat that she hopes some day to own, at the same time efferently noting its details with an eye to building one or making a wise purchase. But Rosenblatt and others assert that the aesthetic stance is neglected in education. Efferent purpose setting, efferent instruction, and efferent assessment have overshadowed it. Only recently has there been a deliberate effort to balance the two stances.

With what results? Much of the theorizing is directed at secondary, young adult levels, yet ethnographies and other studies of reader response more often involve younger children. These reveal what some theorists seem disinclined to believe: elementary-age children can, under suitable conditions, respond to their reading in ways that correspond to the entire transactional model. Suitable conditions include conscious effort to include aesthetic stance in teaching (Zarrillo, 1991), theme-based selection of text so that readers can more readily compare one transaction with another, and many ways of nurturing voluntary reading. Literature-strong reading programs with these attributes are better documented than in the past. Dare we hope that longitudinal study is finally possible, so that a tie between transactional theory and lifelong mature reading can be explored?

For now, reader response theory must deal with other questions and doubts. Probst (1991) notes that "response patterns mature within a cultural context that reinforces some patterns and discourages others," while Purves (1993) argues that "school literature" must take into account a

(continued)

▓▓▓▓▓▓▓▓▓▓▓▓▓▓▓▓▓▓▓▓▓▓▓▓

Reader Response (cont'd.)

broader range than response theory has afforded. How to encourage response to be individualistic but at the same time to illuminate cultural context, how to fit response theory into school settings without artificiality, how to generate self-realization in place of group-think as we implement the model or its successors—these are concerns unresolved.

Sam Leaton Sebesta

reading difficulty level **1.** a judgment, estimate, or prediction of the degree to which reading material will be difficult to understand, usually expressed as a grade level; comprehensibility; readability. **2.** the estimated grade level or other index value resulting from the application of a readability formula, cloze procedure, or a traditional comprehension test.

reading disability **1.** reading achievement that is significantly below expectancy for both an individual's reading potential and for chronological age or grade level, sometimes also disparate with a person's cultural, linguistic, and educational experiences. **2.** reading achievement significantly below what could reasonably be expected of a person; a marked ability-achievement discrepancy. *Note*: Reading disability is often inappropriately used as a synonym for *reading retardation* or *reading backwardness*. A child whose reading achievement is significantly below grade level is defined as a *retarded reader*, regardless of chronological age or learning potential. A child whose reading achievement is below that attained by the average student at the same chronological or mental age is referred to as a *backward reader*. See also **learning disability**.

reading distance the viewing distance when reading. *Note*: "In near-point reading, ordinary-sized material should be held from 36 to 46 cm [14½ to 18½ in.] from the eyes for clear, comfortable vision" (Tinker, 1965).

reading expectancy an estimated level of reading performance that a given student theoretically should be able to reach. *Note*: Reading expectancy predictions may be based on many factors, as age, grade, IQ, or listening comprehension, or on a formula that uses and weighs several such factors. See also **ability-achievement discrepancy**.

reading flexibility the adjustment of one's reading speed, purpose, or strategies to the prevailing contextual conditions.

reading for details reading to note the specific parts of a passage, especially those that support main points. *Note*: A good reader is skilled in selecting details relevant to the main idea and in generating implied main ideas from detailed information. "Reading for details requires not only a grasp of the main ideas but also a putting together of the smaller ideas to bring about a better-rounded and more nearly accurate understanding" (Betts, 1946).

reading growth a measure of the difference in periodic samplings of a person's reading ability. *Note*: Reading growth may be shown by test scores or through portfolios showing development over time in reading and in the ability to apply ideas in writing gained from reading.

reading interests those topics and content fields about which a person not only shows a desire to read but does read. *Cp.* **reading preferences**; **reading tastes**.

reading inventory a checklist or questionnaire for assessing reading interests, habits, books read, etc.

reading laboratory a facility with materials and programs for the teaching of developmental or remedial reading and study skills.

reading level **1.** an estimate of a student's current level of reading achievement as compared to some criterion or standard. See also **reading achievement**. **2.** See **instructional reading level**.

reading literacy the ability to understand and use those written forms required by society and/ or valued by the individual (Elley, 1992).

reading log a student-kept record of books read during a specified period, usually by date and sometimes including the number of pages in each book.

reading maturity a high level of reading development in which the individual reads expertly, widely, profitably, and responsibly. *Note*: "Maturity in reading as one aspect of total development is distinguished by the attainment of those interests, attitudes, and skills which enable young people and adults to participate eagerly, independently, and effectively in all the reading activities essential to a full, rich, and productive life.... In the satisfaction of interests and needs through reading, a mature reader will continue to grow in capacity to interpret broadly and deeply" (Gray & Rogers, 1956).

reading method **1.** any of several relatively specific procedures or steps for teaching one or more aspects of reading, each procedure embodying explicitly or implicitly some theory of how children learn and of the relationship be-

---

Types of *Reading Methods**

ABC method**
alphabet method
analytic method
clinical method
corneal-reflection method
deductive method
extrinsic method
Fernald(–Keller) method
Gillingham method
gingerbread method
global method
historical method
inductive method
integrated method
intrinsic method
Jacotot method
keyword method
kinesthetic method
Lancastrian method
letter phonics
look-and-say method[†]
manual method
mirror method
Montessori method
object method
Orton–Gillingham method[††]
paired-associates method
peephole method
phonics
phonovisual method
project method
sentence method
Socratic method
spelling method
story method
synthetic method
visual-motor method
word method

---

*Terms are all defined in this dictionary.
Term is defined under **alphabet method.
[†]Term is defined under **word method**.
[††]Term is defined under **Gillingham method**.

---

tween the written and spoken language. *Note*: The history of reading is replete with methods, sometimes referred to as *approaches*, of different types. Some, as *analytic method, synthetic method*, and *global method*, refer to the overall pattern of instruction; others, as *word method, phrase method, sentence method*, and *story method*, refer to the language unit that is emphasized; still others, as *look-and-say method* and *phonic method*, refer to a distinctive mode of instruction. **2.** sometimes, a specific reading program that translates a general approach into specific instructional materials, as the initial teaching alphabet. *Cp.* **reading program**.

reading miscue inventory 1. See **miscue; miscue analysis**. **2.** an analytic procedure for assessing children's reading comprehension based on samples of oral reading. *Cp.* **informal reading inventory**.

reading preferences the kinds of material a person reads when offered a choice. *Note:* Reading preferences may or may not coincide with reading interests. If a reader is given the task of reading one of two books that are equally distasteful, the preference for one does not indicate a reading interest. *Cp.* **reading interests; reading tastes**.

reading process 1. an act of reading taken as a whole; what happens when a person processes text to obtain meaning. **2.** *pl.*, any of the subprocesses, as word identification or comprehension, that are involved in the act of reading.

reading profile a graph of several scores of reading performance for the same subject or of different aspects of reading for a group of subjects.

reading program 1. a plan for facilitating reading development. *Note:* "A reading program should be all-inclusive, incorporating diverse plans, media, and approaches for the provision of a wide range of individual differences in the entire student body of a school or school system" (Melnik, 1980). See also **basal reading program**. **2.** any specific reading plan, developmental, corrective, or remedial.

reading readiness 1. the readiness to profit from beginning reading instruction. **2.** the readiness to profit from reading instruction beyond the beginning reading level. *Note:* According to Smith (1986), the concept of reading readiness was not widely accepted in American public schools until about 1925–1935, when it was championed by Gray and others as an important concept in relation to basal reading programs. The concept of reading readiness is being replaced by emergent literacy. See also **readiness** (*Note*); **emergent literacy**.

reading readiness test any of a number of formal or informal ways of attempting to predict a student's performance on entering a formal reading instruction program, usually administered in first grade. *Note:* Work in the area of emergent literacy has greatly modified the nature, use, timing, and interpretation of reading readiness tests.

Reading Recovery 1. a registered trademark for an early intervention program developed by Clay (1985) for use with children at risk in reading progress after one year of schooling. *Note:* The program requires a highly trained specialist who can accelerate children's rate of learning so they succeed when returned to the regular classroom. **2.** a teacher-education program designed by Clay (1987) in which good teaching is defined as a "theory building process in which good teachers learn to make explicit their assumptions about reading" (Myers, 1991).

reading school 1. a school in Europe and colonial America for the earliest formal instruction in the alphabet, beginning reading, and religion, for which the first instructional material was the hornbook. *Note:* The separation of reading and writing schools, chiefly in the 17th century, was a fairly widespread but by no means universal practice in Europe and colonial America. Boys usually attended both kinds of schools, but girls attended only the reading school. *Cp.* **writing school** (def. 1). **2.** in the late 18th century, a term occasionally used for elementary school.

reading specialist a general term referring to educational personnel with advanced training in reading education. Types of reading specialists include: **a. reading teacher**, one with special skills in developmental reading and often in corrective and remedial reading. **b. reading consultant**, one who works with the teachers and administrators of a school system to carry out a reading program. **c. reading supervisor**, one who oversees the reading program within a school system. **d. reading coordinator**, one who works chiefly to help make the complex reading programs of large school systems work smoothly together. *Note*: The above terms may vary in meaning among school systems.

reading standards a statement of reading objectives, and the levels to which they should be attained by individuals, schools, departments, etc., issued by a governmental or professional agency.

reading tastes **1.** one's personal inclination to enjoy certain kinds of reading materials, irrespective of their quality. *Cp.* **reading interests**; **reading preferences**. **2.** the aesthetic and critically discerning judgments reflected in the choice of materials for reading; especially, the recognition of material of high literary and artistic merit. *Cp.* **critical evaluation**.

reading test any test for assessing silent or oral reading performance.

reading the word the construction of meaning of texts or speech derived from a reader's previous experience. *Note*: *Reading the word* is Freire's term for comprehension influenced by understanding of political and economic situations surrounding the text and which in turn influences how one views political and economic

conditions outside the text (Freire & Macedo, 1987). See also **critical theory**; **reading the world**.

reading the world Freire's extension of the concept of functional literacy "to include personal fulfillment, social progress, and economic development.... This message...implies awareness and acceptance of a much larger perception of self in relation to one's own world and the world of others" (Newman & Beverstock, 1990). *Note*: This is Freire's term for *worldview*, one's personal conception of the universe and of humankind. See also **critical theory**; **reading the word**.

reading to learn the use of reading skills to acquire knowledge, broaden understandings, and develop appreciations. See also **reading-writing relationships**. *Cp.* **writing to learn**.

reading vocabulary the number of different words recognized and understood in silent reading. *Cp.* **listening vocabulary**; **speaking vocabulary**; **writing vocabulary**.

reading-writing relationships the connection, interplay, and mutual influence of reading and writing, including: **a.** common psychological processes. **b.** transactive or interactive influences on each other. **c.** in combination, positive learning and thinking effects. Also **reading-writing connections**. *Note*: Tierney and Shanahan (1991), in summarizing research on this topic, concluded that "reading and writing, to be understood and appreciated fully, should be viewed together, learned together, and used together." See also the box "Reading-Writing Relationships" on p. 214; **reading to learn**; **writing to learn**.

realism *n.* a 19th-century literary movement that accepts the world revealed by the senses and science as fact. *Note*: Realism presents experience to the objective observer without em-

---

Reading-Writing Relationships*

Viewpoint
Reading and writing are:
• composing, constructing, problem-solving.
• vehicles for thinking.
• ways of communicative interacting.
• social process.
• parallel in development.

Special relationships
• Early writing aids reading and promotes invention, while reading exploration stimulates meaningful literary experiences.

Practice
Reading and writing are taught with multiple texts as:
• common, not separate tasks.
• parallel skills and behaviors.
• collaborative activities.
• social processes.
• parallel in development.

Special relationships
• Beginning reading offers writing opportunities, while early writing stimulates language awareness and development.

*After Tierney & Shanahan, 1991.

---

bellishment. Its purpose is to convey life as it appears in a natural world limited by the senses and reason. *Cp.* **naturalism**; **romanticism**. *n.* **realist**. *adj.* **realistic**.

realistic fiction a story that attempts to portray characters and events as they actually are. *Cp.* **fantasy**.

real-world literacy the literacy and numeracy skills needed to survive in the nonacademic world.

rebus *n.* the use of a picture or symbol that suggests a word or a syllable, as *U R the* ⊤–◻ *2 my* ♥ suggests *you are the key to my heart.*

recall **1.** *n.* the act or process of bringing back from memory a representation of prior learning or experience by images or words. **2.** *v.* to so bring back from memory. See also the box "Types of Recall" in the next column.

recall item a test item that requires the formulation of a response from memory. *Cp.* **recognition item**.

Types of *Recall*
aided
cued*
delayed*
free*
immediate*

---

*Term is defined in this dictionary.

Received Pronunciation (*Brit.*) the distinctive pronunciation of speakers of Received Standard English.

Received Standard (English) (*Brit.*) the speech of the elite British class.

recency effect **1.** the tendency for that which is more recent to be remembered better than that which is less recent. **2.** the tendency for a specific stimulus to arouse newer rather than older associations.

receptive aphasia difficulty in perceiving and comprehending spoken or written language, as in Wernicke's aphasia.

receptive competence knowledge or understanding of the linguistic, cultural, and interactive conventions that apply in a variety of communication settings, as the effects of social class, age, sex, occupation, religion, etc., on communication. *Note*: Appropriate communicative behavior demands an understanding of the wide range of forms of language use but not necessarily the ability to produce them. *Cp.* **communicative competence**; **productive competence**.

receptive language the receipt of a message aurally or visually. *Cp.* **expressive language** (def. 3).

receptive processes the action of the sense organs or cognitive systems responsive to incoming stimuli, as in seeing and hearing in reading.

receptive vocabulary the comprehension vocabulary actually used by a person in silent reading and listening. *Cp.* **expressive vocabulary**.

reciprocal pronoun a pronoun expressing a mutual relationship, as *each other* and *one another*. See **pronoun**.

reciprocal teaching a teaching strategy in which "students are involved in summarizing, question-generating, clarifying, and predicting as they read texts and observe phenomena... [and] both teacher and students share responsibility for the conduct of the discussion" (Palincsar & Brown, 1985).

recode *v.* **1.** to change information from one code into another, as writing into speech. *Note*: No necessary assumption about meaning is made in this process. See also **decode** (def. 1); **encode** (def. 1). **2.** to identify, relate, and then combine, or chunk, two or more symbols, as *re-*

code 3 and 9 into 39, presumably in long-term memory. *n.* **recoding**.

recognition item a test item that requires identification of the correct choice from among several possibilities. *Cp.* **recall item**.

recognition vocabulary the number of different words known without word analysis; words understood quickly and easily; sight vocabulary. See also **sight word**.

recollection *n.* the conscious recall of past experience(s). *v.* **recollect**.

reconstruction *n.* **1.** See **internal reconstruction**. **2.** the modification in comprehension that may result from continued reading or retelling. *v.* **reconstruct**. *adj.* **reconstructive**.

reconstructive processes the processes involved in selecting, evaluating, and organizing ideas of writers and speakers in the receptive acts of reading and listening.

recreational reading voluntary reading for personal satisfaction at unscheduled periods at any age; leisure reading. *Cp.* **community literacy**.

recursiveness *n.* **1.** a characteristic of all languages that enables their grammars to produce an infinite number of sentences. **2.** in transformational-generative grammar, the property that enables a sentence to be expanded indefinitely by repeatedly applying the same rule, as using infinitely more adjectives to modify a noun; iteration; recursion. *Cp.* **embedding**. *adj.* **recursive**.

recursive process in creating a written composition, moving back and forth among the planning, drafting, and revising phases of writing.

redundancy *n.* **1.** the occurrence of essentially the same information in more than one form, often built into a message to provide greater assurance that the message will be understood, as in the repetition of plurality by *those*, *girls*, and *are* in *Those girls are reading*. **2.** a needless and possibly distracting repetition of words or linguistic forms, as *hurriedly raced*. **3.** the linguistic property that "enables a reader with experience and knowledge about the written code to know that only certain patterns of letters are possible out of all possible combinations" (Hodges & Rudorf, 1972). *adj.* **redundant**.

reduplication *n.* **1.** the creation of compound-like words whose parts rhyme or contain repeated sounds, as *fuddy-duddy*, *ding-dong*, *super-duper*; reduplicative compound. **2.** See **neologism**. *adj.* **reduplicative**.

re-entry program **1.** a program for adults wishing to continue their education without having to return to a high school. *Note*: Such programs are usually designed to cover missing subject areas or levels to allow someone entrance to college or technical school and often give credit for experential learning. **2.** a job upgrading program that usually includes literacy training.

reference **1.** *n.* a source or direction to a source of information, as *an encyclopedia reference*. **2.** *v.* to give sources in a book or article. **3.** *n.* what a linguistic symbol represents. See also **referent** (def. 1). **4.** *n.* language represented by graphemes in a writing system. *Note*: The reference of graphemes is generally to phonemes in alphabetic writing systems, to syllables in syllabaries, and to morphemes, or words, in logographic systems. **5.** *n.* in cohesion analysis, linguistic items that make reference to something else for their interpretation, as personal pronouns (*he*, *she*), demonstrative pronouns (*this*, *that*) and comparative adjectives and adverbs (*good*, *more*). *Note*: Halliday and Hasan (1976) distinguish between *textual* references, in which items can be interpreted by referring to something in surrounding text (see **anaphora**, def. 1; **cataphora**; **endophora**), and

situational references, in which items can be interpreted by referring to the context in which they are used (see **exophora**).

reference book a book designed to be consulted for specific items of information, as a yearbook, atlas, or dictionary.

referent *n.* **1.** the object or event to which a word or other symbol refers, as ▱ is the referent of English *book*, French *livre*, Italian *libro*, German *Buch*. **2.** in semiotics, the object or range of objects to which a sign refers. Also **referend**. *v.* **refer**.

reflection *n.* **1.** the process or result of seriously thinking over one's experiences, especially those valued. **2.** an approach to problem solving that emphasizes the careful consideration of the nature of the problem, the thorough planning of procedures to solve the problem, and the monitoring of the processes used in reaching a solution. **3.** in Rosenblatt's (1978) transactional theory of reading, a late or final phase of the reading process in which the significance of the reader's evocation of the text is reviewed and evaluated. *Cp.* **evocation**. **4.** a sign. **5.** introspection. *v.* **reflect**. *adj.* **reflective**.

reflective abstraction in cognition, the reworking of cognitive constructions at lower levels of development into a higher level cognitive structure. *Cp.* **physical abstraction**.

reflective writer in writing instruction, a writer who tends to rework a composition with the needs of an audience in mind.

reflexive pronoun a pronoun object that refers back to the subject, as *herself* in *Amanda cut herself*. See **pronoun**.

refraction *n.* **1.** the power of the eyes to bend light rays to achieve a clear image. See also **ametropia**. *Cp.* **visual acuity**. **2.** the identification of refractive errors in the eyes in prescribing corrective lenses. *adj.* **refractive**.

refrain *n.* a verse or phrase repeated at intervals in a poem or song, usually at the end of a stanza; chorus.

regional dialect a variety of a given language, which contains shared features, used by most individuals in a geographical region, as the German-English dialect called Pennsylvania Dutch.

register **1.** *n.* the language variety determined by social circumstances. *Note:* Most persons have a repertoire of registers. While an employee chatting with other workers might say, "The boss's latest memo doesn't make any sense at all," he or she would likely use a more respectful register in speaking to his employer, as "I'm having a bit of difficulty understanding your memo." See also **casual speech**; **key** (def. 1); **style of discourse**. **2.** *n.* the tonal range of a voice or musical instrument. **3.** *n.* the exact alignment of inks in color printing. **4.** *v.* to make such an alignment. **5.** *n.* the memory storage unit of a computer; sometimes, the hardware for storing some specific type or category of data. **6. reading register**, the special terminology used to teach reading; the terms needed to develop metalinguistic awareness.

register switching the change from one language variety to another to fit perceived changes in social situations. See also **register** (def. 1).

regression *n.* **1.** movement backward; specifically, a backward eye movement in reading continuous text. See also **eye-movement pattern**. **2.** See **regression toward the mean**. **3.** the return to an earlier developmental state or condition. *v.* **regress**. *adj.* **regressive**.

regression analysis a statistical procedure for the analysis of variables as predictors, and for determining the degree of relationship between an independent and a dependent variable. *Note:* For example, an attempt to predict students' grade point averages from membership in one of the three categories of work habits might involve regression analysis.

regression coefficient **1.** the coefficient of any independent variable in a regression equation. **2.** the constant in a mathematical equation giving the slope of a regression line that shows the relationship between the variables being measured.

regression equation a mathematical formula that expresses the most probable value of one variable when that of the other variable(s) is known.

regression toward the mean the shift in scores toward the mean that occurs on repeated or correlated measures, as of predicted scores.

regular verb a verb that follows a regular pattern of conjugation, as *talk*, *talks*, *talked* as forms of *to talk*; weak verb. *Cp.* **irregular verb**.

rehearsal *n.* in writing, the process in which a writer mentally tries out more than one version of a composition before selecting the one preferred. *v.* **rehearse**.

reinforcement *n.* **1.** the strengthening of something, especially by increased response depth or frequency. **2.** the conditioning process of increasing the probability of a response by rewarding the desired behavior; positive reinforcement. **3.** the facilitation of a neural impulse by the simultaneous arousal of another neural impulse. **4.** that which so strengthens; reinforcer. **5.** simple repetition or repeated practice. **6.** in programmed materials and computer learning programs, feedback about the correct or incorrect responses; knowledge of results. *v.* **reinforce**.

reinforcement schedule a time plan, either regular or intermittent, for rewarding behavior.

Note: Many schedule variations have been developed for specific purposes. For example, a schedule for operant conditioning depends on the response behavior and is intermittent. The schedule may be of two kinds: ratio reinforcement, based on number of responses, or interval reinforcement, based on some time interval. See also **conditioning**.

reinforcer *n.* a stimulus or event that increases the probability of strengthening a response. *Note*: A *primary reinforcer* is a stimulus or event that directly or innately increases the probability of strengthening a response, as *food* or *water*. A *secondary reinforcer* is a stimulus that indirectly increases the probability of strengthening a response because of a previous reinforcing role, as *money* or a *gift*.

relational thought a form of thinking that proceeds by analogy and indirection rather than by strictly logical expectations. *Cp.* **conjunctive thought**; **disjunctive thought**.

relative clause a dependent clause that modifies a noun or noun phrase, as *who wrote the poem* in *The girl who wrote the poem. Cp.* **nonrestrictive clause**; **restrictive clause**.

relative pronoun a pronoun that refers to an antecedent, as *whom* in *the man whom you were talking to*. See **pronoun**.

reliability *n.* consistency in measurements and tests; specifically, the extent to which two applications of the same measuring procedure rank persons in the same way. *v.* **reliable**.

reliability coefficient an index, usually a correlation coefficient, expressing the consistency with which a test measures from one testing condition to another, involving differences in such things as day of testing, test items, and raters. *Note*: Reliability coefficients may be run between scores on two test forms, between scores on repeated test administrations, or between scores on the two halves of a test. See also **coefficient of correlation**.

reluctant reader a euphemism for one who does not like to read. *Note*: A reluctant reader may not have the ability or skills to read, or may have the skills but choose not to read.

remedial reading **1.** specialized reading instruction adjusted to the needs of a student who does not perform satisfactorily with regular reading instruction. **2.** intensive, specialized reading instruction for students reading considerably below expectancy. *Note*: Remedial reading is usually highly individualized reading instruction conducted outside the classroom in a special class, school, or clinic by a teacher trained in the use of clinical methods in reading. Eligibility for some remedial reading programs may be determined by legal definitions or by criteria established by the school or school district. **3.** developmental reading instruction set at a different pace and designed for an individual student or a selected group. *Cp.* **corrective reading**.

remedial reading program **1.** the curriculum and operation of a program designed to provide intensive remediation in reading, usually by a teacher with advanced training and in a setting that allows flexible adjustment of materials and methods to individual differences. **2.** any set of curriculum materials, usually commercially prepared, for the remediation of reading skill deficits.

remediation *n.* **1.** teaching that includes diagnosis of a student's reading ability and corrective, remedial, or clinical approaches to improve that ability. **2.** the process of correcting a deficiency.

repartee *n.* **1.** a quick, witty retort; bon mot. **2.** a conversation marked by such retorts.

repeated measures design an experimental design in which the same experimental group of subjects is exposed to more than one treatment; dependent sample design. *Cp.* **independent groups design**.

repertoire of registers a tacit knowledge of the range of language varieties appropriate to respective social circumstances, topics, etc. See also **register** (def. 1).

replication *n.* **1.** a copy; duplicate. **2.** the repetition of an experiment, often in different settings, to compare and verify findings. *v.* **replicate**.

representamen *n.* in semiotics, a sign. See **sign** (defs. 6, 7).

representational level the relative degree of concreteness or abstractness of an idea or image.

representative sample an experimental sample that reflects to a high degree the composition of the population from which it is drawn. *Cp.* **stratified sample**.

research method any of several general types of systematic inquiry into a subject or problem in order to discover, verify, or revise relevant facts or principles having to do with that subject or problem. See also the box "Types of Research Methods Used in Education" in the next column.

residual **1.** *adj.* left over; remaining. **2.** *n.* in statistics: **a.** the difference between a predicted and an observed value. **b.** the variance remaining in a correlation matrix after the variance of each factor has been removed.

residual gain a measure of individual differences in improvement through training of subjects who have been statistically equated on the basis of pretraining measurement.

residual hearing any hearing possessed by a person with a hearing impairment.

Types of *Research Methods* Used in Education*

action
applied
basic
correlational
crosscultural
cross-sectional
ethnographic
field
historical
laboratory
longitudinal
naturalistic**
observational**
qualitative
quantitative

---

*Terms are all defined in this dictionary.
Term is defined under **ethnographic research.

---

resource center a library or educational site at which materials, often on specific themes or subjects, are located. *Cp.* **instructional materials center**; **media center**.

resource unit **1.** a collection of materials on a single topic from which a teacher can draw in developing a teaching unit. **2.** (*Brit.*) a resource center.

respelling *n.* **1.** a repeated or different spelling of a word. **2.** the spelling of words in a new, usually phonemic, system. See **augmented alphabet**. **3.** a new spelling system, usually phonemic and simpler than its precursor.

response (R) *n.* **1.** a written or spoken answer to a question. **2.** an overt or covert reaction to stimulation. *Cp.* **stimulus** (defs. 1, 2). *Note*: All responses are considered measurable, either by direct inspection or through some electrochemical or mechanical means. **3.** the class of reactions to which def. 2 refers. *v.* **respond**. *adj.* **responsive**.

response discrimination the consistent selection of an appropriate response from alternative stimuli.

response generalization the tendency of a learned response to a stimulus to make that stimulus more likely to call forth similar responses. *Cp.* **stimulus generalization**.

restricted code a term coined in the 1960s by the British sociologist Basil Bernstein to describe the private language used by speakers in informal and intimate settings where strong group membership is shared. *Note*: A restricted code is identified by its high reliance on context for understanding and its predictable syntax and lexicon. *Cp.* **elaborated code** (*Note*).

restricted literacy the specialized use of language characteristics of a particular social class or group. *Note*: Historically, certain types of literacy have always been restricted, as in the use of Latin by Roman Catholic priests, professional jargon by doctors and lawyers, and often esoteric vernacular by artisans in highly technical trades.

restrictive clause a dependent clause that limits or specifies the meaning of a noun, as *who had a camera* in *The man who had a camera took our picture. Cp.* **nonrestrictive clause**; **relative clause**.

retelling *n.* **1.** in discourse analysis, a measure of comprehension. **2.** in miscue analysis, the process in which the reader, having orally read a story, describes what happened in it. *Note*: The purpose of including retelling in miscue analysis is to gain insight into the reader's ability to interact with, interpret, and draw conclusions from the text. *v.* **retell**.

retention curve in a learning task, the graphic representation of performance plotted in relation to time since the last learning practice;

forgetting curve. *Note*: Performance is usually plotted on the vertical axis and time on the horizontal axis of the graph. *Cp.* **learning curve**.

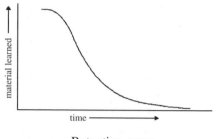

Retention curve

retention test a delayed assessment of learning to discover its relatively long-term effects.

retina *n.* the sense organ for sight; specifically, an extension of the optic nerve inside the eyeball in a thin layer of cells sensitive to light and color.

retinal image the representation of the visual field formed on the retina by the refractive system of the eye.

retinoscope *n.* an instrument for determining the refractive power of the eye, thus enabling eye specialists to prescribe proper corrective lenses; skiascope.

retroactive inhibition the interfering effect of later learning on learned material, especially in remembering similar material; fan effect. *Cp.* **proactive inhibition**.

return sweep the diagonal eye-movement, or saccade, from the end of one line of print to the start of the next. See also **eye-movement pattern**.

reversal *n.* **1.** a turnabout in direction, or rotation. **2.** the misreading or miswriting of letters, numbers, or words by the rotation of a symbol, as *d* for *p* in *pot*, or by an error in the direction of word identification, as *bat* for *tab*. *Note*: Technically, a change in rotation is called a *static reversal*, as *b* for *d*, and a change in direction is called a *kinetic reversal*, as *n* for *u*. *v.* **reverse**.

reversibility *n.* in Piagetian theory, the principle that for every operation there is an inverse or counter operation.

reversible *adj.* referring to forms or to sequences of letters or words that can be meaningfully perceived in more than one direction, as the reversible word *eye*. See also **palindrome**.

review **1.** *v.* to study again for better understanding or retention. **2.** *n.* the act of studying again. **3.** *n.* a critical report, as *a book review*. **4.** *v.* to make a critical report. **5.** *v.* to make a survey of something, as *review the research on reading readiness*. **6.** *v.* to look back on, as *review one's experiences in reading*.

rheme *n.* in functional grammar, "that part of a clause in which the theme is developed" (Halliday, 1985), as *a popular sport worldwide* is the rheme of the sentence that develops the theme of soccer in *Soccer is a popular sport worldwide*. *Note*: In this perspective, the rheme elaborates the meaning of a message, while the theme establishes its topic or tells what it is about. *Cp.* **theme** (def. 4).

rhetoric *n.* **1.** the art or science of using language in prose or verse. **2.** the effective use of language in oratory to influence or persuade an audience. **3.** the study of the theory and principles of effective communication. *Cp.* **discourse analysis**. *adj.* **rhetorical**.

rhyme **1.** *n.* identical or very similar recurring final sounds in words within or, more often, at the ends of lines of verse. **2.** *n.* verse or recurring words that represent such sounds. **3.** *v.* to write words or lines of verse with such recurring sounds.

rhyme scheme the pattern of rhyme in verse, usually coded, to represent identical or highly similar final sounds in lines of verse, as the pattern *aabba* for a limerick.

rhythm *n.* **1.** the pattern of recurring strong and weak syllabic stress in speech. **2.** a recurring emphasis in the flow of spoken or written speech; beat; cadence; as *the rhythm of iambic pentameter*. **3.** metrical form. **4.** the planned recurrence of a motif, as a symbol or theme, in literature or in other art forms. *adj.* **rhythmic**; **rhythmical**.

right brain the right cerebral hemisphere, usually the controlling center for spatial and nonverbal concepts as well as for neuromuscular activity on the opposite side of the body. *Cp.* **left brain**.

rime[1] *n.* rhyme.

rime[2] *n.* a vowel and any following consonants of a syllable, as /o͝ok/ in *book* or *brook*, /īk/ in *strike*, and /ā/ in *play*. *Cp.* **onset**.

rising diphthong *n.* a diphthong in which the second element of the diphthong is stressed, as /o͞o/ in *view*.

ritual *n.* a speech event comprised wholly of routine language forms, interpreted only in terms of the social context in which it occurs, as at religious ceremonies. *Cp.* **routine**.

robust *adj.* referring to a stable statistical procedure. *n.* **robustness**.

rod *n.* any of the light-sensitive but only slightly color-sensitive cells in the retina that are needed especially for peripheral vision and for seeing in dim light. *Note*: Vision by rods is primarily in shades of gray. *Cp.* **cone**.

romance **1.** *n.* a novel or other narrative, often in an imaginary or historical setting, that tells of great deeds, pageantry, courtly love, etc.; especially, a medieval story, often written in verse, as *The Song of Roland*. **2.** *n.* a love story. *adj.* **romantic**.

Romance language any of the Italic Indo-European languages derived from Latin in the Middle Ages; chiefly French, Spanish, Italian, Portuguese, and Romanian.

romanization *n.* the transliteration of the orthography of a language, such as that of Arabic, into Latin alphabetic letters. See also **transliteration** (def. 1). *v.* **romanize**.

romanticism *n.* a literary movement in late 18th- and early 19th-century England and Europe that rejected Enlightenment rationalism and advocated transcendence through imagination and ecstatic experiences. *Note*: Romanticism is associated with the French Revolution and the initial acceptance of democratic ideals. It also cultivates a nostalgia for the Middle Ages and turns increasingly toward religion and conservative traditions.

root *n.* **1.** the basic part of a word that usually carries the main component of meaning and that cannot be further analyzed without loss of identity. **2.** in a complex word, the meaningful base form after all affixes are removed. *Note*: A root may be independent, or free, as *read* in *unreadable*, or may be dependent, or bound, as *-liter-* (from the Greek for *letter*) in *illiterate*. *Cp.* **bound morpheme**; **free morpheme**. **3.** in historical linguistics, a language component reconstructed as part of a protolanguage, as Indo-European *gerbh-* from which are derived *grammar*, *graph*, *graffiti*, etc.; radical. **4.** in a hierarchal computer system, the basic directory from which all other directories branch.

rotation *n.* **1.** continuous movement around an axis or pivotal point. **2.** one such complete turn. **3.** a recurring series, as the rotation of the days

of the week. **4.** a static reversal in reading or writing, as *p* for *d*. **5.** in factor analysis, the shifting of factor axes and their hyperplanes after factor extraction.

rote learning the acquisition of information or behaviors by repetitive drill rather than by understanding. *Note*: The chief value of rote learning is in producing automatic psychomotor responses.

rote memory the process of exact recall of what was learned, often with no guarantee of understanding.

round-robin reading the outmoded practice of calling on students to read orally one after the other. *Note*: Periods of uninterrupted silent reading offer a constructive alternative to round-robin reading.

routine *n.* in language use, fixed utterances or sequences of utterances that are appropriate to a communicative situation, as greetings, a sales pitch, etc.; formulaic expression. *Note*: Routines are learned and interpreted as single units of expression and meaning. See also **ritual**.

rule *n.* **1.** a guiding principle of behavior. **2.** a generalized grammatical statement of conventional usage. **3.** a prescription for correct or preferred language use, as in prescriptive grammar. **4.** in transformational-generative grammar, a phrase structure rule or rewrite rule. **5.** a thin line.

rune *n.* **1.** a letter in the futhork, or runic, alphabet. See also **futhork** (definition and illustration). *Cp.* **ogham**. **2.** a poem, riddle, or incantation written in runic characters. **3.** any occult character or incantation. *adj.* **runic**.

running record a cumulative account of selected behavior, as of that of a student noted by a teacher over time.

running words 1. an uninterrupted series of words in a text. *Note*: *Running words* is a term used in describing the development or application of some readability formulas, informal reading inventories, cloze procedures, etc. **2.** See **tokens** (def. 2). See also **type-token ratio**.

run-on sentence two independent clauses joined without any punctuation or conjunction to separate them, as the omission of a period after *door* in *I walked in the door she was sitting by the fire*. See also **comma fault**.

S

S *n.* **1.** See **stimulus**. **2.** an experimental subject. **3.** in transformational-generative grammar, a sentence. **4.** See **specific factor**.

saccade *n.* the quick, jumping movement of the eye as it shifts fixation from place to place, usually without awareness of the viewer, as in searching a visual field or in moving along a line of print in reading. *Note*: If you look over the top of a page at someone reading, you will see the quick eye movements that alternate with the longer fixations during which print is actually viewed. The eye is essentially blind during these eye movements. See also **eye-movement pattern**. *Cp.* **fixation**; **fixation point**. *adj.* **saccadic**.

saga *n.* **1.** a narrative of heroic deeds and events, usually of a person or family; especially, a medieval story of Icelandic and Scandinavian origin, passed on through oral tradition. *Cp.* **epic** (def. 1). **2.** a modern story of a family.

sample **1.** *n.* a part that represents a whole. **2.** *n.* in experimentation, that part of a population selected for observation. *Note*: Special types of samples, as *stratified sample*, are defined under the describing term. **3. sampling**, the act of getting an experimental sample. **4.** *v.* to examine or test something by considering only a part of a larger whole, as *The effective reader knows when to sample and when to read material in detail.*

sampling error any difference between a sample and the population from which it is drawn that makes the sample inaccurate.

sandhi *n.* **1.** a modification of a sound in a morpheme, as *gimme* for *give me*. *Note*: The term comes from a Sanskrit word meaning *joining* or *juncture*. **2.** a phonological modification occurring especially at a word boundary. *Cp.* **assimilation** (def. 5); **dissimilation**.

sarcasm *n.* **1.** a harsh form of irony, intended to taunt or hurt. **2.** a harsh or cutting remark. See also **irony** (def. 1); **satire**. *adj.* **sarcastic**.

satire *n.* **1.** the use of ridicule or scorn, often in a humorous or witty way, to expose vices and follies. **2.** a literary example of such ridicule or scorn. **3.** the class of such writings. See also **burlesque** (defs. 1–3); **caricature**; **parody**; **travesty** (def. 1). *Cp.* **irony** (def. 1); **lampoon**; **sarcasm**. *adj.* **satirical**.

scaffolding *n.* in learning, the gradual withdrawal of adult (e.g., teacher) support, as through instruction, modeling, questioning, feedback, etc., for a child's performance across successive engagements, thus transferring more and more autonomy to the child. *Note*: "Support activities are called scaffolding because they provide support for learning that can be taken down and removed as learners are able to demonstrate strategic behaviors in their own learning activities" (Herrmann, 1994). This concept is based on Vygotsky's (1978) emphasis on the importance of learning assistance that is adjusted to the learner's potential development. See also **zone of proximal development**.

scale **1.** *n.* any device, or representation thereof, for measuring quantity in a series of ordered units, as *a metric scale*, *a map scale*. **2.** *n.* a standard of measurement. **3.** *n.* a graded series of tasks or tests for measuring performance, as *the Wechsler Intelligence Scale*. **4.** *v.* to make or place on a scale.

scan **1.** *v.* to examine or read something quickly, but selectively, for a particular purpose; skim. **2.** *v.* to examine or read something carefully; look at closely. *Note*: The contrasting meaning of defs. 1 and 2 depend on the context for their interpretation. **3.** *n.* the act or result of making a detailed survey, as *a brain scan*. **4.** *v.* to analyze the metrical structure of verse. **5.** *v.* to follow, in verse, the rules of meter.

scansion *n.* a way of analyzing verse to note rhythmic effects and rhyme scheme; scanning.

scatter **1.** *v.* to spread out; disperse. **2.** *n.* the degree of spread or dispersion of test scores; variance. **3.** *adj.* referring to such a spread. **4.** *n.* the spread or variability of item difficulty in a test.

scatter diagram a crosstabulation or graph that shows the joint distribution of two sets of scores in terms of score intervals; scattergram. See also **joint distribution**.

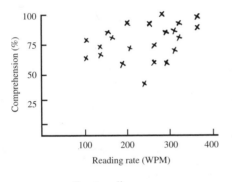

Scatter diagram

schema *n., pl.* **-mata** **1.** a generalized description, plan, or structure, as *a schema of the reading process*. **2.** a system of cognitive structures stored in memory that are abstract representations of events, objects, and relationships in the world. **3.** in Piagetian theory, an image representing reality that is held in thought but not transformed through thought.

schema theory a view that comprehension depends on integrating new knowledge with a network of prior knowledge. *Note:* In schema theory, reading is seen as "an active process of constructing meaning by connecting old knowledge with new information encountered in text" (Anderson & Pearson, 1984). Several varieties of schema theory have been proposed, each of which includes encoding processes (selection,

abstraction, interpretation, and integration) and a retrieval process (reconstruction).

schematic **1.** *n.* a diagram or plan, as a flow chart in a science textbook. See also **schema** (def. 1). **2.** *adj.* referring to such a diagram or plan.

scheme *n.* in Piagetian theory, in the structure of operational thought patterns of logical thinking, activities that can be repeated and generalized in an action.

schwa *n.* **1.** in English, the midcentral vowel in an unaccented or unstressed syllable; as the first vowel sound in *alone*. See also **short vowel**. **2.** the graphic symbol (ə) commonly used in phonetic alphabets and pronunciation keys to represent such a vowel.

science fiction imaginary writing based on current or projected scientific and technological developments, as Jules Verne's *20,000 Leagues under the Sea* or Ray Bradbury's *Fahrenheit 451*.

scope *n.* the breadth or range of content covered by a lesson, unit, course, curriculum, etc. See also **scope and sequence**. *Cp.* **sequence**.

scope and sequence a curriculum plan, usually in chart form, in which a range of instructional objectives, skills, etc., is organized according to the successive levels at which they are taught. See also **sequence**.

score **1.** *n.* the credits or points earned on a test. **2.** *n.* an item of credit on a test. **3.** *v.* to achieve a given score. **4.** *v.* to assess the credits or points earned. See also the box "Types of Score" on p. 228.

scotopic vision vision under conditions of dim light that relies mostly on the rods around the edge of the retina and is thus not very sensitive to color; night vision. See also **rod**. *Cp.* **photopic vision**.

Types of _Score_

composite score*
converted score
criterion score*
critical score
cutting score*
derived score*
factor score*
raw score*
standard score*
true score*
T score
z-score**

---

*Term is defined in this dictionary.
Term is defined under **standard score.

---

scribal literacy a level of literacy in writing that is confined to copying.

scribble **1.** *v.* to write carelessly, without attention to the shape or legibility of the letters, accuracy of the spelling, or grammatical correctness. **2.** *v.* to produce meaningless written marks. **3.** *n.* careless written marks or writing; scribbling. See also **scribble writing**.

scribble writing graphic signs produced by children to communicate meaning in the early stages of writing development. *Note*: Although the writing may be meaningless to adults, children will usually produce an interpretation.

script **1.** *n.* a set of graphic forms used in a writing system, as Latin alphabet, Cyrillic alphabet, Japanese kana, Chinese logographs, etc. *Note*: A given script may have many variant forms, as manuscript, cursive, uppercase, lowercase, italic, boldface, etc. *Cp.* **orthography**; **writing system**. **2.** *n.* the letters or characters used in handwriting. **3.** See **cursive handwriting**. **4.** *n.* the text of a manuscript. **5.** *n.* a text used to guide the speech and actions of performers, as in a play, motion picture, etc. **6.** *v.* to write the text of a play, television show, etc. **7.** *v.*

to transform a novel or play into a television or motion picture script. **8.** *n.* a typeface that looks like handwriting. **9.** *n.* in cognitive psychology, a person's knowledge of sequences, events, and actions related to particular situations, as eating at a restaurant, attending a funeral, etc. See also **schema** (def. 2); **schema theory**. *n.* **scripter**.

script activation the arousal of particular knowledge structures suitable to a given situation. See also **script** (def. 9).

secondary *adj.* with reference to educational difficulties, having an emotional, physical, or environmental basis, rather than a neurological one. *Cp.* **primary**.

secondary accent **1.** the vowel or syllable in a word, phrase, or metrical foot with the second strongest and loudest emphasis; secondary stress. See also **stress** (def. 2). **2.** an orthographic symbol placed above a vowel grapheme or adjacent to a syllable (') or (") or above a syllable in a line of verse (˘) to indicate a weak stress. See also **accent** (def. 2a); **diacritic mark**. *Cp.* **primary accent** (def. 2).

secondary school a school ranking between elementary school and college; high school, usually either grades 9–12 or 7–12.

second-language acquisition the process of gaining facility in a language different from one's native tongue.

self-contained classroom a classroom in which the same teacher teaches all or nearly all subjects.

self-mediation *n.* the active role of the learner in mediation in contrast to the more neutral "linking" role of mediation in stimulus-response theory. *Note*: "In higher forms of human behavior, the individual actively modifies the stimulus situation as a part of the process of responding to it" (Vygotsky, 1978).

---

self-monitoring *n.* in writing, the conscious awareness of the progress of the text, marked by rereading and reflection on features of the text needed to communicate effectively to an audience. See also **metacognitive awareness**.

self-regulation *n.* in Piagetian theory, a sub-principle of equilibration that refers to the active tendency to keep things in balance biologically and through cognitive operations; autoregulation.

self-report any information supplied by oneself, as on a questionnaire, checklist, etc.

self-talk **1.** the mental rehearsal of ways of expressing ideas in writing. **2.** the rehearsal of positive beliefs, as "I can do it," in an effort to substitute positive attitudes for self-defeating ones and to avoid attributing blame to others.

semantic aphasia **1.** See **receptive aphasia**. **2.** See **expressive aphasia**.

semantic count a record of how often different meanings for words appear in a representative sample of reading material.

semantic cue evidence from the general sense or meaning of a written or spoken communication that aids in the identification of an unknown word. *Cp.* **syntactic cue**.

semantic factor the meaning dimension in material to be comprehended, as the measure of the number of hard words that is commonly used in readability formulas. *Cp.* **syntactic factor**.

semantic feature analysis (SFA) in vocabulary instruction, the use of a grid or matrix with target words on the vertical axis and possible features or attributes on the horizontal axis to determine relevant meaning relationships.

semantic field a classification or category of the meanings of words or concepts, as a classification used in a thesaurus; lexical field.

Planets in Earth's solar system

	Closer to sun than Earth	Larger than Earth	Has moon	Has rings	Orbits the sun	Inner planet
Earth	−	−	+	−	+	+
Jupiter	−	+	+	−		−
Mars		−	+	−	+	+
Mercury	+	−		−	+	+
Neptune	−	+		−		−
Pluto	−	+		−		−
Saturn	−	+		+		−
Uranus	−			−		−
Venus	+	−	+	−	+	

From P. Cunningham & J. Cunningham, Content area reading-writing lessons. *The Reading Teacher*, February 1987, p. 509.

Semantic feature analysis

semantic mapping a graphic display of a cluster of words that are meaningfully related. *Note*: Semantic mapping is especially valuable in the prereading and vocabulary-building phases of content area reading.

semantic memory a comprehensive form of meaningful memory; "general, encyclopedic memory of the world and language" (Best, 1989); conceptual memory. *Note*: Semantic memory appears to involve a network of several specific types of memory. *Cp.* **episodic memory**.

semantics *n. (with sing. v.)* **1.** the study of meaning in language, as the analysis of the meanings of words, phrases, sentences, discourse, and whole texts; linguistic semantics. *Cp.* **pragmatics**. **2.** the study of the origin of verbal symbols and their validity with respect to logical consistency and to truth or falsity; philosophical semantics. **3.** in semiotics, the study of the relationships between signs and their objects. **4.** the study of meaning in artificial language systems; pure semantics. **5.** See **generative semantics**.

semantic triangle a model developed by Ogden and Richards (1953) in the 1920s in which meaning is construed as a three-part relationship between a referent, a concept, and a linguistic form.

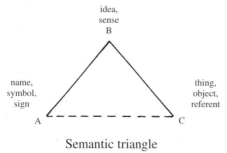

Semantic triangle

semiliterate **1.** *adj.* able to read and write only with difficulty. **2.** *adj.* able to read but not write. **3.** *adj.* not proficient or not well informed in lit-eracy acts. **4.** *n.* a person with any of these characteristics. *n.* **semiliteracy**.

semiosis *n.* **1.** a term coined by Peirce (1931–1958) to indicate the active or dynamic nature of signs. *Note*: In this perspective, signs are not merely inert instruments of communication but are capable of shaping human thought and feeling. **2.** the study of how individuals mean; semiotics.

semiotics *n. (with sing. v.)* **1.** "a general philosophy of communication" (Eco, 1993). **2.** the "formal doctrine of signs" (Peirce, 1984). **3.** the analysis and theory of signaling systems and signs (Morris, 1971). **4.** the theory of signs and their relations and manifestations, comprised of the sub-branches of syntactics, semantics, and pragmatics. See these terms. **5.** the study of how groups come to share meanings. Also **semiotic**; **semeiotic(s) semiology**. *Note*: The field of semiotics has both European and American roots. The Swiss linguist Ferdinand de Saussure (1857–1913) developed a field of inquiry he called *semiologie*. He proposed that a *sign* contains an arbitrary relationship between two parts: a *signifier* (e.g., a word) and a *signified* (e.g., the concept or object, etc., a word represents). Saussure also was instrumental in founding structuralism as an analytic approach. The American philosopher Charles Peirce (1839–1914) developed what he called *semiotic*, a doctrine in which signs have a three-part construction—a *sign*, *object*, and *interpretant* (see these terms). Peirce is also generally credited as one of the developers of the philosophical doctrine of pragmatism. Contemporary semioticians include Umberto Eco (Italy) and Thomas Sebeok (U.S.). See also **sign** (defs. 1, 6). *adj.* **semiotic**.

semivowel *n.* **1.** a speech sound with features of both a consonant and a vowel; specifically, a consonantal resonant; as /w/ in *wash*, /m/ in *spasm*, /y/ in *yes*. *Cp.* **syllabic consonant**. **2.** a sound that can serve as either a vowel or consonant, /y/ or /w/. **3.** a letter representing any of these sounds. *adj.* **semivocalic**; **semivowel**.

sensationalism *n.* the use of verbal or graphic media to create striking or shocking impressions intended to excite interest or attention. **2.** the theory or doctrine that all ideas derive solely from sensory experience. *adj.* **sensational**.

sense 1. *n.* literal or cognitive meaning; denotation. **2.** *n.* semantic meaning; connotation. *Cp.* **meaning** (defs. 1, 2). **3.** *n.* the meaning relationships between lexical elements and sentences; the meaning of a word as established by the context in which it occurs; as the different meanings of *head* in *The baby has a full head of hair*, *Alicia is at the head of her math class*, and *Let's head in that direction*. *Cp.* **referent** (def. 1). **4.** *n.* any of the means, as sight, hearing, smell, etc., by which one perceives stimuli outside or within the body. **5.** *v.* to perceive by the senses. *adj.* **sensory**.

sensorimotor stage in Piaget's theory of mental development, the developmental period from birth to approximately two years during which intellectual development relies primarily on sensory input and motor activities prior to the attainment of symbolic functioning and representational thought. *Cp.* **stage** (def. 2).

sensorineural deafness deafness caused by disease or damage to the inner ear or auditory nerve; nerve deafness. *Cp.* **conduction deafness**.

sensory memory nonsymbolic memory of impressions gained from the senses.

sensory register the store of impressions in sensory memory; sensory store.

sentence (s) *n. Note:* A sentence is more easily identified in writing than in speech; yet most speakers of a language appear to know what a

sentence is, even though grammarians and linguists continue to grapple with its definition. **1.** operationally, a grammatical unit of one or more words, with little necessary syntactic relation to surrounding grammatical units, often punctuated in speech by pauses and marked by recognizable intonation patterns, and typically expressing an independent statement, question, command, etc. **2.** "an expression of thought or feeling by means of a word or words used in such form and manner as to convey the meaning intended" (Curme, 1931). **3.** in transformational-generative grammar, the largest linguistic unit, containing at least one subject and predicate, that is not part of a larger comparable linguistic form and that follows the rules of syntactic formation. See also **sentence pattern**.

Types of *Sentences**
cleft
complex
compound
compound-complex
pseudocleft
simple

---

*Terms are all defined in this dictionary.

---

sentence combining *n.* a teaching technique developed by O'Hare to improve writing skills in which complex sentence chunks and paragraphs are built from basic sentences by means of syntactic manipulation. *Note:* "Sentence combining is essentially a rewriting skill" (O'Hare, 1973).

sentence method a method of teaching reading in which "the sentence first being presented as a whole, the words are discovered, and after that the letters composing the word" (Farnham, cited in Huey, 1908). *Note:* Variations on this method include beginning with phrase or story units.

sentence modifier a word, phrase, or clause that qualifies or limits the meaning of an entire sentence, as *Fortunately* in *Fortunately, the rain stopped*.

sentence pattern any of a number of basic sentence types in a language. *Note*: In traditional grammar, sentence patterns are described in terms of function, as *statement, question, exclamation, command*, etc. In structural grammar, sentence patterns are described in terms of a noun, kind of verb, and the number and kind of elements following the verb, as *N, V, Adv.* to describe *The dog ate quickly*. In transformational-generative grammar, the nature of the verb and the kinds of transformations the sentence may undergo determine its pattern.

sentence transformation in transformational-generative grammar, the rearrangements, deletions, and copyings of elements in phrase-structure grammar that are part of the process of generating a sentence.

sequel *n.* a story, complete in itself, that continues an earlier story. *Cp.* **prequel**.

sequence *n.* in curriculum organization, the arrangement or ordering of subject matter content for presentation and study over a selected period, as a unit, semester, year, etc. *Note*: In its fullest sense, sequencing of content is not merely a linear arrangement but involves provision for revisiting key concepts and skills so that each successive encounter deepens students' understanding or proficiency. Common approaches to sequencing are chronological, developmental, easy to difficult, part to whole, simple to complex, thematic, and whole to part. *Cp.* **scope and sequence**; **spiral curriculum**. *adj.* **sequential**.

sequencing *v.* the structuring of successive speech acts according to their sociocultural functions, as in the temporal sequence *"Hello," "You look fine," "Good bye."*

sequential analysis the analysis of incoming sample data to determine when there is suffi-cient information to accept or reject an experimental hypothesis. *Cp.* **trend analysis**.

sequential constraint in generative phonology, a restriction as to what may occur next in a sequence of phonological features, as, in English, when an initial consonant cluster begins with /s/, the next sound must be a voiceless consonant (/p/, /t/, /k/, etc.), as in *spin, stop, skip*. *Note*: Sequential constraints are also apparent in English orthography, as in the initial consonant cluster /skr-/, /k/ is conventionally spelled *c*, as in *scratch, scream*, etc. *Cp.* **phonotactics**.

sequential relationship an association, stated or implied in a communication, of successive order among ideas or events.

serial **1.** *n.* a story or play presented in parts in writing or on television, radio, or motion pictures, etc. **2.** *n.* any periodical planned and issued as an indefinite series of numbered, consecutive parts. **3.** *adj.* referring to a series. *v.* **serialize**.

serial processing the sequential transformation of a cognitive code.

seriation *n.* **1.** the sequential ordering and processing of language signals, as words in sentences. **2.** in Piagetian theory, the ability to logically order a set of objects.

series *n.* a set of related publications, as a set of textbooks ordered in difficulty or a set of books with a common theme.

series book **1.** one of a group of books having a common set of elements, written by the same author or by a succession of authors. **2.** one of a collection of informational books, usually with the same format but on different subjects.

set **1.** *n.* any coherent group of items, as *a set of cardinal numbers, an alphabetic set, a set of books*. **2.** *n.* a tendency to selectively attend to and respond to certain stimuli rather than to others. **3.** *adj.* in a habitual, stereotyped manner, as *a set speech.* **4.** See **setting** (def. 3). **5.** *v.* to place; adjust; arrange.

set reading (*Brit.*) material assigned to be read for a course or examination.

setting *n.* **1.** the physical and psychological background against which the action in a story takes place. **2.** the time and place in which a narrative occurs. **3.** the scenery and stage effects for a drama, motion picture, etc.; set. **4.** context.

shape constancy the tendency to perceive the shape of an object as the same regardless of angle of view. See also **perceptual constancy**. *Cp.* **size constancy**.

shared reading an early childhood instructional strategy in which the teacher involves a group of young children in the reading of a particular big book in order to help them learn aspects of beginning literacy, as print conventions and the concept of *word*, and develop reading strategies, as in decoding or the use of prediction.

shibboleth *n.* **1.** a distinctive or peculiar use of some aspect of speech that identifies a social group. **2.** an old slogan, catchword, or common saying that has lost meaning or relevance, as *You're the cat's pajamas* from the 1920s.

shortening *n.* **1.** in historical linguistics, a process by which distinctively long vowels or consonants become short. **2.** in phonetics, any reduction in the time duration of a linguistic segment. **3.** in grammar, the omission of a segment from a word. *Cp.* **clipping**; **syncope** (def. 1).

shorthand *n.* a system of rapid handwriting, used generally for taking dictation in office settings, that uses abbreviations and symbols other than standard letters to represent sounds, syllables, words, or phrases; stenography.

short story a brief fictional prose narrative designed to create a unified impression quickly and forcefully, as in Edgar Allan Poe's "The Tell-Tale Heart" or Guy de Maupassant's "The Necklace." *Note*: The modern short story often uses unresolved situations instead of the more familiar narrative pattern in which there is resolution of the action. *Cp.* **novel**; **novella**; **tale** (def. 2).

short-term memory (STM) memory that lasts only briefly, has rapid input and output, is very limited in capacity, and depends directly on stimulation for its form, as memory developed after one has attended to a stimulus array but before one has mastered all its details. *Note*: In current models of reading behavior, STM is seen to enable the reader to keep parts of the reading material in mind until enough text has been processed for deeper comprehension. *Cp.* **long-term memory**.

short vowel **1.** in teaching practice, the sound qualities of /a/, /e/, /i/, /o/, and /u/ heard in *bat*, *bet*, *bit*, *bob*, and *bub*. See also **schwa**. **2.** in phonetics, the relatively short duration of a vowel sound. See also **checked** (def. 2). *Cp.* **long vowel**.

sight conservation special measures taken to preserve existing vision in those who have limited sight, as in the provision of reading materials in large-print formats.

sight-read *v.* to read a text or play music one has not seen before. *Note*: An oral reading test measures one's ability to sight-read.

sight word **1.** a word that is immediately recognized as a whole and does not require word analysis for identification. See also **recognition vocabulary**. **2.** a word taught as a whole. *Note*: Words that are phonically irregular or are important to learn before students have the skills to decode them are often taught as sight words.

sigma *n.* **1.** standard deviation for a population, represented by the symbol δ. **2.** the sum of, represented by the symbol Σ.

sign **1.** *n.* anything used to represent something else, as a grapheme, phoneme, word, Arabic number, etc. **2.** *n.* the phonic or graphic representation of a word with a meaning referent; linguistic sign. *Cp.* **symbol** (def. 4). **3.** *v.* to communicate by signs or sign language. **4.** *adj.* having to do with such a type of communication. **5.** *n.* something that represents or signifies something beyond itself. **6.** *n.* in semiotics: **a.** "something which stands to somebody for something in some respect or capacity" (Peirce, 1931–1958). **b.** an umbrella term for signs and sign systems in general. **7.** *n.* the positive or negative value of a mathematical expression. See also **signal**; **signification** (def. 1).

signal **1.** *n.* a sign that occurs in immediate association with that which is signified, as a stop sign. *Cp.* **symbol** (defs. 1, 2). **2.** *n.* a message encoded by a transmitter and sent over a channel, as a television signal. **3.** *v.* to communicate by signal.

sign function something that acts like a sign or is taken to be one. *Note*: *Sign function* is preferred over *sign* by some semioticians because *function* suggests a dynamic quality of signs, as *a sign serving different functions in different contexts*. *Cp.* **sign** (def. 6).

significant difference any between-sample difference, as between means, test-retest performance, etc., that is unlikely to have arisen by chance.

significate *v.* **1.** to stand for or represent. **2.** to suggest; symbolize. *adj.* **significative**.

signification *n.* **1.** the relation between a linguistic symbol and the concept or concrete object to which it refers. See also **appellation** (def.

3); **semantics**; **semantic triangle**; **signifier** (def. 1). **2.** the intended meaning or sense. **3.** the implying or revealing of meaning. **4.** in semiotics, the process by which signs and their meanings are produced or generated.

signified *n.* in semiotics, the conceptual or meaning component of a sign, as the word *dictionary* represents the concept or meaning of a book listing words of a language, usually in alphabetical order. *Cp.* **signifier**.

signifier *n.* **1.** the verbal or graphic symbol used to indicate or label a referent, either concrete or abstract. See also **referent** (defs. 2, 3); **sign** (def. 2). **2.** in semiotics, the perceptual component of a sign, as the letters *s-p-e-a-k* for the written word *speak*, or the sounds /spēk/ for the spoken word *speak*. *Cp.* **signified**.

signify *v.* to stand for; to serve as a sign or representation of something. *adj.* **signified**.

sign language a system of gestures used as alternatives to spoken and written communication. *Note*: Sign languages are most commonly developed for communication among the deaf or between deaf and hearing persons. Such systems should be distinguished from manual systems such as finger spelling which are developed primarily for educational purposes. With sound absent, hands, head, facial expressions, and body orientation can be brought into play in sign communication to express words and syntax.

sign reading the interpretation of graphic signs. *Note*: The term usually refers to the recognition of simple signs and directions, such as stop signs, road signs, etc., rather than to alphabetic letters.

silent letter in common usage, a letter used in the spelling of a word but which seemingly represents no sound in that word, as *h* in *ghost*. *Note*: Originally some silent letters in English represented sounds that for various reasons have ceased to be pronounced, as *k* in *knife* and *e* in *name*. See also **final e**.

silent reading test a test in which the student responds to items typically designed to measure word-meaning and passage comprehension, and sometimes study skills and speed of comprehension, in several content fields.

simile *n.* **1.** a comparison of two things that are unlike, usually using the words *like* or *as, as "O my love is like a red, red rose"* (Robert Burns, "A Red, Red Rose"). **2.** such a figure of speech. *Cp.* **metaphor**.

simple predicate a predicate consisting of a single verb phrase, as *was singing* in *He was singing. Cp.* **compound predicate**.

simple sentence a sentence with one subject and one predicate, as *The dog ate my homework*.

simple subject a noun, singly or in a noun phrase, or a pronoun that is the subject of a sentence, as *computer* in *The computer lost my homework*.

simplified vocabulary in reading programs, the substitution of easy-to-understand words for words or concepts that are presumed to be difficult for students to comprehend.

single-subject curriculum a curriculum organized around the study of one subject without regard to related fields.

singular *n.* a grammatical category of number referring to one or an uncountable mass, as *boy* in *The boy fished alone*, or *sand* in *The sand felt warm*. See also **number**. *Cp.* **plural**.

sinistrad writing writing that proceeds from right to left, as Hebrew. *Cp.* **dextral** (def. 1).

size constancy the tendency to perceive the size of an object as the same regardless of angle of view or distance. See also **perceptual constancy**. *Cp.* **shape constancy**.

skill *n.* **1.** an acquired ability to perform well; proficiency. *Note*: The term often refers to finely coordinated, complex motor acts that are the result of perceptual-motor learning, as handwriting, golf, or pottery. However, skill is also used to refer to parts of acts that are primarily intellectual, as those involved in comprehension or thinking. See also **basic skills**. **2.** a craft or activity requiring a high degree of competence, as *the skill of making fine jewelry. adj.* **skilled**; **skillful**.

Types of *Skills**
basic skills
study skills
subskills
visual-motor skills

---

*Terms are all defined in this dictionary.

---

slang *n.* **1.** informal speech composed of newly coined words or expressions or of common words and expressions whose meanings are changed or extended; popular speech. **2.** speech used by social or professional peer groups for in-group communication; jargon; cant; argot.

slanting *n.* the use of words to reflect a certain attitude, point of view, or bias, usually intentionally to influence a special audience. *v.* **slant**.

slot *n.* in grammatical analysis, a place or position in a series or sequence into which a class of items can be placed, as a noun in the empty space in *This _____ is delicious*.

slow learner a person whose intellectual functioning is between one and two standard deviations below the mean, usually between 70 and 80 IQ. See also **intelligence quotient**; **mental retardation**.

slurring *n.* the act of speaking indistinctly by running sounds together, as in hurried, careless, or mumbling speech. *v.* **slur**.

smoothing *n.* in a frequency curve or a trend line, the construction of a curve to fit the major trend of the data without distorting it.

Snellen test a test to determine visual acuity by identifying successively smaller lines of letters or numbers, usually conducted for far-point testing at 6 meters (20 feet), under presumably standard light conditions. Also **Snellen rating**.

social constructionism a method in composition and modern rhetoric that views learning and language as a product of social collaboration. *Note*: Social constructionism is vaguely Marxist. It separates itself from cognitive and expressionist theories of rhetoric and composition. Political criticism naturally emerges from social constructionism as a pedagogical technique for teaching writing.

social construction of knowledge in critical pedagogy, the view that knowledge is constructed symbolically by the mind through social interaction with others and is heavily dependent on culture, context, custom, and historical specificity (McLaren, 1989). *Cp.* **constructivism** (def. 1).

social issue story a narrative, usually a novel, with a focus on a major problem of society, as S.E. Hinton's *That Was Then, This Is Now*.

socioeconomic status (SES) a person's position or standing in a society because of such factors as social class, level of education, income, and type of job.

sociolect *n.* a variety of speech used primarily by members of a given social group. See also **dialect**. *Cp.* **nonstandard dialect**; **prestige dialect**.

sociolinguistics *n. (with sing. v.)* the study of the relationships between linguistic behavior and other aspects of social behavior; the study of language as a social phenomenon. *Note*: Sociolinguists examine such relationships as those between an individual's speech and that of others in a speech community; the linguistic identity of social groups; and the effects of political, social, and economical power structures on the perception of language differences. *n.* **sociolinguist**. *adj.* **sociolinguistic**.

sociology *n.* the study of human society; particularly, the study of group relationships and societal institutions. See also **politics of literacy**. *n.* **sociologist**.

sociology of reading **1.** the study of the effects of social forces, as socioeconomic status, and social institutions, as the family, on reading behavior and instruction. **2.** the study of the effects of reading on a reader's habits and attitudes; the interaction between people and print. **3.** the study of the characteristics of the print media; content analysis. **4.** the study of organizations and their effects on reading acquisition and use.

sociometric *adj.* **1.** having to do with measuring social relationships in a group. **2.** having to do with Moreno's (1956) technique for measuring and showing diagrammatically the expressed likes and dislikes of group members toward one another. *n.* **sociometrics**; **sociometry**.

Socratic method the pedagogical technique of asking leading questions to stimulate rational thinking and illuminate ideas.

soft c in phonics, the /s/ sound that the letter *c* represents, as in *cymbal*, *percent*. *Cp.* **hard c**.

soft consonant a voiceless consonant; one produced without vibration of the vocal cords, as *f* in *face*. *Cp.* **hard consonant**.

soft g in phonics, the /j/ sound that the letter *g* represents, as in *gentle, giant. Cp.* **hard g**.

solecism *n.* a violation of prescriptive grammar, as *he don't. Note*: Solecisms vary with culture, literary style, and period as grammatical usage changes.

soliloquy *n.* in drama, a speech given by a character while or as if alone; literally, "talking to oneself." *Cp.* **monolog** (def. 1).

sonnet *n.* a poetic form or poem of 14 lines, usually in iambic pentameter and rhyming according to a formal scheme, which expresses a thought or feeling in a complete and unified way. *Note*: The earliest sonnet form, the Italian or Petrarchan sonnet, has two divisions: the first eight lines called the *octave* and the last six lines called the *sestet*. The later English or Shakespearean sonnet has four divisions: three sets of four lines, or *quatrains*, and a final set of two lines, or a *couplet*.

sound **1.** *n.* energy transmitted as pressure waves or vibrations through an elastic medium as air or water. **2.** *n.* the sensory response to vibration in the inner ear that is transmitted to the brain by the auditory nerve. **3.** *n.* a discretely perceived hearing sensation. **4.** See **phone**; **phoneme**. **5.** *n.* a distinctive feature of a speech sound. **6.** *n.* in teaching practice, how a letter is pronounced. **7.** *v.* to speak; articulate; pronounce. **8.** *n.* recorded audio material, as on film or tape.

sound out the application of phonics skills in reproducing the sound(s) represented by a letter or letter group in a word.

sound symbolism the use of sound for certain literary effects, as in onomatopoeia and synaesthesia.

Spache readability formula a method developed by Spache and originally published in 1953 for estimating the difficulty of primary level reading materials based on average sentence length in words and number of words. *Note*: The formula has undergone several revisions since 1953, chiefly in the list of words used. *Cp.* **Dale–Chall readability formula**; **Flesch readability formula**; **Fry readability graph**.

span of attention **1.** the number of items an individual can correctly reproduce after a single short exposure, either visual or oral; memory span; span of perception. *Cp.* **span of recognition**. **2.** the length of time that an individual can concentrate on one thing or activity; interest span.

span of recognition in the continuous reading of a passage, the average number of words taken in per eye fixation. *Cp.* **span of attention** (def. 1).

spatial organization the arrangement of ideas, images, etc., in a graphic pattern to indicate their relationships, as the graphic representation of cognitive maps or networks. *n.* **spasticity**.

speaking *n.* **1.** the act of communicating through speech. **2.** the giving of a public address or lecture. **3.** productive oral-aural language. *v.* **speak**.

speaking vocabulary the number of different words ordinarily used by a person for meaningful oral communication; oral vocabulary. *Cp.* **listening vocabulary**; **reading vocabulary**; **writing vocabulary**.

Spearman–Brown formula a formula showing the relationship between test length and test reliability. *Note*: The formula is commonly used to estimate the reliability of a whole test from the correlation between the two halves of the test, or the split-half reliability.

special education schooling for those who are very different in one or more ways in intellectual, physical, social, or emotional development from the usual student. *Note*: Special education includes a variety of adjustments in content, method, and facilities to meet the needs of atypical students. See also **atypical learner; mainstreaming; mental retardation**.

special needs student(s) any student or group that is physically handicapped, mentally retarded, learning or behaviorally disabled, or has multiple handicaps and thus needs special attention or consideration in learning. See also **inclusion; mainstreaming**.

specific *adj.* referring to a presumed neurological condition, developmental in nature but without demonstrable brain damage, as *specific developmental dyslexia, specific learning disability*.

specific factor (s) a factor hypothesized by Spearman (1904) to be unique to a given intellectual activity; s factor.

speech *n.* **1.** a medium for transmitting language; spoken language. **2.** the act of speaking. **3.** something spoken; utterance. **4.** an utterance for a particular purpose, as *a graduation speech*. **5.** a single utterance by an actor. **6.** the dialect or language of a particular region or social group; speech community; as *Ulster Scots* speech in Northern Ireland. **7.** the way in which someone speaks. **8.** the study of the theory and practice of oral communication.

speech act in linguistics, the analysis of an utterance in relation to the behavior of speaker(s) and hearer(s) in their interpersonal communication. *Note*: The term is taken from a theory of the role of utterances in human communication developed by the philosopher Austin (1962). Speech acts may be classified by their function: **a.** a *commissive*, which commits the speaker to a future course of action, as making a promise. **b.** a *declarative*, which changes conditions, as pronouncing someone guilty. **c.** a *directive*, which causes a listener to do something, as making a request or command. **d.** an *expressive*, which signifies feelings or attitudes about something, as extending an apology. **e.** a *representative*, which describes or declares something, as an assertion or report. See also **illocutionary act; locutionary act; perlocutionary act**.

speech and language therapy a comprehensive term for the study and correction of speech, language, and voice disorders by a speech and language therapist. Also **speech correction; speech pathology; speech therapy**.

speech community **1.** in ethnography of communication studies, the group to which a particular ethnographic description applies; a group that shares rules of speaking. *Note*: A person can belong to many speech communities, as a college student might be "a resident of a particular dormitory, a student at a particular college, a black person, an American, and a member of a Western European society, all at the same time" (Fasold, 1990). **2.** all those who communicate by a common language or variety of a language. *Note*: The term is often used to identify some subgroup that shares a common dialect or argot not used by the majority of the population, as the Cajuns in Louisiana or the Basques in France and Spain.

speech discrimination in speech audiometry, the assessment of the ability to distinguish different sounds, words, sentences, etc., presented at a constant level, usually about 40 dB above the threshold for speech. *Cp.* **speech reception**.

speech disorder any deviation of speech that seriously interferes with normal oral communication or that causes adjustment problems for the speaker or listener; speech impediment; deviant speech; "an impairment of the articulation of speech sounds, fluency, and/or voice" (Guidelines of the American Speech-Language-Hearing Association, 1982). *Note*: "Speech is abnormal when it deviates so far from the speech of other people that it calls attention to itself, interferes with communication, or causes the speaker or his listener to be distressed" (Van Riper, 1978). Since speech disorders are defined in relation to the existing speech community, a particular form of speech deviation may be considered a disorder in one community but normal in another.

speech event a particular instance of linguistic interaction between persons, as conversation, questioning, etc. See also **ethnography of communication**.

speech frequencies that portion of the sound frequency spectrum that includes most speech sounds, usually from 125 to 8000 Hz.

speech organs the body structures used to produce speech sounds; specifically, the articulators (tongue, lips, teeth, palate), the larynx, the resonators (pharynx, nasal cavity, oral cavity, trachea), and the lungs.

speechreading *n.* the process of interpreting a speaker's message, with or without hearing his or her voice, by watching his or her lips, facial expressions, gestures, and body posture. *Note*: The teaching of speechreading has largely replaced the teaching of lipreading among the deaf because of its broader focus on aspects of body language in communication. *Cp.* **lipreading**.

speech reception in speech audiometry, the assessment of the threshold level at which two-syllable words can be repeated correctly at least half of the time. See also **spondee words**. *Cp.* **speech discrimination**.

speech rehabilitation speech and language therapy for restoring a lost speech function.

speech spectogram in phonetics, a graphic record of speech sounds. See also **visible speech** (def. 3).

speech-to-print match an understanding of the one-to-one correspondence between the printed words on a page and the words as they are read aloud. *Note*: Children often demonstrate such understanding by pointing to words as they are read aloud by another.

speed of comprehension the rapidity with which one understands what is read, usually when reading silently. *Note*: Speed of comprehension is usually measured in relation to the number of passages successfully understood. The speed score is not converted to a words per minute score. See also **rate of reading**.

speed reading reading that is faster than a person's normal rate of reading; (*Brit.*) accelerated reading. *Note*: Speed reading is often used for specific purposes, as to locate essential information only, to get an overview of text, etc. The concept that an invariant, high-speed rate of reading comprehension applicable to all materials can be obtained or is desirable has been largely discredited. Rather, reading rate is seen as a function of the nature of the text and the reader's purpose, interests, etc. Also **accelerated reading**.

speed test a test with time limits so short that a substantial number of persons cannot attempt all items. *Cp.* **power test**.

spelldown 1. *n.* a game or contest in which a student who misspells a word is eliminated; spelling bee. See also **spelling-school**. **2.** *v.* to eliminate a competitor in a spelling contest by spelling a word correctly when the competitor has failed to do so.

speller *n.* in the United States, a spelling textbook. See also **spelling book** (def. 1).

spelling *n.* **1.** the process of representing language by means of a writing system, or orthography. **2.** See **orthography** (def. 3). **3.** the study of writing words according to their correct letters or graphemes. See also **orthography** (def. 2). **4.** the way a word is spelled on a particular occasion, whether correct or incorrect. **5.** reciting the letters composing a word, in their correct sequence, as in *s-p-e-l-l*. *v.* **spell**.

spelling book **1.** a textbook with exercises for learning to write words in standard orthography. See also **speller**. **2.** an early type of children's textbook designed primarily for reading instruction, and secondarily for spelling instruction. *Note*: Spelling books traditionally included the alphabet, syllabarium, and "tables" (lists of words organized by increasing number of syllables) interspersed with "lessons" (reading matter mainly based on words in the preceding lessons). *Cp.* **abecedarium**.

spelling demon a common word that is particularly difficult or tricky to spell correctly.

spelling method **1.** any of several approaches to teaching students to spell. **2.** a way of teaching reading. See also **alphabet method** (def. 1).

spelling pronunciation saying a word on the basis of its standard spelling rather than its standard pronunciation, as /komp trō' lər/ rather than /kən tro' lər/ for *comptroller*. *Note*: Spelling pronunciations occur when sounds are attributed to each letter of a written word regardless of whether each letter represents a speech sound. Some spelling pronunciations have become acceptable in spoken language, as /of' tən/ for *often*.

spelling reform an individual or organized effort to augment, simplify, or devise an orthography, generally one based on a correspondence of phonemes and graphemes, so that spelling conforms to pronunciation, and vice versa. See also **augmented alphabet**; **modified alphabet**.

spelling-school *n.* a spelling competition popular in the United States in the 19th century, held outside normal school hours and in which both children and adults completed.

Spencerian script a handwriting style named after an early 19th-century American handwriting expert, Platt Rogers Spencer, characterized by rounded ornate letters slanting to the right.

spiral curriculum **1.** a curriculum designed to present important concepts, skills, topics, etc., for additional, more complex study at successive levels of student maturity. **2.** (*Brit.*) concentric curriculum/method.

split-half reliability coefficient a test reliability coefficient obtained by correlating scores on one-half of a test, as on even-numbered items, with scores on the other half of the test, as on odd-numbered items, and applying a correction formula such as the Spearman–Brown formula. See also **internal consistency**.

split infinitive an English infinitive verb form in which *to* is separated from the verb by an adverb or adverbial phrase, as *to carefully read*. *Note*: Split infinitives occur commonly in daily speech and writing even though such constructions are considered incorrect in prescriptive grammar.

spoken language **1.** language used in speaking as distinct from writing. **2.** that style of language that is written as if spoken, as in conversation. *Cp.* **sign language**; **written language**.

spondee words words of two equally stressed syllables, as /good´ bye´/, /sun´ shine´/, etc., used in testing speech reception. See also **speech reception**.

spontaneous concept in Vygotsky's theory of cognitive development, an early stage of concept development in children's play. *Note*: "In play, a child spontaneously makes use of his ability to separate meaning from an object without knowing he is doing it, just as he does not know he is speaking in prose but talks without paying attention to the words. Thus, through play the child achieves a functional definition of concepts or objects, and words become a part of a thing" (Vygotsky, 1978). *Cp.* **nonspontaneous concept.**

spoonerism *n.* the accidental transposition of initial sounds or syllables of two words, usually with humorous results, as *roaring pain* for *pouring rain. Note*: The word comes from Dr. W.A. Spooner (1844–1930), a warden of New College at Oxford University, who is said to have made many such transpositions.

SQ3R *n.* a series of steps to be used in reading a textbook for study purposes. *Note*: The term derives from *s*urvey the assignment to note the points emphasized; pose a *q*uestion initially on the first section (and later on successive sections); *r*ead to answer the question; *r*ecite the answer to the question; and, after several questions and answers, *r*eview the material read. This study method was first introduced by Robinson in *Effective Study* (1946), but it has since been adapted by many other writers and programs.

stage 1. *n.* a single and qualitatively distinct period in a process or series. **2.** *n.* in Piaget's theory of intellectual development, one of four developmental periods (*sensorimotor*, birth–2 years; *preoperational*, 2–7 years; *concrete operations*, 7–11 years; *formal operations*, 11–15 years), each characterized by certain types of mental activities or operations. *Note*: These stages are sequential because each is necessary for the formation of the following one. The ages given for each stage are approximate. **3.** *n.* a platform or area for performing plays, music, etc. **4.** *v.* to present a performance in such a place. **5. the stage,** the theatrical profession.

stance *n.* **1.** in transactional or reader response theory, a selective attitude that expresses the reader's intent or purpose and guides the reader's attention. *Note*: "In the reading act, whether the reading event will produce a literary or a nonliterary work depends...on the reader's stance toward the contents of consciousness during the transaction with text. The same text can be read, either 'efferently'...or 'aesthetically'" (Rosenblatt, 1978). See also **aesthetic reading**; **efferent reading. 2.** the position or attitude taken by a person toward something.

standard American English 1. that variety of American English in which most educational texts, government, and media publications are written in the United States. **2.** English as it is spoken and written by those groups with social, economic, and political power in the United States. *Note*: Standard American English is a relative concept, varying widely in pronunciation and in idiomatic use but maintaining a fairly uniform grammatical structure. See also **prestige dialect.**

standard deviation (SD) a measure of the variability of a distribution; specifically, the square root of the mean of the squares of the deviations of all scores from the mean of a test or set.

standard error (SE) an estimate of the variability in a statistic. Also **S.E.** See also **standard error of estimate; standard error of mean; standard error of measurement; true score.** *Cp.* **probable score.**

standard error of estimate an estimate of variability of predictions made from a regression line of one variable to another; specifically, the standard deviation of the differences of actual values from those predicted by a regression line. *Note*: The standard error of estimate allows the development of a confidence band about a predicted score. *Cp.* **standard error of measurement.**

standard error of mean an estimate of the variation in means to be expected in successive samples.

standard error of measurement (SEM) in classical test theory, the standard deviation of "the differences between observed scores and true scores" (Cronbach, 1984). *Note*: The standard error of measurement decreases as the reliability of the instrument increases. *Cp.* **standard error of estimate**.

standardization *n.* **1.** the process, act, or result of establishing criteria for the evaluation of something; specifically, in educational testing, the building of tests to meet established criteria with respect to validity, reliability, curriculum relevancy, etc. **2.** the building of standardized tests. See also **standardized test**.

standardized test **1.** a test with specified tasks and procedures so that comparable measurements may be made by testers working in different geographical areas. **2.** a test for which norms on a reference group, ordinarily drawn from many schools or communities, are provided.

standard language **1.** a culturally dominant language in a country or region; language of well-educated people; standard variety. *Note*: Standard language is usually the language specifically recognized in grammars and dictionaries for use in education, government, and business. **2.** a variety of language favored by the well educated in socially important situations, as Standard American English or Received Standard English. **3.** the established dialect or style of any language variety.

standard score a derived score used to "express the individual's distance from the mean in terms of the standard deviation of the distribution" (Anastasi, 1976). *Note*: A significant value of standard scores is that they allow comparison of relative performance on tests having unequal units of measurement, as those for reading rate and quality of penmanship. Stanines and z-scores are standard scores.

Stanford–Binet Intelligence Scale (S–B) an individual test of general mental ability, published as a revision of the Binet–Simon scales by Terman and others in 1916 with later revisions in 1937 and 1960, and renormed in 1972. *Cp.* **Wechsler Intelligence Scale**.

stanine *n.* a normalized standard score representing an interval in a 9-point scale, with a mean of 5 and a standard deviation of 2.

stanza *n.* a group of lines in a poem or song with an identifiable pattern of meter and often rhyme.

state-dependent memory retrieval of information that is improved when learners are in a similar psychological state when retrieving as they were when encoding.

stations approach a classroom or laboratory in which a number of stations or centers are set up, each with its own directions, materials, and tasks, to be used by students who move from station to station either at their own choosing and pace, or as a result of the teacher's diagnosis and direction. *Cp.* **learning center** (def. 2).

statistic *n.* **1.** a score or value based on one or more samples that represents a parameter of a population, as a mean, a standard deviation, etc. **2.** any single score or value in a set that has been derived as the end product of the quantitative analysis of other variables. See also **statistics** (def. 1).

statistical analysis the process or result of applying a set of mathematical operations to determine relationships among data gathered from a sample population. *Note*: The interpretation of the results of a statistical analysis is strictly a matter of making inferences from these results.

statistical significance a statistical expression of the probability that an experimental finding did not happen by chance. See also **confidence level**.

statistics *n.* **1.** (*with sing. v.*) the science of collecting and mathematically analyzing data so that the random effects of chance may be estimated or controlled in seeking to establish significant facts and relationships. **2.** (*with pl. v.*) data thus collected, as *statistics on high school dropouts*.

stem *n.* **1.** the part of a word to which an inflectional suffix is or can be added. See **base word**; **root** (defs. 1, 2). **2.** portion of the brain under the cerebellum and cerebrum that controls many involuntary physical activities. Also **brainstem**. **3.** the heavy, usually vertical line of a typeface.

stereograph *n.* a visual target of two photographs or drawings side by side which, when seen through a stereoscope, may appear as a single three-dimensional image. Also **stereogram**. See also **stereoscope**.

stereoscope *n.* an instrument for vision testing and training that allows each eye to see only one of a pair of pictures slightly displaced laterally on a stereograph so that, normally, stereopsis or depth perception occurs and a single picture is seen as three dimensional. See also **stereograph**. *adj.* **stereoscopic**.

stimulus (S) *n., pl.* **-li** **1.** anything that arouses sensory activity leading to a response. *Cp.* **response** (def. 2). **2.** the class of such reactions. **3.** an incentive.

stimulus generalization the extension of a stimulus response to other stimuli that previously did not call forth such a response. *Cp.* **response generalization**.

stop **1.** *n.* in speech sound production, any complete halt and sudden release of the air flow, usually, but not always, referring to a stoppage anywhere in the vocal tract, as a plosive, a glottal stop, a click, etc. **2.** *n.* a consonant speech sound made by stopping the air flow and then suddenly releasing it through the mouth; plosive. *Note*: The English stops are /p/, /b/, /t/, /d/, /k/, and /g/. *Cp.* **continuant**. **3.** *adj.* referring to such a speech sound.

story *n.* **1.** a prose or poetry narrative; tale. **2.** an imaginative tale shorter than a novel but with plot, characters, and setting, as a short story. **3.** the plot of a novel, poem, etc. **4.** a branch of literature. **5.** something narrated.

storyboard *n.* **1.** the telling of a story by a bas-relief carving on wood. *Note*: The storyboard is a popular way of preserving stories in the islands of the South Pacific, especially Palau. **2.** a panel on which sketches show the scene and plan of action for the production of a motion picture, television show, etc.

story grammar in text analysis, a formal device or grammar used for specifying relations among episodes in a story and to formulate rules for generating other stories.

story map **1.** a time line showing the ordered sequence of events in a text. **2.** a semantic map showing the meaning relationships between events or concepts in a text, regardless of their order.

story method an extension of the sentence method of teaching reading introduced toward the end of the 19th century in which students first learn a whole story before attending to its parts. *Cp.* **Jacotot method**; **memory reading**.

story schema the pattern of organization in narration that characterizes a particular type of story, usually in simplified terms such as problem, action, goal, setting, and outcome. Also **story structure**. *Cp.* **text structure**.

storytelling *n.* the art of telling a story orally rather than reading it aloud.

story theater a dramatic presentation with few or no props or costumes in which players pantomime the action of a story while it is narrated.

strabismus *n.* heterotropia; squint. *Cp.* **heterophoria**.

strategy *n.* in education, a systematic plan, consciously adapted and monitored, to improve one's performance in learning.

stratificational grammar a system of linguistic analysis based on the work of Lamb (1966) in which language is presumed to have two components—meaning and sound—with several interrelated levels in between, including phonemic, morphemic, and lexemic strata.

stratified sample a sample, selected from a population, that has been divided into categories. *Note*: A stratified sample contains members from each category in approximately the same proportion that the category bears to the entire population. *Cp.* **representative sample**.

streaming *n. (chiefly Brit.)* **1.** ability grouping within classes; homogeneous grouping. **2.** placement in an academic or vocational program after testing.

stream of consciousness **1.** in psychology, a term coined by William James to describe the random but continuous flow of thoughts, feelings, memories, etc., through a person's mind at a given moment or interval. **2.** in literature, a technique of presenting a character's thoughts and feelings as they develop, as in Laurence Sterne's *Tristram Shandy* and James Joyce's *Ulysses*; free association.

stress **1.** *n.* emphasis; importance; significance; urgency; concern. **2.** *n.* the emphasis from increased force of breath that makes a syllable, word, or group of words stand out; accent. *Note*: Stress, often considered as *sentence stress* and *word stress*, is a major marker of meaning in speech. Sentence stress changes meaning, as *I did not say that* vs. *I did not **say** that*. Word stress may likewise change meaning, as /ob' ject/ vs. /ob ject'/, or may simply mark pronunciation of a word. In the latter sense, several levels of stress are recognized: **a. primary stress**, / ´ /, marks the greatest emphasis. **b. secondary stress**, / ˆ /, is moderate and less emphatic. **c. tertiary stress**, / ` /, marks little emphasis, but the vowel sound is still distinct. **d. weak** or **minimal stress**, or **unstressed** or **not marked**, / ˘ /, are terms used to indicate the least force, as for a neutral vowel or schwa. *Ĕlĕvătŏr ôpĕràtór* demonstrates all four levels of stress. See also **accent** (def. 2); **suprasegmental**. **3.** *v.* to accent one's speech; to emphasize parts of an utterance; to pronounce strongly. **4.** *v.* to emphasize. **5.** *n.* a physiological response to a disturbance in the balanced functioning of body processes. **6.** *n.* the psychological tension associated with physiological stress.

stressed syllable **1.** a syllable having the greatest stress in the word or phrase in which it is located, as in the first syllable in *decent*, /dē´ sənt/, or the second syllable in *descent*, /di sent´/. **2.** any syllable that has any degree of stress. See also **stress** (def. 2).

string *n.* a linear sequence of grammatical units, as article + adjective + noun + auxiliary verb + verb + noun. See also **terminal string**.

structural analysis the identification of word-meaning elements, as *re* and *read* in *reread*, to help understand the meaning of a word as a whole; morphemic analysis. *Note*: Structural analysis commonly involves the identification of roots, affixes, compounds, hyphenated forms, inflected and derived endings, contractions, and, in some cases, syllabication. Structural analysis is sometimes used as an aid to pronunciation or in combination with phonic analysis in word-analysis programs.

structural grammar **1.** a descriptive model of the grammar of speech; descriptive linguistics; structural linguistics. **2.** an approach to the study of language that analyzes its sounds, word formation, and syntactic structure. *Cp.* **prescriptive grammar**.

structuralism *n.* a form of linguistic study that views language as an internally consistent system of rules unrelated to history. *Note*: Structuralism began with the work of Ferdinand de Saussure early in the 20th century in opposition to historical linguistics. His methods were extended to anthropology by Claude Lévi-Strauss in the late 1940s. Literary criticism followed suit in the 1960s and early 70s. All versions assume that structure is objective and independent. See also **deconstruction**; **poststructuralism**. *adj.* **structural**; **structuralist**.

structural linguistics **1.** the study of language in terms of its form and the distribution of elements within its parts, as the form and distribution of phonemes and morphemes in English. **2.** the study of language at a particular point in time; synchronic linguistics. See also **descriptive linguistics**.

structured overview a form of graphic organizer in which important concepts of a topic or unit of study, as reflected in its vocabulary, are displayed visually to anticipate, revise, and confirm relationships among the concepts. *Note*: A structured overview "actually serves as an advance organizer, a process organizer, and as a post organizer in content area reading" (Earle, 1969).

student journal a running record kept by a student that is usually shared with the teacher.

study guide **1.** any one of several specific sets of suggestions to help students in the efficient examination and comprehension of subject matter content. **2.** a commercially prepared guide to develop skills and strategies necessary for effective reading or "an understanding of a significant segment of a content area" (Wood et al., 1992).

study-habits inventory a checklist or questionnaire on strategies, methods, and conditions of study.

study skills a general term for those techniques and strategies that help a person read or listen for specific purposes with the intent to remember; commonly, following directions, locating, selecting, organizing, and retaining information, interpreting typographic and graphic aids, and reading flexibly.

study strategy a systematic process for the intensive study of a selection for retention and recall, as SQ3R. Also **study technique**.

stutter **1.** *n.* spasmodic, involuntary, blocked speech marked by hesitation and by sound prolongations or repetitions; stammer. *Note*: A severe stutter is often accompanied by bodily tension, as facial grimaces, clenched hands, and rigid posture. **2.** *v.* to engage in such speech; stammer. *n.* **stutterer**.

style *n. Note*: Style as applied to writing and speaking is an elusive and subtle concept. In the broadest sense it refers to the characteristic way in which a person conceives and expresses ideas through language. Great writers and speakers develop fresh ideas and ways of thinking about them which they express in unique ways. Thus when their works are "simplified" or translated, style is distorted: neither the ideas nor the way they were expressed are truly represented. **1.** the characteristics of a work that reflect its author's distinctive way of writing. **2.** an author's use of language, its effects, and its appropriateness to the author's intent and theme. **3.** the manner in which something is said or done, in contrast to its message, as Hemingway's terse, blunt, conversational style. **4.** the particular identifying characteristics of something, as *a flowing style of speaking*, *a formal style of writing*. **5.** the particular way in which a person uses language in a given social environment. **6.** a set of rules for preparing published material, as the University of Chicago Press *Manual of Style*.

style of discourse language use as determined by the roles taken or assumed by speaker and listener, or by writer and reader. See also **casual speech**; **register** (def. 1).

stylistic variation **1.** See **register** (def. 1). **2.** differences in structure among literary forms.

stylistics *n.* (with sing. v.) **1.** in linguistics, the study of the grammatical, phonological, and practical aspects of style in written and spoken language as used in situational contexts. **2.** the study or practice of the art of using linguistic devices to make communication more precise, connotative, or personal. *adj.* **stylistic**.

subject *n.* **1.** a topic of discussion, thinking, observation, etc. **2.** an area of learning and study; discipline. **3.** the main topic of a sentence or proposition; that to which a predicate refers; as *day* in *The day was hot*. *Cp.* **nominative case**; **object** (def. 1). **4.** a person or animal that is observed, experimented on, created, etc., as *the subject of the experiment*. **5.** in philosophy: **a.** mind, as distinguished from that which is thought about. **b.** an essential substance that possesses qualities and attributes, as *the subject of excellence*.

subject centered referring to a curriculum approach in which teaching-learning experiences are selected from and organized around systematic areas of study, as English, mathematics, etc.

See also **curriculum**. *Cp.* **activity curriculum**; **child centered**.

subject interest attraction to the content of what is read as opposed to the tone in which it is conveyed. *Note*: "Subject interest, plus accessibility and readability, are the major determining factors in our reading" (Waples et al., 1940).

subject matter **1.** broadly, a content area or field of study and the learning associated with such a discipline. **2.** a specific topic in the curriculum or in the course of study.

subordination *n.* the joining of a dependent clause, introduced by such words as *unless*, *because*, *that*, *when*, etc., to an independent clause, as the first clause is joined to the second in *Unless we start now, we'll be late*. *v.*, *adj.* **subordinate**.

subskill *n.* a skill that is part of a more complex skill or group of skills.

substantive **1.** *n.* a noun, pronoun, or noun phrase that functions as a noun; nominal. **2.** *adj.* referring to a noun.

substitution *n.* **1.** See **consonant substitution**. **2.** the replacing of one or more words in the oral reading of text with another word or words, one of several types of errors commonly recorded in testing oral reading. *Note*: Substitutions often make contextual sense to the reader but bear little or no phonic resemblance to the word or words they replace. See also **insertion** (def. 1); **mispronunciation**; **omission**. **3.** an adjustment mechanism, conscious or subconscious, wherein an unacceptable or unattainable behavior or goal is replaced with a behavior or goal that is acceptable or attainable. *n.*, *v.*, *adj.* **substitute**.

subtest *n.* a division or section of a longer test, usually containing items on a similar topic or type of problem, as *Vocabulary Meaning* may be a subtest on a silent reading test.

subvocal *adj.* referring to ideas thought but not spoken.

subvocalization *n.* the movements of the lips, tongue, and larynx during silent reading. *Note*: Excessive subvocalization hinders fluent silent reading. *Cp.* **implicit speech**.

suffix *n.* an affix attached to the end of a base, root, or stem that changes meaning or grammatical function of the word, as *-en* added to *ox-* to form *oxen*. See also **affix**; **derivational suffix**; **inflectional suffix**. *Cp.* **prefix**.

summary *n.* a brief statement that contains the essential ideas of a longer passage or selection.

summation *n.* **1.** a numerical total of a series or group of things, represented by the symbol Σ (sigma). **2.** any cumulative effect or joint action, as the effect of several rapid light stimulations being perceived as one. **3.** a summary; a bringing together of all the relevant information.

summative evaluation the final evaluation, usually quantitative in practice, of the degree to which the goals and objectives of a program have been attained. *Note*: Different types of evidence, as the final test score of students and the statistical analysis of program results, may enter into summative evaluation. *Cp.* **formative evaluation**.

supernatural story **1.** a narrative about situations and events that cannot be explained by known natural causes. **2.** a narrative about ghosts and other unworldly beings. **3.** a secret, magic, or mysterious narrative.

supplementary reading **1.** reading material added to that used in the basic reading program to provide more extensive reading experience. **2.** seatwork exercises, as for reading practice.

suppletion *n.* in morphology, the use of an unexpected and structurally unrelated word form to complete a grammatical paradigm, as *go*, *went*, *gone* or *good*, *better*, *best*. *adj.* **suppletive**.

suprasegmental *n.* a phonological feature that extends over more than one speech sound, as pitch, stress, and juncture, and contributes to meaning; superfix; suprasegmental phoneme.

surface structure **1.** in transformational-generative grammar, the structural level that contains all the syntactic and lexical elements needed to convert a sentence into speech or writing. *Note*: Two sentences may have the same deep structure but different surface structures, as *Bill broke the window* vs. *The window was broken by Bill*. *Cp.* **deep structure**. **2.** what is actually said, written, heard, or read.

surrealism *n.* a French artistic movement in the early 20th-century that cultivates irrational experience by systematically distorting ordinary perception. *adj.* **surreal**.

survey test a test, usually a group test, designed to sample knowledge or proficiency, usually broadly, in a given area. *Cp.* **diagnostic test**.

survival literacy minimal reading, writing, and often numeracy skills needed to get by in everyday life in the target language, either first or second. Also **survival language**.

survival story a narrative, real or imagined, that describes the courageous spirit of characters who overcome the problems of frontier life, war, dangerous adventure, etc.

suspense *n.* the sustained interest in a narrative or drama created by delaying the resolution of the conflict. *adj.* **suspenseful**.

syllabogram *n.* one of a set of graphic characters that represents a syllable in a syllabary.

syllabarium *n., pl.* **-ia** a list of nonsense syllables, organized alphabetically, that followed the alphabet in the hornbook, primer, and spelling book, as *ab eb ib ob ub / ba be bi bo bu /* etc. *Note*: Syllabaria were read orally. Students advanced to lists of increasing numbers of syllables as each preceding list was mastered. See also ABC **book**; **abecedarium**; **alphabet method**; **hornbook**.

syllabary *n.* **1.** a writing system in which orthographic symbols represent syllables, as Japanese kana or the Cherokee orthography created by Sequoyah. **2.** a list of syllables or of the characters representing syllables in a given language. **3.** a writing system, such as ancient Sumerian, in which orthographic symbols represent either a syllable or a syllable sequence. See also **syllable**; **writing system**. *Cp.* **alphabetic writing**; **ideography**; **logography**; **logosyllabic writing**; **pictography**.

syllabic *adj.* **1.** referring to syllables. **2.** in linguistics, referring to any sound that serves as the nucleus of a syllable. *Note*: In English, *syllabic* is normally applied to vowels although it is sometimes applicable to liquids and nasals. *Cp.* **syllable**.

syllabication *n.* the division of words into syllables. Also **syllabification**. *v.* **syllabicate**; **syllabify**.

syllabic consonant a consonant sound that, in the absence of a vowel sound, has sufficient energy or sonority to function as a syllable, as /m/ in *prism*. *Cp.* **semivowel** (def. 1).

syllabic verse verse in which one pays attention to the number of syllables in a line, as in haiku, rather than to stressed and unstressed syllables.

syllable *n.* in phonology, a minimal unit of sequential speech sounds comprised of a vowel sound or a vowel-consonant combination, as /a/, /ba/, /ab/, /bab/, etc. *Note*: In most languages, vowels play a central role in syllable formation since, by definition, a syllable always contains a vowel or vowel-like speech sound. In consonant-vowel-consonant syllable forms, as /bab/, the opening segment is called the *onset*, the final segment, the *coda*, and the central or most prominent segment, typically a vowel, the *nucleus*. The *onset* and *coda* are sometimes collectively called *syllable margins*. In metrical phonology, the nucleus and coda are regarded as a single unit called a *rime*.

symbol *n.* **1.** anything that represents something else, often by indirect association or by the convention of an emblem, token, word, etc. **2.** anything recognized as a sign. **3.** an idea or mental image. **4.** any arbitrary, conventional, written or printed mark intended to communicate, as letters, numerals, ideographs, etc. **5.** the disguised form of unconscious thoughts, feelings, and experiences, often appearing in dreams. **6.** in semiotics, a conventionalized sign. *Cp.* **sign** (def. 6a). *adj.* **symbolic**.

symbolic function in Piagetian theory, the ability to represent something not presently perceived by symbols or signs, as language, gesture, drawings, mental imagery, etc.; semiotic function.

symbolism *n.* **1.** the use of one thing to suggest something else; specifically, the use of symbols to represent abstract ideas in concrete ways. **2.** the implied meaning of a literary or artistic work. **3.** (*cap.*) the writing style and themes of the European Symbolists of the later 19th and early 20th centuries. **4.** the psychoanalytic theory that symbols may be used to bring material from unconsciousness into consciousness. *n.* **symbolization**. *v.* **symbolize**.

synchronic linguistics the study of a language at a particular stage of its development, without regard to historical changes. *Cp.* **diachronic linguistics**.

syncope *n.* **1.** the omission or loss of one or more sound segments from the middle of a word; as the loss of /w/ in *coxswain*, now pronounced /kok´ sən/. **2.** the omission of a syllable from a poetic foot, often balanced by extending an adjacent syllable. **3.** a brief loss of consciousness; faint. *Cp.* **apherisis**; **aphesis**; **apocope**; **contraction** (def. 1). *adj.* **syncopic**.

syncretism *n.* **1.** in the historical development of language, the merging of different inflectional forms into one form. **2.** in Piagetian theory, the linking in a complex configuration of unrelated ideas into some total impression without details or logical organization. See also **egocentric logic**. **3.** any attempt to reconcile or merge inconsistent or conflicting ideas. *v.* **syncretize**. *adj.* **syncretic**.

synecdoche *n.* a specific metaphor in which a part represents the whole or the whole represents a part, as *all hands on deck*.

syneresis *n.* the contraction of two syllables into one, as *diamond* is pronounced /dī´ mənd/ rather than /dī´ ə mənd/, or two vowels into one, as in a diphthong. Also **synaeresis**. *Cp.* **epenthesis**; **metathesis**; **tmesis**.

synesthesia *n.* **1.** a type of psychological association experienced by some persons in which stimulation in one sensory mode produces images in another mode, as in hearing sounds in color. **2.** a description of one sensation in terms of another, as "But the creaking empty light / Will never harden into sight" (Edith Sitwell, "Aubade"). Also **synaesthesia**.

synonym *n.* **1.** one of two or more words in a language that have highly similar meanings, as *sadness*, *grief*, *sorrow*, *etc. Cp.* **antonym**. **2.** a word used in a figurative sense, as *the deep* for *water*, *a heel* for *an untrustworthy person*, *etc.*; metonym. *adj.* **synonymous**.

synopsis *n.* a brief summary.

syntactic awareness the cognizance of grammatical patterns or structures, a phase of metalinguistic awareness.

syntactic cue evidence from knowledge of the rules and patterns of language that aids in the identification of an unknown word from the way it is used in a grammatical construction. *Cp.* **semantic cue**.

syntactic factor the grammatical complexity dimension in material to be comprehended, as the number of clauses in a sentence. *Cp.* **semantic factor**.

syntactics *n. (with sing. v.)* the branch of semiotics concerned with the relationships among the formal properties of signs.

syntagmatic *adj.* referring to a linear relationship between elements in a phrase or clause, as in *Go* and *away* in the sentence *Go away. Cp.* **paradigmatic**.

syntax *n.* **1.** the study of how sentences are formed and of the grammatical rules that govern their formation. **2.** the pattern or structure of word order in sentences, clauses, and phrases. **3.** the rules for determining how a computer language will be used to formulate and operate a program. *adj.* **syntactic(al)**.

synthetic language a language in which syntactic features are expressed primarily by affixes rather than words, as in Latin. *Cp.* **analytic language**.

synthetic method a way of teaching beginning reading by starting with word parts or elements, as letters, sounds, or syllables, and later combining them into words. *Note:* "The beginning emphasis in a synthetic method is learning the sound-symbol correspondence" (Dallman,

1974). See also **phonics** (def. 1); **word method**. *Cp.* **analytic method**.

synthetic phonics a part-to-whole phonics approach to reading instruction in which the student learns the sounds represented by letters and letter combinations, blends these sounds to pronounce words, and finally identifies which phonic generalizations apply; inductive phonics. *Cp.* **analytic phonics**; **whole-word phonics**.

systematic error repeated bias or distortion, especially in the collection or analysis of data; constant error.

systematic phonemics a theory that one's knowledge of spoken language includes knowledge of how different forms of words are phonologically related, as *divine-divinity; academy-academic*, etc. See also **morphophonemics**.

systemic grammar a theory of grammar developed by M.A.K. Halliday (1985) in which a speaker's or writer's use of meaningful language is seen as a result of interactions between the grammatical system and the environment. Also **systemic linguistics**. *Note*: In this theory, one's grammatical choices in constructing meaning are influenced by the social setting, mode of expression, and register.

systems approach an approach to designing a lesson, course, or curriculum in which all components are designed to work together as an integrated instructional plan. *Note*: A systems approach involves such steps as stating the objective in behavioral terms; designing, selecting, and integrating possible approaches to attaining the objective; and evaluating the effectiveness of the planned steps, or system, in reaching it.

T

tachistoscope *n.* any mechanical device for the controlled and usually very brief exposure of visual materials, as pictures, letters, numbers, words, phrases, and sentences. *adj.* **tachistoscopic**.

tacit knowledge knowledge that one has, but of which one is not consciously aware.

tactile *adj.* **1.** having to do with the sense of touch; tactual. *Cp.* **kinesthesis**. **2.** capable of being felt; providing information to the sense of touch; tangible; as Braille. *Note*: A *tactile approach* refers to any teaching method that involves touching the material to be learned, as the use of sandpaper letters or words on felt.

tag *n.* a grammatical construction, usually an auxiliary verb and a pronoun, added to a sentence to form a question for confirmation, as *wasn't it* in *That was a great movie, wasn't it?*; tag question.

tagboard *n.* a strong cardboard used especially in making charts in the primary grades; oaktag.

tagmemics *n. (with sing. v.)* a theory of language developed by Pike (1967) that views language as part of patterned general cultural behavior, both verbal and nonverbal, and composed of three levels: *sound* (phoneme), *unit* (morpheme), and *function* (tagmeme). *adj.* **tagmemic**.

tale *n.* **1.** a relatively short and detailed story of a real or imagined event. **2.** a literary example of such a story. See also **folktale**; **tall tale**.

talk **1.** *v.* to speak; communicate by speaking. **2.** *n.* speech; conversation; parlance. **3.** *v.* to discuss. *adj.* **talkative**.

talking book a sound recording of a publication.

tall tale a story about impossible or exaggerated happenings related in a realistic, matter-of-fact, and often humorous way, as the tales of Paul Bunyan. See also **tale**.

target language **1.** a language selected to be learned. **2.** the language into which a text is translated.

task analysis a systematic study of the components of a skill or other activity for determining a sequence for learning.

tautology *n.* the repetitious or unecessary use of words that do not provide new information in an utterance, as *Hear, hear!* or *I myself said....* *Note*: Tautologies occur commonly in everyday speech. *adj.* **tautologous**.

taxonomy *n.* the systematic classification of organisms, characteristics, processes, etc., into hierarchical groups, as described in *Taxonomy of Educational Objectives: The Cognitive Domain* (Bloom et al., 1956).

teacher center a place where professional and instructional materials are gathered for teacher use.

teacher evaluation those processes used in judging a teacher's adequacy as a professional: **a.** on entry to the profession, judgment as to the appropriateness of the teacher-situation match, with respect to learners and the schools. **b.** formative evaluation of the first few years of teaching, often with mentoring and support. **c.** summative evaluation with respect to granting tenure. *Note*: In the United States, the National Board of Professional Teaching Standards proposes innovative evaluation procedures for the certification of master teachers. See also the essay "Evaluation in Education" on pp. 77–78.

teacher expectation the mental set through which teachers filter perceptions of individual student performance.

teacher-librarian a teacher with special training in library science who manages a school library and educates students in the pleasures, use, and care of library materials; school library supervisor.

teacher's edition (T.E.) a comprehensive teacher's guide or manual to an instructional series of publications that also includes the student text. *Note*: Teacher's editions ordinarily include the philosophy and objectives of the series or program, as well as specific instructional suggestions, tests, and supplementary material.

teaching English as a second language (TESL) 1. a set of philosophies and approaches for teaching English to those with another first language. **2.** a department in a college or university devoted to research and teaching within the framework of such philosophies and approaches. Also **teaching of English to speakers of other languages (TESOL)**. See also **English as a second language**.

team teaching an instructional technique in which several teachers plan and carry out an integrated teaching approach.

technical school a school offering applied arts and science courses that bridge the gap between the skilled trades and the professions. *Cp.* **vocational school**.

technical word 1. a word with a specialized meaning in one or more content fields, disciplines, or professions. Also **technical term**. *Cp.* **jargon; terminology. 2.** a meaning of a common word form specific to a content field, as the technical meaning of *mean* in statistics.

technical writing writing to communicate specific information, as a scientific description of a computer operation.

telegraphic speech 1. a stage in language development in which all but the essential words of an utterance are omitted as in a telegram, as *Mommy give cookie* for *Mommy, give me one of those cookies*. See also **caretaker speech; child-directed speech. 2.** a communication technique that uses simple constructions and omits nonessential words, as in closed-captioned television broadcasts.

telescoping *n.* contracting a word, word part, or phrase, as *WYSIWYG* from *What you see is what you get*, analogous to closing a telescope. See also **acronym**.

teletext *n.* an electronic system using telephone, television, or other communication devices in which the user can select what is presented next. *Cp.* **videotex**.

television literacy 1. competence in using television to enhance daily life and to acquire social power. Also **teleliteracy**. *Note*: Buckingham (1993) observes that television literacy differs from conventional print literacy in that television is ungrammatical because it lacks syntax and leads to inferences that are drawn from graphic images. However, television literacy shares some features of conventional literacy: the medium is a means of communication; it has meaning; it serves social and cultural purposes; it is constantly evolving in conception; and it is subject to historical change. **2.** competence in interpreting the successive patterns, or mosaics, of television stimuli that are characterized by low visual orientation and high involvement with maximal interplay of all the senses. *Note*: This view, based on the writings of Marshall McLuhan (McLuhan & Fiore, *The Medium Is the Massage*, 1967), attempts to identify the psychological processes involved in television viewing that differentiate it from those involved in reading text. See also **literacy; visual literacy**.

tempo *n.* the rate of articulation of speech sounds, especially syllables. *Note*: In English, the tempo of unstressed syllables speeds up rather than remaining relatively constant, as in French.

temporal *adj.* **1.** referring to time. **2.** temporary. **3.** referring to verbal time. See also **tense** (def. 1).

tenor of discourse the relationships among persons engaged in a language interaction, especially the extent of formality used in the interaction. See also **field of discourse**; **mode of discourse**.

tense **1.** *n.* how verbs indicate time of action. *Note*: Some languages, as Chinese, do not directly indicate tense, but most languages have several tense forms. English uses two major tense forms, past and nonpast, traditionally called *past tense*, as *Ivan wrote a poem*, and *present tense*, as *Ivan writes poems daily*. A so-called *future tense* or *aspect* is formed with the use of one or more auxiliaries, as *will* in *Ivan will write another poem soon*. See also **aspect**; **modal auxiliary**; **modality** (def. 2). **2.** *adj.* having considerable muscle tension in the tongue and vocal tract walls when making speech sounds, as /ē/ in *eat*, /t/ in *tense*. **3.** *adj.* referring to a distinctive feature in the analysis of speech sounds in which the sound is prolonged and has clearly defined resonance, as /ē/ in *feet*, /o͞o/ in *cool*. *Cp.* **lax** (def. 1).

terminal objective a statement of an expected behavioral outcome of a specified learning experience.

terminal sound the ending sound(s) of a word; usually, the sound represented by the final consonant, digraph, or blend, but in some cases the last vowel sound and its following construction, as /ōpe/ in *rope* or /asm/ in *chasm*.

terminal string in transformational-generative grammar, the product of a series of phrase structure rules, as Nom(inal) + Vt (verb transitive) + Det(erminer) + Nom(inal), which could become the sentence *Felicia wrote the report*, to which transformational rules may be applied. See also **phrase-structure rule**; **string**.

terminology *n.* **1.** the technical words and expressions used in a special field. *Cp.* **technical word**. **2.** the science of developing a system of terms for a special field, subject, etc.; nomenclature.

test **1.** *n.* a set of systematic tasks or questions yielding responses that may be quantified so performance can be interpreted. **2.** *n.* a measurement, as *a hearing test, a statistical test*. **3.** *n.* a criterion to determine the truth or accuracy of something. **4.** *n.* procedures for determining whether a hypothesis is tenable. **5.** *v.* to put to a trial. **6.** *v.* to undergo a trial. See also the box "Types of Tests" on p. 255. *n.* **testing**. *adj.* **testable**.

test battery **1.** a group of selected tests used together to examine a given aspect of behavior. **2.** a group of tests standardized on the same population.

test bias the differences in test scores, or predictions from those scores, between two or more subgroups of the population that are matched on the underlying construct being measured.

test equating the statistical process of placing scores from different forms of a test on a common scale.

test item a single statement, question, or problem to be responded to on a test.

test manual a guide or handbook to the administration, scoring, and interpretation of a particular test.

test-retest reliability coefficient a reliability coefficient obtained by correlating the scores on two suitably separated administrations of the same test.

Types of *Tests**
achievement test
aptitude test
auditory-discrimination test
culture-fair test
diagnostic test
equivalency test
essay examination *or* test
free-association test**
free-response test
F test
goodness-of-fit test
group test
hearing test
individual test
intelligence test
mastery test
matching test
minimum competency test[†]
nonverbal test
objective test
oral reading test
paper-hole test
performance test
pointing test
posttest
power test
pretest
projective test
readiness test
reading readiness test
reading test
retention test
silent reading test
Snellen test
speed test
standardized test
subtest
survey test
t test
verbal test
vocabulary test
word-association test
word-recognition test

---

*Terms are all defined in this dictionary.
Term is defined under **word-association test.
[†]Term is defined under **minimum competency survey**.

---

tetrachloric correlation a correlation between two variables assumed to be continuous and normal in distribution, but both of which have been divided into only two classes, as a correlation between tall-short and fair-dark persons. *Cp.* **biserial correlation**; **point-biserial correlation**.

text *n.* **1.** the entirety of a linguistic communication, as a conversation and its situational context. **2.** *n.* a segment of spoken or written language available for description or analysis. **3.** the original spoken or written words or wording, in contrast to translations, abridgments, introduced errors, etc. **4.** the main part of a written communication, other than title, footnotes, etc. *Note: Internal text* refers to the author's words; *external text* refers to the meaning of an author's words as constructed by the reader. "The content of an internal text embellishes but also reflects the external text" (Durkin, 1993). **5.** the topic or theme of a discourse, as *a text of a lecture*. **6.** written or printed matter on a page or in a book, in contrast to illustrations; words. **7.** a textbook. **8. text hand**, handwriting that uses large, bold lettering. *adj.* **textual**.

text analysis the analysis of the structural characteristics of text, as coherence, hierarchical organization, concept load or density, etc., as they relate to comprehensibility. Also **text structure analysis**. *Cp.* **content analysis**.

text anxiety feelings of insecurity and fear in attempting to cope with text that is considered too challenging.

textbook **1.** *n.* a book used for instructional purposes, especially in schools and colleges. *Cp.* **trade book**. **2.** *adj.* as in a textbook in style and content, as *a textbook definition of literacy*.

text linguistics a branch of linguistics in which a unit of speech or writing, as a conversation, road sign, poem, etc., is studied in terms of the organization of its parts and the semantic relationships among them. Also **textlinguistics**. *Note*: Text linguistics is a chiefly European development. Some linguists make little distinction between text linguistics and discourse analysis although others distinguish text from discourse in terms of length, form (speech or writing), and participants (monologue or dialogue). *Cp.* **discourse analysis**.

text processing any of several theoretical views of the direction of the construction of comprehension by the reader: **a. top-down processing**, reading comprehension that begins with and is controlled by the experiences and expectations that the reader brings to text; inside-out theory; reader driven. **b. bottom-up processing**, reading comprehension that begins with and is controlled by the text, as in letter and text decoding; outside-in theory; text driven. **c. interactive processing**, reading comprehension that involves both the accurate, sequential processing of text and the experiences and expectancies that the reader brings to the text, each acting on and modifying the other. *Note*: In interactive processing, comprehension is generated by the reader under the stimulus control of the print. *Cp.* **interactive-compensatory hypothesis**.

text signal any typographical device, as italics or boldface, special symbols or headings, or special format arrangements that are used to call the reader's attention to particular aspects of written material.

text structure the various patterns of ideas that are embedded in the organization of text. *Note*: Common patterns of text structure are expository, cause-effect, comparison-contrast, problem-solution, description, and sequence. *Cp.* **story structure**.

theater of the absurd an avante-garde type of drama in which the usual conventions of plot, characterization, and theme are distorted, often to stress the isolation of man in an irrational, chaotic world, as in Samuel Beckett's *Waiting for Godot*. *Cp.* **black comedy**.

thematic teaching the organization of instruction around themes or topics, instead of around subject areas such as mathematics or history.

theme *n.* **1.** a topic of discussion, writing, etc. See also **thesis** (def. 3). **2.** a major idea or proposition broad enough to cover the entire scope of a literary or other work of art. *Note*: A theme may be stated or implicit, but clues to it may be found in the ideas that are given special prominence or tend to recur in a work. **3.** a short school composition; informal essay. **4.** in linguistics, the topic of a sentence, as *John* in *John talked on the telephone*. **5.** in functional grammar, the starting point of meaning for a clause; what the clause is about; "one element in a particular structural configuration which, taken as a whole, organizes the clause as a message" (Halliday, 1985). *Note*: A theme can be a noun phrase, an adverbial phrase, or a prepositional phrase. *Cp.* **rheme**. *adj.* **thematic**.

thesis *n., pl.* **-ses 1.** a formal piece of writing, sometimes required for a bachelor's degree, commonly so for a master's degree, and usually so for a doctorate. *Cp.* **dissertation** (def. 2). **2.** the basic argument advanced by a speaker or writer who then attempts to prove it. **3.** the subject or major argument of a speech or composition. See also **theme** (def. 1).

think-aloud *n.* **1.** oral verbalization. **2.** in literacy instruction, "a metacognitive technique or strategy in which the teacher verbalizes aloud while reading a selection orally, thus modeling the process of comprehension" (Davey, 1983). *Cp.* **visualization**.

think-aloud protocol the recording of a writer's spoken thoughts during the writing act to provide insight into the thinking processes involved in writing.

thinking **1.** *n.* the process(es) or product(s) of cognition; ideational thought. See also **cognition**; **conjunctive thought**; **disjunctive thought**; **relational thought**. **2.** *n.* any use of symbols or percepts in cognition. **3.** *n.* ideational problem solving. **4.** *n.* meditation or reflection on an idea or problem. **5.** *adj.* rational. *v.* **think**.

Types of *Thinking**
abstract (reasoning)
concrete (reasoning)
convergent
creative
critical
divergent

---
*Terms are all defined in this dictionary.

---

thought *n.* **1.** See **thinking** (defs. 1, 4). **2.** any part of thinking activity. **3.** the thinking that is or was characteristic of a given place, class, or time, as *Greek thought*.

threshold *n.* the minimum stimulation necessary to produce awareness or a response; the minimum change necessary for recognition of a difference, either absolute or differential.

tilde *n.* **1.** the diacritic mark (˜) placed above an *n* in some orthographies to indicate a palatalized sound, as in Spanish *cañon*. **2.** the same mark placed above a vowel in phonetic transcription to indicate that the vowel is nasalized. See also **nasal** (def. 2); **palatal**.

tinnitus *n.* a hearing disorder "in which individuals hear noises with varying characteristics" (Schow & Nerbonne, 1989), frequently accompanied by sensorineural hearing loss.

Title I the federally funded compensatory education program in the United States, intended to serve children of lower socioeconomic back-

grounds who may be at risk of school failure, particularly in the elementary grades. Formerly **Chapter 1**.

tmesis *n.* the insertion of one or more words between parts of a compound word, as *Where I go ever* for *Wherever I go*. *Cp.* **epenthesis**; **metathesis**; **syneresis**.

token *n.* **1.** a specific observed instance of language use, as a spoken or written word, a speech sound, a mathematical symbol, etc., as in the proposition *A is to B as B is to C* the Bs represent two tokens of the same type. **2. tokens**, the number of running words in a passage as contrasted to the number of different words, or types. *Cp.* **type** (defs. 1, 2); **type-token ratio**.

token system the overt reinforcing of desirable actions, particularly in a behavior-modification program, so named because tokens are given as rewards for work completed or time on task.

tone *n.* **1.** any sound of well-defined pitch, quality, and duration. **2.** the quality or character of such a sound. **3.** the effect produced by a regularly repeating sound wave. *Cp.* **noise** (def. 2). **4.** the inflections that mark the speech of a person or region; accent. **5.** the functioning of pitch on words. *Cp.* **intonation**. **6.** the pitch or pitch changes in a word that distinguish it from similar words in tonic languages, as Thai. **7.** a particular style in writing or speaking. *Note* In literary analysis, there is a difference of opinion about the distinction between *tone* and *mood*. The terms are sometimes used synonymously, but certain authorities use *tone* to apply to the author's attitude reflected in the style of the written word, reserving *mood* to refer to the effect created by the author's use of various literary devices. See also **mood**[1] (defs. 1, 2). **8.** the characteristic style of a period. **9.** elegance of style. *adj.* **tonal**.

tone deafness difficulty in or lack of tonal discrimination.

tone language a language that uses differences in tone to distinguish words otherwise phonetically identical, as Mandarin or Cantonese Chinese. *Note*: Nontonic languages, such as English, use tone as a suprasegmental phoneme. Also **tonic language**.

tool subject a subject made up of skills and abilities useful in studying other subjects; tool; as reading and other language arts.

topic *n.* the general category or class of ideas, often stated in a word or phrase, to which the ideas of a passage as a whole belong; theme. See also **thesis** (def. 3).

topic sentence a sentence intended to express the main idea in a paragraph or passage.

topic string an ordered sequence of ideas used in planning a writing or speaking task.

toponomy *n.* the study of place names, as *Newark* is a toponym. *Cp.* **onomastics**.

total communication the philosophy and methods of educating deaf students that encourage the use of all modes of communication, as sign language, finger spelling, speech, speechreading, and amplification. *Cp.* **manual method**; **oralism**.

tract *n.* a religious or political leaflet.

trade book **1.** in the United States and Canada, for example, a book published for sale to the general public. *Cp.* **textbook** (def. 1). **2.** commercial books, other than basal readers, that are used for reading instruction.

traditional orthography (T.O., t.o.) **1.** the standard writing system of a language. **2.** in English, the use of the conventional alphabet rather than an augmented alphabet such as the Initial Teaching Alphabet to spell words.

tragedy *n.* **1.** a play, or the dramatic form it represents, in which the leading character suffers intense conflicts and a wretched fate, often because of some weakness. **2.** any literary work that presents a somber or serious theme in a story that leads to an unfortunate, if not catastrophic, conclusion, as Gustave Flaubert's *Madame Bovary*.

tragic flaw a flaw or defect in a tragedy's hero or heroine that eventually causes his or her downfall.

tragicomedy *n.* **1.** a play or other literary work that contains elements of both tragedy and comedy. **2.** a play that initially progresses as a tragedy but, because of the turn of events, ends as a comedy, as Shakespeare's *The Merchant of Venice*.

trainable mentally retarded (TMR) referring to a person with moderate to severe mental retardation; specifically, one with an IQ between 3 and 5 standard deviations below the mean, usually between 25 and 50 IQ. *Note*: The trainable mentally retarded are not usually able to maintain themselves economically; however, they can be taught self-care, oral communication, and social adjustment skills so that they may function in a sheltered environment. See also **educable mentally retarded**; **mental retardation**.

training *n.* all of the instructional procedures and circumstances used to induce learning. *Note*: This psychological meaning is often viewed with suspicion by educators because of the presumed implication of narrowly focused, authoritarian, rote drill as distinguished from the broader meaning of *education*. *Cp.* **education** (defs. 2, 3). *v.* **train.** *adj.* **trainable**.

trait *n.* **1.** any characteristic tendency toward a behavior determined by an enduring motivation or habit, as one that can be measured by a personality test. **2.** an inherited characteristic. **3.** in statistics, a term sometimes used to refer to a variable.

transaction *n.* the view that human activities and relationships represent a fusion of individual, cultural, and natural factors so that the knower, the knowing, and the known all become aspects of a common communicative process. See also **transactional theory**. *v.* **transact**. *adj.* **transactional**.

transactional theory the view that meaning is constructed in communication through language by an active, fluid interchange of ideas within a given context, as between reader and text or between speaker and audience. Also **transactional model**. *Note*: According to Rosenblatt (1978) *transaction* designates "an ongoing process in which the elements or factors are...aspects of a total situation, each conditioned by and conditioning the other." See also the essay "Reader Response" on pp. 209–210. *Cp.* **constructivism**.

transactional writing a term used by Britton et al. (1975) to describe "language to get things done: to inform people...to advise or persuade or instruct people." See also **expressive writing**; **poetic writing**. *Cp.* **exposition** (def. 1).

transcription *n.* **1.** in linguistics, the act or result of making a written copy of spoken language, using phonetic or phonemic symbols or standard orthography. **2.** transcript. **3.** an electronic reproduction on magnetic tape. *v.* **transcribe**.

transductive reasoning in Piagetian theory, irreversible reasoning characteristic of preoperational thought. *Note*: Transductive reasoning is neither deductive nor inductive, is full of undetected contradictions, and relies on analogy.

transfer **1.** *n.* in general, the carryover process, or effect, of one response or set of responses on another, as the transfer of certain reading skills to writing skills. *Note*: The carryover may be positive, negative, or zero. Special types of transfer, as *negative transfer*, are given under the describing term. **2.** *v.* to so transfer. **3.** *n.* the process or effect of the carryover of grammatical forms from language to language, often in an interfering way. **4.** *n.* the change of spoken language into another medium of expression, as writing. **5.** *n.* a metaphor. **6.** *n.* a design to be carried over onto another surface, as by a printing press, a decal, etc. *adj.* **transferable**.

transfer of training the doctrine that training or learning can be carried over into stimulus situations that the learner recognizes as similar to one(s) previously learned. Also **transfer of learning**. *Note*: This concept has a long history in educational theory and practice. Thorndike (1914) proposed that such transfer involved the recognition of identical elements. Judd (1908), on the other hand, proposed that such transfer takes place through a process of generalization. Both positions have profoundly influenced instructional practice. See also **transfer** (def. 1)

transformation *n.* **1.** in cognition, the conversion of the physical stimulation of print or speech into a meaningful symbolic pattern or cognitive code. **2.** in transformational grammar, the process or result of change from one linguistic construction to another according to syntactic rules, as the transformation of the declarative structure *That is funny* to the interrogative *That is funny?* **3.** the process that converts a deep structure to a surface structure. **4.** a change in the nature or form of symbols according to the formal rules of logic or mathematics. **5.** a change in a mathematical expression without altering the values represented, as *2 + 3* is the same as *3 + 2*. **6.** a conscious expression of a disguised feeling that is usually opposite to one's repressed feelings. *v.* **transform**. *adj.* **transformational**.

transformational-generative grammar a theory of grammar that contains a set of rules for producing all possible grammatical—and no ungrammatical—sentences in a language to reveal the grammatical competence possessed by a native speaker. *Note*: Transformational-generative grammar, based on the work of Chomsky (1957), originated as an attempt to discover the universal characteristics of language. It has since gone through a number of revisions and reformulations. *Cp.* **government/binding theory**. See also **sentence transformation**; **transformation** (def. 2).

transformation rule in transformational-generative grammar, a set of instructions for converting one grammatical pattern to another. See also **transformation** (def. 2).

transitive verb a verb that takes a direct object, as *read* in *Francesca read the book. Cp.* **intransitive verb**.

transitivity *n.* in Piagetian theory, the understanding developed after the age of seven or eight that when *A* has a quantitative relationship to *B* which *B* also has to *C*, *A* has the same relationship to *C*.

translation *n.* **1.** the process of converting the meaning of phrases, sentences, etc., from one language to another. **2.** the completed material in the translated form. *Note*: Translation, whether free or literal, is seldom if ever successful in capturing entirely the meaning and spirit of the original. See also the essay "Problems in Translation" on p. 261; **free translation**; **literal translation**. *v.* **translate**.

transliteration *n.* **1.** the representation of orthographic symbols of one writing system by those of another writing system. **2.** a written message or text resulting from such a change. *Cp.* **romanization**. *v.* **transliterate**.

transposition *n.* a change in sequence of two or more language units, as in reading *the brown little dog* for *the little brown dog*, in writing *desrcibe* for *describe*, or in sounding *spaghetti* as though it were spelled *pshgetti. v.* **transpose**.

travesty *n., pl.* **-ties 1.** an extreme form of burlesque in which a grand style is used to treat a simple subject or a vulgar style is used to treat a grand subject. See also **burlesque** (def. 1). **2.** an extremely poor imitation of another work.

treatise *n.* a formal and systematic statement in writing of the principles of a subject, generally longer and more detailed than an essay but shorter than a book.

treatment *n.* **1.** in education, instruction given to an individual, based on needs determined by diagnosis. **2.** any form of medical or therapeutic aid by self or professionals. **3.** the manner of expression toward something, as Molière's satiric treatment of the clergy in *Tartuffe*. **4.** the independent variable in an experiment. **5.** the systematic handling of data to determine statistical relationships.

tree diagram 1. in phrase-structure grammar, a graphic illustration of the successive layers of parts that make up a sentence, as by using branches to show relations among these parts. See also **phrase marker** (def. 1). **2.** a graphic illustration of the historical relationship among related languages.

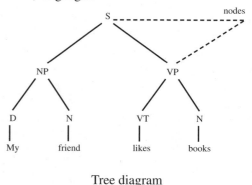

Tree diagram

Problems in Translation: A Japanese-to-English Example

A literal translation does not always convey the equivalent meaning of a word in the original language. This is especially true when the cultures in which the languages are used are quite different. Here are some examples of this problem that might be encountered when translating from English into Japanese or vice versa.

Dokusho

The equivalent Japanese word for *reading* is *dokusho*, but this word is not used when Japanese refer to the reading of chapters, paragraphs, sentences, phrases, words, or alphabets since it originally had the connotation of "book reading" only. For the same reason, to speak of *dokusho* in connection with the reading of newspapers, magazines, comic strips, instruction manuals, documents, signs, and so on is incorrect in Japanese. The verb *yomu*, however, which means "to read," can be used in conjunction with any of the instances mentioned above.

Dokusho shido

Dokusho means "reading" and *shido* means "guidance" or "instruction" but *dokusho shido* is neither "reading guidance" nor "reading instruction" in the sense that these terms would be understood in English. In addition to such activities as selecting and encouraging the reading of a suitable book, *dokusho shido* includes encouraging a child to attain the author's presumed higher stage of character or personality by engaging in a mental conversation with the author during the process of reading.

Dokusho kanso-bun

This term would be literally translated as "reading-impression composition." In addition to writing a summary of a book and giving their thoughts and feelings about it, Japanese children are encouraged to write their views on the relationship between the theme of the book and their own past and future life and are taught to try to attain the author's exemplary level of character or personality. In this respect, *dokusho kanso-bun* is very different from a book report written by pupils in English-speaking countries, even though both terms describe compositions written after doing some reading.

Dokusho jinkaku

Dokusho is "reading" and *jinkaku* is "character" or "personality." Rendered into English, however, "reading personality" or "reading character" does not really have any meaning. *Dokusho jinkaku* is the ultimate goal of *dokusho shido* and connotes the reader's reaching a very high stage of character of personality whereby he or she becomes able to hold a mental conversation with the author without any outside help and is able to improve his or her character beyond the level of the author by reading more books.

Difficulties in translating these terms highlight the important role of culture in language. In traditional Japanese culture, the function of character building is the principal object of reading instruction. Translators, therefore, should be aware of such cultural differences and not always attempt to translate culture-specific terms into the target language. Instead, they might use the original term followed by an explanatory phrase after the first occurrence.

Takahiko Sakamoto

trend analysis the observation and evaluation of changes in some variable over some period to determine long-term rather than short-term variations. *Cp.* **sequential analysis**.

trial **1.** *n.* a single opportunity for response; especially, one of a series of such opportunities. **2.** *n.* a completed response pattern in an experiment or test. **3.** *adj.* used as a sample. *v.* **try**.

trial-and-error learning a pattern of learning efforts in problem situations that is unsystematic and apparently unplanned. *Note*: This term, which was introduced by Thorndike to describe animal behavior, is felt by many psychologists and educators to be less appropriate in describing goal-oriented human behavior than is *approximation and correction*, a term suggested by Cronbach. *Cp.* **approximation and correction**.

trigram any sequence of three alphabet letters independent of their sound representations. *Note*: Trigrams are used by some psychologists to study such factors in reading as effects on word recognition of word length, frequency distribution, etc. *Cp.* **trigraph**.

trigraph *n.* a sequence of three letters representing a single speech sound or phoneme, as *sch* for /sh/ in *schmaltz*, or *eau* for /o/ in *beau*. *Cp.* **digraph** (def. 1); **trigram**.

triphthong *n.* a vowel sound generally regarded as a single sound made up of three vowel qualities, as in some pronunciations of *power*. *Note*: Triphthongs are generally restricted in English speech to words containing a *vowel + r* combination, as *power* /pow ə/. Some other languages, as Thai, make more substantial use of triphthongs. *Cp.* **diphthong**; **monophthong**.

trope *n.* a rhetorical or literary technique of using words in other than their literal sense; figure of speech.

true score in classical test theory, a hypothetical score, never obtained, that is free of measurement error, used for estimating measurement error. *Cp.* **standard error**.

t **test** the ratio of a statistic to its standard error, often used to determine the significance of the difference between two means.

type **1.** *n.* in linguistics: **a.** the generic class or category to which an observed linguistic unit, or token, belongs, as a sentence, word, grammatical class, phoneme, etc. **b.** one such representative token used as a model of a class or category. **2.** **types**, the number of different words in a passage as contrasted to the number of running words, or tokens. *Cp.* **token**; **type-token ratio**. **3.** *n.* in metal typography, a block, usually of metal, with a typeface for printing. **4.** *n.* in computerized typography, a computer code for type forms. **5.** *n.* a collection of computerized or metal type. **6.** *n.* typeface of the same style, as *italic type*. **7.** *n.* characters printed or typewritten, not handwritten. **8.** *v.* to print by keyboard.

Type I error rejection of the null hypothesis when it should be accepted. See also **alpha risk**.

Type II error acceptance of the null hypothesis when it should be rejected. See also **beta risk**.

type-token ratio (TTR) the number of times a particular linguistic item (token) occurs in a text in relation to the linguistic class (type) to which it belongs, as of all the noun entries in this dictionary compared to all the entries; lexical density. *Note*: The TTR is usually expressed as a percentage. See also **vocabulary diversity**; **word-frequency count**.

typographical signal a print cue to meaning. *Note*: "Typographic signals include underlining, italics, boldface, indented lines, as well as punctuation marks" (Durkin, 1993). See also **print conventions**.

typology *n.* a system of classifying all languages into broad classes based on phonological or grammatical criteria. *adj.* **typological**.

umlaut *n.* **1.** a change of a vowel sound occurring as the result of assimilating some feature of a following vowel or semivowel sound, as the *ö* in German *Töpfer* ("potter") from *Topf* ("pot"). See also **assimilation** (def. 5). **2.** a vowel that has undergone such a change. **3.** the orthographic mark (¨) placed directly above a vowel in some languages to indicate a change in vowel pronunciation; dieresis.

Umwelt *n.* in semiotics, the environment in which an organism exists to the extent that the organism is able to perceive it. *Note*: The term was coined by the German biologist von Uexkull and roughly translates as "surrounding world or environment" (Colapietro, 1993). *Umwelt* is not merely the objective environment but includes what an organism perceives and can act upon. See also *Lebenswelt*.

unaccented syllable 1. See **unstressed syllable**. **2.** a syllable without a strong beat in a literary rhythmical pattern composed of strong and weak beats.

uncial 1. *n.* a style of handwriting characterized by rounded capitals, found especially in Greek and Latin manuscripts of the fourth to eighth centuries A.D. **2.** *n.* a letter produced in this style. **3.** *n.* a medieval capital letter. **4.** *adj.* referring to such letter or style of writing.

unconscious motivation a motivating force or drive that is apparent to others but not to the subject.

underextension *n.* in the early acquisition of words and their meanings, the application of a word only to a particular object or to an instance of the class to which an object belongs, as *dog* to the family pet, but not to other dogs. *Cp.* **overextension**.

understanding *n.* **1.** the process or result of acquiring or constructing meaning; comprehen-

sion. **2.** intelligence; mind; especially, superior power of abstract thought. **3.** particular knowledge or skill. *v.* **understand**.

understatement *n.* **1.** the representation of something as less than it actually is. See also **litotes**. **2.** a form of irony or humor. *v.* **understate**.

ungrammatical *adj.* speech or writing that is incorrect according to prescriptive grammar criteria or the usage of competent speakers and writers.

uninterrupted sustained silent reading (USSR) a period of time during the school day when children in a class or in the entire school read books of their own choosing. Also **sustained silent reading** (SSR). *Note*: In some schools, everyone—students, teachers, principal, secretaries, custodians, etc.—stops to read, usually for 30 minutes.

unique 1. *adj.* not shared by others; singular; idiosyncratic; nonuniversal. *Cp.* **universal** (def. 2). **2.** *n.* the quality of being singular; specifically, the goal of cognitive development that an individual will possess certain nonuniversal, or unique, traits as well as universal traits.

unit *n.* **1.** a part of a course or subject that is taught as a whole, as *a short story unit in the English literature curriculum.* **2.** a basic part of the structure of linguistic knowledge, as phonology and grammar.

unit plan a teaching approach in which materials from one subject or from several subject areas are related to a central theme. Also **unit approach**.

unity *n.* **1.** oneness; the combining of the parts of something to make a whole. **2.** the harmony among the parts of a work in literature or the arts that reflects an organic whole and produces a single, major effect on the reader. *Note*: Literary unity may be the result of a single unifying element, as plot, character, mood, etc., or some combination of these.

universal **1.** *adj.* referring to the whole of any category, area, or sphere. **2.** *adj.* characteristic of all. *Cp.* **unique** (def. 1). **3.** *n.* a characteristic of all languages, as *the convention of assigning arbitrary meaning to symbols is a language universal*. See also **universal grammar**. **4.** *n.* a proposition in logic that applies to all members of a class.

universal grammar (UG) a theory of grammar proposed by Chomsky (1986) to discover and demonstrate the linguistic properties common to all languages. See also **core grammar**; **government/binding theory**.

universe of discourse all that is referred to in a discussion.

unlettered *adj.* **1.** See **illiterate** (defs. 1, 2). **2.** uneducated.

unread *adj.* **1.** See **illiterate** (def. 4). **2.** not knowledgeable in a specific subject.

unstressed syllable in polysyllabic words, the syllable(s) with least stress or emphasis, as the last two syllables in *syllable*.

uppercase letter a letter form, as *A, B, C*, that is usually larger than and different from a lowercase letter; majuscule. *Cp.* **lowercase letter**.

usage *n.* **1.** the way in which the native language or dialect of a speech community is actually used by its members. **2.** the sum of all idiolects within a language or language variety.

usage label a word or phrase in a dictionary entry that describes the appropriateness of that entry for specific contexts, as *informal*, *Brit.*, etc.

Usher's syndrome congenital nerve deafness.

utterance *n.* an actual production of a meaningful sequence of words; speech act. *v.* **utter**.

validation *n.* **1.** the process of attempting to assess the degree of test validity. **2.** the process of attempting to get objective evidence, as of a logical proposition.

validity *n.* **1.** a truthful or factual condition. **2.** a logical argument. **3.** the evidence that the inferences drawn from test results are accurate. **4.** the evidence that inferences from evaluation of program effectiveness and teacher competence are trustworthy; curriculum validity. *adj.* **valid**.

Types of *Validity**
concurrent
construct
content
convergent
curriculum
differential
discriminant
empirical
face
instructional
predictive

---

*Terms are all defined in this dictionary.

---

validity coefficient any correlation between a test and an appropriate criterion.

validity generalization the use of prior information in conjunction with test data for a given sample to estimate the extent to which the estimate of validity may be generalized to other samples. See also **predictive validity**.

value **1.** *n.* the relative worth, merit, or usefulness of something. **2.** *n.* something thought to be worthy for its own sake. **3.** *v.* to show or express the worth of something. **4.** *n.* in phonetics, the phonetic equivalent of a letter or grapheme, as /e/ in *bet*. **5.** *n.* a quantity given to a mathematical symbol or expression. **6.** *n. pl.*, the ideals, institutions, customs, etc., with which a group or a culture identifies either positively or negatively.

values of reading **1.** the general outcomes of reading that foster a sense of personal, social, or intellectual worth, as inspiration to do good, environmental awareness, or appreciation of literature. **2.** the particular merits of the reading act and its outcomes in gaining access to a full range of ideas. *Note*: The values of reading are described this way by Waples et al. (1940): "Print, to be sure, is not the only effective means of mass communication. It is probably not even the most important means of reaching the entire population directly.... But print still remains the only vehicle of communication which is not restricted to particular times and places, which can present ideas of all sorts to anyone who can read, and which can develop a subject to any desired fulness of detail."

variability *n.* **1.** changeableness, as *reading rate variability*. **2.** the dispersion, spread, or scatter of scores or values in a distribution, usually about the mean.

variable **1.** *n.* any quantity that is subject to variation. **2.** *n.* anything that is subject to quantitative change, as behavioral responses, temperature, etc. **3.** *adj.* changeable. **4.** *adj.* fickle. **5.** *n.* in sociolinguistics, a language unit, as a word, sound, or grammatical element, that is most susceptible to social or stylistic variation. **6.** *n.* in linguistics, a word whose change in form expresses a grammatical function, as *book* vs. *books*. **7.** in grammar and semantics, something that functions as any value member in a set of values.

Types of *Variables**
criterion
dependent
independent
intervening
predictor

---

*Terms are all defined in this dictionary.

---

variance *n.* a measure of variability; specifically, the square of the standard deviation (σ^2).

variant *n.* **1.** a subset of a linguistic class that shares features but also differs in some way from other members of the class, as the different forms of the English past-tense morpheme. *Cp.* **allomorph**; **allophone** (def. 1). **2.** an alternate pronunciation of a word, as /har'əs/ vs. /həras'/ for *harass*.

variation *n.* **1.** change, or the process of change; especially, change from the normal or typical. **2.** the spread or dispersion of scores in a distribution. **3.** in sociology, deviation from the structure or characteristics of the parents or from the group to which the individual belongs. **4.** a modified theme or pattern, especially in music. *v.* **vary**.

vegetative sounds coughs, burps, sneezes, etc., produced by infants during the first few weeks of life.

venereal noun a collective noun indicating a group or gathering. *Note*: The term is derived from *venery* ("hunting"). Venereal nouns range from the facetious, as an *exaltation* of larks, to the mundane, as a *herd* of cows, to the humorous, as a *flush* of plumbers.

Venn diagram in semantic mapping, overlapping circles that show those features either unique or common to two or more concepts.

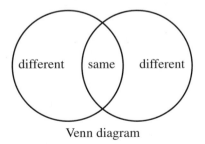

Venn diagram

verb *n.* in English, a word expressing an action or state that occurs in a predicate, can be inflect-

ed for tense, aspect, voice, and mood, and shows agreement with subject or object.

verbal **1.** *adj.* having to do with words. **2.** *adj.* oral. **3.** *adj.* referring to the use of words without regard to content or reality, as *a purely verbal argument*. **4.** *n.* a word in verb form that is used like a noun, adjective, or adverb, as *Reading* in *Reading is fun*. See also **gerund**. *Cp.* **participle**.

verbal ability the ability to understand or reason with language.

verbal fluency **1.** ease in the use of spoken and written language. **2.** speed in making word associations.

verbal IQ the IQ score for language-based tasks, as on the Wechsler Intelligence Scale. See also **intelligence quotient**. *Cp.* **nonverbal IQ**.

verbalization *n.* **1.** expressing oneself in words; making an utterance. **2.** the conversion of a part of speech into a verb, as *white* to *whiten*. *v.* **verbalize**.

verbal test **1.** the language-based portion of an intelligence test, as on the Wechsler Intelligence Scale. **2.** any scale or test for which the understanding or use of language is necessary. Also **verbal scale**. *Cp.* **nonverbal test**.

verbal thought thinking in words. *Note*: Vygotsky (1962) describes verbal thought as "a complex, dynamic entity [within which] the relation of thought and word...[is] as a movement through a series of planes...from the motive which engenders a thought to the shaping of the thought, first in inner speech, then in meanings of words, and finally in words."

verbiage *adj.* excessively wordy. *n.* **verbosity**.

verb phrase (VP) **1.** in traditional grammar, a group of auxiliary and main verbs that act together as a single verb, as *may have been talking*. **2.** in transformational-generative grammar, the complete predicate, as *raised their hands* in *Some students raised their hands. Cp.* **noun phrase**.

vergence *n.* **1.** for a single eye, the movement of the eyeball by any of the extraocular muscles. **2.** for both eyes, convergent or divergent ocular movements to maintain single binocular vision. *Cp.* **convergence** (def. 3); **divergence** (def. 3).

vernacular **1.** *n.* the native, spoken language or dialect of a speech community. **2.** *n.* the common language of a speech community as distinguished from its literary language. See also **dialect**; **register** (def. 1). **3.** *n.* the special way words are used by a class or profession, as *legal vernacular*. **4.** *adj.* having to do with the common language of a speech community.

vernacular literacy the ability to read, write, and sometimes speak the common language of a speech community; popular literacy.

vers de société *(Fr.)* a form of humorous light verse that usually deals with fashions and social relationships with grace and sophistication, as "Out upon it, I have loved / Three whole days together; / And am like to love three more / If it prove fair weather" (John Suckling, "A Poem with the Answer").

verse **1.** *n.* one line of a poem. **2.** *n.* a metrical composition. **3.** *n.* poetry without imaginative and conceptual power. See also **poetry** (def. 2 *Note*). **4.** *adj.* referring to verse. *n.* **versification**. *v.* **versify**.

version *n.* **1.** translation, as *an English version of Edmond Rostand's* Cyrano de Bergerac. **2.** any of several variations of a story, play, etc., sometimes in different media, as *the film version of Sir James Barrie's* Peter Pan.

vertical imbalance an oculomotor imbalance or deviation in which one of the eyes turns up or down. *Cp.* **lateral imbalance**.

vicarious experience indirect, imagined participation in events in the experience of others, of which reading is a prime source.

videotex *n.* an interactive presentation of text and graphics on a video screen, often with touch-screen selection of choices by user and occasionally with an exchange of longer messages. *Cp.* **teletext**.

vignette *n.* **1.** a decorative design often found on the title page or at the beginning or end of a book chapter. **2.** an illustration without borders that fades into its background. **3.** a short, descriptive sketch or "word picture."

virtual reality **1.** the simulation of a realistic environment by sophisticated computer programs. **2.** the use of such a technique by writers to create a fictional world and tell a story. Also **augmented reality**.

visible speech **1.** the use of symbols to indicate the proper placement of the speech organs to produce specific sounds in teaching the deaf to speak. **2.** the use of both speech and signing in communication; combined method. **3.** the electronic conversion of audible speech into visual patterns that may be read. See also **speech spectogram**.

vision *n.* **1.** the act or power of seeing; sight; visual acuity. **2.** something seen. **3.** something imagined and pictured; hallucination. **4.** having the imaginative intelligence or foresight to anticipate the future consequences of present behaviors and trends.

visual *adj.* **1.** having to do with the use of the eyes or with sight. **2.** referring to information gained by sight, as *visual impressions*. **3.** capable of being seen; seeable; visible; as *a visual alphabet*. **4.** optical, as *a visual illusion*. **5.** referring to projected or displayed representations such as pictures, models, charts, etc., used for educational purposes, as *visual aids*.

Types of *Vision**
binocular
distance
foveal
perimacular
peripheral
photopic
---
*Terms are all defined in this dictionary.

---

visual acuity the sharpness of seeing resulting from the clarity of the image falling on the retina, the sensitivity of the retina and the nervous system, and the keenness of perception. See also **Snellen test**. *Cp.* **refraction** (def. 1).

visual closure the process or ability to fill in missing parts of a visual stimulus; especially, the process of supplying a letter missing from a word or a word missing from a sentence. See also **closure** (def. 1). *Cp.* **auditory closure**.

visual coordination the smooth working together of both eyes; binocular coordination.

visual cue a distinctive sight feature that triggers a response; especially, a distinctive shape that aids in identification of a letter, letter group, or word. See also **configuration clue**; **visual perception**.

visual-cue reading in early reading development, the selection of meaning of words based on some visual clue (Ehri, 1991); logographic reading; as by the recognition of *yellow* by its two high marks in the middle or of *McDonald's* by its "golden arches" logo. *Cp.* **cipher sight-word reading**; **phonetic-cue reading**.

visual discrimination **1.** the process of perceiving similarities and differences in stimuli by sight. **2.** the ability to engage in such a process. *Note:* An educational aspect of this processing ability is that of acquiring sensitivity to the distinctive features of common printed material, as letters, words, and phrases. This may lead to students' more rapid and accurate processing of those stimuli in the future. If such features as the difference between *m* and *w* or *then* and *than* are not learned, errors of letter or word identification will tend to persist and block reading progress. See also **auditory discrimination**; **word discrimination**.

visual fatigue eyestrain; tiredness presumably due to excessive or improper use of the eyes. *Note*: *Visual fatigue* is an inexact descriptive term, not a diagnostic one. It may refer to many symptoms of tiredness associated with the eyes, as in the neck, back, etc. Experiments concerning visual fatigue while reading conducted by Dearborn (1906) and others at the turn of the century suggest that the external eye muscles are remarkably resistant to fatigue in adults with normal vision. However, Vernon (1978) notes that "the eye of the child is much more liable to fatigue and strain than that of the adult."

visual feature (of print) a print convention, as the punctuation and capitalization of letters, used to signal meaning in the writing process.

visual field the entire area visible to an eye without shifting fixation. *Note:* When the eye is looking straight ahead, the range of this field is normally about 65° upward from the center of the eye, 95° outward, 75° downward, and 60° inward. *Binocular visual field* refers to the total area seen when both eyes are looking at one spot.

visual impairment **1.** the loss of acuity of the visual field because of a physical or physiological defect. **2.** visual acuity of 20/200–20/70 in the better eye after correction; partially sighted.

visualization *n.* the process, or result, of mentally picturing objects or events that are normally experienced directly. *Note*: Encouraging students to use visualizations before and during writing is a device sometimes used to stimulate productive writing. See also **imagery** (def. 1). *Cp.* **think-aloud**. *v.* **visualize**.

visual literacy the ability to interpret and communicate with respect to visual symbols in media other than print, as visual literacy in viewing television, art, nature, etc. See also **literacy**; **television literacy**.

visually handicapped 1. having serious loss of useful sight. **2.** See **visual impairment** (def. 2).

visual memory the retention, recall, or recognition of things seen. *Note*: In reading and writing, visual memory is helpful in learning letter forms and their sequence in words.

visual memory span the number of items that one can recall, usually in the correct order, immediately after seeing them. *Cp.* **auditory memory span**.

visual-motor method a modified kinesthetic method of learning to identify printed words that emphasizes seeing and writing them without tracing. *Cp.* **Fernald(–Keller) method**.

visual-motor skills skills requiring a specified degree of visual-motor coordination, usually tested by having a person copy a design.

visual perception the extraction of information about things, places, and events in the visible world; the process of seeing such characteristics of things as shape, color, size, distance, etc., and identifying them meaningfully. See also **form perception**; **word perception**.

visual processing the full range of mental activity involved in reacting to visible stimuli, es-

pecially in reading. *Note*: The nature and operation of visual processing continues to be under intensive study in research in reading comprehension. *Cp.* **auditory processing**.

visual span 1. See **span of attention** (def. 1). **2.** all that can be perceived in an instant in the visual field.

visual suppression failure to use, or the inhibition of, the vision of one eye to avoid double vision or visual confusion. *Note*: Visual suppression may involve cortical inhibition of all or part of the neural information coming from the retina of one eye due to failure in binocular fixation or, in some cases, hysteria. See also **amblyopia**.

visual tracking the process or ability to follow lines of print.

vocabulary *n.* **1.** a list of words, as in a dictionary or glossary; lexicon. **2.** those words known or used by a person or group. **3.** all the words of a language. **4.** nonverbal forms of expression, as *the vocabulary of the painter*. **5.** (*cap.*) a subtest of several intelligence and reading tests. See also **lexical item**.

Types of *Vocabulary* *
controlled**
core
expressive
listening *or* hearing
meaning
reading
receptive
recognition *or* sight
simplified
speaking *or* oral
writing

*Terms are all defined in this dictionary.
See **vocabulary control.

vocabulary burden **1.** the degree to which the number of difficult words, their rate of introduction, and their comprehensibility affects readability. **2.** the frequency of hard words, as determined by specific criteria, used as a variable in readability formulas. Also **vocabulary load**. *Cp.* **concept load** (def. 2).

vocabulary control the practice of limiting the rate of introduction of new words, as in basal reading texts.

vocabulary development **1.** the growth of a person's stock of known words and meanings. **2.** the teaching-learning principles and practices that lead to such growth, as comparing and classifying word meanings, using context, analyzing word roots and affixes, etc.

vocabulary diversity the extent to which different words are used in writing or speaking; lexical variety. See also **type-token ratio**.

vocabulary test any test of word knowledge, active or passive, oral or silent.

vocal *adj.* **1.** sounded with an unblocked air flow between the vocal cords and the lips, as during vowel production. **2.** referring to any aspect of speech, as *vocal organs*, *vocal tract*, etc. **3.** outspoken.

vocalization *n.* **1.** causing the vocal folds to vibrate during speech; voicing. **2.** voice production; utterance; phonation. **3.** subvocalization. **4.** any sequence of speech sounds without regard to its structure. **5.** supplying vowel indicators in writing systems that do not use vowels, as in Hebrew. *v.* **vocalize**.

vocal play a stage in early language acquisition in which the infant initiates and repeats consonant-vowel sequences.

vocational school an occupationally oriented school with courses, usually comprehensive, in the more highly skilled trades or occupations. *Cp.* **technical school**.

vocative case the case form in inflected languages that indicates the person or personified object being directly addressed.

voice **1.** *n.* any sound produced by the vocal tract of a vertebrate, or a sound similar to it. **2.** *n.* the speech sounds, or their range, produced by the larynx and modified by the resonators. **3.** *n.* the ability to produce such speech sounds. **4.** *v.* to make such sounds; talk; speak. **5.** *n.* the distinctive features of a person's speech and speech patterns. **6.** *n.* in many languages, a syntactic pattern that indicates the verb-subject relationship. *Note*: The principal voices in English and many other languages are *active* and *passive*. In the active voice, the subject of the verb carries out some action, as *He hit the ball*. In the passive voice, the subject of the verb is the receiver of some action or state indicated by the verb, as *He was hit by the ball*. **7.** *n.* in some languages, as in Latin, the inflection of verb forms to show verb-subject relationships. **8.** See **personal voice**.

voice disorder a difficulty in one or more aspects of voicing or resonation, serious enough to interfere with ease of communication. *Note*: A severely guttural, strident, or hoarse voice may represent a voice disorder. This term does not cover articulatory or fluency problems, for which the more general term "speech disorder" is used.

voicing *n.* **1.** the conversion of the energy of the moving air flow in speech into acoustic energy in the larynx; phonation. **2.** the vibration of the vocal cords during speech, as in the production of vowels and certain consonants. See also **vocalization** (def. 1).

volunteer literacy programs programs in adult basic education that "are staffed by volunteers, as in the pioneer work of Alfred Fitzpatrick in Canada, the 'moonlight schools' of Cara Stewart, the 'citizenship schools' of Miles Horton in the United States, and the Literacy House of Welthy Honsinger Fisher in India" (Newman & Beverstock, 1990). See also **citizenship schools**; **moonlight schools**.

vowel *n.* **1.** a voiced speech sound made without stoppage or friction of the air flow as it passes through the vocal tract. *Note*: Vowels are generally classified by specifying tongue position and elevation, and by the position of the lips. **2.** the most prominent sound in a syllable, as /ō/ in *Joan*. *Note*: The greater loudness and resonance helps distinguish vowels from consonants. **3.** a letter representing any such sounds. *Note*: Special types of vowels, such as *long vowel*, are defined under the describing term. *Cp.* **consonant**.

vowel cluster in teaching practice, a sequence of two or more vowel sounds in a word, as in *aorta*, or a sequence of two or more vowel letters, as *oa* in *boat*.

vowel controller the letters *r*, *l*, and, in some phonic systems, *w*, when the sounds they represent modify an immediately preceding vowel sound in the same syllable, as in *fir*, *fall*, *saw*. See also **r-controlled vowel sound**.

vowel digraph a spelling pattern in which two or more adjoining letters represent a single vowel sound, as *eigh* for /ā/ in *sleigh*, *ea* for /e/ in *bread*, or *aw* for /ô/ in *saw*. *Cp.* **diphthong**.

W

webbing *n.* in planning writing, the use of diagrams or maps to show the relationships among the ideas to be included. See also **mapping** (def. 1).

Wechsler Intelligence Scale any of several individually administered general mental ability tests developed by Wechsler that give separate verbal and nonverbal IQs as well as a total IQ. *Note*: The three scales in current use are the Wechsler Preschool and Primary Scale of Intelligence (WPPSI), the Wechsler Intelligence Scale for Children–Revised (WISC–R), and the Wechsler Adult Intelligence Scale (WAIS). See also **Stanford–Binet Intelligence Scale**.

weight 1. *n.* the numerical coefficient by which a score or value is multiplied to give it a desired relative importance. **2.** *n.* the relative contribution made to the variance of a test. **3.** *v.* to give statistical weight to a variable.

weighting *n.* the determination or assignment of weights to scores to produce a desired total score or to improve the predictive ability of an equation.

western *n.* a work of fiction featuring the frontier setting and action of the American West, as Walter Clark's *The Ox-Box Incident*. Also **Western**.

whimperative *n.* a request or command that is superficially stated as a question; indirect speech; as *Why don't you close the door?*

whole language See the essay "Whole Language" on pp. 279–281.

whole-part relationship an association, stated or implied in a communication, between a general idea and one or more of its subordinate ideas.

whole-word methodology an approach to reading instruction that deals with the learning of words as wholes. *Cp.* **eclectic methodology**; **letter phonics**; **word method**.

whole-word phonics an analytic approach to reading instruction in which the sounds represented by certain letters and groups of letters within whole words are compared and contrasted to those in other whole words, avoiding the separate sounding of word parts. *Cp.* **analytic phonics**; **cluster phonics**; **letter phonics**; **synthetic phonics**.

Whorfian hypothesis the view advanced by Whorf that the structure of a language organizes and influences the thought and behavior of its speakers; Sapir–Whorf hypothesis. *Note*: According to Whorf (1940), "We dissect nature along lines laid down by our native language." The strongest form of this view, *linguistic determinism*, holds that language relentlessly determines the way we think. The weaker version, *linguistic relativity*, maintains that language shapes the way we perceive and remember but that people can transcend language differences.

wh- word a word that commonly begins a question, as *who, what, when, where, why*. Note: *How* is sometimes added to these five words to form "the five Ws and H."

word *Note*: A word is a key language unit of meaning in reading, as it is in listening, speaking, and writing. It is not, however, the only meaningful unit with which the reader must deal. "It should constantly be remembered that words are functional, and that their main function is to help express a total meaning which always requires or implies their association together with other words" (Huey, 1908). Although people generally know what a word is in actual use and can identify a word in the speech of others, its precise definition is less certain, and, like language, is subject to the theoretical or subjective views of the definer. **1.** *n.* "a morpheme or group of morphemes that is regarded as a pronounceable and meaningful unit" (Wardhaugh, 1966). **2.** *n.* "segments of language recorded as independent entities in dictionaries" (Lehmann, 1976). **3.** *n.* "any linguistic form considered to be independent in distribution and meaning" (Francis, 1958). **4.** *n.* a phoneme or series of phonemes or their written representations that conveys meaning and consists of at least one free morpheme, as the main entry of a dictionary. **5.** *n.* in writing, "a sequence of letters with a white space on either side" (Smith, 1975). **6.** *n.* in word identification, "a complex of features, a composite representation of five classes of information: graphic, phonological, orthographic, semantic, and syntactic" (Gibson & Levin, 1975). *Note*: The authors go on to say that "full recognition of a word depends upon the extraction of all these kinds of information." **7.** *n.* the smallest lexical unit of meaning in speech and writing; more technically, a morpheme or unit of morphemes that can be used in syntactic constructions; "a minimum free form (morpheme)" (Bloomfield, 1933). *Note*: Single morphemes may be combined in compounds, as *black* and *bird* to form the word *blackbird*. Some types of words, as *are*, *the*, *very*, *of*, etc., usually depend on their relation to other words for meaning, except in such references as the *the* in *Watch the parade*. **8.** the smallest unit of grammar that can stand alone as a complete utterance (Crystal, 1992). **9.** *n. pl.*: **a.** an insincere speech with little significance; prattling. **b.** the lyrics of a song. **c.** angry, quarrelsome speech, as *The rivals exchanged heated words*. **10.** *n.* a short talk or conversation, as *May I have a word with you?* **11.** *n.* an expression, as *word of praise*. **12.** *n.* a promise, as *I give you my word*. **13.** *n.* news; information; as *What word do you bring?* **14.** *n.* a verbal signal, as a password. **15.** *n.* an order; command; as *His word was law*. **16.** *n.* (*cap.*) the Bible. Also **the Word**. **17.** *v.* to put into words. **18. in a word**, in summary; in short. **19. in so many words**, literally. **20. by word of mouth**, speaking. *Note*: Special types of words, as *compound words*, are defined under the describing term.

Whole Language

In recent years, no educational movement has produced as much interest, activity, and controversy as that of whole language. It has had a major impact on how the reading education community thinks and talks about instruction today.

Whole language is both a professional movement and a theoretical perspective. It embodies a set of applied beliefs governing learning and teaching, language development, curriculum, and the social community. Historically, whole language may be viewed as part of a long tradition of progressivism in education that reflects concern and discontent with prevailing practice. Whole language teachers have been influenced by theorists such as Lev Vygotsky, Louise Rosenblatt, Kenneth Goodman, and Frank Smith, among others. They make use of the implications drawn from language research, including studies of the writing process, sociolinguistics, psycholinguistics, and emergent literacy. Yet, while many disciplines and theories have influenced whole language, its proponents are quick to point out that it is not synonymous with any of them. Rather, it is a unique and evolving framework, rare among educational movements in that the great majority of its proponents are drawn from the ranks of classroom teachers.

(continued)

Concerns and Controversies

Issues surrounding phonics and the teaching of discrete skills evoke the most heated discussions about whole language. Because whole language teachers believe that all language systems are interwoven, they avoid the segmentation of language into component parts for specific skill instruction. The use of strategies taught in meaningful contexts is emphasized. Phonics is taught through writing and by focusing on the patterns of language in reading—and students are taught only as much phonics as they need. Invented spelling is viewed as the best demonstration of the development of phonics relationships. Assessment focuses on authentic demonstrations of each student's ongoing work.

Critics of whole language would opt for a more systematic and hierarchical approach to phonics in the belief that instruction in sound-symbol relationships is foundational to learning to read. They express concern that invented spelling encourages sloppy habits and reinforces incorrect behaviors. While there is a growing interest among all educators in more authentic approaches to assessment, standardized test scores remain the key indicator of success in literacy and the major determiner for decisions regarding promotion and placement. Thus, many teachers are reluctant to adopt whole language approaches. Instead they say, "We cannot teach one way and assess another."

The applicability of whole language to the upper grades is another concern. Although whole language advocates recommend it for all levels, its use is concentrated primarily in the lower grades. This comes as no surprise. Most early childhood and elementary teachers have some knowledge of child growth and development. Therefore, the principles and practices associated with whole language come more "naturally" to them. In the upper grades, where teachers are more likely to focus on curricular content, whole language theory with its blend of process and product may seem too indirect and inefficient. Even those who readily agree that learning the definition of *adjective* and acquiring the ability to locate one in a sentence has virtually nothing to do with writing a descriptive paragraph may opt to have students memorize definitions and identify parts of speech because they can be readily taught, learned, and tested.

Future of Whole Language

It has been said that whole language is for all children, but not for all teachers. There may be far more than a grain of truth in this. Because whole language theory is closely aligned to the way children learn their first language, it makes good sense to those who have taken the time to study it. Unlike a parent, who usually deals with one child at a time, however, teachers find themselves in classrooms with as many as 30 or more students, all with varying needs and abilities. They ask how a single teacher can apply whole language principles with so many diverse individuals. In response, of course, one can point to the many teachers who are doing just that. Conversely, there are many others who will probably never be willing, because of philosophical differences, or capable of doing so. The question of capability probably has less to do with intelligence or motivation than it has to do with the tremendous staff development required to make the far-reaching changes asked of some teachers who wish to move toward whole language. Most school districts underestimate the time and

(continued)

Whole Language (cont'd.)

effort required to effect meaningful change. In discussing plans for staff development, a very enthusiastic school principal once said to me, "Well, we did whole language last year. What do you suggest we do next?"

I believe that the effects of the whole language movement are both profound and enduring. At the same time, the controversy and confusion surrounding whole language will also have an exasperatingly long run. Ironically, evidence of the influence of whole language will increasingly appear under the heading of various less controversial terms, such as *literature-based reading* or *integrated language arts*, while the term *whole language* will be increasingly "borrowed" for use as a descriptor for "whole language thinking kits" and "whole language phonics workbooks." Ultimately, the future of whole language will rest in the educational community's commitment to look well beyond labels to examine thoughtfully the theory and practice whole language represents.

Dorothy Strickland

word analysis a general, imprecise label applied to word identification or decoding. *Note*: Now seldom used, the meaning of *word analysis* varied in use among reading specialists: **a.** to Vernon (1978), "usually the analysis of words into their constituent parts." **b.** to Gray (1960), "sight vocabulary, phonics, structural analysis, context clues, and dictionary skills."

word-association test a projective test, chiefly in clinical and experimental use, in which a person is asked to say quickly the first word that each of a series of stimulus words suggests; free-association test. *Cp.* **projective test**.

word attack an outmoded term for word identification or decoding.

word bank **1.** a file of words mastered or being studied by a student. **2.** a personal dictionary, as a student's own record of words used in constructing messages.

word blindness **1.** alexia. **2.** dyslexia. *Note*: The concept of word blindness has a long history, being a convenient label for the inability to

read the simplest words, presumably because of some neurological defect. The term is now seldom used except in a metaphorical sense, as in one Chinese expression of the concept of illiteracy. See also **illiteracy** (def. 1).

word-by-word reading **1.** a halting, labored type of oral reading with a very slow rate of word identification, poor phrasing and comprehension, and sometimes mispronunciations; word calling. *Note*: In word-by-word reading, the reader "just bumps along from word to word without any notion of what he is reading" (Anderson & Dearborn, 1952). **2.** very slow silent reading, often with lip and head movements that suggest a narrow span of recognition.

word calling **1.** See **word-by-word reading** (def. 1). **2.** proficiency in the mechanics of oral reading with little or no attention to meaning, often the result of an overemphasis on word analysis, oral reading, and drill on isolated words. *Note*: Problems of word calling are often ignored under the presumption that because a reader can pronounce the individual words, comprehension also occurs.

word class a set of words that share the same grammatical, morphological, or semantic properties. See also **form class** (def. 1); **part of speech**.

word discrimination the process of noting differences in words; especially in their visual outlines or overall shapes. *Note*: Teachers often use the term to refer to the noting of similarities as well as differences. See also **auditory discrimination**; **visual discrimination**; **word identification**; **word perception**; **word recognition**.

word family **1.** a group of words sharing a common phonic element, as /īt/ spelled *ite* in *bite*, *kite*, *despite*. See also **phonogram** (def. 2). *Cp.* **phonic cue**. **2.** a group of words sharing the same root or base, as *phon-* in *phonemic*, *phonation*, *telephone*.

word form the form of a word that serves a particular grammatical function, as the past-tense form of a verb.

word formation **1.** the production of new words in a language by invention, onomatopoeia, borrowing, etc.; specifically, the production of new words in a language by morphological processes, as by using derivational affixes, as in *happiness*, or by compounding, as in *cupcake*. **2.** the regular morphological rules of a language. *Cp.* **morphology**.

word-frequency count a list showing how often words appear in a sample of reading material. Also **word-frequency list**. *Note*: Word-frequency counts vary in comprehensiveness and purpose. The Dolch list of 220 basic sight words (1936) identified the most common words in beginning reading. On the other hand, *The Educator's Word Frequency Guide* (1995), a word count of over 17 million words (tokens) and over 164,000 different word types in reading materials of all kinds, kindergarten through college, serves many teaching and research purposes. See also **type-token ratio**.

word history an explanation of the origin and development of the meaning or meanings of a word. *Cp.* **etymology**.

word identification the process of determining the pronunciation and some degree of meaning of an unknown word. *Note*: Word-identification skills commonly taught are phonic analysis, structural analysis, context clues, configuration clues, dictionary skills, and sometimes picture clues. Some reading authorities, as Tinker (1965) and Durkin (1993), make a sharp distinction between the *identification* of an unknown word and the *recognition* of a word previously met. See also **word analysis**; **word discrimination**; **word perception**. *Cp.* **word recognition** (def. 2).

wordless book a picture book with no text.

word meaning the concept or concepts associated with a spoken or written word. *Note*: "In word meaning...thought and speech unite into verbal thought" (Vygotsky, 1962).

word method **1.** a way of teaching reading in which a substantial number of words are learned as whole units before word analysis is started; a "words-to-reading" system (Mathews, 1966). *Note*: "The word method, beginning with the *Orbus Pictus*,...was very little used in America until 1870.... The pictures of the *Orbus Pictus* were intended to suggest the names printed below, without using any tedious spelling" (Huey, 1908). "This is a modern system, known since the close of the eighteenth century, but put into wide-spread practice about 1900.... In the 1830s and 1840s it was called the new method, later the word method, and later still the look-and-say method.... The method is that of starting children in reading by having them memorize words without analyzing them into letters and sounds" (Mathews, 1966). **2.** a way of teaching reading that begins with whole words but either immediately subjects them to word analysis or introduces a parallel phonics program; a "words-to-letters" system (Mathews, 1966). **3.** any analytic approach or method for teaching reading; sight method. *Note*: "If the word method is not accompanied by the analysis of words into their elements, it should not be classified as an analytic method" (Gray, 1956). See also **analytic method**; **eclectic method**. *Cp.* **alphabet method** (def. 1); **synthetic method**; **whole-word methodology**.

word order   the sequential arrangement of words in a phrase, clause, or sentence. *Note*: In languages with few inflections, as English, sentence meaning is usually dependent on word order, as *The boy hit the ball* vs. *The ball hit the boy.*

word perception **1.** the visual or auditory identification of a word and some degree of meaning. **2.** the understanding of the appropriate meaning of a word following its identification or recognition. *Note*: "The perception of words...depends upon the meanings that are present in the identification and recognition of the words" (Tinker, 1965). See also **word discrimination**; **word identification**; **word recognition**.

word play **1.** the witty use of words, especially in conversation. **2.** punning. **3.** in early language development, a child's manipulation of sounds and words, sometimes for pleasure or for purposes of language exploration and practice.

wordprocessing the use of computers, with appropriate software programs and printers, to create, edit, and print text. Also **word-processing**; **word processing**.

wordprocessor a person, machine, or computer program that does wordprocessing. Also **word-processor**; **word processor**.

word recognition **1.** the process of determining the pronunciation and some degree of meaning of a word in written or printed form. See also **word perception**. **2.** the quick and easy identi-

fication of the form, pronunciation, and appropriate meaning of a word previously met in print or writing. *Cp.* **word identification**. See also **word discrimination**.

word-recognition test **1.** a test of ability to identify words already learned. **2.** a test of ability to identify words not learned before by applying word-identification techniques. *Note*: A word-recognition test may be informal or formal. An informal test may merely list words to be identified. A formal test may also measure competence in phonics, structural analysis, dictionary use, and use of context clues.

word sort a vocabulary-development and word-study activity in which words on cards are grouped according to designated categories, as by spelling patterns, vowel sounds, shared meanings, etc.

words per minute (WPM) rate of reading or speaking in terms of the average number of words covered in one minute. *Note*: For ease of computation, most speed-reading estimates are expressed as words per minute even though ideas are not evenly spread over the words in text.

word study **1.** vocabulary-building exercises. **2.** practice in word identification, as in phonics, structural analysis, etc. **3.** spelling practice.

word-superiority effect in word recognition, "the superior ease of recognizing a target letter embedded in a word" (Gibson & Levin, 1975).

word wheel a device with two concentric circles of cardboard or stiff paper fastened together, each with a series of word elements on it which, when one element is aligned with another by rotation, make up words for practice in word analysis.

workbook *n.* **1.** a book, usually paperbound and expendable, with practice lessons on one or more skills or concepts. **2.** a supplementary exercise book for skill development in a basal reading program.

workplace literacy literacy that "focuses attention on individuals in relation to the societal and economic concerns of a nation" (Yarborough, cited in Newman & Beverstock, 1990); workforce literacy. See also **literacy**. *Cp.* **academic literacy**.

worksheet *n.* **1.** an exercise sheet containing directions and space for student response. **2.** any sheet for recording work done, ideas, plans, etc.

workshop *n.* a seminar or special course for productive activity, either on a common topic or on topics of interest to individuals in the group. *Note:* The workshop in education arose as an alternative to formal courses that did not adequately relate to practical teaching problems.

writer's anxiety feelings of insecurity and fear arising from doubts about one's control over the writing process (e.g., the ability to express what one wants to say) or about audience reaction to one's written efforts.

writer's block the inability, usually temporary, to continue generating ideas to satisfactorily advance the text of a composition.

writer's cramp the painful muscle spasm in the hand and wrist that may follow an overlong period of handwriting or an improper grip on the writing instrument.

writers' workshop a block of school time devoted to student planning, drafting, and editing compositions for publication, often involving peer collaboration. Also **writing workshop**.

writing *n.* **1.** the use of a writing system or orthography by people in the conduct of their daily lives and in the transmission of their culture to other generations. **2.** the process or result of recording language graphically by hand or other means, as by letters, logograms, and other symbols. **3.** a meaningful set of ideas so expressed. *Cp.* **composition** (def. 2). **4.** *pl.*, literary works or forms. **5.** a person's distinctive style of graphically recording language; handwriting. *v.* **write**.

Types of *Writing**
alphabetic
boustrophedon
creative
cursive
expressive
logosyllabic
manuscript
mirror
phonetic**
pictorial†
poetic
process
sinistrad
syllabic††
transactional

---

*Terms are all defined in this dictionary.
Term is defined under **phonetic transcription.
†Term is defined under **pictography**.
††Term is defined under **syllabary**.

---

writing acquisition the developmental progression in learning to write for purposes of communication, from the young child's use of scribbles and drawings in an effort to communicate to the sophistication of the mature writer who has gained control of writing processes and has developed a sense of audience. Also **writing development**.

writing approach to reading the encouragement of children to write to help them understand that words are written-down speech. *Note:* The writing approach to reading stresses meaning over grapheme-phoneme correspondences and interprets invented spellings as attempts by the student to understand the code system. See also **experience approach** (def. 1).

writing center a classroom area that provides students with tools for writing, illustrating, editing, and sharing written communications.

writing conference a meeting between the writer and a teacher or peer for help with questions that arise during the writing process.

writing cycle in the writing process, the recurring phases of writing and revision until a satisfactory communication is achieved.

writing portfolio a collection of written composition samples, usually selected by the student, that may be used to assess progress in planning, drafting, revising, and editing writing.

writing process the many aspects of the complex act of producing a written communication; specifically, planning or prewriting, drafting, revising, editing, and publishing. See also **process writing**.

writing school 1. from the late 16th century, schools to which elementary school boys were sent at specific times each day to learn writing and arithmetic. *Note*: In American colonies, the most famous of these schools were the three Writing Schools of Boston, which survived until the end of the 18th century. They gave instruction to girls as private students when the boys were not there. *Cp.* **reading school** (def. 1). **2.** in the 19th century, a private school offered by an itinerant teacher who provided a few weeks of penmanship instruction for those unable to write or who wrote poorly.

writing system 1. a standardized set of graphic symbols used to represent the speech sounds,

historical development of writing systems is believed to have evolved from *pictorial writing* (up to 3500 B.C.) to *logography*, as in Egyptian hieroglyphics (3000 B.C.) and Chinese characters (1500 B.C.), to *logosyllabic writing*, as in the Sumerian and Hittite cuneiform (2500 B.C.), to *syllabic writing*, as in Japanese kana, to *alphabetic writing*, as in Phonecian (1000 B.C.), Greek (800 B.C.), Arabic and Gothic (A.D. 400), and Cyrillic (A.D. 900) writing systems. See also **alphabetic writing**; **ideography**; **logography**; **logosyllabic writing**; **pictography**; **syllabary** (defs. 1, 3). *Cp.* **orthography**; **script** (def. 1).

writing task the production of a written communication; specifically, the selection of a theme or topic, the mode of discourse to be used, and those writing processes needed to advance the creation of text.

writing to learn the use of writing to "facilitate learning with text by helping students to explore, clarify, and think deeply about ideas and concepts encountered in reading" (Vacca & Vacca, 1993). *Note*: In this view of writing, the relationship between writing and reading is intimate and interactive. In writing to read, students help themselves read; in reading to write, students help themselves write. See also **reading-writing relationships**. *Cp.* **reading to learn**.

writing vocabulary the number of different words ordinarily used in writing. *Note*: The writing vocabulary is usually but not always smaller than the reading, speaking, and listening vocabularies. *Cp.* **listening vocabulary**; **reading vocabulary**; **speaking vocabulary**.

writing workshop 1. an intensive seminar on how to write. **2.** See **writer's workshop**.

written language 1. the representation of lan-

X̄Y̅Z

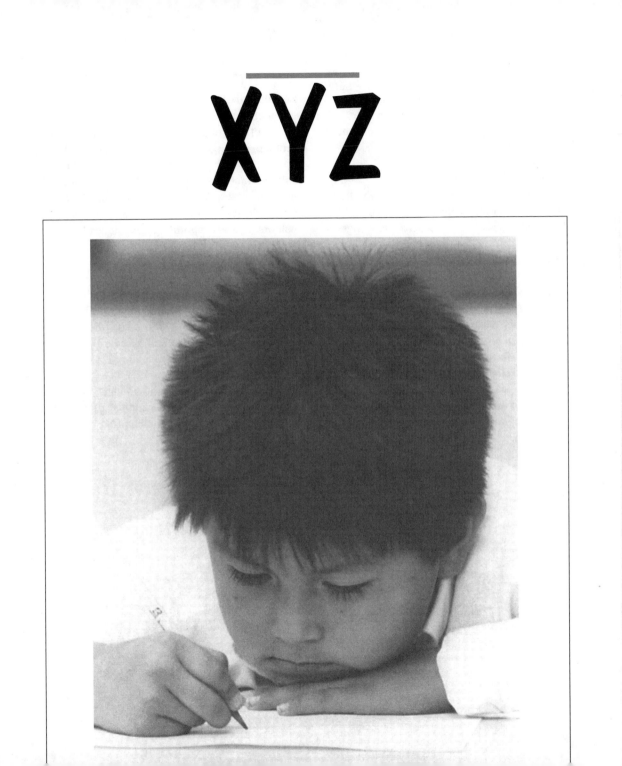

X **1.** raw score. **2.** a signature mark made by persons who cannot write their names. **3.** a mark indicating an error or a mistake, used, for example, in correcting a test.

Young Adult Literacy Survey (YALS) a 1985 survey in the United States of the literacy skills of 21- to 25-year-olds conducted by the National Assessment of Educational Progress.

young adult literature books selected for reading by young adults, ages 13 to 18, whether published specifically for them or for the general adult public. Also **adolescent literature**. *Note*: Young adult literature includes many types of books in which the protagonist is usually a teenager. *Woodsong* by Gary Paulson was written especially for young readers; on the other hand, *The Kitchen God's Wife* by Amy Tan was written for an adult audience but has become a popular young adult selection. *Cp.* **children's literature**.

zone of proximal development (ZPD) "the distance between a child's actual developmental level as determined through independent problem solving and [his or her] potential development [level] as determined through problem solving under adult guidance or a collaboration with more capable peers" (Vygotsky, 1978). *Note*: The concept of the zone of proximal development is an important cornerstone of social-constructivist theories of human learning and development (McCarthey & Raphael, 1992).

zoosemiotics *n.* a branch of semiotics devoted to the study of the use of signs throughout the animal world; "the scientific study of signaling behavior in and across animal species" (Sebeok, 1972).

z score a standard score in which a raw score is expressed in terms of the number of standard deviations it deviates from the mean.

Appendix A Wordex

For definition of	See
ABC	ABC book
abcee-book	ABC book
ABC method	alphabet method
abecedary	abecedarium
absey-book	ABC book
absolute blindness	blindness
abstract thinking	abstract reasoning
accelerated reading	speed reading
accelerator, reading	pacer
accent, primary	primary accent
accent, secondary	secondary accent
acoustic feature	distinctive feature
acoustic modality	modality
acquired dyslexia	dyslexia
acrolect	creole
action	plot
active voice	voice
adolescent literature	young adult literature
advanced literacy	cultured literacy
aesthetic effect	effects of reading
affective meaning	connotation
affixation	affix
agglutinative language	agglutination
aided reading	assisted learning
alpha	coefficient alpha
alphameric	alphanumeric
alveoli	alveolar ridge
American New Criticism	formalism; New Criticism
The American Spelling Book	Blue-Back(-ed) Speller
anaphor	anaphora
anonym	pseudonym
antonymmy	complementarity
aphaerisis	apherisis
apostrophe	punctuation mark
assessment, clinical	clinical assessment
assessment-curriculum alignment	curriculum validity
assisted reading	assisted learning
attention span	span of attention

For definition of	See
auding level	listening comprehension level
auditory center	auditory area
auditory comprehension	listening
auditory masking	masking
auditory modality	modality
Augmented Roman Alphabet	augmented alphabet
author's purpose	author's intent
author's voice	personal voice
autoregulation	self-regulation
baby talk	caretaker speech
back *or* backward reference	anaphora
backward reader	reading disability
basal reading scheme	basal reading program
base	base word
base form	base word
base rule	phrase-structure rule
basilect	creole
battery, test	test battery
Bay Psalm Book	New England Primer
beat	rhythm
bell curve	normal (frequency) curve
bias, item	item bias
bias, test	test bias
binding theory	government/binding theory
Binet–Simon Scale	Binet Scale
binocular coordination	visual coordination
binocular visual field	visual field
biological adaptation	adaptation
blocked syllable	closed syllable
blocked vowel	closed vowel
blown-up book	big book
body language	kinesics
bon mot	repartee
book corner	book nook
Book Week	National Children's Book Week
bottom-up processing	text processing
bounding theory	government/binding theory
braces	punctuation mark
brackets	punctuation mark
brainstem	stem
Brodmann's area	angular gyrus

For definition of	See
cadence	rhythm
capital letter	uppercase letter
cartouch	cartouche
case conference	case history
case study	case history
case theory	government/binding theory
casual style	casual speech
causative verb	verb
cesura	caesura
Chapter 1	Title I
c, hard	hard c
chart, experience	experience chart
checked syllable	closed syllable
checked vowel	closed vowel
Children's Books in Print	*Books in Print*
Christ-cross-row	hornbook
classical conditioning	conditioning
click	stop
climax	plot
closed-captioned television	captioning
coda	syllable
cognitive leap	intuition
cognitive meaning	denotation
collaborative reading	collaborative learning
collaborative writing	collaborative learning
colon	punctuation mark
combined method	visible speech
comics	comic strip
comma	punctuation mark
comma splice	comma fault
comment	rheme
commissive	speech act
comparative degree	degree
comparative historical linguistics	historical linguistics
comparative reconstruction	internal reconstruction
complex genre	genre
compound	compound word
computer-managed instruction	computer-based instruction
concentric curriculum/method	spiral curriculum
concept burden	concept load
concept density	concept load
concepts of print	print awareness

For definition of	**See**
conceptually driven	text processing
conceptual meaning	denotation
conceptual memory	semantic memory
concord	agreement
concrete thinking	concrete reasoning
connective	conjunction
consequence	causal network theory
consonant blend	consonant cluster
consonant doubling	geminate
consonant rhyme	consonance
constancy, perceptual	perceptual constancy
consultative style	consultative speech
content area	content field
contentive	content word
context effects	context
context sensitive	context bound
contrast	opposition
controlled vocabulary	simplified vocabulary; vocabulary control
conventional literacy	functional literacy
conversational implicature	conversational maxim
conversion	functional shift
cooperative principle	conversational maxim
cooperative reading	cooperative learning
coordinating conjunction	conjunction
Coptic alphabet	Greek alphabet
correlative conjunction	conjunction
correlation coefficient	coefficient of correlation
Corridos	ballad
cortical localization	cerebral localization
covariance, analysis of	analysis of covariance
critical period	feral children
cross-age grouping	grouping
crossclass grouping	grouping
c, soft	soft c
cultural relativism	literary criticism
cumulative frequency distribution	cumulative frequency curve
curriculum integration	integrated curriculum
dangling participle	dangling modifier
dash	punctuation mark
data driven	text processing
declarative	speech act

For definition of	See
declarative mood	mood[1]
declarative sentence	sentence pattern
deductive phonics	analytic phonics
deductive reasoning	deduction
deep meaning	deep structure
definite article	article
definitional knowledge	declarative knowledge
denotative meaning	denotation
denouement	plot
dependent sample design	repeated measures design
derived form	derivative
descriptive meaning	denotation
details, reading for	reading for details
developmental alexia	developmental
developmental aphasia	developmental
developmental dyslexia	dyslexia
developmental imbalance	developmental lag
deviant speech	speech disorder
diacritical mark	diacritic mark
diaeresis	dieresis
directed reading-thinking activity	directed reading activity
directional orientation	directionality
directive	speech act
direct speech	direct discourse
disabled reader	reading disability
dissyllable	disyllable
Dolch list	word-frequency count
dominant eye	eye dominance
double vision	diplopia
doubling	geminate
Drop Everything and Read	uninterrupted sustained silent reading
DRTA	directed reading activity
dull normal	mental retardation
dumb	mute
echoic word	onomatopoeia
echophrasia	echolalia
echo reading	assisted learning
ecology of the classroom	classroom climate
economic literacy	functional literacy
educational media center	instructional materials center
educational mentally handicapped	educable mentally retarded

For definition of	See
educational scaffolding	scaffolding
egocentric speech	egocentric language
electronic mail	e-mail
The Elementary Spelling Book	Blue-Back(-ed) Speller
ellipsis	punctuation mark
emotive meaning	connotation
empty word	function word
encyclopedic reader	eclectic reader
en dash	punctuation mark
English for speakers of other languages	teaching English as a second language
English sonnet	sonnet
enunciation	diction
environmental text	environmental print
equating, test	test equating
equivalent form	alternate form
error of estimate	standard error of estimate
e, silent	final e
essay test	essay examination
ethnography of speaking	ethnography of communication
ethnolinguistics	ethnography of communication
exceptional child	atypical learner
exclamation mark	punctuation mark
exclamatory	exclamation
exclusive	inclusive
expression jargon	conversational babble
expressive	speech act
external evaluation	critical evaluation
external motivation	motivation
external text	text
extrinsic motivation	motivation
eye fixation	fixation (defs. 1, 2)
eye-movement photography	eye-movement camera
fan effect	retroactive inhibition
feltboard	flannelboard
feminine gender	gender
field study	field research
finger spelling	dactylology
flash device	flashcard
flexibility, reading	reading flexibility
flicker fusion	fusion
flummery	gibberish

For definition of	See
focal point	focus
folk story	folktale
footedness	handedness
forgetting curve	retention curve
formal style	formal speech
formative	bound morpheme
formulaic speech	formulaic expression
forward reference	cataphora
fovea	foveal vision
free-association test	word-association test
frozen speech	frozen style
full word	content word
functional adult literacy	functional literacy
functions of reading	effects of reading
functor	function word
funnies	comic strip
futhark	futhork
future tense	tense
future perfect aspect	aspect
future progressive aspect	aspect
general semantics	generative semantics
generative grammar	transformational-generative grammar
generative-transformational grammar	transformational-generative grammar
gestalt	form (def. 4)
g, hard	hard g
global approach	global method
gradation	ablaut
grade school	elementary school
The Grammatical Institute, Part I	Blue-Back(-ed) Speller
grammaticalness	grammaticality
grammatical word	function word
groupements	grouping
g, soft	soft g
head term	head
hearing vocabulary	listening vocabulary
hemianopsia	hemianopia
hero(-ine)	protagonist
hexameter	prosody
higher mental functions	higher mental processes
hi(gh)-lo(w)	high interest–low load
high school	secondary school

For definition of	See
high vowel	vowel (def. 1)
historical novel	historical fiction
Hittite	dead language
holophrastic speech	holophrase
homeostasis	equilibrium
horizontal *décalage*	*décalage*
humbug	gibberish
hyphen	punctuation mark
iambic pentameter	prosody
idea density	concept load
ideogram	ideograph
ideological literacy	literacy (def. 5)
idyl	idyll
immediate comprehension *or* knowledge	intuition (def. 1)
imperative mood	mood[1]
imperative sentence	sentence
indicative mood	mood[1]
inductive phonics	synthetic phonics
inductive reasoning	induction (def. 1)
inferential statistics	statistics; Bayesian statistical inference
innate(-ness) theory	nativist theory
in print	print
inside-out theory	text processing
instructional scaffolding	scaffolding
instrumental conditioning	conditioning
instrumental effect	effects of reading
interactive learning	interactive
interactive processing	text processing
interclass grouping	grouping
interest span	span of attention
interlinear gloss	gloss
intermental plane	interpsychological plane
internal evaluation	critical evaluation
internal motivation	motivation
internal speech	implicit speech
internal text	text
interrogative mood	mood[1]
interrogative sentence	sentence
interval	class interval
interval reinforcement	reinforcement schedule
intervention research	dyslexia

For definition of	See
intraclass grouping	grouping
intramental plane	intrapsychological plane
intrinsic motivation	motivation
isolating language	analytic language
Italian sonnet	sonnet
item, test	test item
iteration	recursiveness
junior book	junior novel
keyword	keyword method
kinesthetic approach	kinesthetic method
kinesthetic modality	modality
kinetic reversal	reversal
lalling	lallation
language competence	competence
language function	function
language learning	language acquisition
language *or* linguistic performance	parole; performance
language universal	universal
lateral dominance	cerebral dominance
lateralization	cerebral dominance
Latin	dead language
learning style	cognitive style
legal blindness	blindness
legasthenie	legasthenia
leisure reading	recreational reading
leptokurtosis	kurtosis
letter method	alphabet method
letter-sound correspondence	grapheme-phoneme correspondence
level of confidence	confidence level
level of significance	confidence level; statistical significance
lexeme	lexical item
lexical density	type-token ratio
lexical meaning	content word
lexical variety	vocabulary diversity
lexicon	vocabulary (def. 1)
license, poetic	poetic license
linguistic competence	competence
linguistic determinism	Whorfian hypothesis
linguistic divergence	linguistic convergence
linguistic environment	context

For definition of	**See**
linguistic relativity	Whorfian hypothesis
linguistic semantics	semantics
linguistic sign	sign
linking verb	copula
listening comprehension	listening (def. 2)
literacy, politics of	politics of literacy
literary ballad	ballad
literary theory	literary criticism
literature of adolescents	young adult literature
living language	dead language
loan translation	calque
logogram	logograph
logographic reading	visual-cue reading
longhand writing	cursive writing
look-and-say method	word method
low vowel	open vowel
magical realism	magic realism
main clause	independent clause
maintenance bilingual programs	bilingual education
main topic	main idea
majuscule	uppercase letter
masculine gender	gender
measure	foot
media literacy	literacy
meiosis	litotes
memory system	mnemonic
mental deficiency	mental retardation
mental dictionary	mental lexicon
mental set	set
mesokurtosis	kurtosis
mesolect	creole
metacomprehension	metacognitive awareness
metaphysics	neo-Aristotelian criticism
metonym	synonym
metre	meter
minimal contrast	minimal pair
minimum competency test	mastery test; minimum competency survey
minuscule	lowercase letter
misplaced modifier	dangling modifier
modal	modal auxiliary
modulated babble	conversational babble

For definition of	See
monitorial school	Lancastrian method
monitoring, comprehension	comprehension monitoring
monophthong	monosyllable
morphophonology	morphophonemics
motherese	caretaker speech
mother tongue	native language (def. 1)
multiethnic literature	multicultural literature
multilingual	polyglot
multiple meaning	polysemy
muscular imbalance	heterotropia
narrow diphthong	diphthong
nativism	nativist theory
nativist hypothesis	nativist theory
naturalistic assessment	authentic assessment
naturalistic research	ethnographic research
nearsightedness	myopia
negative diagnosis	diagnosis
negative pronoun	negation
negative transfer	interference
nerve deafness	sensorineural deafness
nesting	embedding
neuter gender	gender
neutral vowel	schwa
node	causal network theory
nom de plume	pseudonym
nomen	figura
noncount noun	mass noun
nonlanguage test	nonverbal test
nonliterate	illiterate
normal vision	emmetropia
novice processes	naive processes
nucleus	syllable
oaktag	tagboard
object language	metalanguage
observational research	ethnographic research
occult story	supernatural story
octave	sonnet
ocular motility	ocular mobility
ogam script	ogham
onset	syllable
open juncture	juncture

For definition of	See
operant conditioning	conditioning
ophthalmometer	keratometer
optical image	image
optic disk	blind spot
optometric training	orthoptics
oral-aural method	oralism
oral literacy	oracy
oral method	oralism
oral vocabulary	speaking vocabulary
orthographic cipher	cipher
Orton–Gillingham method	Gillingham method
out of print	print
outside-in theory	text processing
overcorrection	hypercorrection
overgeneralization	overextension
overregularization	overextension
paired reading	assisted learning
paracentral vision	perimacular vision
parallel form	alternate form
parametric statistics	statistics
parlance	talk
partially sighted	visual impairment
partner reading	assisted learning
passive voice	voice
past participle	participle
past perfect aspect	aspect
past progressive aspect	aspect
past tense	tense
pausing	hesitation phenomenon
Pavlovian conditioning	conditioning
peer conferences	peer response
pen name	pseudonym
pentameter	prosody
perceptual decentration	decentration
perfect aspect	aspect
performance-based assessment	performance assessment
performance objective	behavioral objective
performance standard	cut score
period	punctuation mark
personal dialect	idiolect
Petrarchan sonnet	sonnet

For definition of	See
petrogram	petroglyph
petrograph	petroglyph
phantasy	fantasy
Ø (phi)	phi coefficient
philosophical semantics	semantics
phonemic alphabet	phonetic alphabet
phonemic notation	phonemic transcription
phonetic notation	phonetic transcription
phonetic variant	allomorph; phoneme
phonetic writing	phonetic alphabet; phonetic transcription
phonic approach	linguistic reading program
phonological coding	dyslexia
phonological feature	distinctive feature
phoria	heterophoria
pictogram	pictograph
pictorial writing	pictography
picture writing	pictography
pie chart *or* graph	circle graph
pivot grammar	open class
planning	prewriting
platykurtosis	kurtosis
plosive	stop
plot structure	plot
plurilingualism	multilingualism
polysemantic	polysemy
polysyllabic word	polysyllabic
popular literacy	vernacular literacy
popular speech	slang
positive degree	degree
positive diagnosis	diagnosis
potentes	figura
pragnanz, law of	law of pragnanz
predicate noun	predicate nominative
present participle	participle
present perfect aspect	aspect
present progressive aspect	aspect
present tense	tense
prestige effect	effects of reading
pretend reading	emergent reading
preterite	preterit
primary language	native language
primary reinforcer	reinforcer

For definition of	**See**
primary stress	stress
printing	manuscript writing
printout	print
print-rich environment	print-immersion curriculum
printscript	manuscript writing
private language	restricted code
production systems	production rules
programmed learning	programmed instruction
progressive aspect	tense
Project Head Start	Head Start
projective technique	projective test
pronominal	pronoun
proofread	read (def. 20)
propositional operations	formal operations
Proto-Indo-European	Indo-European languages
prototypical	genre
proximal development, zone of	zone of proximal development
psychometrist	psychometric
public language	elaborated code
pure semantics	semantics
pyramidal system	motor area
question mark	punctuation mark
quotation mark	punctuation mark
radical subjectivism	literary criticism
rate of comprehension	speed of comprehension
ratio reinforcement	reinforcement schedule
read between the lines	read (def. 5)
reader driven	text processing
reader-unfriendly writing	reader-friendly writing
reading accelerator	pacer
reading beyond the lines	reading the world
reading consultant	reading specialist
reading coordinator	reading specialist
reading corner	book nook
reading disorder	reading disability
reading effects *or* functions	effects of reading
reading, rate of	rate of reading
reading retardation	reading disability
reading scheme	reading program
reading span	span of recognition
reading, speed of	rate of reading

For definition of	See
reading register	register
reading supervisor	reading specialist
reading teacher	reading specialist
reading to write	writing to learn
reading versatility	reading flexibility
reading-writing connections	reading-writing relationships
rebus reading	reading development
recognition span	span of recognition
recursion	recursiveness
reduplicative compound	reduplication
referend	referent
referential meaning	denotation
reflective thinking	reader response (theory)
regulation	self-regulation
reinforcement effect	effects of reading
remedial centre	reading clinic
representative	speech act
required literacy	pragmatic literacy
resolution	plot
respite effect	effects of reading
response journal	dialogue journal
response to literature	reader response (theory)
retarded reader	reading disability
rewrite rule	phrase-structure rule
rich interpretation	open class
Roman alphabet	Greek alphabet; Latin alphabet
root creation	neologism
runic alphabet	futhork
Sanskrit	dead language
Sapir–Whorf hypothesis	Whorfian hypothesis
scanning	scansion
scattergram	scatter diagram
scholastic ability	academic ability
scholastic aptitude	academic ability
school library supervisor	teacher-librarian
science fantasy	science fiction
scotoma	blind spot
secondary reinforcer	reinforcer
secondary stress	stress
second person	person
see-and-say	analytic method

For definition of	See
self-correction	correction strategy
semantic indicator	determinative
semantic webbing	semantic mapping
semicolon	punctuation mark
semiology	semiotics
semiotic function	symbolic function
sensory fusion	fusion
sensory store	sensory register
sentence factor	syntactic factor
sentence stress	stress
service word	function word
sestet	sonnet
S factor	specific factor
Shakespearean sonnet	sonnet
sight method	word method
sight vocabulary	recognition vocabulary
silent e	final e
silent reading	reading
Simitic alphabet	Greek alphabet
sinistral	dextral
situational reference	reference
skiascope	retinoscope
skim	scan (def. 1)
social accommodation	accommodation
social adaptation	adaptation
social class	class (def. 3)
social dialect	sociolect
sociology of language	sociolinguistics
sound-symbol correspondence	phoneme-grapheme correspondence
space perception	depth perception
span of perception	span of attention
specific developmental dyslexia	specific
specific language disability	specific
specific learning disability	specific
specific reading disability	dyslexia; specific
spectrogram	speech spectrogram
speech audiometry	speech discrimination
speech correction	speech and language therapy
speech defect	speech disorder
speech deviation	speech disorder
speech impediment	speech disorder
speech pathology	speech and language therapy

For definition of	**See**
speech therapy	speech and language therapy
speed of reading	rate of reading
spelling bee	spelldown
spelling-sound correspondence	grapheme-phoneme correspondence
spirant	fricative
stammer	stutter
standard dialect	standard language
static reversal	reversal
stem *or* affix boundary	boundary
stenography	shorthand
stereopsis	stereoscope
story structure	story schema
strategic learning	strategy
stress mark	accent
strong verb	irregular verb
structure word	function word
student assessment	learner assessment
study technique	study strategy
study-type reading	study skills
stylebook	style
subjunctive mood	mood[1]
subordinate clause	dependent clause
subordinating conjunction	conjunction
superfix	suprasegmental
superlative degree	degree
superordinate	hypernym
suprasegmental phoneme	suprasegmental
survival language	survival literacy
sustained silent reading	uninterrupted sustained silent reading
syllabification	syllabication
syllabic writing system	syllabary
syllable boundary	boundary
syllable margin	syllable
synaeresis	syneresis
syntactic(-al)	syntax
synthesis	analysis (def. 1)
systemic linguistics	systemic grammar
tactile approach	tactile
tactual	tactile
tagmeme	tagmemics
tag question	tag

For definition of	See
teacher induction	teacher evaluation
teacher research	action research
teacher's aide	paraprofessional
teacher selection	teacher evaluation
teacher's guide *or* manual	teacher's edition
teacher tenure	teacher evaluation
teaching of English to speakers of other languages	teaching English as a second language
technical term	technical word
terminal juncture	juncture
tertiary stress	stress
tetrameter	prosody
text driven	text processing
text hand	text
text-structure analysis	text analysis
textual constraint	contextual constraint
textuality	critical theory
textual reference	reference
thematic contrast	binary feature
theta theory	government/binding theory
third person	person
three Rs	R
time-compressed speech	compressed speech
top-down processing	text processing
toponym	toponomy
tracking	ability grouping
traditional grammar	prescriptive grammar
transact	transactional theory
transactional model	transactional theory
transfer of learning	transfer of training
transformational-generative linguistics	transformational-generative grammar
transition	juncture
transitional bilingual programs	bilingual education
transition reading	reading development
transmediation	mediation
triadic	intelligence
tropia	heterotropia
tumbling E	illiterate E
T-unit	minimal terminal unit
unattached modifier *or* participle	dangling modifier
underlying structure	deep structure

For definition of	See
unit approach	unit plan
unstressed	stress
VAKT	Fernald(–Keller) Method
value word	abstract noun
variance, analysis of	analysis of variance
verbal coding	dyslexia
verbal foliage	verbiage
verbal scale	verbal test
verb marker	auxiliary verb
vers libre	free verse
vertical *décalage*	*décalage*
vibration	acoustic phonetics
vision therapy	orthoptics
visual analysis	visual discrimination
visual fusion	fusion
visual image	image
visual modality	modality
visual training	orthoptics
visuospatial	cerebral dominance
vocabulary load	vocabulary burden
vowel, long	long vowel
vowel, short	short vowel
weak stress	stress
weak verb	verb
Wernicke's aphasia	auditory aphasia
wide diphthong	diphthong
word blindness	alexia
word boundary	boundary
word configuration	configuration clue
word deafness	auditory aphasia
word fluency	verbal fluency
wordiness	verbiage
word list	word-frequency count
word map	mapping
word origins	etymology
word stress	stress
word-study skills	study skills
word-type reading	study skills
word writing	logography
workforce literacy	workplace literacy

For definition of	See
writer-based reading	reader-friendly writing
writing development	writing acquisition
writing to read	writing to learn
x-bar theory	government/binding theory

Appendix B Common Abbreviations and Their Meanings

ABE	adult basic education
ADD	attention-deficit disorder
ADHD	attention-deficit hyperactivity disorder
ALAN	Assembly on Literature for Adolescents
ALBSU	Adult Literacy and Basic Skills Unit
ANCOVA	analysis of covariance
ANOVA	analysis of variance
APL	adult performance level
ASL	American Sign Language
AV	audiovisual
BEV	Black English Vernacular
CA	chronological age
CAI	computer-assisted instruction
CCTV	closed-circuit television
CD	compact disk
CD-ROM	compact disk—read only memory
CDS	child-directed speech
CNS	central nervous system
cpi	characters per inch
CR	critical ratio
CVC	consonant-vowel-consonant
dB	decibel
DEAR	Drop Everything and Read
df	degrees of freedom
DRA	directed reading activity
DRTA	directed reading-thinking activity
DTP	desktop publishing
ECE	early childhood education
EEG	electroencephalogram
EFL	English as a foreign language
EMG	electromyogram
EMR	educable mentally retarded
ERIC	Educational Resources Information Center
ERIC/RCS	Educational Resources Information Center/ Center for Reading and Communicating Skills
ESL	English as a second language
ESOL	English for/to speakers of other languages
ESP	English for specific/special purposes
ETV	educational television
EVS	eye-voice span

F	*F* test
g	general factor
gb	government/binding
GED	General Educational Development
GPA	grade point average
IBBY	International Board on Books for Young People
IEP	Individualized Educational Plan
IMC	instructional materials center
IPA	International Phonetic Alphabet
IPI	individually prescribed instruction
IQ	intelligence quotient
IRA	International Reading Association
IRI	informal reading inventory
IRT	item-response theory
ISBN	International Standard Book Number
ISSN	International Standard Serials Number
i.t.a. *or* i/t/a	initial teaching alphabet
JOBS	Job Opportunity and Basic Skills Program
JTPA	Job Training and Partnership Act
k	coefficient of alienation
ku	kurtosis
LAD	language-acquisition device
LAP	learning activity package
LC	Library of Congress
LCSH	Library of Congress Subject Headings
LEA	language experience approach
LEP	limited English proficiency/proficient
LES(A)	limited English speaking (ability)
LTM	long-term memory
M	mean
MA	mental age
MARC	machine readable cataloging
MBD	minimal brain dysfunction
Md	median
MLU	mean length of utterance
NAEP	National Assessment of Educational Progress
NALS	National Adult Literacy Survey
NBPTS	National Board of Professional Teaching Standards
NCAL	National Center on Adult Literacy
NCTE	National Council of Teachers of English
NEP	non-English proficiency/proficient
NIL	National Institute of Literacy
NP	noun phrase

OCR	optical character recognition
OPAC	on-line public access catalog
PE *or* P.E.	probable error
R	multiple-correlation coefficient; response
r	product-moment correlation
S	sentence; specific factor; stimulus
S–B	Stanford–Binet (Intelligence Scale)
SD	standard deviation
SDI	current awareness service
SE *or* S.E.	standard error
SEM	standard error of measurement
SES	socioeconomic status
SFA	semantic feature analysis
SLD	specific language disability
SSR	sustained silent reading
STM	short-term memory
TABA	The American Book Awards
TDD	telecommunication device for the deaf
T.E.	teacher's edition
TESL	teaching English as a second language
TESOL	teaching of English to speakers of other languages
TMR	trainable mentally retarded
T.O. *or* t.o.	traditional orthography
TTR	type-token ratio
TTY	teletypewriter
TV	television
UG	universal grammar
UNESCO	United Nations Educational, Scientific, and Cultural Organization
USBBY	United States Board on Books for Young People
USSR	uninterrupted sustained silent reading
V	verb
VAKT	visual-auditory-kinesthetic-tactile
VP	verb phrase
W	coefficient of concordance
WAIS	Wechsler Adult Intelligence Scale
WISC—R	Wechsler Intelligence Scale for Children—Revised
WPM	words per minute
WPPSI	Wechsler Preschool and Primary Scale of Intelligence
X	raw score
YALS	Young Adult Literacy Survey
ZPD	zone of proximal development

Appendix C Selected Bibliography

Adams, M.J. (1990). *Beginning to read: Thinking and learning about print.* Cambridge, MA: MIT Press.

Aitchison, J. (1987). *Words in the mind: An introduction to the mental lexicon.* Oxford, England: Blackwell.

American Psychiatric Association. (1994). *Diagnostic and statistical manual of mental disorders* (4th ed.). Washington, DC: Author.

Anastasi, A. (1989). *Psychological testing* (6th ed.). New York: Macmillan.

Appleyard, J.A. (1990). *Becoming a reader: The experience of fiction from adolescence to adulthood.* New York: Cambridge University Press.

Bakhtin, M. (1986). *Speech genres and other late essays.* Austin, TX: University of Texas Press.

Barker, R.L. (1995). *The social work dictionary* (3rd ed.). Washington, DC: National Association of Social Workers Press.

Barr, R., Kamil, M.L., Mosenthal, P.B., & Pearson, P.D. (Eds.). (1991). *Handbook of reading research* (Vol. 2). New York: Longman.

Beach, R. (1993). *A teacher's introduction to reader-response theories.* Urbana, IL: National Council of Teachers of English.

Beach, R., & Bridwell, L.S. (Eds.). (1984). *New directions in composition research.* New York: Guilford Press.

Beach, R., Green, J.L., Kamil, M.L., & Shanahan, T. (Eds.). (1992). *Multidisciplinary perspectives on literacy research.* Urbana, IL: National Council of Teachers of English.

Bennett, T., & Woolacott, J. (1987). *Bond and beyond: The political career of a popular hero.* New York: Routledge.

Berger, A. (1992). *Popular culture genres.* Newbury Park, CA: Sage.

Berkenkotter, C., & Huckin, T. (1993). Rethinking genre from a sociocognitive perspective. *Written Communication, 10,* 475–509.

Bernstein, B.B. (1971–1975). *Class codes and control* (Vols. I–III). New York: Routledge.

Bernstein, B.B. (1990). *The structuring of pedagogic discourse: Class codes and control* (Vol. IV). New York: Routledge.

Bettelheim, B. (1976). *The uses of enchantment: The meaning and importance of fairy tales.* New York: Knopf.

Bloom, B.S., Engelhart, M.D., Furst, E.J., Hill, W.H., & Krathwohl, D.R. (1956). *Taxonomy of educational objectives: The cognitive domain* (Handbook 1). New York: Longman.

Bloome, D. (Ed.). (1987). *Literacy and schooling.* Norwood, NJ: Ablex.

Bloome, D. (Ed.). (1989). *Classrooms and literacy.* Norwood, NJ: Ablex.

Cazden, C.B. (1988). *Classroom discourse: The language of teaching and learning.* Portsmouth, NH: Heinemann.

Chomsky, N. (1982). *Some concepts and consequences of the theory of government and binding.* Cambridge, MA: MIT Press.

Chomsky, N. (1986). *Knowledge of language: Its nature, origin and use.* New York: Praeger.

Colapietro, V.M. (1993). *Glossary of semiotics.* New York: Paragon.

Comrie, B. (Ed.). (1987). *The world's major languages.* New York: Oxford University Press.

Cooper, C.R. (Ed.). (1985). *Researching response to literature and the teaching of literature: Points of departure.* Norwood, NJ: Ablex.

Cronbach, L.J. (1984). *Essentials of psychological testing* (4th ed.). New York: HarperCollins.

Crystal, D. (1987). *The Cambridge encyclopedia of language.* Cambridge, England: Cambridge University Press.

Crystal, D. (1991). *A dictionary of linguistics and phonetics* (3rd ed.). Oxford, England: Blackwell.

Crystal, D. (1992). *An encyclopedic dictionary of language and languages.* London: Penguin.

Daiute, C. (1993). Youth genres and literacy: Links between sociocultural and developmental theories. *Language Arts, 70,* 402–416.

Dearborn, W.F. (1906). The psychology of reading. *Columbia University contributions to philosophy and psychology, 14*(1).

de Saussure, F. (1966). *Course in general linguistics* (C. Bally & A. Sechehaye, with A. Reidlinger, Eds.; W. Baskin, Trans.). New York: McGraw-Hill. (Original work published 1916)

Durkin, D. (1993). *Teaching them to read* (6th ed.). Boston, MA: Allyn & Bacon.

Elkonin, D.B. (1963). The psychology of mastering the elements of reading. In B. Simon & J. Simon (Eds.), *Educational psychology in the U.S.S.R.* (pp. 165–179). New York: Routledge.

Ferreiro, E., & Teberosky, A. (1982). *Literacy before schooling.* Portsmouth, NH: Heinemann.

Flood, J., Jensen, J.M., Lapp, D., & Squire, J.R. (Eds.). (1991). *Handbook of research on teaching the English arts.* New York: Macmillan.

Freire, P., & Macedo, D.P. (1987). *Literacy: Reading the word and the world.* Westport, CT: Greenwood.

Galda, L., Cullinan, B.E., & Strickland, D.S. (1993). *Language, literacy and the child.* Orlando, FL: Harcourt Brace.

Gee, J.P. (1990). *Social linguistics and literacies: Ideology in discourses.* London and New York: Falmer.

Gee, J.P. (1992). *The social mind: Language, ideology, and social practice.* Westport, CT: Greenwood.

Giroux, H.A. (1983). *Theory and resistance in education: A pedagogy for the opposition.* South Hadley, MA: Bergin & Garvey.

Goodman, K.S. (1965). A linguistic study of cues and miscues in reading. *Elementary English, 42,* 639–643.

Goodman, K.S., & Smith, E.B. (1987). *Language and thinking in school: A whole-language curriculum* (3rd ed.). New York: Owen.

Gough, P., Ehri, L., & Treiman, R. (Eds.). (1992). *Reading acquisition.* Hillsdale, NJ: Erlbaum.

Halliday, M.A.K. (1985). *An introduction to functional grammar.* London: Arnold.

Halliday, M.A.K., & Hasan, R. (1976). *Cohesion in English.* London: Longman.

Harste, J.C., Pierce, K.M., & Cairney, T. (Eds.). (1985). *The authoring cycle: A viewing guide.* Portsmouth, NH: Heinemann.

Heath, S.B. (1983). *Ways with words: Language, life, and work in communities and classrooms.* Cambridge, England: Cambridge University Press.

Hirsch, E.D., Jr. (1987). *Cultural literacy: What every American needs to know.* Boston, MA: Houghton Mifflin.

Holman, C.H., & Harmon, W. (1992). *A handbook to literature* (6th ed.). New York: Macmillan.

Huck, C.S., Hepler, S, & Hickman J. (1993). *Children's literature in the elementary school* (5th ed.). New York: Holt.

Huckin, T., Haynes, M., & Coady, J. (Eds.). (1993). *Second language reading and vocabulary learning*. Norwood, NJ: Ablex.

Huey, E.B. (1968). *The psychology and pedagogy of reading*. Cambridge, MA: MIT Press. (Original work published 1908)

Hunt, M. (1993). *The story of psychology*. New York: Doubleday.

Husen, T., & Postlethwaite, T.N. (Eds.). (1985). *The international encyclopedia of education: Research and studies* (Vols. 1–10). Oxford, England, and New York: Pergamon.

Jackson, P.W. (Ed.). (1992). *Handbook of research on curriculum: A project of the American Educational Research Association*. New York: Macmillan.

Joos, M. (1967). *The five clocks*. Orlando, FL: Harcourt Brace.

Judd, C.H. (1908). The relation of special training to general intelligence. *Educational Review, 36,* 28–42.

Kitchener, R.F. (1986). *Piaget's theory of knowledge: Genetic epistemology and scientific reason*. New Haven, CT: Yale University Press.

LeCompte, M.D., Millroy, W.L., & Preissle, J. (Eds.). (1992). *The handbook of qualitative research in education*. San Diego, CA: Academic.

Lemke, J. (1990). *Talking science: Language, learning, and values*. Norwood, NJ: Ablex.

Lévi-Strauss, C. (1967). Structural anthropology (C. Jacobson & B.G. Schoepf, Trans.). New York: Doubleday.

Locke, J. (1910). Some thoughts concerning education. In C.W. Eliot (Ed.), *English philosophers of the seventeenth and eighteenth centuries* (pp. 141–142). New York: Collier.

Lyons, J. (1977). *Semantics* (Vols. 1–2). Cambridge, England: Cambridge University Press.

McArthur, T. (Ed.). (1992). *The Oxford companion to the English language*. Oxford, England: Oxford University Press.

McLaren, P. (1989). *Life in schools: An introduction to critical pedagogy in the foundations of education*. New York: Longman.

McLuhan, M., & Fiore, Q. (1967). *The medium is the massage*. New York: Random House.

McNally, D.W. (1974). *Piaget, education and teaching*. Lewes, England: New Educational Press.

McNeill, D. (1992). *Hand and mind: What gestures reveal about thought*. Chicago, IL: University of Chicago Press.

Menyuk, P. (1988). *Language development: Knowledge and use*. Boston, MA: Little, Brown.

Moll, L.C. (Ed.). (1990). *Vygotsky and education: Instructional implications and applications of sociohistorical psychology*. New York: Cambridge University Press.

Monaghan, E.J. (1983). *A common heritage: Noah Webster's blue-back speller*. Hamden, CT: Shoe String Press.

Moreno, J.L. (1956). *Sociometry and the science of man*. New York: Beacon House.

Morris, C. (1971). *Writings on the general theory of signs*. The Hague: Mouton.

Nagy, W.E. (1988). *Teaching vocabulary to improve reading comprehension*. Urbana, IL, and Newark, DE: National Council of Teachers of English, and International Reading Association.

Nakanishi, A. (1980). *Writing systems of the world*. Boston, MA: Tuttle.

Newman, A.P., & Beverstock, C. (1990). *Adult literacy: Contexts and challenges*. Newark, DE, and Bloomington, IN: International Reading Association, and ERIC Clearinghouse on Reading and Communication Skills.

Ogden, C.K., & Richards, I.A. (1953). *The meaning of meaning: A study of the influence of language upon thought and of the science of symbolism* (10th ed.). New York: Routledge.

Olson, D.R. (1994). *The world on paper*. New York: Cambridge University Press.

Ong, W.J. (1982). *Orality and literacy: The technologizing of the word*. London: Methuen.

Pearson, P.D., Barr, R., Kamil, M.L., & Mosenthal, P. (Eds.). (1984). *Handbook of reading research*. New York: Longman.

Peirce, C.S. (1931–1958). *Collected papers* (Vols. 1–8) (C. Hartshorn, P. Weiss, & A.W. Burks, Eds.). Cambridge, MA: Harvard University Press.

Pike, K.L. (1967). *Language in relation to a unified theory of the structure of human behavior*. The Hague: Mouton.

Purves, A.C. (1993). Toward a reevaluation of reader response and school literature. *Language Arts, 70*, 348–361.

Purves, A.C., Papa, L., & Jordan, S. (Eds.). (1994). *Encyclopedia of English studies and language arts: A Project of the National Council of Teachers of English* (Vols. 1–2). New York: Scholastic.

Rabinowitz, P. (1987). *Before reading: Narrative conventions and the politics of interpretation*. Ithaca, NY: Cornell University Press.

Reid, I. (Ed.). (1988). *The place of genre in learning: Current debates*. Geelong, Australia: Deakin University Press.

Richard, J.C., Platt, J., & Platt, H. (1992). *Longman dictionary of language teaching and applied linguistics* (2nd ed.). Harlow, England: Longman.

Rieben, L., & Perfetti, C.A. (Eds.). (1991). *Learning to read: Basic research and its implications*. Hillsdale, NJ: Erlbaum.

Robeck, M.C., & Wallace, R.R. (1990). *The psychology of reading: An interdisciplinary approach* (2nd ed.). Hillsdale, NJ: Erlbaum.

Robinson, F.P. (1946). *Effective study*. New York: HarperCollins.

Rosenblatt, L.M. (1978). *The reader, the text, the poem: The transactional theory of the literary work*. Carbondale, IL: Southern Illinois University Press.

Rosenblatt, L.M. (1983). *Literature as exploration* (4th ed.). New York: Modern Language Association.

Ruddell, R.M., Ruddell, M.P., & Singer, H. (Eds.). (1994). *Theoretical models and processes of reading* (4th ed.). Newark, DE: International Reading Association.

Samuels, S.J., & Farstrup, A.E. (Eds.). (1992). *What research has to say about reading instruction* (2nd ed.). Newark, DE: International Reading Association.

Saville-Troike, M. (1989). *The ethnography of communication: An introduction* (2nd ed.). Oxford, England: Blackwell.

Shannon, C.E., & Weaver, W. (1949). *The mathematical theory of communication*. Urbana, IL: University of Illinois Press.

Smith, N.B. (1986). *American reading instruction*. Newark, DE: International Reading Association.

Smith, F. (1988). *Understanding reading: A psycholinguistic analysis of reading and learning to read* (4th ed.). Hillsdale, NJ: Erlbaum.

Soares, M.B. (1992). *Literacy assessment and its implication for statistical measurement*. Paper prepared for the Division of Statistics, UNESCO, Paris.

Spearman, C. (1904). General intelligence objectively determined and measured. *American Journal of Psychology, 15*, 201–293.

Sticht, T.G., & Mikulecky, L. (1984). *Job-related basic skills: Cases and conclusions*. Columbus, OH: The National Center for Research in Vocational Education.

Strickland, D.S., & Morrow, L.M. (Eds.). (1989). *Emerging literacy: Young children learn to read and write*. Newark, DE: International Reading Association.

Teale, W.H., & Sulzby, E. (Eds.). (1986). *Emergent literacy: Writing and reading*. Norwood, NJ: Ablex.

Temple, C., Nathan, R., Temple, F., & Burris, N.A. (1993). *The beginnings of writing* (3rd ed.). Boston, MA: Allyn & Bacon.

Templeton, S., & Bear, D.R. (Eds.). (1992). *Development of orthographic knowledge and the foundation of literacy: A memorial festschrift for Edmund H. Henderson*. Hillsdale, NJ: Erlbaum.

Thorndike, E.L. (1913). *Educational psychology* (Vol. 2). New York: Columbia University, Teachers College.

Thurstone, L.L. (1938). *Primary mental abilities*. Chicago, IL: University of Chicago Press.

Tierney, R.J., Readence, J.E., & Dishner, E.K. (1990). *Reading strategies and practices: A compendium*. Boston, MA: Allyn & Bacon.

Tinker, M.A., & McCullough, C. (1968). *Teaching elementary reading* (3rd ed.). New York: Appleton-Century-Crofts.

Tolman, E.C. (1932). *Purposive behavior in animals and men*. New York: Appleton-Century-Crofts.

UNESCO. (1978). *Revised recommendation concerning the international standardization of educational statistics*. Paris: Author.

Venezky, R.L., Wagner, D.A., & Ciliberti, B.S. (Eds.). (1990). *Toward defining literacy*. Newark, DE: International Reading Association.

Vygotsky, L. (1978). *Mind in society: The development of higher psychological processes* (M. Cole, V. John-Steiner, & E. Souberman, Eds.). Cambridge, MA: Harvard University Press.

Vygotsky, L. (1986). *Thought and language* (rev. ed.) (A. Kozulin, Ed.). Cambridge, MA: MIT Press. (Original work published 1962)

Wiener, N. (1948). *Cybernetics, or the control and communication in the animal and the machine*. New York: Technology Press and Wiley.

Williams, J.M. (1990). *Style: Toward clarity and grace*. Chicago, IL: University of Chicago Press.

Winterowd, W.R. (1989). *The culture and politics of literacy*. New York: Oxford University Press.

Winthrop, R.H. (1991). *Dictionary of concepts in cultural anthropology*. New York: Greenwood Press.

Wolman, B.B. (Ed.). (1989). *Dictionary of behavioral science (2nd ed.)*. San Diego, CA: Academic.

Zarrillo, J. (1991). Theory becomes practice: Aesthetic teaching with literature. *The New Advocate*, *4*, 221–234.